CW01654542

Sustainable Construction Techniques

Edition **DETAIL** Green Books

Sustainable Construction Techniques

From structural design to interior fit-out:
assessing and improving the environmental impact of buildings

Sebastian El khouli
Viola John
Martin Zeumer

Imprint

MANCHESTER
METROPOLITAN
26 MAY 2016
UNIVERSITY LIBRARY

Authors:
Sebastian El khouli, Dipl.-Ing.
Viola John, Dr. sc. ETH Zürich, Dipl.-Ing.
Martin Zeumer, Dipl.-Ing.

Co-author:
Franziska Hartmann, Dipl.-Ing.

Project management:
Jakob Schoof, Dipl.-Ing.

Editiorial work and layout:
Jana Rackwitz, Dipl.-Ing.
Jakob Schoof, Dipl.-Ing.

Illustrations:
Ralph Donhauser, Dipl.-Ing. (FH)

Cover design:
Cornelia Hellstern, Dipl.-Ing. (FH)

Translation:
Sharon Heidenreich, Dipl.-Ing. (FH)

English proofreading:
J. Roderick O'Donovan, B. Arch.

This work is subject to copyright. All rights are reserved, whether the whole or part of the material is concerned, specifically the rights of translation, reprinting, recitation, re-use of illustrations and tables, broadcasting, reproduction on microfilms or in other ways, and storage in data banks.
Duplication of this publication is only permitted under the provisions of the German Copyright Law in its current version. A copyright fee must always be paid. Violations are liable for prosecution under the German Copyright Law.

DTP & layout:
Roswitha Siegler

Reproduction:
ludwig:media, Zell am See

Print:
Kösel GmbH & Co. KG, Altusried-Krugzell
1st edition 2015

Institut für internationale
Architektur-Dokumentation GmbH & Co. KG
Hackerbrücke 6, D-80335 München
Telephone: +49/89/38 16 20-0
Telefax: +49/89/39 86 70
www.detail.de

© 2015 Institut für internationale
Architektur-Dokumentation GmbH & Co. KG, Munich
A specialist book from Redaktion DETAIL

ISBN: 978-3-955532-38-3 (Print)
ISBN: 978-3-95553-239-0 (E-Book)
ISBN: 978-3-95553-240-6 (Bundle)

MIX
Papier aus verantwortungsvollen Quellen
FSC® C013736

The FSC-certified paper used for this book is manufactured from fibres proved to originate from environmentally and socially compatible sources.

Contents

What is sustainable construction?

In the whole history of building nothing has been more contentious than the choice of materials. Up until the beginning of the Industrial Revolution, the number of building products available was very restricted. The possibilities and technologies concerning their implementation were improved over centuries and perfected down to the last detail. The industrial era introduced new production methods and more efficient ways of transportation. These, coupled with the later emergence of the "International Style", released architecture from dependence on a mainly regional mix of materials. The development of materials has accelerated considerably since then, and probably more products have been introduced during the last 20 years than during the entire earlier history of materials science.
From the end of the 1970s, the energy efficiency of buildings has been one of the most important driving forces behind the development of new construction materials. In recent times, more and more "sustainable building products" have come on to the market. However, sustainability is interpreted in a variety of ways. Regional products, products made from renewable resources, materials with a low primary energy content, extremely durable products or products which are particularly easy to recycle – all are marketed under the sustainable banner.
There is a clear indication that the environmental and biological assessment of construction materials will gain even greater importance in future. The German law on life cycle management (Kreislaufwirtschaftsgesetz), for example, is intended to promote a closed material cycle, and the EU Construction Products Regulation refers to hygiene, health and environmental protection, as well as the sustainable use of natural resources, as being fundamental in the development of new buildings. Increasingly stringent statutory requirements ensure that buildings consume less energy for heating, cooling, ventilation and lighting. It is for this reason that, when taking into account the total life cycle of a development, the production and re-use of construction materials and buildings has become increasingly important.
Meanwhile, many planners and clients are showing themselves open to new concepts and requirements in terms of materials. However, they are often handicapped by a lack of appropriate background knowledge. Our experience from project work and consultations on building materials has shown that many planners perceive the field of materials science as vast and confusing, and would therefore very much appreciate clear statements and simple instructions. A very superficial analysis of this topic already shows that, due to the complexity of the subject matter and the large number of assessment criteria and methods available, it is extremely difficult to meet these needs. This, among other things, was one of the reasons why we gladly accepted the request to publish a book in the DETAIL Green Books series on the topic "Sustainable construction techniques". We were quite aware that the term "sustainability" embraces a broad range of meanings in architecture. Thus, in order to narrow down the scope in a meaningful way, we decided to concentrate on the conservation and efficient use of resources and building materials which pose no risk to health.

Approach to a complex problem

There are many standard reference books on construction issues. So how can this selection be complemented in a meaningful way? What really distinguishes sustainable construction materials from others? Is it true that the amount of embodied energy in a building can be reduced through the construction, and, if so, by how much? Should the impact on health be assessed in a different way to the impact on the environment, and, if so, how?
For the most part, in relation to building components and construction, it is not possible to give unequivocal answers to these questions. The main objective of this book is therefore to bring together and compile up-to-date information with regard to the sustainable implementation of building materials. It is directed towards specialist planners, in particular architects, with the intention of making environmentally improved building design and the selection of green sustainable construction techniques more accessible. With this book, we hope to make an important contribution towards more objective discussion and to generally improve the basic know-how on the subject. The latest assessment criteria for construction materials make the statement by Walter Gropius, "Designing means: dancing in shackles", even more relevant than ever before. Taking account of environmental factors when selecting building products is one of the core tasks in architecture; a task which can only be accomplished successfully by assessing each design individually.
It is for this reason that we have not placed special emphasis on the specific properties of individual construction materials, as has been the case in previous publications on materials science. Instead, the book focuses on the various life cycles and design processes in construction – the material life cycle, the building life cycle, as well as the various processing cycles in the design and in the development of a life cycle assessment. The link to individual construction materials derives, in general, from consideration of specific reference projects.

Book contents

The introduction to this book focuses on the criteria that have been used to assess construction materials in the past and the developments that have made the selection of materials – for centuries a key task in architectural work – such a challenging and complex process today.

The following chapter "Environmental objectives, criteria and assessment methods" looks into new assessment criteria for construction materials and sheds light on their background. The life cycle assessment is a key focus in this respect. To many, the LCA method is still a closed book and its results are understandable only to the initiated. Thus, the chapter offers step-by-step instructions for the development and evaluation of a life cycle assessment and tries to make the findings more accessible by using comparisons. A number of other assessment criteria and standards – in particular those concerning building biology – are introduced in the same chapter. An overview of the most important design tools, databases and quality labels completes this section.

The chapter "Strategies for material use in the construction process" examines the life cycle of materials and buildings one by one and highlights fundamental strategies for improving building biology and ecology-related aspects. What is evident here is that the requirements concerning upkeep and maintenance, the durability of construction materials and the ultimate deconstruction of built structures can only be assessed in association with the specific use. The cost-benefit ratio of the selected measures is also always dependent on the individual situation.

The chapter "Design phases and processes" identifies the most important tools for designing environmentally improved buildings. It is structured according to the design phases and explains the various approaches for improvement, their sequence and possible interdependencies. The chapter also includes an overview of software tools and databases for the design phase of buildings.

To date, most of the discussion has been limited to the category of assembly units. In the chapter "Environmental impact of building components" we therefore provide advice on the selection of materials for the more important components from an ecological point of view. Equal weight is given to the aspects of building biology and building ecology in order to ensure a holistic approach to the assessment. This method highlights the fact that the requirements concerning the environmental and health aspects of building products are rarely contradictory.

The final chapter, "Case studies", features a range of different buildings. These were chosen because in them the selection of materials plays a central role and also because of the detailed documentation of the assessment criteria, the design stages and results. Some projects have a focus on avoiding pollutants, whereas others were developed using a life cycle assessment or specific concepts with regard to recycling. The number of reference projects has been restricted to just a few so that each one can be documented in a detailed and comprehensive way.

The environmental improvement of constructions is always related to the context. Depending on the requirements of a building and its components, very different solutions may therefore be referred to as "correct". This book should therefore be considered as a tool for further thought and study. The field of sustainable construction techniques has not yet been fully explored and is undergoing constant further development. The more planners and architects contribute their own experience to this subject, the more the building industry will benefit as a whole.

0.1 Single family home in Nyborg (DK) 2013, Lendager Arkitekter. In comparison to a conventional construction, the consistent use of recycled materials in this experimental building reduced the amount of embodied CO_2 emissions by more than 80 %.

0.1

- Architecture and its materials
- Between tradition and innovation
- Development of sustainability models for buildings
- Principles and fields of action

Architecture and its materials

Building is inextricably linked to the use of materials, and the materials used are always an integral part of the creative concept. It is therefore with good reason that, in the planning process, this phase is often referred to as "materialisation of the design idea".
It is becoming more and more difficult to construct a building using only a single material (fig. 1.1). This is mainly due to the ever increasing demands being made on buildings and the bewildering number of products now available. Nevertheless, there are limits here too. An "anything goes!" approach in this context would invariably mean ignoring the technical and creative features of construction materials in the same way as aspects that are well-established in the history of building, such as conservation of resources, reduction of environmental impact and health hazards. Finally, from a sustainability viewpoint, the changing scene will place greater emphasis on the selection of materials.

On the one hand, the manufacturing industry is developing faster than ever before resulting in an increasingly wide range of construction materials. New products, on the other hand, are often not called into question until later, and then, attract a great deal of public interest. The development of nanomaterials, for example, shows how new technologies transform from being a trend, to extremely controversial and then become a standard solution within a particular field of application (e.g. facade coating). Other processes develop almost unobserved. For example, the proportion of volatile organic compounds in solvents and other substances used in the building industry rose within the total amount of man-made VOC emissions in Germany from 30 % to 50 % between 1990 and 2003 [1] (fig. 2.7, p. 18). The introduction of quality labels for building products and building certification systems (e.g. LEED or DGNB) was a first step towards the improvement and definition of new quality standards in the building industry.

1.1

Construction materials are often caught between the conflicting priorities of technical progress and social values. It is the planners' task to face this challenge and balance the needs simply because most solutions are directly related to a specific project.
The well-considered use of resources and energy is the overriding goal. Both of these aspects will continue to grow in importance. This can already be detected in the implementation of more stringent energy-related building standards. In the case of new builds, the energy demand for the building's operation is still the prime focus. The further tightening of energy-related building regulations has however revealed a new emphasis on a balance between embodied and operating energy. According to the objective of the EU Energy Performance of Buildings Directive (EPBD), all new builds completed in Central Europe as of 2021 will be permitted to use only the same low amount of energy for the construction of the building as for its operation during a 50-year period (fig. 1.2). In some instances raw materials are already becoming scarce. When, for example, krypton light bulbs were introduced in automobiles, it became difficult to get hold of thermal insulating glazing with the highly efficient gas-filled cavities. Dwindling resources will not affect every raw material. However, it is a fact that it will no longer be possible to focus on construction materials in an isolated manner. The effect of the material in a greater context is of importance for its application. When performing a sustainability assessment of a building according to the German DGNB system, more than 50 % of all criteria are more or less directly influenced by the choice of construction materials (fig. 1.3). More than 30 % of all aspects incorporated in the LEED certification system can be attributed to mate-

rial [2]. And the environmental impact of the construction can differ by as much as 30 % in a single project without making any fundamental changes to the design [3]. Furthermore, the term “sustainable construction materials” can also be interpreted as only the “sustainable use of construction materials”. In this case, it is not the construction material itself but the concept in terms of usage which decides whether the result is sustainable or not.
It is a fact that the conflicting arguments presented by interests groups – some of whom favour new, innovative materials while others advocate traditional and environmentally friendly materials – appear only superficially as a conflict between innovation and environmental policy. In practice, this conflict is not reflected in guidance on construction materials.
Based on the overriding goals of sustainability, future strategies can develop in various directions either by increasing efficiency in production processes, developing resource-related local identity or improving and increasing the use of recycling processes (fig. 1.14, p. 14).
This book aims to present current methodology and future trends, to contribute towards bringing back together the varied approaches to the environment, energy efficiency, sustainability and building in general that have been followed since the 1960s and to rediscover a common basis for construction work. The reason is that the construction and materials of buildings offer a unique opportunity to incorporate solutions to important future issues into existing building traditions.

Between tradition and innovation

Our cultural achievements in architecture are closely linked to the availability of raw materials and resources, as well as to energy, climate conditions, cultural identity and social attitudes. Autochthonous building traditions and vernacular architecture have bestowed us with an incredible diversity of typologies and building materials. The identity of towns and regions are also often directly linked to these underlying circumstances. Traditional buildings are consistent with our current understanding of sustainability, simply because their development was determined by restrictions and constraints.
In reference to the use of resources, there was often a debate about the value and merits of construction materials. In the Middle Ages, the value of limited resources was already used to express a particular feature of a building. Stone, for example, became a very representative material due to its moisture resistance, durability and the many different ways in which it could be worked (in contrast to the more commonly used timber frames). New construction materials did not come into use until the industrialisation. New manufacturing techniques for bricks, steel and glass increased the volume of production tremendously, which in turn enabled the construction of large and impressive buildings, such as factories, workers' housing estates and town houses. In Germany this innovative power is best expressed in the railway stations, market halls and the Reichstag building in Berlin (Paul Wallot, 1894).

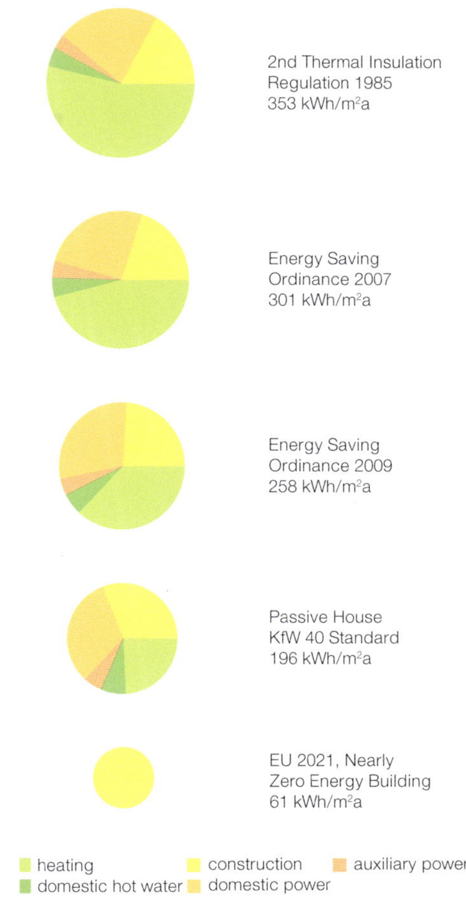

1.2

1.1 Facades in Speicherstadt featuring a creative use of brickwork, Hamburg (D) around 1890
1.2 Development of primary energy demand in residential building and its allocation to different functions
1.3 Spheres of sustainability and a reference to the use of material according to the DGNB system for office and administrative buildings 2012

Environmental Quality (ENV)

- ■ 1.1 Life cycle assessment – risks caused by emissions
- ■ 1.2 Risks to the local environment (groundwater, surface water, ground, air)
- ■ 1.3 Environmentally friendly extraction of materials (wood, natural stone)
- ■ 2.1 Life cycle assessment – primary energy
- ☐ 2.2 Domestic water consumption and volume of waste water
- ☐ 2.3 Area demand

Economic Quality (ECO)

- ■ 1.1 Building-related life cycle costs
- ■ 2.1 Flexibility and suitability for third-party use
- ☐ 2.2 Marketability (location, market situation)

Sociocultural and Functional Quality (SOC)

- ■ 1.1 Thermal comfort (winter and summer)
- ■ 1.2 Indoor air quality
- ■ 1.3 Acoustic comfort
- ■ 1.4 Visual comfort
- ☐ 1.5 Occupants' extent of control
- ☐ 1.6 Quality of exterior space
- ■ 1.7 Safety and risk prevention
- ☐ 2.1 Barrier-free access
- ☐ 2.2 Accessibility
- ☐ 2.3 Convenience for cyclists
- ☐ 3.1 Procedures to introduce creative and urban concepts
- ☐ 3.2 Art in architecture
- ☐ 3.3 Quality of layouts

Technical Quality (TEC)

- ■ 1.1 Fire protection
- ■ 1.2 Sound insulation
- ■ 1.3 Quality of building envelope's thermal and moisture insulation
- ☐ 1.4 Adaptability of technical systems
- ■ 1.5 Suitability for upkeep and repair
- ■ 1.6 Suitability for deconstruction, reuse and recycling

Process Quality (PRO)

- ☐ 1.1 Quality of project preparation
- ☐ 1.2 Integrated planning process
- ☐ 1.3 Optimisation and complexity in the design approach
- ■ 1.4 Evidence of sustainability in the tendering process
- ☐ 1.5 Provision of conditions for perfect use and operation
- ■ 2.1 Construction site and processes
- ■ 2.2 Quality of workmanship
- ☐ 2.3 Systematic commissioning

Site Quality (SITE)

- ☐ 1.1 Conditions of the micro climate
- ☐ 1.2 Image and condition of site and neighbourhood
- ☐ 1.3 Traffic connections
- ☐ 1.4 Vicinity to user-specific facilities

■ directly affected by the choice of material
■ indirectly affected by the type of material application
☐ not affected by building materials

1.3

1.4

1.5

1.6

1.7

New Objectivity

In the German-speaking world the emergence of this new era is best expressed by the foundation of the German Werkbund in 1907. Born out of desperate social issues and the possibilities provided by new materials, the New Objectivity movement expressed a standard which incorporated important aspects of today's understanding of sustainability, such as material conformity, fitness for purpose and durability [4].

The Werkbund coined the term "New Objectivity" to pursue the objective of totally reforming architecture by making use of rationalisation, standardisation and new materials. In terms of social responsibility, this was achieved by incorporating what were at first thought to be life-reforming principles, such as "light, air and sun" into the architectural designs. The Glass Chain group (1919/20) spent most of its time discussing these social aspects of architecture [5]. The material glass represented the emergence of this new era throughout the world (fig. 1.4). Concrete, however, played the most important role in the New Objectivity movement. Le Corbusier, in particular, experimented with this so-called precision material. The system "Dom-ino" (1914), invented by Le Corbusier for the industrial production of houses, introduced the separation of load-bearing structure, fit-out and facade – a method applied frequently several years later. The system allowed for total flexibility in the layouts, providing advantages in the case of third-party use, which is still a key aspect of sustainability today.

Modernism

Le Corbusier's dream of using concrete as a precision material was not fulfilled in those early days – the quality simply could not meet expectations. So it was the modern movement's task to reinforce the radical change of building materials with suitable design concepts according to the principles "truth and honesty". Frank Lloyd Wright argued that considering the inherent nature of a material was the best method to resist change. At the same time, he believed this was the sa-fest way to discover a new architectural style, because, as Frank Lloyd Wright states, "Every new material means a new form, a new use, if used according to its nature" [6]. This process is best expressed in the work of Le Corbusier, who through exploration of the production techniques of concrete, recognised the creative properties of the material and employed its coarse and rough structure as a design feature. He used a sequence of rough shuttering boards tacked together with nails which left traces of their wooden grain on the surface of the concrete (fig. 1.5). Le Corbusier called it "beton brut" and paved the way for today's perception of exposed concrete and the term "Brutalism" later coined by Hans Asplund.

Many other protagonists of architecture contributed towards creating a new conception of materials. In his designs Frank Lloyd Wright, for example, selected materials that embrace local features. Similar notions were later also adopted by Alvar Aalto and Sverre Fehn. Aalto, in particular, tried to reconcile the relationship between human being and built environment through the sensual appreciation of materials. Alongside visual aspects, he also emphasised the haptic features of his designs (fig. 1.6). Thus, he can be regarded as an important pioneer of the building biology-related debate in architecture (see p. 16).

The approaches taken by Le Corbusier concerning industrial prefabrication made headway in the 1920s: Ernst May was the first in Germany to make use of the prefabricated panel construction system in his project Neues Frankfurt (1925–1930) [7].

Post-war era

After the Second World War, destroyed houses and approximately 12 million homeless people brought about a reorientation in Germany with regard to the development of towns and housing estates and the mass production of residential space. Adopting ideas of the modern movement, one of the main aims was to encourage healthy building [8]. The concept of prefabrication was taken up in both East and West Germany where, in the 1950s and 60s, numerous new modular construction systems were developed for residential buildings (fig. 1.8). New facade systems with energy-efficient features were introduced during the same era: in France, Félix Trombe and Jacques Michel built a special wall to make use of passive solar energy. Designed back in 1956, it is nowadays known as a "Trombe wall". Technological innovations were encouraged by the fact that former metal construction businesses were on the lookout for new markets after the war (fig. 1.7). The know-how was especially useful for the development of innovative structural facades. The plastics industry also

entered the market of building products and supplied houses, sanitary units, interior finishes and furniture. These developments increased the speed of construction and the rate of prefabrication. And, even though the quality of workmanship rose in comparison to that of the post-war era, it was possible to reduce the size of the workforce. So, all in all, a classic example of economic optimisation.
In industrial building, engineers, such as Heinz Isler and Konrad Wachsmann, carried out investigations into more efficient load-bearing structures. With the aim of finding a perfect solution for everything, Fritz Haller created the modular furniture systems Maxi (1960), Mini (1967) and Midi (1972–1976). His concepts combined construction and building services by, for example, integrating solutions for cable management (fig. 1.9, p. 12). With his membrane constructions Frei Otto contributed towards plastics becoming a visible feature in buildings (e.g. the roof of the Olympic stadium in Munich).

The search for a new paradigm

Following the economic miracle in Germany, a new direction was needed in the building industry. This is where Buckminster Fuller can be seen as a pioneer of sustainability. By 1928, he had already started to develop material-efficient construction principles, which allowed for maximum material performance at minimum use of material, under the name of "dymaxion" (dynamic maximum tension (fig. 1.10). With "An integral function of the universe", Fuller raised questions about the meaning of modern life, which he then answered, for example, in his book "Operating Manual for Spaceship Earth" [9]. Due to his long-term collaboration with Norman Foster between 1968 and 1983, his theses were also incorporated in built architecture [10].
Predominantly formal aspects came into play in post-modern architecture – mainly without addressing any specific material properties. However, at the same time, the layered structure of components became more differentiated as was later expressed in the era of Deconstructivism and High-tech architecture. The exposure of layers and their independent designs revealed, on the one hand, the instability of the overall construction and, on the other hand, the separate creative features relevant to their function (fig. 1.12, p. 13).
It was at the same time that the interaction of humans and the environment came to the fore again and was much discussed as a reaction to environmental destruction, catastrophes like the Seveso disaster (1976), and the dangers posed by nuclear power (fig. 1.11, p. 13). The Werkbund accompanied this process, for example, by hosting a congress in 1968 on "The generation and its responsibility for our environment". The book "Das gesunde Haus" (The Healthy House) published by Hubert Palm was a first reference work on the subject building biology [11]. The Institute for Building Biology in Rosenheim, which is still active today, was founded at the beginning of the 1970s. The universities reacted by performing more research in the field of green, environmentally friendly building design. The objectives pursued deliberately involved decentralised, labour-intensive building processes and the opportunity to complete projects as self builds [12]. This was complemented by a return to renewable and low-pollutant construction materials, like timber and clay. The comprehensive development of preservation orders for historic buildings and monuments and the beginnings of energy-efficient building can also be attributed to this time. In the 1980s, for example, Wolfgang Feist developed the Passive House standard and introduced a method for making a detailed calculation of a building's energy demand. Subsequently, the legislators tightened the energy requirements of buildings, which, although initially perceived as "green and bohemian", were gradually woven into the building culture. Building with renewable resources and the grading of pollutants was distinguished by similar, possibly less conspicuous developments.

Sustainability as an integrated tool

Back in the 1970s Otl Aicher, co-founder and senior editor of the architect's journal Arch+, endeavoured to bring together concepts of efficient building, Passive House design and glass architecture to form a meaningful whole. Aicher coined the term "integrated design" to express this ambition [13]. It is since then that the task of compiling a variety of requirements to form a whole resides with architects. Walter Gropius' legendary statement "Designing means: dancing in shackles" is more valid today than ever before, and the construction materials industry should also take into consideration this integrated approach. So far, the industry has contributed greatly towards the development of environmental specifications and has also, across a broad spectrum, advanced the industrialisation of renewable materials, such as engineered wood and cellulose insulation. Nevertheless, there is still a long way to go when it comes to the systematic integration of material properties in modular energy-efficient systems, for example making use of solar thermal energy [14].

Current developments

Due to the diversity and complexity of the subject matter, it is possible to take a look at only some of the current trends: some projects apply new assessment methods, such as the life cycle assessment, in order to make decisions on design-related matters (fig. 3.3, p. 53, 4.9, p. 72). This in turn leads to new solutions concerning components, which can be reintroduced into the material cycle once they have fulfilled their original purpose.
Another approach involves balancing the creative potential of modular systems and manufacturing techniques. This is achieved, for example, by analysing bespoke prefabrication techniques (see fig. 1.13, p. 13 and Single-family home on Taylor Island, pp. 103ff.)
Comparing the durability of the building envelope with that of the building services develops a further focus. The possibility, in this case, to reduce the use of building services through the performance of

1.4 Curtain wall facade of the Van-Nelle factory, Rotterdam (NL) 1931, Brinkman & Van der Vlugt
1.5 "Beton Brut" at the Unité d'Habitation, Marseille (F) 1952, Le Corbusier
1.6 Interior of dwelling Villa Mairea, Noormarkku (FIN) 1939, Alvar Aalto
1.7 "MAN-Stahlhaus", prefabricated house designed by MAN, market entry: 1948, end of production: 1953, quantity: 230, here in Mainz (D)
1.8 Residential housing block with sculptured concrete frame and prefabricated concrete panels, Interbau 1957, Hansaviertel Berlin (D) 1956–1958, Hans Schwippert

1.8

materials represents a further opportunity for improvement. The prototype office building "2226" designed by Baumschlager Eberle features an exterior shell made of a 76-cm-thick two-leaf brick wall, but does not have an active heating system. A ventilation system using sensor-controlled vents is incorporated in the facade (fig. 1.15, p. 15).
Analysing the results of these new approaches will be exciting. Experiments will continue to be an important aspect of creative design work – simply because this is what creates the competitive edge, or as the American architect James Timberlake puts it: "If you're clever, you'll try new things" [15].

Development of sustainability models for buildings

Sustainability is based on the incorporation of various approaches deriving from different professional and technical backgrounds (fig. 1.11). At first, politics was the driving force, and it was the Brundtland Report, published in 1987, which coined the term "sustainable development" [16]. The Earth Summit in Rio de Janeiro in 1992 implemented the action plan "Agenda 21" to ensure sustainable development, especially with regard to problem solving on a local level [17]. This approach was already familiar in Germany from the environmental movement, but was nevertheless useful to reinforce the main principles.
The second UN Conference on Human Settlements (Habitat II), held in Istanbul in 1996, focussed on transferring the objectives of sustainable development to an urban scale. In terms of material, the most important objectives determined at the conference were prevention of environmental destruction, the implication of limited resources, protection of public health and minimizing the damage caused by natural disasters [18]. The need to move away from undifferentiated planning methods was also a subject of discussion at the conference.
What followed was a broadly based development of systems to perform sustainability assessments. The British standard BREEAM was introduced back in 1990. It therefore had a considerable influence on the following assessment systems of the first generation (e.g. LEED), each of which was distinguished by a country-based focus. To date, BREEAM and LEED are among the most widespread systems throughout the world. With the introduction of the "Code for Sustainable Homes" in 2006, the United Kingdom was the first country to make sustainability assessments for buildings mandatory. The reference to materials in these early certification systems was generally achieved by integrating requirements concerning the deconstruction and reuse of products, the origin and recycled content of materials, as well as by encouraging the use of low-emission materials for the fit-out (fig. 1.11). All in all, the selection of materials can influence the assessment result by up to 30% [19].
The Swiss system Minergie-Eco, first introduced in 2006, was the first building certification system to incorporate extensive environmental requirements for construction materials. A life cycle assessment was integrated into the calculations of a building's energy performance in 2013 in order to provide a comprehensive overview of the building's environmental impact.
The development of German assessment systems, DGNB (Deutsche Gesellschaft für Nachhaltiges Bauen) and BNB for federal buildings (Bewertungssystem Nachhaltiges Bauen), was taken up in 2007. These certification systems were the first to make the analysis of the building's entire life cycle mandatory, for example by making use of a life cycle assessment or a life cycle cost analysis. Moreover, they included a scale to determine the content of pollutants in construction materials. Thanks to this new feature, it has become possible to provide measurable proof of reductions in the environmental impact and the content of pollutants (fig. 1.11).
In future, the environmental impact of a building will presumably shift from the operation phase to the construction, maintenance and return of the construction materials to the material cycle. As a consequence, the international standard for certifications, ISO/TS 21931-1:2010 Framework for methods of assessment for environmental performance of construction works, has also determined the life cycle analysis as the most important assessment system.

Health-related aspects as an assessment tool

In 1958, Max von Pettenkofer, known as a pioneer of hygiene and public health, suggested using the CO_2 content of indoor air as an indicator for its quality. The studies of air quality and indoor climate made by Ole Fanger in the 1970s and 80s were then largely adopted in building physics standards (mainly DIN EN ISO 7730).
This was followed in 1980 by the founding of AGÖF, the Association of Ecological Research Institutes, which developed scientific principles for the emerging environmental movement in the building industry. AGÖF published its first report in 1990 on "Indoor air contamination – identification, evaluation and remediation". Since 2004, AGÖF has been providing guideline values to identify the content of pollutants in indoor air, which have been adopted in the DGNB and BNB certification systems [20].

1.9

1.10

1.9 Residential building made from MINI modular system in Mörigen am Bielersee (CH) 1971, Fritz Haller; refurbishment: 2013, 2bm Architekten
1.10 Dome over Manhattan Island (USA) 1960, Richard Buckminster Fuller and Shoji Sadao
1.11 Development of political sustainability, assessment systems for sustainability and health-related issues in building design in relation to important historical milestones
1.12 Centre Georges Pompidou in Paris (F) 1977, Renzo Piano/Richard Rogers: exterior-mounted structural system as a design feature
1.13 Office and commercial building on Welfenstraße, Munich (D) 2010, Hild und K: plastic appearance of composite thermal insulation system to accommodate functional principles (objective: better shedding of rainwater)

Health-related issues were first considered in product manufacturing processes when the European Building Products Directive came into effect in 1989 [21]. In Germany this legislation was then transferred into national law (BauPG1992). These events were followed by analyses of pollutants and their effects, which were undertaken in the main by the European Collaborative Action (ECA) "Indoor air quality and its impact on Man". In 1992, based on public health in the workplace, the Senate Commission provided the German Research Foundation (DFG) with maximum workplace concentrations (formerly known as MAK values, today AGW values) and biological tolerance values (formerly known as BAT values, today BGW values) for the further examination of health hazards at work.
The ad-hoc Working Group set up by the Federal Environment Agency in Germany in 1993 specified uniform guideline values (RW I – precautionary value, RW II – health hazard value) for the quality of indoor air which are still valid today. In 2000, the Committee for the Health-related Evaluation of Building Products (AgBB) finally introduced parameters for the assessment of VOC emissions from building products indoors, including so-called LCI values (Lowest Concentration of Interest) [22]. These parameters have been integrated in the approval guidelines for the health-related evaluation of building products issued by DIBt, the German Institute for Building Technology, since 2004.
As a consequence, the debate on the environmental properties of building products increased. DIN ISO 14020, published in 2001, determined three categories for the classification of building products (see Tools for planners, p. 21). Type 1 labels for products with an emphasis on health, such as the eco-label "Blauer Engel", are most widely used and frequently implemented by the industry as a marketing tool (fig. 2.15, p. 22). The European Construction Products Directive, introduced in 2012, further specified requirements for building products. The main focus is on the consideration of the total life cycle, extending from the production to the operation and, finally, the demolition of the building, which then includes preventing the release of hazardous and climate-damaging emissions (e.g. greenhouse gas) [23].

Environmental impact as an assessment tool
The material life cycle can also be considered an assessment tool for sustaina-

	Historical events	Development of sustainability concept	Development of sustain ability assessments in building	Development of health and safety matters in building
	1961 Thalidomide disaster	1962 "Silent Spring", Rachel Carson 1969 "Operating Manual for Spaceship Earth", Buckminster Fuller		1968 "The Healthy House", Hubert Palm
1970	1973 first oil crisis 1976 Seveso disaster 1980 Dying Forest Syndrome 1986 Chernobyl disaster	1972 "The Limits to Growth", Dennis Meadows et al. 1978 foundation of the first German Ministry for the Environment 1987 "Our Common Future", Brundtland Report	1974 introduction of Cumulative Energy Demand (CED)	1978 introduction of German eco-label "Blauer Engel" (D) 1980 foundation of AGÖF, Association of Ecological Institutes (D)
1990	1991 oil spill in Persian Gulf 1997 El Niño – southern oscillation 1999 Hurricane Lothar	1992 Earth Summit in Rio de Janeiro, Agenda 21; foundation of Commission on Sustainable Development 1993 "Factor 10 – The Essentials for a Sustainable Economy", Friedrich Schmidt-Bleek 1995 "Factor 4: Doubling Wealth, Halving Resource Use", Ernst Ulrich von Weizsäcker 1996 Habitat II Conference in Istanbul 1997 Kyoto Protocol resolution	1990 introduction of BREEAM certification system 1991 first Passive House in Germany; introduction of Minergie label (CH) 1994 introduction of LEED certification system (US)	1990 general asbestos ban for all new products in Austria and Switzerland 1992 definition of MAK values (D) 1993 formation of Ad-Hoc Working Group to assess quality of indoor air; Chemicals Prohibition Ordinance (D)
2000	2002 Elbe flooding 2005 Hurricane Katrina 2007 Hurricane Kyrill	2002 World Summit in Johannesburg 2005 ratification of Kyoto Protocol 2007 Nobel Peace Prize for Intergovernmental Panel on Climate Change (IPCC) and Al Gore	2000 introduction of life cycle assessment method 2001 eco-label definitions 2002 EU Energy Performance Directive 2004 introduction of AgBB for health-related evaluation of building products (D); Code For Sustainable Homes (UK) 2006 introduction of Minergie-ECO (CH) 2009 introduction of DGNB certification system (D)	2000 development of AgBB rating system (D) 2004 definition of AGÖF guideline values 2005 first EU-wide Asbestos Prohibition Regulation
2010	2010 Deepwater Horizon oil rig disaster 2011 Fukushima nuclear disaster	2010 international definition of two degrees goal	2010 review of EU Energy Performance of Buildings Directive; ISO/TS 21931 Assessment methods for environmental performance of construction works 2012 European Building Products Directive	

1.11

1.12

1.13

ble building design. The phases raw material extraction, production, processing, transportation, use, re-use and disposal are part of a system which can be seen as a tool to improve processes involved in the use of materials (see Optimisation of the material life cycle, pp. 44ff.).
The introduction of the MIPS concept (Material Input Per Service) in 1994 can be regarded as a first milestone in this respect [24]. It assesses the material input required for the production and use of a building component in the form of material intensities. This was the first time that necessary processes were analysed according to their consumption of abiotic resources [kg], biotic resources [kg], earth movement [kg], water [l] and air [m^3]. The total material input, also often referred to as the environmental rucksack, results from the weight of the product and its material intensity factors. Thus, the MIPS concept provided a framework that made it possible and worthwhile to reduce the environmental burden of a product. The method, however, focused exclusively on the mass of material, and not yet on the environmental impact.
The standards DIN EN ISO 14040 and 14044 on the principles of life cycle assessments, introduced in 2000, laid the foundation stone for today's evaluation of the environmental impact of processes. Like the MIPS concept, a life cycle assessment analyses the whole life cycle of a product from cradle to grave. In addition, it takes into consideration the environmental impact (e.g. emissions) and functions as a basis to describe the overall effects deriving from use of the product. As a result, hundreds of different emissions can be expressed by a few equivalents.
As a constituent part of building certification systems, this method has been used in project design since 2008. As a consequence, manufacturers are often required to present the pollutant content and LCA data of their products in a comprehensible way. Nowadays, most companies have come to appreciate the value of LCAs. They highlight the potential for improvement in processes and make it possible to operate and market products in a more environmentally friendly way.

Principles and fields of action

Architects and other building professionals have always had to contend with building materials. In recent years, traditional parameters regarding function and design have increasingly been complemented by sustainability-related factors. Meanwhile, a comprehensive range of tools for applying these new strategies has become available (fig. 2.41, p. 43). While adjustments may still be made concerning the scope of the evaluation or pollutant-related criteria, a fundamental change in the assessment methodology is not expected in the near future. This means that the principles for examining the environmental impact of building materials incorporated in a design have been established. The two main points of an environmental material analysis, building ecology and building biology, can be likened to the two sides of a coin. On the one hand, they stand for a rational approach to elusive environmental factors (building ecology) and, on the other hand, for an approach which is difficult to generalise, but is focused on the occupant (building biology). What is interesting is that they are usually concerned with different aspects of the building and are therefore rarely in conflict. And when one of the two approaches fails to lead to a satisfactory result, the other usually gives an indication of how to proceed in a meaningful way.

Principles of the building life cycle
The principle of closed material cycles has already been incorporated into various ordinances and regulations, such as the European Building Products Directive, take-back systems and the Circular Economy Legislation. The sustainable use of materials must refer to the entire life cycle, and buildings made from these materials must also become an integral component of the natural material cycle. It goes without saying that most buildings, simply to meet statutory requirements, already have to reduce their consumption of resources during the operation phase.
In this case, it is necessary to consider all phases of the life cycle and understand the consequences of applying an optimisation measure to only one part of the life cycle. It sometimes helps to change the perspective and to consider first the building life cycle and then the material life cycle, or vice versa. Generally this strategy highlights the important factors and their significance within the system, thus making it easier to identify the consequences (see Optimisation of the material life cycle, pp. 44ff.).
Out of all the phases in a building's life cycle, the operation and re-use phases are the ones least addressed by planners. This presumably means that the interfaces between architecture and facility management will lead to new findings for the sustainable design of buildings in years to come. A close analysis of the opportunities for re-use and deconstruction of buildings will also be of great importance in future. And as, for example, research on plattenbau in the former GDR has shown, re-use must not necessarily involve the entire building, but can also be limited to a few easily recyclable components [25] (see Return to the material cycle, p. 55). A third option is building material recycling. However, a true cycle is only achieved, if all the required energy comes from renewable sources.

Dimension	Consistency	Sufficiency	Efficiency	Life cycle optimisation	
	nature and health-compatible design	demand analysis	increase of functional performance	building life cycle	material life cycle
Building	reduce environmental impact during life cycle	create awareness for changes of use	increase space efficiency	reduce production through re-use	provide measures for deconstruction
Unit	use materials that are non-hazardous to health	reduce space requirements and envelope surface area (compact design)	improve design for optimised operation (reduction of operating energy; simple upkeep and maintenance systems)	neutral utilisation of space	improve durability
Room		reduce quality of fit-out		reduce repairs by introducing maintenance plan	
Component	increase proportion of renewable resources	reduce amount of technology	increase efficiency of construction	use standard dimensions	make use of prefabrication/modular systems
Material	use alternative resources	reduce detailing	increase technical performance of materials	improve project documentation	minimise material flow by choosing materials carefully

1.14

1.14 Aspects of a resource-saving building design with regard to different scales and separated according to the three categories consistency, sufficiency and efficiency
1.15 Office building 2226, Lustenau (A) 2013, Baumschlager Eberle: solid structure without heating system
1.16 Efficiency House Plus with Electric Mobility in Berlin (D) 2012, collaboration between Universität Stuttgart (Institute for Lightweight Structures and Conceptual Design, Institute for Building Energy, Chair for Building Physics as well as the Institute for Work Science and Technology Management) and Werner Sobek Stuttgart and Werner Sobek Green Technologies: experimental building with energy-plus standard and recyclable structure

1.15

1.16

Life cycle assessment as a tool

Over the years, the non-renewable primary energy demand and the global warming potential have become established as key parameters for a life cycle assessment (see Selecting impact categories and indicators, pp. 29ff.).
If, in future, fierce competition arises in the usage of renewable resources (e.g. between food and energy supply systems), a further assessment category could well emerge.
To date, the question concerning the potential for optimising the building structure in an environmentally friendly way yields only an approximate answer. In the case of some components, particularly those relevant to appearance, the life cycle assessment indicators of different design variations can differ by a factor of at least 10 [26]. According to current knowledge, there is an optimisation potential of more than 50 % so long as there is flexibility in the design [27]. And even if modifications to the design are not possible, the potential for improvement is around 30 % (see Ceiling constructions, pp. 90ff.).
The path to the future is in this case largely set. We know all about the environmental impact of most construction materials. The task now is to incorporate the knowledge gained so far, step by step, into the design process. Not until sufficient experience concerning this matter has been gathered for all performance phases of a development will it be possible to make full use of the knowledge of sustainable building design. One of the problems we are facing today is that the environmental impact of the construction and the operation are seen as two separate optimisation issues. However, the most effective material concepts are usually those developed when both of these aspects of the life cycle assessment are taken into consideration at the same time (fig. 1.15, 1.16).
On the other hand, when building is referred to as a whole, the situation is very simple: the energy tied up in the German building stock is almost equal to the amount of energy required to operate these buildings for 25 years [28]. But the more efficiently this stock is operated, the higher the value: by the middle of the century, it could already be as high as 50 years. So, the resource "construction material", which we are dealing with here, will actually increase in value over time.

Health-based building design

The well-know pollution issues in buildings (e.g. asbestos contamination, ingress of pollutants through wood preservatives, formaldehyde emissions from wood-based materials) have determined the significance of low-pollution design. The sensitivity of the public in all spheres of life (furniture, clothes, food etc.) has also forced the building industry to rethink its approach. Health-related aspects should become an integral part of every building design simply for the sake of conserving the value of buildings.

Recycling-based building design

As was the case in modernism, we are currently at a stage where new findings prompt new questions. The return of construction materials into the material cycle is an important consideration in this respect. But it is precisely this field that is still burdened by many unresolved issues. Is there a possibility, for example, to recover the metal coating used in high-quality glazing systems? Is it really necessary to recover the metal, or will a new material, precious metal-enriched molten glass, be created through the processing cycle? It is at the very least debatable whether all components of a building have to be returned to their original state in the material cycle. The value of each component is, after all, linked to the value of the resource at the time of removal. In the same way as the building industry continues to evolve, the recycling industry will also explore new avenues. And in this case, a learning process must take place in order to find an optimal global solution appropriate to society as a whole. Nevertheless, the recycling industry will only be able to operate effectively if appropriate amounts of material and clear descriptions of the resources are made available. Thus, a new way of documenting all parts built and installed is the minimum requirement in this respect.

Resource-saving design and construction processes

Peter Sloterdijk wrote about sustainable building design: "The next architecture will have to be an architecture of atmospheric respect and ecological restraint" [29]. There are no "sustainable construction materials" per se. The issue is more about providing a consistent material concept in which construction materials have a far-reaching and sustainable effect. The optimisation strategy can vary according to the type of use (see Optimising the building life cycle, pp. 57ff.). Based on the three aspects of sustainability (consistency, sufficiency and efficiency), consistency – a design method which makes use of technologies that are compatible with nature and eco systems without destroying them – can be determined as the basis for design and construction work. In addition, the planner can set priorities within both the efficiency concept (resource productivity) and the sufficiency concept (reduction of resource consumption)(fig. 1.14). It is indisputable that the task of selecting materials is a fundamental skill that must be fully embraced by architects and all other planning professionals.

- Environmental objectives and assessment criteria
- Life cycle assessments of buildings
- Tools for the ecological assessment of buildings

Environmental objectives and assessment criteria

We spend most of our lives in buildings. Due to their construction and the intensive use of resources involved (raw materials and energy), it follows that our way of life impacts on both immediate and wider environment and, in consequence, on the existing ecosystem. At the same time, the newly built environment has a strong influence on public health and wellbeing. The three environmental objectives of green building can be derived from these interdependencies [1]:
- protection of public health
- protection of ecosystems
- protection of resources

Based on these objectives, the building industry distinguishes between the two fields building biology and building ecology (fig. 2.1 and 2.2).

In building biology, the occupant is determined as the most important factor, and strategies are implemented to assess, for example, the impact of pollutants on public health and prevent the use of pollutant sources in building (impact of the building on the occupant). The main task of a building biologist is therefore to improve the performance of buildings in terms of their impact on public health by pursuing an integrated design approach. Building ecology, in contrast, assesses the impact of buildings and construction materials on the environment and develops strategies to minimise the corresponding negative effects during the life cycle of the building (impact of the building on the environment).

A common goal of the two fields is the conservation of natural resources. The slightly more qualitative analysis of building biology and the quantitative assessment of the environmental impact characteristic of building biology complement one another. However, if a holistic approach is aimed for in the building design, the two areas of consideration must be treated as equivalents.

Close attention should be paid to balancing and weighting the various aspects of building biology and building ecology in accordance with the specific project design. As a rule, structural components and materials seldom satisfy all criteria concerning building biology and building ecology in equal measure. The task of influencing and improving the decision making process with regard to the load-bearing structure and the choice of materials in terms of both of these aspects is a real challenge for architects.

With the intention of providing support for the decision making process, this chapter introduces the environmental objectives and assessment criteria characteristic of building biology and building ecology, including their relationships and interdependencies. In the case of building biology, there is a clear focus on the evaluation of pollutants; in the case of building ecology, on the life cycle assessment (LCA), which enables a quantitative estimate of the environmental impacts caused by construction materials and buildings.

2.1 Objectives and activity areas of building biology and building ecology
2.2 Protection goals of building biology and building ecology
2.3 "Tree Hotel" in Harads (S) 2010, Tham & Videgård Hansson: escapism or ideal concept of human habitat in tune with the natural environment?
2.4 Objectives and strategies of building biology

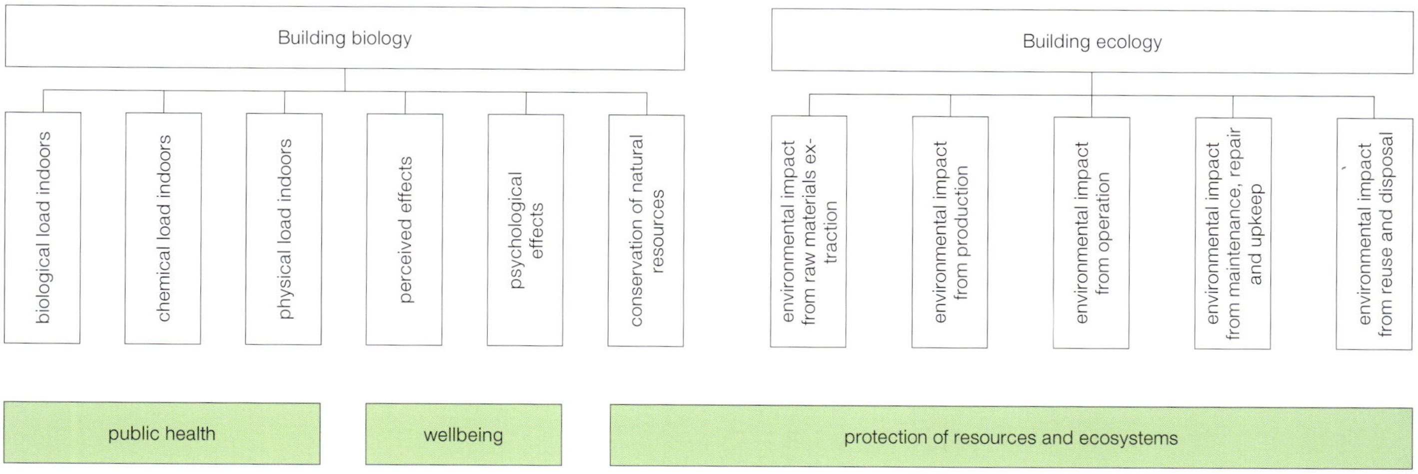

2.1

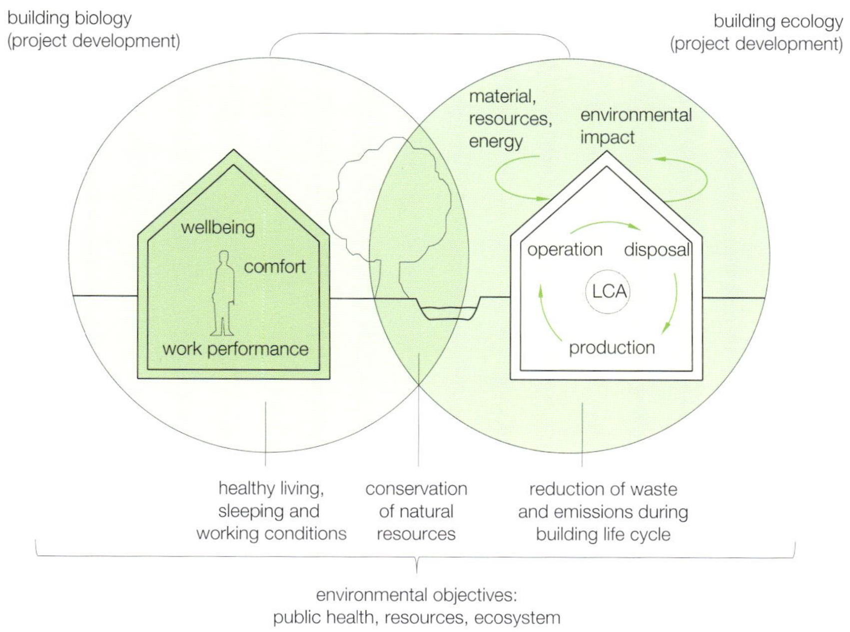

2.2

2.3

Protection of public health		Detailed definition of the environmental objective and necessary measures
biological load indoors	prevent indoor mould, fungi and bacteria growth; reduction of allergens	Mould can, through its spores and metabolic products, have a toxic effect on humans and lead to infections and allergies. The aim is therefore to prevent, as far as possible, conditions promoting mould growth in buildings (≤ 80 % relative humidity). For this purpose, there should be no significant thermal bridges or other flaws (e.g. damage to water pipes) in the building construction. Any build-up of moisture (e.g. from the kitchen, bathroom or perspiration) should be removed from the interior space by exchanging the indoor air at regular intervals.
chemical load indoors	reduction of pollutants	According to present knowledge, it is almost impossible to totally avoid the use of human toxic (risk to human health) and ecotoxic (risk to environment) substances in buildings. By using product groups with a low level of pollutants (e.g. products that are free from solvents and heavy metals) and avoiding substances that are hazardous to health, such as formaldehyde, VOCs and biocides, a considerable reduction of harmful emissions can be achieved indoors. Pollutants should be removed from the interior by exchanging the indoor air at regular intervals.
physical load indoors	reduction of low-frequency electric and magnetic fields	Electric fields exist wherever electric current flows, for example in cables, electrical appliances, as well as plugs and sockets. They can be reduced by compensatory measures (e.g. phase exchange), shielding cables and switching off electrical appliances and circuits (e.g. by using a demand switch). It is helpful in this case to provide separate earth and neutral conductors (e.g. by using a TNS system) and a star network rather than a ring network. In contrast to electric fields, magnetic fields arise from the motion of electric charges, especially in the case of transformers, charging devices, motors, coils as well as in the absence of forward and reverse current. The measures used to reduce electric fields are usually also effective for magnetic fields. However, the most simple method for reducing magnetic fields is to increase the distance to the source. Significant emission can arise from, for example, electricity use in neighbouring buildings, traction power supply or power lines.
	reduction of high frequency electric and magnetic fields	High-frequency electromagnetic fields arise from, for example, wireless communication, radio or radar systems. The negative effects caused by emission sources in buildings can be reduced by repositioning appliances (e.g. outside of bedrooms), redirecting, shielding or switching them off. In terms of protection from outside sources, it is either possible to shield only certain functional areas or the whole facade by making use of conductive materials.
	reduction of radon levels	Radon is a natural, radioactive noble gas, which is produced when small amounts of uranium and radium in soil and rocks decay. It can be drawn into the building through the ground. The risk of adverse health effects from radon exposure can be mitigated by extracting the gas before it penetrates the building (e.g. installing a drainage system and a radon well for removal purposes), sealing cracks (e.g. use of radon-proof coatings, seals, covering natural basement floors with a new layer of concrete) or increasing the ventilation in basement rooms (e.g. better natural or mechanical ventilation systems). Local radon maps provide information on the risk level in specific areas.

Protection of natural resources	Detailed definition of the environmental objective and necessary measures
conservation of material resources	Material resources, such as water, fossil fuels and minerals, should be used in an environmentally responsible way. Resource depletion can be slowed by consciously limiting material use to a minimum, using building products that are manufactured in a resource-efficient and environmentally friendly way, implementing renewable raw materials and making optimal use of all properties (e.g. use of durable materials with long renewal cycles).
conservation and rehabilitation of land and soil	Surface sealing should be minimised as far as possible. The aim should be to create compact and appropriately dense structures and to increase the local infiltration of rainwater (e.g. by using permeable paving systems in exterior zones and planted roofs). These methods help to maintain the local water balance and improve the local microclimate. In some cases, the possibility of unsealing paved surfaces should be considered.
sustainable management and conservation of biosphere	Interference in existing ecosystems should be minimised. In order to retain natural biotopes and support biological cycles (e.g. the natural water cycle), it is necessary to examine local situations during the early planning stages.
transformation of anthroposphere	Waste that is not reused has a negative impact on the anthroposphere and contributes to economic loss. Constructions which can be broken down into recyclable materials do not create waste at the time of deconstruction. Thus, suitable strategies for deconstruction should be considered during the design phase.

2.4

2.5

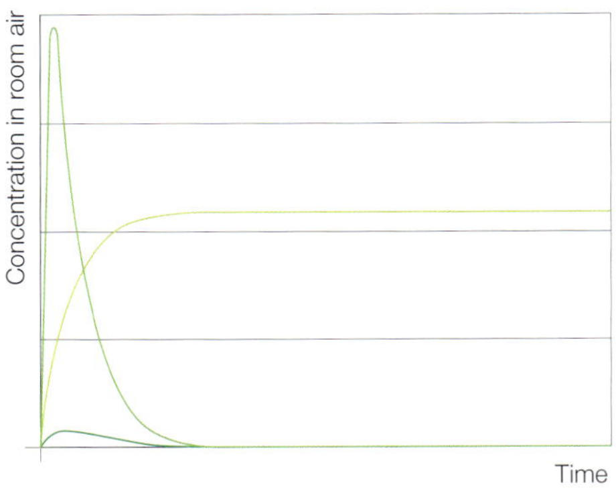

— typical emission performance of mineral building materials (e.g. gypsum, mortar, concrete, etc.)
— typical emission performance of fairly nonvolatile compounds, which outgas over long periods (e.g. SVOCs in wood preservatives, adhesives, varnishes, etc.)
— typical emission performance of wet materials (e.g. paint, primers)

2.6

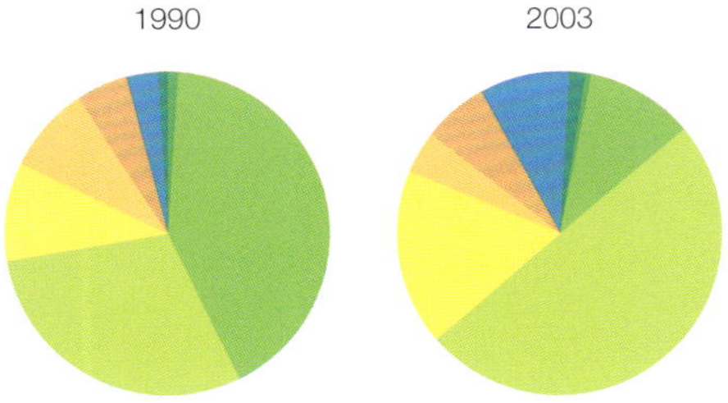

- transport
- solvents and other product applications
- agriculture
- emissions from fuel burning
- homes and small-scale consumers
- industrial processes
- energy industry
- manufacturing industry

2.7

2.5 Chapel in Valleacerón (E) 2001, Sancho-Madrilejos Arquitectos: exposed concrete construction with stunning atmosphere achieved by the interaction of indoors and outdoors and the minimalist range of materials
2.6 Typical emissions performance for a variety of construction materials
2.7 Proportion of different sources in the anthropogenic VOC emissions in Germany in 1990 and 2003
2.8 Ufogel holiday residence in Nußdorf-Debant (A) 2013, Peter Jungmann: example of optimising material use according to aspects of comfort and wellbeing. Larch wood is used almost entirely throughout the house.
2.9 Selection of pollutants and their sources in buildings (chemical load)

Building biology

Building biology is defined as the study of holistic interrelationships between humans and their living environment. It is a synonym for the environmentally friendly and pollution-free development of buildings, which are, at the same time, able to meet the occupants' requirements for a comfortable and healthy living environment. If nothing else, the individual perception of the occupants is of greatest importance in this context. Building biologists work as consultants and/or planners by, for example, giving advice on healthy conditions for living rooms, offices or bedrooms, but also on the conservation of natural resources and the promotion of a responsible approach to nature. They also perform tests in buildings, for example, to research into possible health hazards caused by noise, pollutants, mould, radon, electric and magnetic fields, and other sources.

Healthy environments for living, sleeping and working

The aim is to achieve greater

- comfort (wellbeing, happiness through aspects related to the living and working environments): among other things, it is possible to assess the impact of indoor air and surface temperatures, air humidity or the colour and light concepts applied within the building and affecting the occupants.
- wellbeing (physical and psychological health): this incorporates the
  - analysis of biological, chemical and physical loads indoors
  - taking measurements of pollutant emissions deriving from construction materials (volatile organic compounds (VOC), formaldehyde, biocides, etc.)
  - investigation into the concentration of dust and pollutants in indoor air
  - surveying rooms for mould infection (e.g. by taking material or air samples to detect mould spores, or performing mould swab tests)
  - analysis and reduction of hazards caused by radon and electrosmog indoors
- performance (assessment of capacity to do work): an important aspect of building biology is to avoid the so-called "Sick Building Syndrome", which is generally caused by indoor air pollution, carelessly maintained air conditioning units, which can in turn lead to allergies, headaches, tiredness, infections and asthma.

Protection of natural resources

The protection of natural resources includes the following aspects:

- conservation of material resources
- conservation and rehabilitation of land and soil
- sustainable management and conservation of biosphere
- promotion of building materials recyclability.

Figure 2.4 (p. 17) shows an overview of these objectives together with possible strategies for their implementation. Thus, planning according to building biology principles generally involves an integrated planning approach and making design-related adjustments. Notwithstanding the above, the matter of "pollutants in buildings" is an important consideration and explained in the following.

Analysis of pollutants

A lot of construction materials release pollutants into the air, which are then absorbed by occupants through their respiratory systems. The most noteworthy substances in this context are volatile hydrocarbon compounds (Volatile Organic Compounds, VOC). This chemical substance group includes, for example, solvents which are contained in various paints and varnishes and generally take a long time to outgas from the coated material. Formaldehyde, used for the production of synthetic resins, also contributes to the pollutant load of indoor air. It is contained in many laminated wood products and furniture, but also in adhesives, processed textiles, insulation materials and paper products. Formaldehyde can cause headaches, allergies and depression, it is also suspected of being carcinogenic. In order to avoid damage to health, the Federal Office of Public Health (FOPH) in Switzerland recommends that the concentration of formaldehyde should not exceed 0.1 ppm, which corresponds to 125 micrograms of formaldehyde per cubic metre of room air (μg/m^3) [2]. Chemical wood preservatives are a further source of pollution in buildings. If these are used in indoor areas, the biocides contained in the preservatives can severely impair the human nervous system.
In order to ensure a harmless environment for occupants, buildings should be completed with as few pollutants as possible. When choosing construction materials that are non-hazardous to health, it is important to understand that some pollut-

2.8

ants are incorporated into the building without at first being recognised, and do not develop their harmful effect until years later (fig. 2.6). One example of this phenomenon is the ageing process of adhesives and sealants, which can release pollutants years later when the material starts to decay.
Even construction materials in existing buildings which are in actual fact non-hazardous can become an emitter of pollution following long-term contamination. These secondary hazards can either be caused by user-related issues (e.g. spilled liquids, detergents) or primary pollution deriving from other construction materials. A building biologist can in this case carry out a comprehensive survey as a basis to determine suitable measures for the remedial treatment of the building.
Because these procedures are usually extensive and costly, the planner's main aim should be to avoid the ingress of pollutants into the building from the outset of the project development. This strategy also helps to ensure long-term maintenance of the property value. In the case of new builds, planners can already avoid potential material problems when selecting the type of construction and building products if they are sufficiently aware of the most important health and safety concerns. Health risks can, for example, stem from surface finishes and coatings, varnishes, primers and sealants, which are all characterised by an intensive use of solvents. Most of the building materials known to cause health problems are contained in these indirect, auxiliary construction materials, which make up only about five mass per cent of the today's total building stock [3].
Figure 2.7 shows the role of solvents as a source of anthropogenic VOC emissions in Germany according to information published by the German Federal Environment Agency, (UBA), and illustrates how this role has grown within only a few years.
Based on these facts, it is definitely worth striving to reduce the use of such auxiliary construction materials. For example, simply by laying fitted carpets and elastic floor coverings with fasteners rather than adhesives avoids a potential source of pollution. This measure also makes it easier to replace the floor covering later on (see Optimising replacement processes, pp. 64ff.). A further example concerns the rust proofing of steel components, where galvanisation is just as effective as a coat of paint. Because some of these measures also have an impact on appearance, the preselected materials should be considered carefully early on to determine any potential health issues.
Analyses to determine whether building products are hazardous to health or not change continuously in line with the current state of technology. This explains why some construction materials, which were originally thought to be a novel innovation in the building industry, were later identified as a source of pollution (e.g. asbestos fibre products). In terms of pollutants in buildings, it is therefore possible to differentiate between already familiar problems and newly emerging issues.
Figure 2.9 shows an overview of pollutants and their sources currently known to be hazardous to humans in existing and new buildings.

Valuation concepts
With few exceptions, there are to date no legally binding limit values for the pollutant load of indoor air. In order to nevertheless evaluate the danger of a pollutant, guideline values are defined according to two different methods:
- toxicologically derived assessment concepts
- statistically derived assessment concepts

Toxicologically derived assessment concepts
Toxicological assessments are usually performed by using in vivo experiments, in which different concentration levels of a single compound are tested on animals. The experiments help to determine the threshold level of the dose above which organ failure or metabolic disorders occur. The results of the tests are then used to calculate toxicological limit values. A hazard to human health cannot be ruled out, if the value determined is exceeded. However, toxicological limit values are not always suited to present the sum concentration of different substances, their interaction as well as the health risk to humans resulting from

Pollutant	**Possible sources in buildings**
asbestos	sprayed asbestos, plasters and renders, asbestos cement panels (e.g. as a roof covering or facade cladding, window sills and panelling in radiator recesses), elastic floor coverings, fire-resistant cladding, asbestos sheathing felt, stuffing and sealing tape, putties, strings, ropes and ties, fabric membranes and foamed materials, friction linings; electrical insulators, electric off-peak storage heaters, waste water and gas pipes → *banned for all applications in Germany since 1990; Asbestos Regulation since 1996 (D)*
biocides	wood preservatives (e.g. in coatings (paints, varnishes), adhesives, impregnating agents, primers), renders for composite thermal insulation systems, facade paints, paints for damp rooms, carpets, contamination of renewable building materials
bisphenol A (BPA)	plastics (e.g. packaging, multi-layered hollow plastic panels), pipe linings, paint (primers, varnishes), adhesives
formaldehyde	engineered wood products, floor sealers, fitted wardrobes, furniture, acid hardening fixers, wood adhesives, preservatives
artificial mineral fibres (AMF)	insulation materials made of mineral fibres (glass, rock or slag), textile glass fibres, ceramic fibres and fibres for special purposes (glass micro fibres) → *1990 introduction of CI index (CI value ≥ 40 means that product is not carcinogenic) (D)*
polycyclic aromatic hydrocarbons (PAHs)	coal tar (e.g. via parquet flooring adhesives, roofing membrane, asphalt flooring); creosote (e.g. wood preservatives); naphthalene (e.g. moth proofing agents, paints and varnishes) → *1991 creosote ban (D)*
polychlorinated biphenyl (PCB)	sealants and putties, coatings (paints, varnishes), electrical components (capacitors, transformers) → *1989 PCB ban (D), 2004 EC Regulation No. 850/2004*
volatile organic compounds (VOC)	coatings (paints, varnishes), adhesives, sealants, impregnating agents, oils, solvents, plasticisers, plastics

2.9

VOC compound	CAS registration number	Reference value (I) IRK ad hoc working group (UBA) [µg/m³]	Reference value (II) IRK ad hoc working group (UBA) [µg/m³]	New build AGÖF reference value 2013) [µg/m³]
toluene	108-88-3	300	3000	30
styrene	100-42-5	30	300	12
phenol	108-95-2	20	200	3
benzyl alcohol	100-51-6	400	4000	4.6
furfural	98-01-1	10	100	4
formaldehyde	50-00-0	30 [1)]	100/120 [1)]	30 [1)]
benzaldehyde	100-52-7	20	200	15
acetaldehyde	75-07-0	100	1000	ns
methyl isobutyl ketone	108-10-1	100	1000	8
TVOC		300–1000	3000–10000	1000

[1)] these guidance or reference values are not taken from the same source (list of references see p. 144)

2.10

GISCODE	Label	Product groups	Solvent content
RE 0	X_i	epoxy resin dispersion	< 5%
RE 1	C, N	epoxy resin products, sensitising, solvent-free	solvent-free (<0.5%)
RE 2	C, N, R10	epoxy resin products, sensitising, low in solvents	< 5%
RE 2.5	X_n, F	epoxy resin products, contains solvents	> 5%
RE 3	C, N, F	epoxy resin products, sensitising, contains solvents	> 5%
RE 4	C, X_n, N, R_{10}	epoxy resin products, sensitising, with toxic component, low in solvents	< 5%
RE 5	C, X_n, N, R_{11}	epoxy resin products, sensitising, with toxic components, contains solvents	> 5%
RE 6	T, N	epoxy resin products, sensitising, toxic, low in solvents	< 5%
RE 7	T, F, N	epoxy resin products, sensitising, toxic, contains solvents	> 5%
RE 8	T, N	epoxy resin products, sensitising, carcinogenic, low in solvents	< 5%
RE 9	T, F, N	epoxy resin products, sensitising, carcinogenic, contains solvents	> 5%

X_i irritating C corrosive N harmful to environment R_{10} flammable R_{11} easily flammable
X_n harmful to health F easily flammable T toxic

2.11

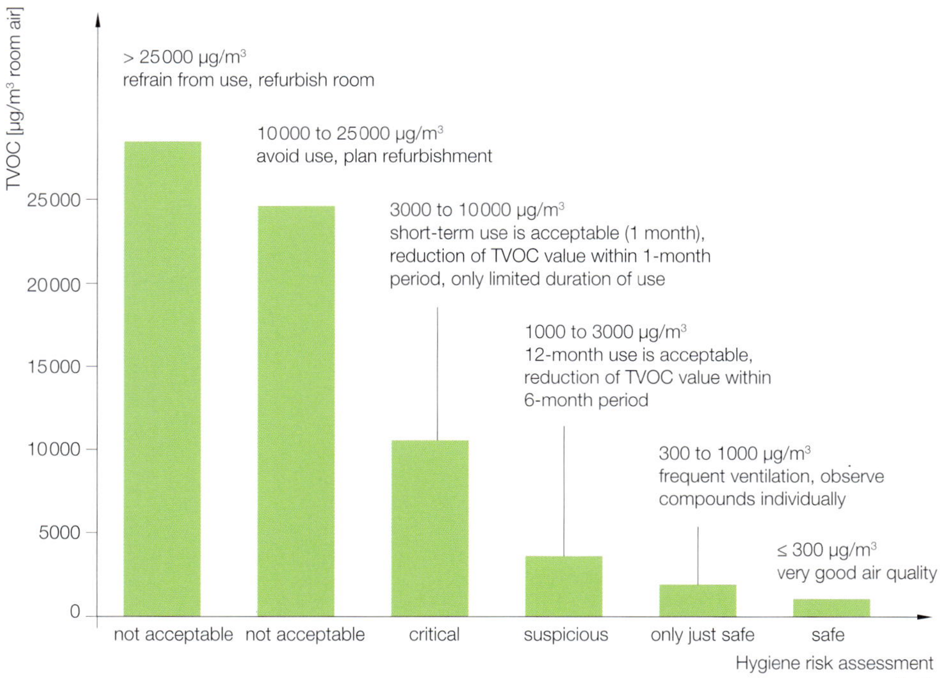

2.12

these. Moreover, it is difficult to simulate the long-term exposure to very low doses typical in the building industry by using in vivo experiments.
The findings from toxicological experiments are, for example, used as a basis in Germany for the concept of guideline values established by the ad-hoc Working Group with experts from the Indoor Air Hygiene Commission (IRK) of the Federal Environment Agency and the Permanent Working Group of the Highest State Health Authorities (AOLG). The concept applies two reference values. Guideline value II (GV II) is a health-related value based on current knowledge about the effect threshold of a pollutant. If the determined concentration level is reached or exceeded, immediate action must be taken and the room may no longer be used for permanent stay. Depending on the effect of the pollutant in question, the value is either identified as a short-term effect value (GV II S) or a long-term effect value (GV II L). The guideline value I (GV I) applies to concentrations ranging between the level at which, according to current know-how, a substance does not give rise to adverse effects even with lifelong exposure, and the level at which precautionary measures must be taken. GV I is obtained by dividing GV II by a factor, which was initially introduced as a convention (usually 10). Thus, GV I can, for example, be used as a maximum value for a refurbishment.

Statistically derived assessment concepts
The statistically derived reference values are the result of a large number of comparative indoor air measurements. Data for individual pollutants is gathered from the measurements, and reference values are established, which, if exceeded, indicate a case of unusual exposure. However, these reference values do not give an immediate indication of the specific health risk to humans.
The Association of Ecological Research Institutes (AGÖF) in Germany has used the statistics to develop a statistically derived assessment concept for the pollutant load of indoor air.

Combined assessment concepts
Only the combined use of toxicologically and statistically derived data enables a comprehensive assessment of the pollution situation in a building and, thus, provides the basis for effective use. Figure 2.10 presents a selection of VOC compounds with the toxicologically

2.13

2.14

derived guideline values and statistically derived reference values. The total of all volatile organic compounds (TVOC) in the air is a perfect example to present these facts:

- toxicological data:
  only just hygienically harmless
  > 300–1000 μg/m³
  hygienically harmful
  > 3000–10000 μg/m³
- statistical data:
  standard concentration (AGÖF 2013): 360 μg/m³
  conspicuous value P 50 (AGÖF 2013): 1572 μg/m³
  reference value P 90 (AGÖF 2013): 1000 μg/m³ [4]

Based on these facts, the Federal Environment Agency's ad hoc working group recommends that, in terms of a long-term objective, the TVOC concentration should range between 200–300 μg/m³ (fig. 2.12). Concentrations above 1000 μg/m³ indicate a general need for action. Concentrations exceeding 10000 μg/m³ are not acceptable from a hygiene point of view and require immediate action.
However, regarding the above-mentioned assessment concepts, it is important to understand that the findings concerning the health hazards of individual pollutants cannot necessary be applied to the additional health risks caused by the possible interaction of compounds in pollutant mixtures. A variety of pollutants from numerous different sources (e.g. smoking, cooking, heating, cleaning) accumulate indoors and mix with those stemming from construction materials and furniture. Due to the complexity of the matter, there are to date no scientifically confirmed findings concerning these interdependencies. Thus, to be on the safe side, all potential sources of pollutants in buildings should be minimised as much as possible.

Planning tools
There are various assessment tools to help planners select building materials and auxiliary building materials that are not hazardous to health. Among these are numerous labels and seals of approval certifying that building products are harmless and safe (so-called Type I Environmental Product Declarations, such as EMICODE or EU Ecolabel). They are based on specific tests and identify products which are, within a particular product group, more environmentally friendly than others concerning specific aspects. However, the overabundance of information in this field is remarkable and not every label provides the originally assumed justification. Credible ecolabels offer transparency on the testing procedures involved in awarding labels, for example by offering a detailed description of the assessment criteria. In addition, they usually include information on the certified products which might be helpful for reference purposes.
Figure 2.15 (p. 22) presents some of the most well-known and recommended ecolabels.
The so-called Type III Environmental Product Declarations, which are based on a life cycle assessment of the product in question, provide information on potential danger that has already been identified but not yet proven. The database WECOBIS [5], which documents the environmental aspects of certain material groups, is also a useful source of information for checking the potential hazards of selected building materials.
The material safety data sheets provided by the manufacturers may also be helpful in answering any questions concerning the pollutants in building materials. Not only do they give a detailed technical description of the product, they also list ingredients and specify any hazardous substances, including possible effects that may occur during processing, installation or disposal. The listing of so-called SVHCs, substances of very high concern, is mandatory. SVHCs have serious and often irreversible effects on human heath (some are, for example, carcinogenic) and/or the environment, and must therefore be avoided at all costs.
A candidate list of hazardous substances is published by the ECHA (European Chemicals Agency) [6] and updated at regular intervals. It includes SVHCs with their corresponding CAS and EC numbers (standard international reference guides for chemical substances (CAS) and enzymes (EC)).
GISBAU, a service provided by the Construction Industry Trade Associations (BG BAU), is a further institution that offers information on hazardous substances by using the so-called GISCODE system [7]. The code categorises products into groups with a comparable level of health risk. It does not, however, consider all factors necessary for the choice of a non-hazardous product. GISCODE provides information, among other things, on the

2.10 Examples of VOC compounds with the corresponding guideline values set by the ad hoc working group and AGÖF guideline values (2013) which consider the total VOC content (TVOC) in buildings
2.11 GISCODE labels for epoxy resin products
2.12 TVOC assessment and recommendations provided by the Federal Environment Agency's ad hoc working group
2.13 Living with a minimum amount of space: prefabricated house "Bunkie" with a floor area of 10 m² made of prefabricated plywood components for self build purposes
2.14 Converted stable, dwelling in Almens (CH) 2010, M. Gujan + C. Pally: use of natural construction materials, such as mud and wood, to improve indoor climate

Ecolables for building products (alphabetical order)	Product groups (the range of application of each is added in brackets)	Assessment criteria
Blue Angel (Blauer Engel) (Federal Environment Agency/RAL German Institute for Quality Assurance and Certification)	Bituminous coatings[1], floor coverings made of wood or wood products (including laminate flooring and wood flour-based linoleum), engineered flooring products[1], insulation materials made of recycled paper and glass, low-emission sealing compounds for interior fit-out[2], wood and engineered wood products (including furniture and inside doors), varnishes/primers[2], masonry blocks and roofing tiles, wallpaper, wall paint[2], composite thermal insulation systems[1], cements/plaster/mortar *highly recommended[3]; awarded in Germany*	Depending on the label: "protection of the environment": impact on the climate, "protection of the environment and public health": impact on the environment and health, "conservation of resources": consumption of resources. Individual assessment criteria for each product group. A detailed list of assessment criteria is available for each product group on the Blue Angel website. *www.blauer-engel.de*
eco-Institut-Label	Coating materials (based on synthetic materials), sealants (based on synthetic materials), wood-based materials/fit-out panels (with surface coatings, e.g. MDF board, particle board, OSB panels), adhesives (based on synthetic materials), mineral building products, wood and cork flooring products, parquet flooring, laminate flooring, panelling (with surface coatings based on synthetic materials), carpets, resilient and exterior flooring products *recommended[3]; awarded worldwide*	Emission assessment for formaldehyde, VOC, TVOC and TSVOC, etc., as well as assessments of hazardous contents, such as heavy metals, pesticides, biocides, plasticisers, etc. Labels relevant for certification:[2] EC1/EC1^{Plus} and EC1-R/EC1^{Plus}-R *www.eco-institut.de/von-der-analyse-bis-zur-qualitaetssicherung/eco-institut-label/*
EMICODE (Association for the Control of Emissions in Products for Flooring Installation, Adhesives and Building Materials)	Adhesives, primers, undercoating paints, surface fillers, underlays, insulation materials, parquet varnishes, screed, etc. *recommended[3]; awarded worldwide*	Emission assessment for VOC, TVOC and TSVOC. *www.emicode.com*
EU Ecolabel (European Commission)	Varnishes/primers, wall paints, flooring products (tiles) *highly recommended[3]; awarded throughout EU*	Individual assessment criteria for each product group *http://ec.europa.eu/environment/ecolabel*
FSC (Forest Stewardship Council A.C.)	Wood/engineered wood products *highly recommended[3]. awarded worldwide*	Environmentally friendly, socially beneficial and economically viable forest management and maintenance. *www.fsc-deutschland.de*
natureplus	Insulation materials, varnishes/primers, wall paints, wood/engineered wood products, floor coverings (made of wood), floor coverings (excluding wood flooring materials), cement/plaster/mortar (plaster, mortar and mineral adhesives), masonry blocks/roof tiles (roof tiles/vertically perforated brick) *highly recommended[3]. awarded throughout EU.*	Climate, health and sustainability: conservation of resources in material extraction and production, emission assessment for VOC and assessments concerning the use of hazardous compounds (e.g. heavy metals). *www.natureplus.org*
PEFC (Programme for the Endorsement of Forest Certification)	Flooring products (made of wood), wood/engineered wood products *recommended[3]; awarded worldwide*	Socially, ecologically and economically acceptable wood management. *www.pefc.de*
GoodWeave	Floor coverings (carpets) *highly recommended[3]; awarded worldwide for carpets from India and Nepal*	The aim is to end child labour, secure incomes and good working conditions, organise social and educational programmes and check that minimum environmental standards are met. *www.goodweave.de*

[1] relevant for certification according to BNB 2011 [2] relevant for certification according to BNB 2011 and DGNB (category: Office and administration building 2012)
[3] recommendation according to www.label-online.de [4] recommendation according to Action Program Environment and Health North Rhine Westphalia (APUG) 2.15

solvent content, not however on the VOC content.
It is not mandatory to list these codes in product brochures or data sheets. Although, manufacturers are usually able to present the GISCODE details fairly quickly upon request.
The higher the number following the product group, the higher the risk posed by the product. Figure 2.11 (p. 20) explains this grading system by using epoxy resin coatings as an example. According to this coding system, epoxy resin dispersions with GISCODE RE0 are less hazardous to health than epoxy resin products with GISCODE RE9.

2.15 Ecolabels for building materials

GISBAU also puts forward recommendations on the proper handling of construction materials in workshops and on building sites.
Figure 2.41 (p. 43) offers a detailed overview of the most important assessment tools for planners.

Building ecology

Ecology is the study of interactions among the living and nonliving components within the environment. By developing, operating and disposing of buildings, humans severely disturb ecological cycles. A building not only consumes raw materials, energy, water and ground during its life cycle, it also it produces vast amounts of pollution and waste. Building ecology is an attempt to depict the life cycle of construction materials, components and buildings from the extraction of raw materials through the erection and operation to the disposal. The aim is to assess the potential environmental impacts resulting from the various phases, as well as the consumption of resources and surface areas. With the help of building ecology, it is therefore possible to quantify the qualitative measures concerning resource conservation methods in the building industry (fig. 2.4, p. 17), which were stated in the context of the building biology aspects, and determine individual improvement strategies for each construction project and building component individually. So resource conservation is the most important link between building biology and building ecology. The building sector, as the largest consumer of resources worldwide,

offers great potential to reduce energy, ground and material consumption, because it is this sector that is responsible for 30 % of global CO_2 emissions and 40 % of global primary energy consumption. Material consumption can be reduced considerably by developing and applying new, more environmentally friendly building products, increasing the possibilities for reuse and recycling, improving their durability, and constructing buildings using comprehensive resource conservation methods. In terms of the building, though, there should by a clear emphasis on optimising the functionality of the overall system. A detailed introduction of suitable strategies for the implementation of resource conservation measures in practice is provided from page 43.
The following sections outline the assessment criteria for construction materials and buildings with regard to building ecology as well as the life cycle assessment methodology, which is used to determine the potential environmental impacts of buildings.

Live cycle assessment of buildings

In recent years, life cycle assessment (LCA) has become an effective tool to evaluate the potential impacts buildings and components have on the environment during their life cycle. The ISO standards 14040 [8] and 14044 [9] describe the general approach and principles of life cycle assessment. The European standard EN 15978 [10] is especially designed for the life cycle assessment of buildings and provides a detailed description of all aspects that are relevant in the context of property development. Life cycle assessments are particularly helpful to architects and other planning professionals in supporting the decision-making process and assisting the selection of materials for specific development schemes. They should therefore be performed at a very early project stage in order to weigh possible alternative solutions and make the best possible decisions in consideration of the building's total life cycle. Life cycle assessment is a method to calculate the material and energy flows, where all inputs (total amount of raw materials and energy used) and outputs (total amount of waste and emissions produced) during the full life cycle of a product system (e.g. a building) are associated with potential environmental impacts (e.g. the environmental impact "climate change", which incorporates the negative impacts of greenhouse gases on climate change). The relation between energy flows and environmental impacts always refers to the specific function that the product system in question has to fulfil during its total life cycle. In the case of a building, this function can be associated with meeting requirements specifically concerning building physics (e.g. energy standard, fire and noise protection). This is defined as the so-called functional unit. The potential environmental impacts are identified according to the individual inputs and outputs and, by using the functional unit, expressed in relation to the objective and scope of the life cycle assessment. "One year and one square metre of a building, which meets the predefined functions" is, for example, a common functional unit. So the results of the life cycle assessment are, in this case, divided by the estimated service life and floor area of the building, which are linked to the predetermined building function.
It is important to understand that life cycle assessments are not suitable for making precise or even absolute predictions of environmental impacts due to the relative and very target-oriented assignment of results to a functional unit and other inevitable uncertainties in the calculation. Inaccuracies in life cycle assessments can result from possible modelling errors (e.g. in the definition of the degree of detail (system boundary), the consideration and selection of the allocation method, the functional unit and the applied databases. They can also derive from assumptions concerning the potential future environmental impacts, not all of which are quantifiable at the time of performing the assessment. The results of a life cycle assessment should therefore always be put into perspective by using a sensitivity analysis, which is designed to clarify critical aspects of modelling and previous assumptions by taking into consideration suitable alternatives. It is for this reason that the following passages offer a closer look at potential uncertainties in the life cycle assessment of buildings. In addition, advice is given on how to recognise critical aspects and avoid making common mistakes in performing and interpreting life cycle assessments. Despite the above-mentioned potential uncertainties, life cycle assessments of buildings are well suited for not only comparing different material or component alternatives, but also life cycle scenarios, which the planner can choose from in certain situations and use to draw conclusions on the potential for improvement available in buildings.
In the case of buildings, it is possible to distinguish between different levels of detail (fig. 2.16). On a material level, the production and disposal of a product are usually the main aspects of consideration. The aim here is to minimise, as far as possible, the use of energy and resources as well as the resulting impact on the environment. On a component level, on the other hand, the focus is on the meaningful combination of different materials (e.g. improving the material configuration of a certain component in terms of its durability and replacement cycles). On a building level, the main interest lies in the interaction of components and building services with regard to the total building as well as the energy required to operate it (e.g. energy for heating, domestic hot water and ventilation). It is on this level that overriding aspects, such as a compact design or the energy standard of a building, have a significant impact on the results of the life cycle assessment, since these are features that affect the size of the envelope surface area and thus the demand for building materials in the construction phase and the energy demand in the operation phase. Moreover, preparatory measures (e.g. excavating and backfilling operations) and transportation of materials to the construction site or place of disposal can be included in a comprehensive building life cycle assessment in order to determine their influence on the total environmental impact of the development. A comparative life cycle assessment considers several buildings simultaneously with the aim of helping the planner to make decisions during the design process.
The life cycle assessment method according to ISO 14040 is divided into four successive phases (fig. 2.18).

- goal and scope definition
- inventory analysis
- impact assessment
- interpretation

The following sections explain the most important stages of a building life cycle assessment according to an example project (fig. 2.17) [11].

Goal and scope definition

The definition of the goal and scope of the assessment is determined in the first phase. The aim is to identify issues and questions which should be dealt with in the life cycle assessment. The information

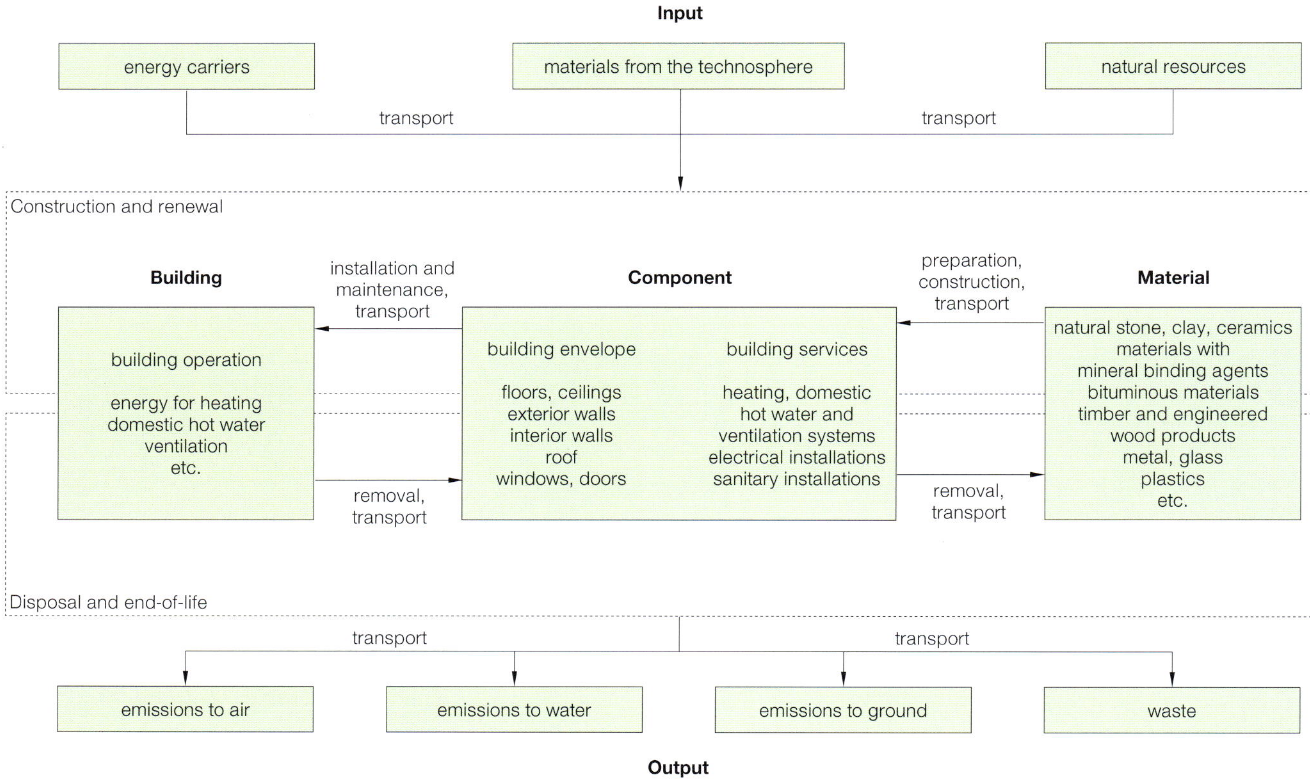

2.16

is then used as a basis to clarify where the system boundary of the assessment lies and which product processes (in the case of a building, for example, construction, replacement and disposal of components) must be considered in order to answer the questions correctly. In the context of buildings objectives and issues can differ fundamentally:

- How can the selection of materials be optimised to increase the service life of building components and improve the replacement thereof?
- Which construction material is most suitable for which purpose or function in a building?
- Which construction materials and building components of a development have the greatest impact on the environment? Where is, therefore, the greatest potential for improvement?
- Which phase of the building life cycle results in the greatest environmental impact?
- In the case of a building comparison: which building fares best in terms of its environmental impact?

The aim of the example life cycle assessment study presented here (fig. 2.17) is to identify the building components and phases which have the greatest influence on the environmental impact over the total 60-year life cycle of the building and thus offer the planner the greatest potential for improvement. (For comparison: the assessment period of the DGNB life cycle assessment is only 50 years.)
Once all objectives and issues have been clarified, the process of the life cycle assessment study is determined. The aim here is to develop a strategy to achieve the previously defined goals and plan the necessary stages. In the example life cycle assessment presented here, the life cycle assessment software SimaPro (version 7.3.0) is used to conduct a comparative life cycle assessment of twelve different multi-unit dwellings. In order to answer all questions correctly, the life cycles of the buildings are modelled in detail on a material level.
The following aspects must be considered carefully when developing the strategy:

- definition of system boundary
- choice of suitable allocation method
- definition of functional unit
- determination of suitable database and data quality
- identification of assumptions for the life cycle assessment modelling approach
- selection of appropriate impact categories and indicators

All of these aspects have an influence on the results of the life cycle assessment. Thus, special care should be taken in the selection process; in particular, in the case of a comparative life cycle assessment of different buildings. In order to ensure comparable results, the same system boundaries must be used and the functional units and databases selected must be identical.
The following information is designed as support for these initial stages.

Definition of system boundary
The system boundary is selected according to the initially defined objectives of the life cycle assessment. A diagram is the best way to express the meaning of a system boundary. Figure 2.19 (p. 26) shows the system boundary of the life cycle assessment, which is used here for demonstration purposes. It examines completed new builds for which precise information was available for all material quantities implemented in the developments. The amount of detail at hand provides a basis for conducting an extremely accurate life cycle assessment. And due to the high degree of precision, it is possible to consider processes in the assessment otherwise often neglected, such as preparatory measures (e.g. excavation and backfill operations), the construction of the building, maintenance work, the disposal of components and materials, as

2.16 Level of detail in the life cycle assessment of buildings: building – component – material
2.17 Goal and scope of the example life cycle assessment presented on the following pages
2.18 Structure of a life cycle assessment

well as the building services. In addition, it takes account of the energy demand for heating, production of domestic hot water and electricity (for the operation phase of the building) and all processes regarding transportation of building materials to the construction site (construction phase) and later to the waste disposal site (deconstruction phase).
Depending on the objective and the degree of detail chosen for the study, further processes can be included within the system boundary, such as the workmanship and energy consumption on the construction site, demolition work and trim waste, or some of the aforementioned processes can even be removed from the analysis. When defining the system boundary, so-called cut-off criteria can be determined. All materials or substances adding up to, for example, less than 1 % of the total building mass can be neglected in the results of the life cycle assessment and can therefore be excluded from the evaluation. However, there is a danger here that precisely those materials that pose a risk to health and environment, such as primers, varnishes and wood preservatives, are left outside the system boundary. It is for this reason that the environmental impacts of hazardous compounds should be taken into account in defining cut-off criteria in order to map even small amounts of critical substances in the life cycle assessment.
The decision on the level of detail of a life cycle study can have a significant bearing on the results. It must therefore be tailored to meet the objective of the assessment and recorded in detail. At the beginning of a project, it is, for example, more realistic to carry out an approximate life cycle assessment since there is usually not sufficient detail at this early stage to record the exact quantities of materials for the structural components and total building. Planning tools like the Swiss electronic building component catalogue [13] can provide a first overview of the expected environmental impact of building components. It does not make sense and is not worthwhile to carry out a detailed life cycle assessment until sufficient information has been accumulated during the planning process. Further information concerning data sources and software solutions to support the planner in performing a life cycle assessment during the different planning phases is offered on page 35 onwards (Tools for the ecological assessment of buildings).

Selecting the allocation method
Allocation is always an issue in a life cycle assessment when several co-products result from one production process (meaning that further products must be dealt with in addition to the product concerned). This can be resolved by sharing the inputs and outputs and therefore the environmental impacts among the product concerned and the co-products or product systems, or, in other words, by allocating the appropriate share to each product. This is particularly important in a building context when producing a life cycle inventory analysis for building mate-

Example life cycle assessment [12]: Goal and scope definition

Question: Throughout the total building life cycle, which building components and life cycle phases have the most influence on the total building's environmental impact?

Goal: Identification of the building components and life cycle phases with the greatest potential for improvement.

Procedure: 12 different multi-unit dwellings (completed after 2006) are examined. The same system boundary is used for all buildings in order to ensure better comparability of the results.

System boundary: see figure 2.19 (p. 26). At the end of the service life, most materials are usually disposed of (that is not reused). In the preparation work, materials are disposed of at a landfill.

Allocation method: cut-off approach at end-of-life. The allocation method of the individual building materials can be taken from the ecoinvent report (www.ecoinvent.ch).

Functional unit: 1 m² of treated floor area per year of the building's design life

Data source and data quality: The ecoinvent database (high degree of transparency) is used as a source for the life cycle inventory data of the material and energy processes in the life cycle assessment; life cycle inventory data for the building services is taken from SIA 2032. The information concerning the material quantities and energy demand was compiled by the corresponding planning practices (variations cannot be fully excluded).

Assumptions: A number of assumptions had to be made, e.g. concerning the bulk density of materials or the thickness of layers in components, the service life of individual materials, transport distances, etc.

Impact categories and impact indicators:
- embodied energy (nonrenewable energy for production, transport and disposal of building materials) and nonrenewable energy for building operation
- embodied emissions (from production, transport and disposal of building materials) and emissions from building operation (GWP 100a).

2.17

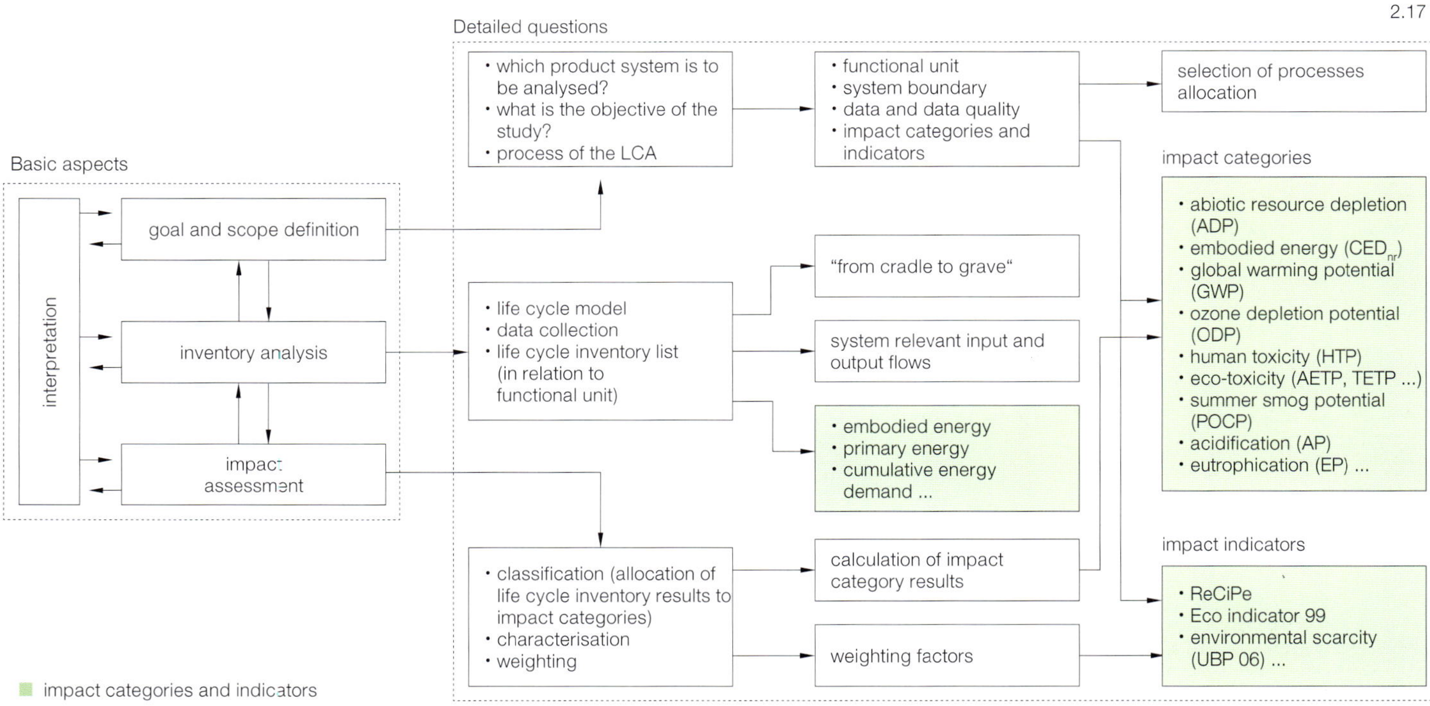

2.18

rials. For example, co-products frequently occur when manufacturing wood products (e.g. saw dust, wood chip).
A further use of allocation in the life cycle assessment takes place when modelling the end-of-life disposal phase - that is if the product concerned is designed for reuse or recycling (fig. 2.21, 2.22). There are different allocation methods which either perform the assignment according to product mass or volume or according to the economic value of co-products (or, in the case of recycling, according to the number of times the material can be reused). The ISO standard 14044 offers a good overview of possible allocation methods.
In order to model the energy processes and the component and material processes in the life cycle assessment, the planer should collect life cycle inventory data sets only from reliable sources. The data sets should provide clear and unambiguous information on the allocation method(s) used to produce them. The life cycle assessment presented here as an example, for instance, uses data sets from the internationally renowned ecoinvent database. It employs the so-called cut-off method for the end-of-use phase. The method implies that all environmental impacts caused by the product until it reaches the end of its life cycle should be allocated to the product concerned rather than, for example, sharing the impact among several future applications, which would be the case in the event of product recycling.

Definition of functional unit
The first phase of a life cycle assessment also includes the definition of the functional unit. The intention is that it determines the specific function(s) that a product system must fulfil during its service life. The functional unit is therefore designed to standardise a life cycle assessment according to the performance of a particular task, including both quantitative and qualitative aspects.
For example, it makes little sense, when performing a life cycle assessment of a building, to compare 1 kg of concrete with 1 kg of roof tiles in terms of quantity only. The comparison of different building materials can only produce meaningful results when associated with a specific structural component or building. Thus, it is more sensible to compare components that fulfil the same qualitative functions in a building (e.g. concerning thermal insulation capacity, noise protection properties, structural requirements, etc.). The selection of materials should then be optimised on the basis of this principle and in conjunction with the other materials incorporated in the component.
Qualitative aspects can have a much greater influence on the life cycle assessment of a building than is evident at first sight. It is precisely for this reason that they should be described in the evaluation of the components and outlined according to their impact only if they are not generally classified. According to this background, it makes sense when choosing the functional unit on a component level (e.g. 1 m² of ceiling, one-way slab with 6.6 m span, floor between apartments, sound insulation $R`_w$=53 dB, fire prevention F 90) to check the effects of the requirements. The impact of the span, for example, on the results of the life cycle assessment in residential building is not as great as the measures necessary to provide noise insulation and fire protection. The following list presents some of the qualitative aspects that can be considered when choosing the functional unit:

System boundary of building life cycle assessment

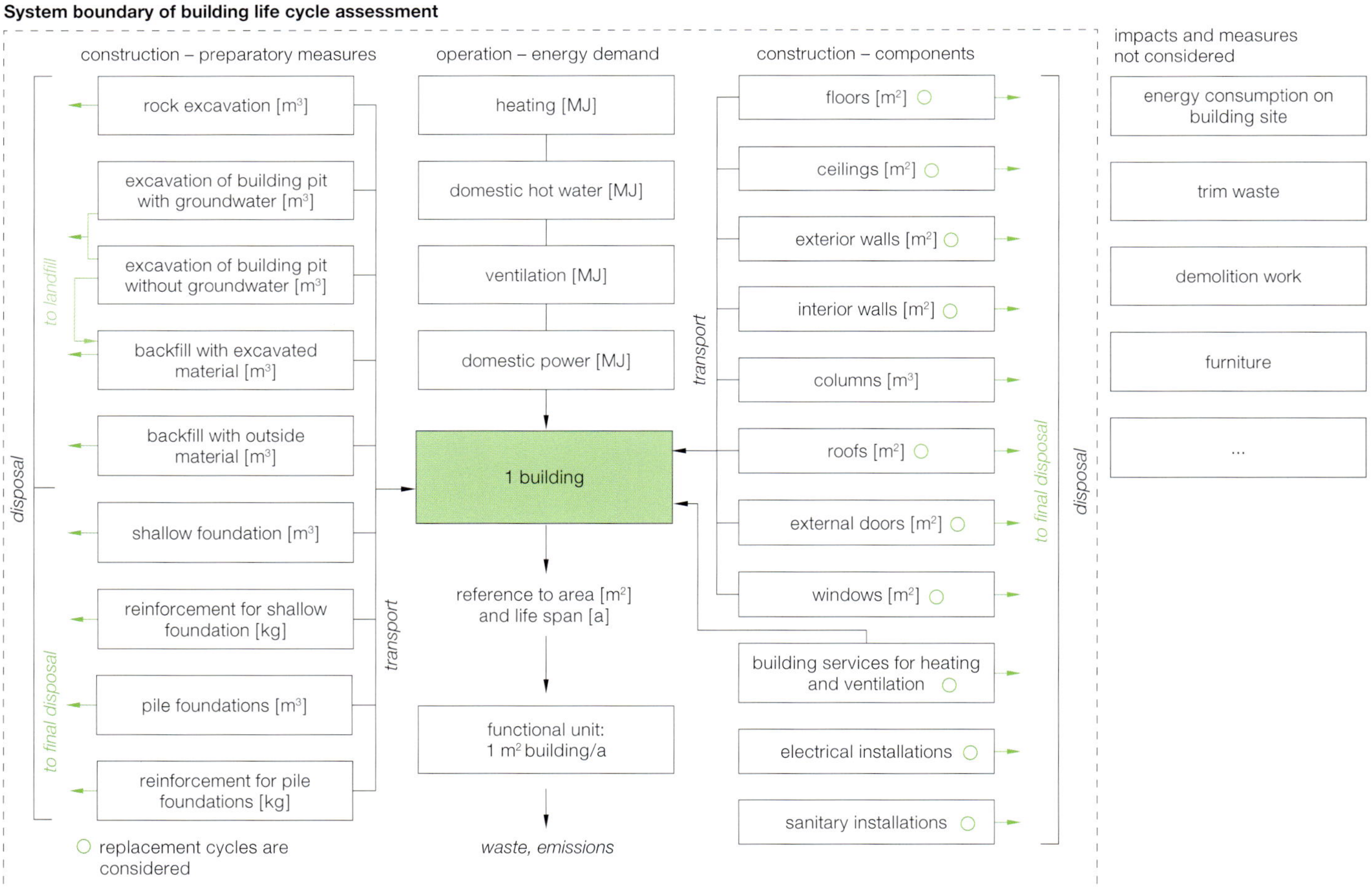

2.19

Functional unit	Possible objectives of study	System function	Examples
unit of mass or volume building material	weak point analysis or optimisation of production processes, EPD development	provision or conditioning of a defined quantity of building material	kg cement, kg reinforcing steel, m³ pumice
area unit of a component	product and quality control	provision of a building material with a defined U-value and g-value	m² window
	component optimisation	provision of a building component with defined statics and U-value	m² wall
	analysis of new or optimised applications	provision of a building component with a defined configuration (insulation X, wall material Y, U-value)	
total building	all-in-one solutions and integral component optimisation	provision of a building component with optimised system behaviour	1 building or 1 m² TFA
	strategic decisions	secure competitiveness	
	improving political framework conditions (legislation)	increase the innovation capacity of the product system or the industry	
	sensitivity or dominance analysis, building comparison	provision of a defined useful floor area with specific framework conditions	1 dwelling with 120 m² of floor area

2.20

2.21

- User flexibility: linear access corridors provide for greater user flexibility in the same way as switch rooms, larger span lengths and higher imposed loads, room heights exceeding 2.75 m and pre-planned wall and ceiling penetrations. The three aspects neutrality of use, pre-planned adaptability and acceptable restrictions of use are important considerations in this context. Neutrality of use generally offers the greatest potential for a flexible design; however, it is also the aspect that leads to an oversizing of components with the effect that the potential of reducing the environmental impact on a component level can no longer be fully exploited. On the other hand, neutrality of use is an important consideration if oversizing leads to added value in the originally planned scheme, for example by being able to provide flexible floor plans.
- Implementation of compensatory measures: in some cases, especially with regard to noise and fire protection, requirements, which would usually be met by applying suitable components, can also satisfied by using compensatory measures. A variety of solutions are available, such as ceiling panels, additional smoke extraction systems, bulkheads or sprinkler systems. If compensatory measures are used, it may be necessary to extend the system boundary of the life cycle assessment by these additional components. The problem arising from this strategy is that the respective material performance and environmental impact can be attributed only partially to a single building component. Planners are therefore recommended to make a rough estimate of any compensatory measures at an early design stage. The results highlight the consequences of a decision and enable clear specifications to be drawn up for the design. This approach also helps to limit the time and effort spent on planning.
- Interdependence of building components: it is virtually impossible to avoid interdependencies between building components, and therefore they occur frequently in design projects. There are numerous examples of interdependencies among building components. For instance, complex floor slab constructions with a correspondingly large construction height result in an increase of the facade surface area (fig. 5.2, p. 87), or a light, wide-span structural system may require a greater input of material at the supports in order to prevent the load-bearing elements (floor slabs or girders) from inducing a punching effect. Technical installations can also have structural consequences, for example when installing lagged water pipes in the impact sound insulation of a floor. In this case, the diameter of the pipes determines the thickness of the insulation. The aim should generally be to prevent point and strip-shaped elements from changing the configuration of a whole layer.

It makes sense at an early stage in the design to create an overview of all interdependencies and links between building components, which will be analysed in the life cycle assessment, and to roughly estimate the significance of the relationships. The results should then allow for the definition of a meaningful system boundary and functional unit that is suited to the general set-up of the assessment.

2.22

2.19 System boundary of the example life cycle assessment presented in this chapter
2.20 Examples of functional units
2.21 Flagship store made of freight containers in Zurich (CH) 2006, spillmann echsle architekten
2.22 Experimental structure made of recycled paper bales in Essen (D) 2010, Dratz & Dratz Architekten

All inputs and outputs of the life cycle inventory analysis as well as the impact analysis results of the life cycle assessment refer to the functional unit. It is important, therefore, to understand that different functional units can be applied to achieve a certain objective. On the other hand, the use of different functional units can produce significant variation in the results. This can, of course, clearly limit the comparability of a study to other life cycle assessments. Moreover, the choice of functional unit can also influence the results of the analysis considerably.
If, for example, the results of a building life cycle assessment refer to 1 m^2 of floor area, the numerical values tend to be much lower than if the study had referred to 1 m^2 of treated floor area, as the treated floor area refers only to a certain part of the floor area. The result is that the environmental impact of a building can appear less severe if it is expressed by a cleverly chosen functional unit. This is definitely something that should be taken into consideration when analysing the results of a completed life cycle assessment or comparing the results of various studies.
The table in figure 2.20 (p. 27) presents a small selection of possible functional units suitable for carrying out a life cycle analysis of buildings, building components or construction materials according to the objective of the study and the determined system function. Further variations can be achieved by changing the modelling approach of the analysis.
The comparative life cycle assessment presented here (fig. 2.17, p. 25) defines the functional unit as follows: "1 m^2 of treated floor area per year for the expected service life of a new multi-family dwelling (developed after 2006)". The treated floor area is in this case determined according to the Swiss standard SIA 380/1. It includes all floor areas above and below ground which are contained within the thermal envelope and require heating or cooling for proper use. In Switzerland, the treated floor area is used as a reference value to calculate the annual space heating demand. The treated floor area is therefore perfectly suited for comparing the environmental impacts caused by operating the building with the environmental impacts caused by the materials used in the building throughout the life cycle. By converting the total result into a square metre of building, no matter which reference area was chosen (i.e. treated floor area or useful floor area), the differences in the sizes of buildings is equalised enabling better comparison.
The design life of the building selected for the presented example is 60 years; the functional unit refers to one year of this total period. This means that the final result of each building is first divided by the size of the relevant treated floor area and then by 60. The requirements regarding building physics that all examined properties had to meet are more or less comparable, since all buildings were completed at roughly the same time (since 2006); furthermore, they had access to same standard of technology. The energy standard, which differs fundamentally in each of the examined buildings, is the only exception. Thus, a life cycle assessment must also include information on the selected energy efficiency standard and the heating system installed in order to compare the findings and bring the results of an individual building in line with those of the model building.

Data and data quality requirements
A further important step, which must be accomplished during the first phase of a life cycle assessment, is the selection of a suitable database, and thus also the quality of data, for all material and energy flows. The quality of data influences the depth and detail of the whole life cycle assessment. Suitable data can, on the one hand, be obtained from professional inventory databases (for general data concerning material and energy flows) and, on the other hand, from commonly available sources and Type III Environmental Product Declarations according to ISO 14025 and ISO 15804 (for certain building products). Primary data can also be obtained from manufacturers and used for life cycle assessments. It is always advisable to use data from a database with a high degree of transparency in order to comprehend the principles that were used to compile the product data. This especially applies if the aim is to publish the results of the life cycle assessment. Figure 2.23 displays a selection of freely available Internet-based building material databases for the performance of building life cycle studies. The pedigree matrix published by Weidema and Suhr Wesnaes (fig. 2.40, p. 42) is a useful tool to assess the quality of life cycle assessment data.
The life cycle inventory data used in the presented life cycle assessment model is derived mainly from the ecoinvent database (version 2.2), which is renowned for its high level of data transparency. SIA 2032 [14] was only used to obtain data for the building services. The information concerning the material quantities and the energy demand of the buildings was provided by the architects' practices. Unfortunately, it was not possible rule out all uncertainty in the figures supplied.

Assumptions for life cycle assessment modelling
A number of assumptions have to be made during the performance of a life cycle assessment, for example if the material quantities, the service life of materials or transport distances can be determined by making only a rough estimate. It is important, if this situation arises, to clearly document and describe the assumptions taken. Furthermore, the impact these have on the results of the life cycle assessment should be checked carefully in a sensitivity analysis, which is designed to compare different scenarios. For example, frequent replacement cycles of building materials and a considerable increase of the building design life result in the maintenance of the building acquiring greater significance than the construction itself. Such assumptions, which often lead to extreme uncertainties in the study and affect the results accordingly, can be put into perspective by making use of a sensitivity analysis.
The assumptions made for the life cycle assessment model (fig. 2.17, p. 25) refer to the thickness, density and design life of materials. It is assumed that the main construction materials (reinforced concrete, masonry and load-bearing timber structures) have a design life of 60 years, whereas most other building materials must be replaced after a period of only 30 years. Assumptions were also made concerning the transport distance of building materials to the construction site. In this case, it was assumed that all locally available materials cover a transport distance of 50 km, whereas a distance of 200 km was selected for all other materials. The building materials are delivered to the construction site by truck, which means that one empty run, for the return journey of the truck once it has been unloaded, is added per trip.

Selecting impact categories and indicators
The first phase of the life cycle assessment is also used for selecting impact categories and indicators. Their task is to help illustrate the environmental impacts

Name of database	Type of database	Contents and use
Datensammlung Dauerhaftigkeit www.nachhaltigesbauen.de/baustoff-und-gebaeudedaten/nutzungsdauern-von-bauteilen.html	• data collection concerning the durability of building components and component layers with different functions • high consistency of data since database is maintained by the Federal Ministry for the Environment, Nature Conservation, Building and Nuclear Safety (BMUB)	• durability of building components and component layers according the type and intensity of use • enables cross references of product service lives for products with similar use and implementation
Institut für Baubiologie und Bauökologie (IBO) www.ibo.at/de/oekokennzahlen.htm	• assessment of a component's technical and environmental parameters	• life cycle assessment data • publications with descriptive diagrams for the comparison of different materials and component configurations
Institut Bauen und Umwelt www.bau-umwelt.de	• information collection concerning the life cycle assessment of building materials • central collection point of EPD data sets and PCR documents • manufacturers' data verified by independent third parties • third-party verification ensures greater transparency in data quality • possibly lower consistency because the assessments are performed by different test centres and definition of system boundary is not 100 % clear • potentially very voluminous since new EPD data sets are added continuously	• life cycle assessment data • information on the environmental impact of building products • enables cross references of environmental impacts for products with similar use and implementation
KBOB-Empfehlung 2009/1: Ökobilanzdaten im Baubereich www.bbl.admin.ch/kbob/00493/00495/	• information collection concerning the life cycle assessment of building materials (approx. 150 data sets), building services (approx. 100 data sets), energy (approx. 70 data sets) and transport (approx. 50 data sets)	• life cycle assessment data • information on the environmental impacts of materials, building services, energy and transport
Ökobau.dat www.nachhaltigesbauen.de/baustoff-und-gebaeudedaten/oekobaudat.html	• information collection concerning the life cycle assessment of building materials and components • data collection independent of manufacturers • high quality, consistency and user security of data since database is maintained by BMUB • extensive: currently more than 1300 data sets (in 2013), of which 724 are generic data sets, 230 EPD data sets (calculated according to the new EN 15804) and 382 older data sets according to ISO 14025	• life cycle assessment data • information on the environmental impacts of materials
WECOBIS – ökologisches Baustoff-informationssystem www.wecobis.de	• information collection concerning building materials during their life cycle • categorisation according to the life cycle phases of building materials • manufacturer-independent data collection • extremely extensive • little help concerning navigation • in some cases very clear evaluation of building materials	• building material information • first information on product and application fields • particularly suited for experienced planners with knowledge of the ecology of building materials
U.S. Life Cycle Inventory Database http://www.nrel.gov/lci/	• information collection concerning the life cycle assessment of materials (more than 900 data sets)	• life cycle assessment data • information on the environmental impacts of materials, energy and transport

2.23

of all products and processes examined. The most important impact categories in a building construction context are presented in the following (fig. 2.24, p. 31).

Primary energy input PEI_{nr}, PEI_r, cumulative energy demand CED and embodied energy [MJ]:
The primary energy input includes the input of primary energy carriers needed to produce a material or product. A difference is made between the use of renewable (PEI_r) and non-renewable (PEI_{nr}) primary energy carriers.
The cumulative energy demand, on the other hand, describes the total input of primary energy required for the production, use and disposal of a product. A difference between renewable and non-renewable energy is made in this case, too. The two categories of cumulative energy demand are therefore "cumulative energy demand, renewable" (CED_r) and "cumulative energy demand, non-renewable" (CED_{nr}). There are various methods of calculating the cumulative energy demand: in Switzerland, for example, it is calculated according to the method established by Frischknecht et al. [15]. The Swiss system should not be mixed with the approach taken by the Association of German Engineers (VDI) [16] since the two methods lead to very different results. Thus it is important to indicate clearly which system is used for the calculations.
According to the Swiss Standard SIA 2032, the embodied energy is defined as the non-renewable primary energy or the non-renewable cumulative energy demand (according to Frischknecht et al.) associated with the production processes and disposal of a product including the necessary transportation of goods. The utilisation phase of the product is not covered in the calculations. With regard to construction work, this means that the operation of the building is not taken into consideration when calculating the embodied energy.

Climate change ⟶ global warming potential (GWP) [kg CO_2 eq.]:
The impact category "climate change" is expressed by the global warming potential (GWP). It is the impact on the Earth's atmosphere associated with the anthropogenic emissions of greenhouse gases (e.g. CO_2, CH_4, CFC). According to the German Federal Environment Agency (UBA) [17], the global annual mean temperature has risen by a total of approximately 0.74 °C since the beginning of the 20th century and, in fact, by 0.13 °C per decade since 1950. Climate researchers proceed on the assumption that a large proportion of the observed climate warming is being caused by human activities and the associated release of greenhouse gases. Greenhouse gases absorb infrared radiation with the effect that the temperature of the troposphere is

2.23 Selection of several freely accessible, Internet-based building material information platforms

increasing (fig. 2.24). This so-called greenhouse effect is caused by a variety of greenhouse gases, each affecting the climate in different ways and to different degrees.
Since, in comparison to other greenhouse gases, CO_2 has the smallest impact, it was chosen as a reference unit for the global warming potential. The impact of all other greenhouse gases is expressed by using characterisation factors, where factor 1 is equivalent to the absorption capacity that 1 kg of CO_2 has on the infrared radiation of the atmosphere. The Institute of Environmental Sciences (CML) at Leiden University has published a detailed list of characterisation factors for a variety of greenhouse gases and different impact periods (20 years, 100 years and 500 years) [18]. A period of 100 years (GWP 100a) is usually applied when performing a building life cycle assessment

Stratospheric ozone depletion → ozone depletion potential (ODP) [kg CFC-11 eq.]:
The ozone depletion potential (ODP) is an indicator for the thinning and destruction of the ozone layer in the stratosphere. The ozone layer filters approximately 99% of the ultraviolet (UV) radiation from the sun and prevents it from entering the Earth's atmosphere. The destruction of the ozone layer reduces the protective shield and increases the risks to human health (e.g. damage to eyes and skin, skin cancer). Chlorinated substances, such as fluorochlorinated hydrocarbon (CFC), are known to be particularly destructive to the ozone layer.
As is the case for the global warming potential, the effect of different substances is expressed with the help of characterisation factors. The reference unit here is 1 kg of CFC-11 (trichlorofluoromethane). Thus, the ozone depletion potential is expressed by the unit CFC-11 equivalent (CFC-11 eq.). Details concerning the characterisation factors have been published by CML [19].

Photochemical oxidant formation → photochemical ozone creation potential (POCP) [kg C_2H_4 eq.]:
Photochemical oxidants, ozone in particular, are referred to as photochemical smog or summer smog. They consist of aggressive pollutants, which are created from substances, such as nitric oxide (NO_x) or hydrocarbons, in the lowest parts of the atmosphere under the influence of sunlight. A high concentration of photochemical smog in the air has a toxic effect on human health.
The photochemical ozone creation potential (POCP) refers to the capacity of 1 kg of ethane (C_2H_4) in forming photochemical oxidants. The impact of other substances, such as nitrous oxides (NO_x) and formaldehyde, are expressed as relative C_2H_4 equivalents. CML has published the individual characterisation factors for a variety of substances [20].
Acidification → acidification potential (AP) [kg SO_2 eq.]:
The acidification potential (AP) addresses the destruction of ecosystems caused by the acidification of ground and water bodies. The effect occurs when certain airborne pollutants, such as sulphur dioxide (SO_2) or nitrous gases (NO_x), are transformed into acids (acid rain). The air contaminants generally derive from the combustion of fossil fuels, such as oil or coal. They lower the pH value of precipitation and mist, which in turn leads to forest dieback and corrosive damage to building materials (e.g. natural stone and metals). The reference unit for the acidification potential is 1 kg SO_2 eq. The impact of other substances, such as ammonia (NH_3) or nitrous oxides (NO_x), are expressed as the relative equivalents of the effect caused by 1 kg of sulphur dioxide (SO_2). Details concerning the characterisation factors of other substances have been published by CML [21].

Eutrophication → eutrophication potential (EP) [kg PO_4^{3-} eq.]:
Airborne pollutants, such as nitrous oxides (NO_x), and nutrients in waste water and agricultural fertilizers (e.g. nitrate (NO_3^-), phosphate (PO_4^{3-})) contribute to the higher concentration of nutrients in the ground and fresh water bodies. An excess of nutrients in water results in the excessive growth of algae and death of fish. Eutrophication of the soil disrupts plant growth and reduces their resistance to infections. The accumulation of nitrate in the ground and drinking water is also an issue in that the nitrate can undergo a chemical reaction and change into nitrite, which has a toxic effect on the human body.
The eutrophication potential is expressed in phosphate equivalents. Consequently, the eutrophication potential of other substances is equivalent to the effect that 1 kg of PO_4^{3-} has on the environment. The characterisation factors for the eutrophication potential have been published by CML [22].

Life cycle inventory

The life cycle inventory (LCI) phase involves developing a detailed model of a product's life cycle. It is performed by using the basic conditions determined during the first phase of the life cycle assessment (goal and scope definition). Ideally, the life cycle model of a building includes everything "from cradle to grave" in order to illustrate all phases throughout the life cycle of a development. All the data concerning the quantities of materials and energy flows (consumption of resources and energy on the input side; waste and emissions on the output side) are compiled during this phase and assigned to the previously defined functional unit. The predetermined product inventory databases, which should ideally feature a high level of transparency, are used as a source of data for recording all necessary processes (e.g. the extraction of raw materials or the disposal of a certain building product, the energy supply, etc.).
The actual modelling of the building's life cycle can then either be performed by using a life cycle assessment software tool (e.g. OpenLCA, SimaPro, LEGEP) or by compiling the data in a simple spreadsheet program.
Figure 2.25 (p. 31) shows an example of the modelling details for a floor structure, as well as an extract of the results obtained through the life cycle inventory analysis. Because the life cycle inventory data in this example was available only in kg and m^3, it had to first be converted into square metres in order to correspond with the surface areas of the building materials. The assumptions made in this context are presented in the last column of the table.
Due to the fact that the total life cycle of the rather complex product system "building" has to be assigned and calculated with such data, the result of the life cycle inventory phase is a long list of inputs and outputs, which functions as a basis for identifying and quantifying the causes of the environmental impacts. Because the list is not a suitable tool for interpreting the potential environmental impacts, a further step must be completed first: the life cycle impact assessment (LCIA), which is explained in the following section.

2.24 Schematic diagram of the most important impact categories in a life cycle assessment
2.25 Extract from a life cycle assessment
a modelling of a floor structure
b extract from a life cycle inventory list for the same component (referring to a component surface area of 100 m^2)

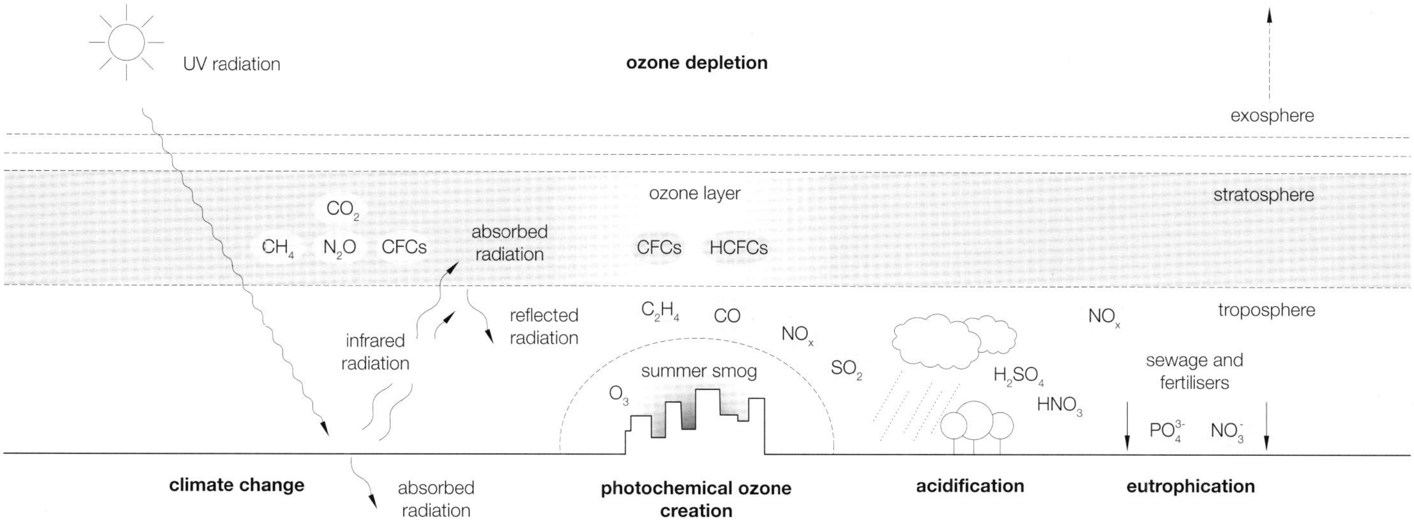

2.24

Construction materials	Quantity [1)]	Unit	Description
cement screed (ex works)	(0.03 · a · 1850)	kg	thickness of layer: 0.03 m; weight density: 1850 kg/m³; service life: 30 years
concrete floor slab (concrete, normal, ex works)	0.4 · a	m³	thickness of layer: 0.4 m; weight density: 2380 kg/m³; service life: 60 years
reinforcing steel for concrete flcor slab (ex works)	0.4 · a · 80	kg	weight density: 80 kg/m³; service life: 60 years
lean concrete (ex works)	0.1 · a	m³	thickness of layer: 0.1 m; weight density: 2190 kg/m³; service life: 60 years
Replacement/renewal of materials			
cement screed (ex works)	(0.03 · a · 1850)	kg	thickness of layer: 0.03 m; weight density: 1850 kg/m³; service life: 30 years
Disposal waste for further treatment			
cement screed (disposal, building, cement (in concrete) and mortar)	(0.03 · a · 1850) · 2	kg	thickness of layer: 0.03 m; weight density: 1850 kg/m³; service life: 30 years
reinforced concrete (disposal, building, reinforced concrete)	(0.4 · a · 2380) + (0.4 · a · 80)	kg	thickness of layer: 0.4 m; weight density of concrete: 2380 kg/m³; reinforcing steel: 80 kg/m³; service life: 60 years
lean concrete (disposal, building, unreinforced concrete)	0.1 · a · 2190	kg	thickness of layer: 0.1 m; weight density: 2190 kg/m³; service life: 60 years

[1)] a = 100 m²; this means that all calculations in this table refer to a component surface area of 100 m².

a

No.	Substance	Environmental compartment	Environmental sub-compartment	Unit	Construction [1)]	Replacement/ renewal [1)]	Disposal [1)]
243	CO_2, fossil	air		kg	13833	846	1443
244	CO_2, fossil	air	emissions in high-density areas	kg	1210	38.51	233
245	CO_2, fossil	air	emissions in low-density areas	kg	1551	35.77	220
246	CO_2, fossil	air	emissions in stratosphere and troposphere (air plane emissions)	mg	83.24	12.95	101
247	CO_2, in air	raw material	in air	kg	154	60.53	4.94
472	formaldehyde	air		g	7.44	0.28	24.56
473	formaldehyde	air	emissions in high-density areas	g	3.88	0.26	0,26
474	formaldehyde	air	emissions in low-density areas	mg	771	50.62	61.83
475	formaldehyde	air	emissions in stratosphere and troposphere	µg	4.16	0.65	5.06
696	methane, fossil	air		g	144	12.66	53.47
697	methane, fossil	air	emissions in high-density areas	g	212	28.83	244
698	methane, fossil	air	emissions in low-density areas	oz	835	27.67	108
699	methane, fossil	air	stratosphere and troposphere	µg	1.32	0.21	1.61
1241	VOC, non-defined origin	water	oceans	g	3.16	0.17	3.39
1242	VOC, non-defined origin	water	rivers	g	13.07	0.86	11.64

[1)] values related to 100 m² component area

b

2.25

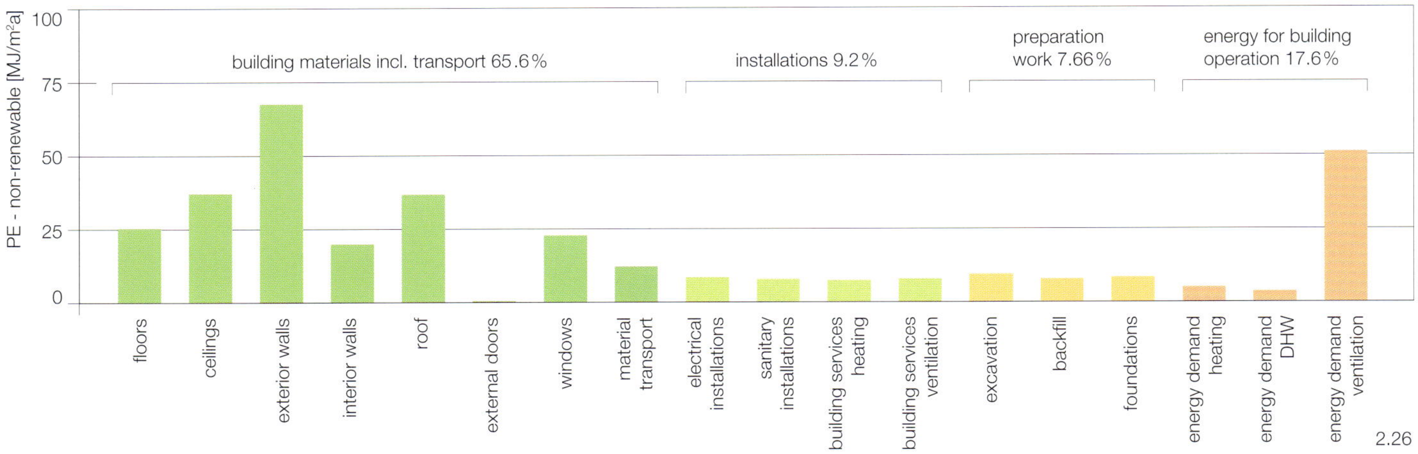

2.26

The results of the life cycle inventory analysis phase can, however, be used to determine the primary energy content, the cumulative energy demand and the embodied energy of a building. Figures 2.26 and 2.28 present the results of the life cycle inventory analysis phase for the comparative building life cycle assessment used here as an example. The diagrams illustrate the embodied energy of the components as well as the proportion of non-renewable energy consumed during the operation phase of the building. Figure 2.26 (p. 32) presents the results for one of the twelve examined buildings; whereas Figure 2.28 (p. 33) shows a direct comparison of the results obtained by all twelve buildings.

2.26 Example life cycle assessment (building mfd02): life cycle inventory results for embodied energy and nonrenewable operating energy during the building life cycle (PE_{nr})
2.27 Example life cycle assessment (building mfd02): results of impact assessment for embodied emissions and emissions from building operation (GWP 100a)
2.28 Example life cycle assessment (building comparison): life cycle inventory results for embodied energy and nonrenewable operating energy during the building life cycle (PE_{nr})
2.29 Example life cycle assessment (building comparison): results of impact assessment for embodied emissions and emissions from building operation (GWP 100a)

Life cycle impact assessment

The life cycle impact assessment (LCIA) is designed to allocate specific environmental impacts to the input and output flows determined in the life cycle inventory analysis phase (i.e. the causes of the environmental burden). This is performed by assigning the individual inventory parameters to so-called impact categories, which represent the potential environmental impacts. The categories cover a variety of aspects, including consumption of resources, effects on human health and ecological hazards. The process of allocating the life cycle inventory items to impact categories is referred to as classification stage. It includes, for example, assigning the greenhouse gases carbon dioxide (CO_2) and methane (CH_4) to the impact category "climate change" or chlorofluorocarbons (CFCs) to the impact category "ozone depletion" (fig. 2.24, p. 31). Some life cycle inventory items are the potential cause for several environmental issues simultaneously and must therefore be assigned to more than one impact category. For example, nitric oxides (NO_x) are responsible for the acidification and overfertilisation of soil and water bodies, but also for the photochemical ozone creation potential.
In a second step, the so-called characterisation phase, the impact categories are used to calculate the impact indicators (e.g. the indicator "impact on climate change", fig. 2.30). This is performed by using the characterisation factors referred to earlier, which assign the impact of a specific substance (e.g. methane) to a certain reference unit (in this case CO_2 as a reference unit for greenhouse gases). The result is the total of greenhouse gas emissions deriving from the life cycle inventory results, which were previously multiplied by their respective characterisation factors.
In addition, there are impact indicators, which combine several impact categories and apply weightings to obtain a single reference value. Approaches using this methodology are, for example, the method of ecological scarcity using environmental loading points (UBP) [23] and ReCiPe [24]. The selection of impact categories and their corresponding weighting varies according to the indicator. Thus, the indicator selected has a direct influence on the results of a life cycle assessment.
The choice of impact categories and indicators assessed is dependent on the objective and the scope of the life cycle assessment. In this context, it is important to understand that the various impact

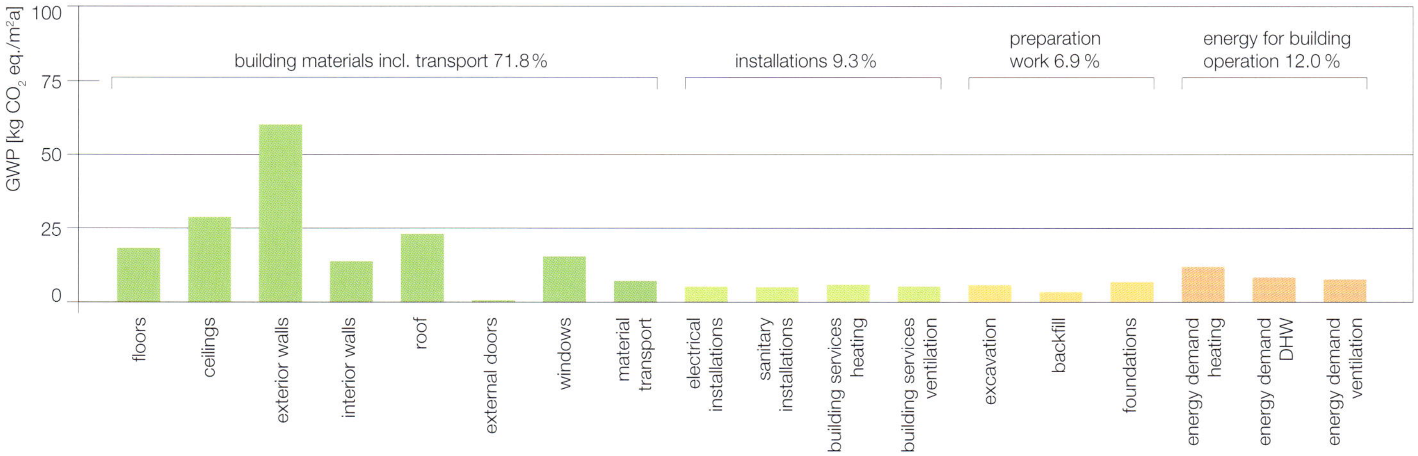

2.27

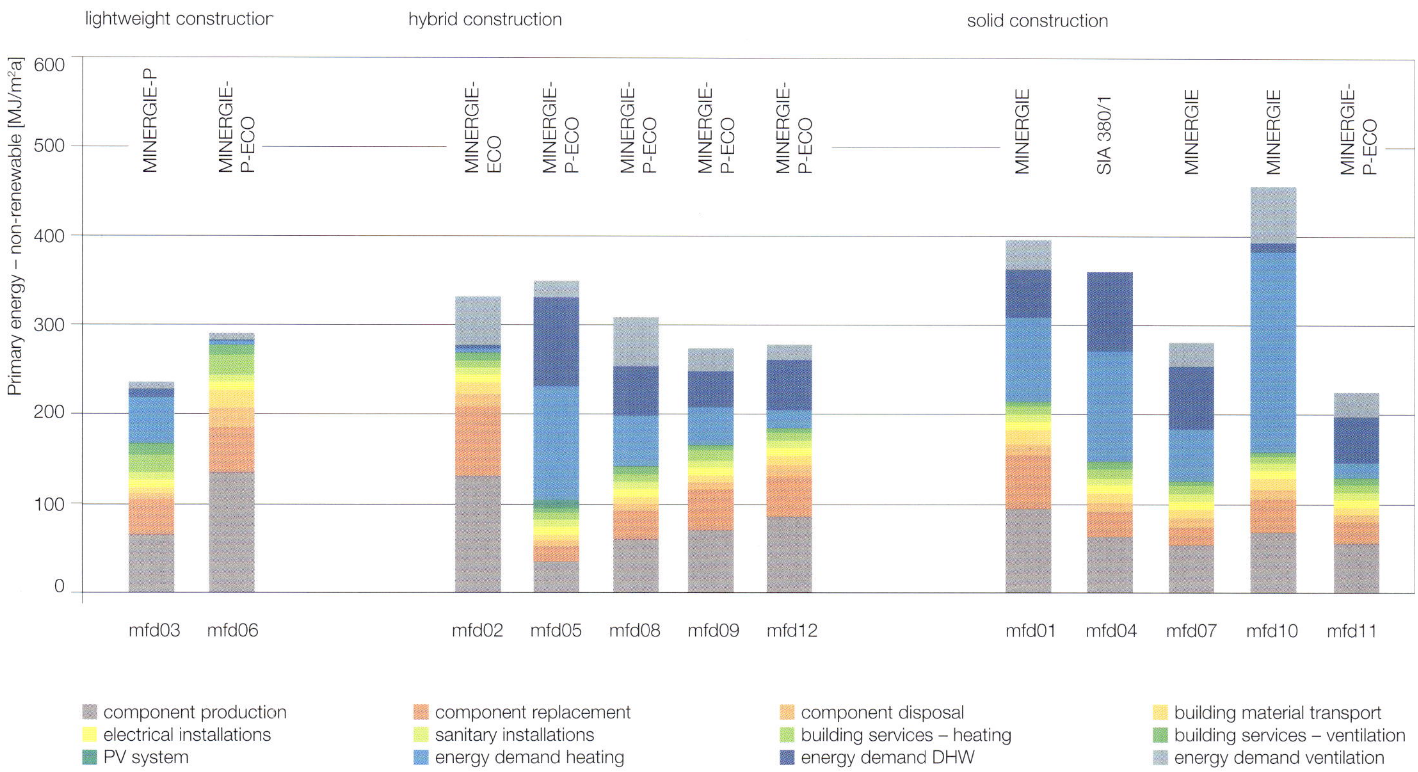

Results: primary energy demand (non-renewable) for household electricity [MJ/m²a]

mfd01	mfd02	mfd03	mfd04	mfd05	mfd06	mfd07	mfd08	mfd09	mfd10	mfd11	mfd12
27.4	17.5	24.6	19.7	19.8	22.5	20.3	16.4	24.0	27.4	22.7	26.2

2.28

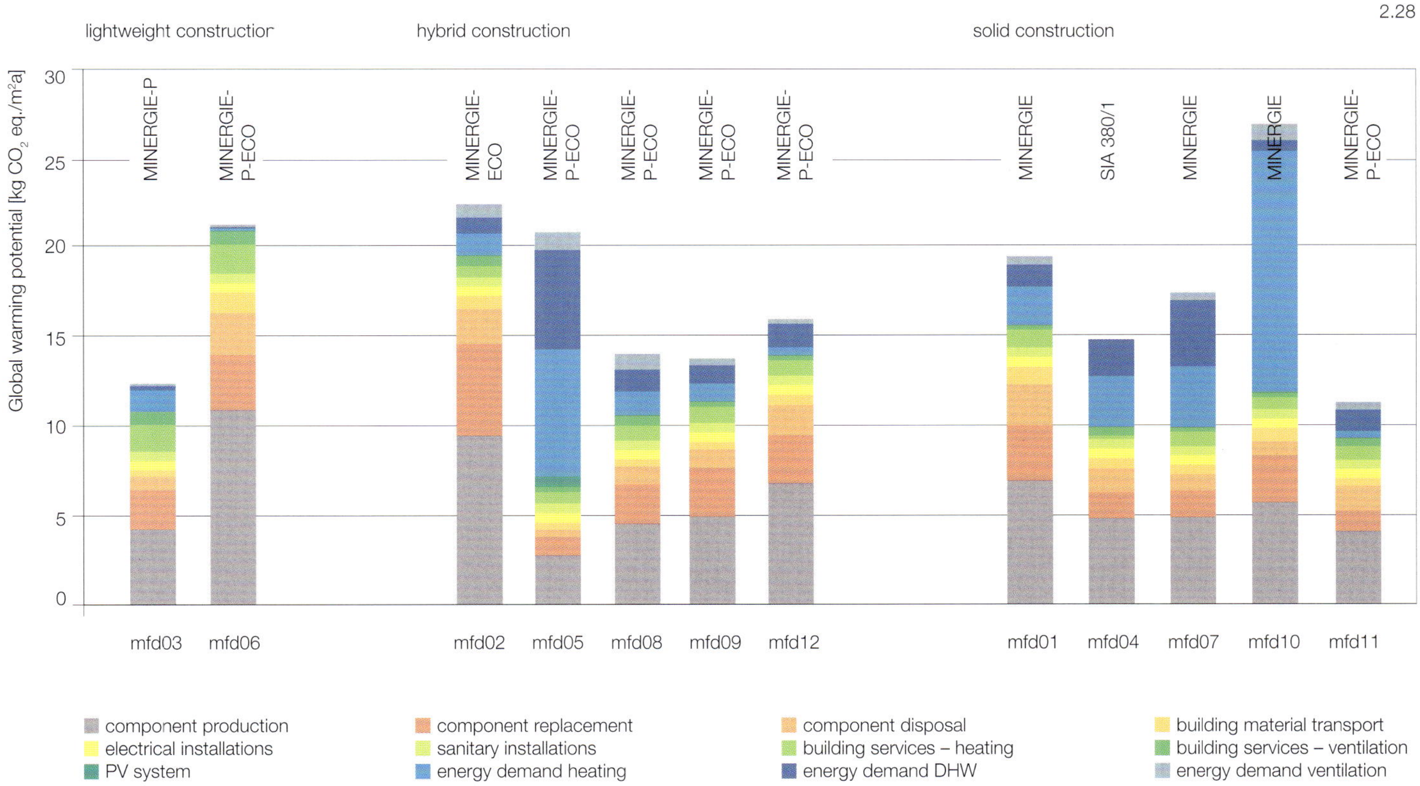

Results: emissions from household electricity (GWP 100a) [kg CO_2 eq./m²a]

mfd01	mfd02	mfd03	mfd04	mfd05	mfd06	mfd07	mfd08	mfd09	mfd10	mfd11	mfd12
36.0	23.0	32.3	25.9	26.0	29.6	26.7	21.5	31.6	35.9	29.9	34.4

2.29

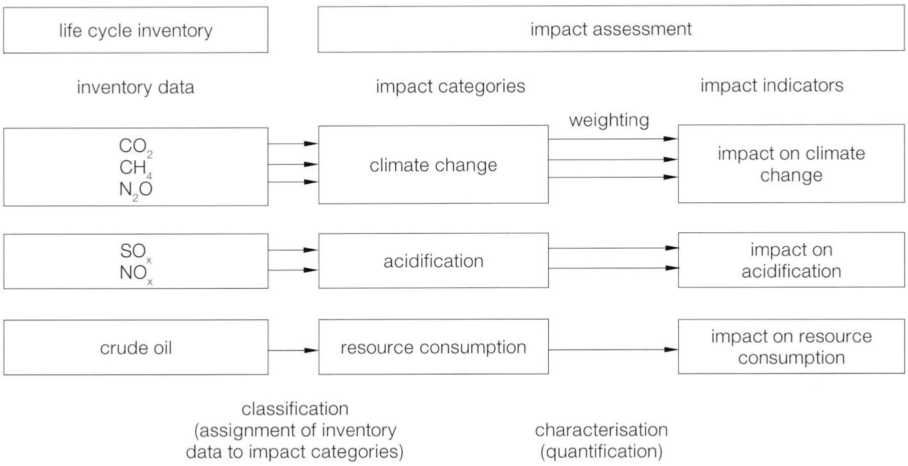

2.30

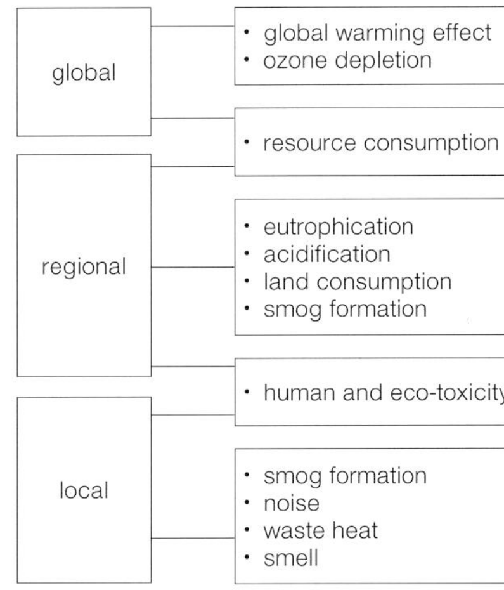

2.31

categories describe environmental impacts with different geographic scales. The greenhouse effect, ozone depletion and resource scarcity, for example, have a global environmental impact, whereas other impact categories, such as over-fertilisation, acidification and land consumption tend to affect the environment only on a regional level. Noise and waste heat, on the other hand, usually have an impact only on the local environment. Smog formation and human toxicity can give rise to environmental issues on both a regional and local level (fig. 2.31). In the light of these aspects, it always makes sense to consider several impact categories and indicators in a life cycle assessment.

The comparative life cycle assessment used here as an example includes a generic calculation of the impact category climate change. It sheds light on the embodied greenhouse gas emissions (i.e. those contained in the building components) as well as the greenhouse gas emissions generated during the building operation phase. The life cycle assessment is performed with the assessment software SimaPro together with the Ecoinvent database [25], which is the implemented life cycle inventory database (advice on software and other helpful tools for the life cycle impact assessment is included in the section "Tools for the ecological assessment of buildings" from page 36 onwards). Professional software has the advantage that only a single mouse click is required to calculate the life cycle assessment results for any chosen impact category or impact indicator. The calculations are based on the life cycle inventory model of the processes concerned throughout their life cycle. The software then performs the classification and characterisation automatically in accordance with the selected method. In this example, the calculations are performed using the method "GWP 100a" (IPCC 2007 GWP100a V1.02 [26]). Thus, all of the results refer to a time period of one hundred years and are expressed by the unit kilograms of CO_2 equivalents. Figure 2.27 (p. 32) illustrates the results for one of the twelve examined buildings; figure 2.29 (p. 33) shows the results of all twelve buildings in a direct comparison.

Life cycle interpretation

Finally, in the life cycle interpretation phase, the results of the inventory analysis and the life cycle impact assessment are analysed, evaluated and used to answer the original questions. The objective of the life cycle assessment presented here was to discover which building components and which life cycle phases of the building examined have the largest impact on the environment. A comparison of the figures 2.26 and 2.27 (p. 32) clearly illustrates the very sizable impact of the exterior walls, the floor slabs, roof and ground slab of building mfd02. The comparison also shows that the operating energy is only of minor importance throughout the total life cycle of the building.

In order to grasp the full significance of the results, the building is described here in greater detail: the residential building analysed incorporates two units and was built using a hybrid construction method. The construction consists mainly of reinforced concrete (ground slab, floor slabs, exterior and interior walls), timber (floor slabs, exterior and interior walls, roof) and limestone brick (interior walls). The insulation materials used are: mineral wool, foam glass granulate, extruded and expanded polystyrene, and polyurethane foam. The building meets the Swiss Minergie-ECO standard; its operating energy is supplied by district heat, which is generated through the combustion of wood chips. The treated floor area of the building amounts to 350 m². Thus, this building is an interesting exception in the direct comparison of buildings (fig. 2.28 and 2.29, p. 33) since the embodied energy accounts for the largest proportion of the total result. In contrast, the most influential factor in the building life cycle of most other examined residential buildings is the operating energy.

The building comparison also highlights that, on a building component level, the construction phase has a much greater influence on the result than the maintenance and replacement phase. In the case of all twelve buildings, on the other hand, the disposal phase carries hardly any weight at all. A sensitivity analysis is performed in this example to assess the impact of the building's design life on the total result and the weighting of the life cycle phases. Instead of 60 years, a design life of 120 years is now assumed for the buildings. Because the replacement cycles are doubled for many of the materials, the maintenance and replacement phase is clearly enhanced and even considered the most important phase on a component level. The results of this analysis are illustrated in figure 2.32.

The sensitivity analysis helps to put the results of the life cycle analysis into per-

2.30 Relation between life cycle inventory and impact assessment
2.31 Geographical scale of environmental impacts
2.32 Results of the sensitivity analysis for the example building
a embodied energy and non-renewable operating energy (PEI_{nr})
b embodied emissions and operating emissions (GWP 100 a)

spective and point out the interdependencies of certain parameters or assumptions. The example illustrates that a life cycle assessment is designed to provide only the answer to a particular question and that the result is therefore valid only for the system boundaries, assumptions and conditions specifically selected. Thus, the sensitivity analysis is not only used to perform a critical analysis of the parameters most significantly affecting the assessment, but also to give an impression of the uncertainties that tend to be characteristic of life cycle assessments.

Life cycle assessment as an iterative process

The four parts of a life cycle assessment presented here are part of an iterative process. From the formulation of a question to the finding of an adequate answer, adjustments have to be made repeatedly to the structure and the modelling of an individual life cycle assessment. It might, for instance, be necessary to adapt system boundaries or select alternative impact categories or indicators. Very different study methods are theoretically suited to answer the same question. So, the detailed documentation of assumptions taken is actually more important than their correctness in order to make a life cycle assessment and its results comprehensible and the uncertainties in the modelling assessable. There are several tools, which support architects and planners in performing the life cycle assessment of components and buildings. Some of the tools are introduced in the following passages. They do not, however, relieve the user of the initial responsibility to reflect upon the object of the study. Because, in the case of a life cycle assessment, the answer to a question can only ever be as good as the question itself.

Tools for the ecological assessment of buildings

A large number of tools are available today to help architects and planners assess the ecological performance of buildings. Standards, guidelines and manuals generally form the basis for establishing the framework conditions and approach used for the life cycle assessment of buildings. The objectives and conditions set out in these are also used as a foundation for building standards and certifications systems, which ultimately help determine and communicate the quality of a building. Furthermore, a variety of data sets and software tools are available to calculate the environmental impacts of buildings, structural components or building materials. These range from life cycle inventory databases and user-friendly building life cycle assessment tools for the practical

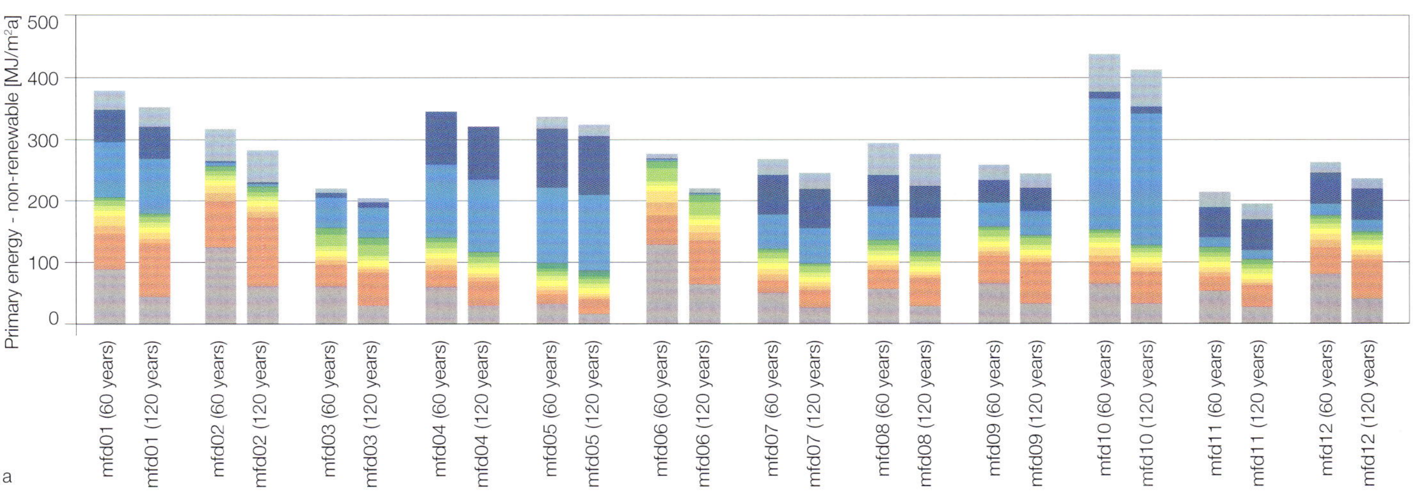

a

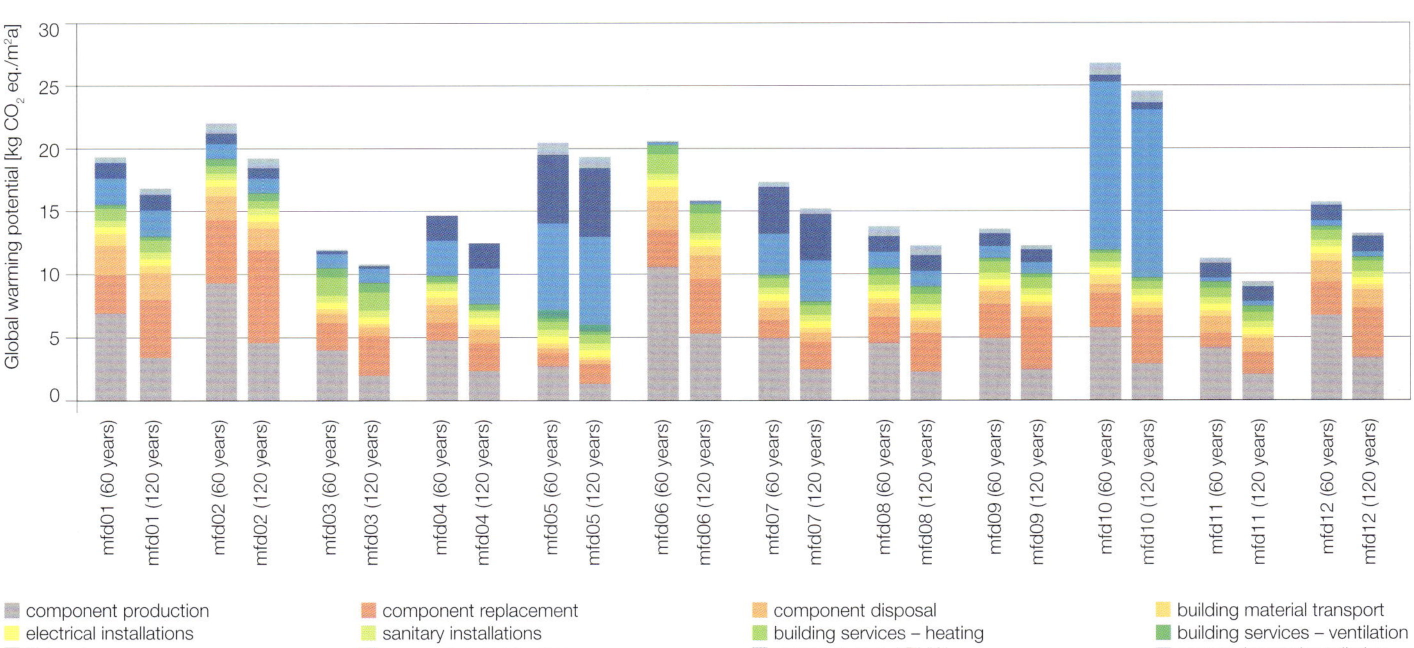

b

2.32

implementation in everyday planning to professional software solutions for the performance of life cycle assessments, which are used mainly for research purposes. The Joint Research Centre (JRC) of the European Commission has published detailed information on life cycle assessment tools [27]. Among other things, JRC provides an overview of the most well-known databases and software tools used within Europe.
The following passages introduce a selection of the most useful tools and illustrate the coherence (fig. 2.41, p. 43). Alongside European standards, there is a focus on the situation in Germany, Austria and Switzerland.

Standards

The European standards EN ISO 14040 and 14044 provide a very general (and not specifically building-related) overview of conceptual definitions, framework conditions and the individual steps required to perform a life cycle assessment. They do, however, as already explained, leave a lot of individual room for interpretation with regard to the very special requirements imposed on building life cycle assessments. The consequence is that, even if the very same item is under examination in a building life cycle assessment, the outcome may still differ fundamentally.
The European standard EN 15978 published in 2011 achieves greater clarity in this confusing situation by providing additional information and a specific calculation method for the environmental quality of buildings. The standard was developed for the assessment of design options and specifications for new builds, existing buildings and refurbishments.
It divides the building life cycle into the following stages (fig. 2.33):

- Product stage: modules A1–A3
- Construction process stage: modules A4 and A5
- Use stage: modules B1–B7
- End-of-life stage: modules C1–C4
- Reuse, recycling and recovery stage: module D

The modular format provides a standardised set of requirements for the development of life cycle scenarios in building life cycle assessments. In addition, it simplifies the communication of the selected system boundary in a life cycle assessment. The standard identifies the factors with the greatest influence on the structure and system boundary of a life cycle assessment as well as the individual life cycle modules. For example, it provides information on the definition of a meaningful functional unit in a building context and points out which data is relevant during which design stage of the building modelling process. The standard also explains how building product data from environmental product declarations (EPD) is used in the development of a building life cycle assessment.
The European standard EN 15804 [28] also contains important information for the performance of a building life cycle assessment. Among other things, it incorporates the basic principles for the creation of environmental product declarations (EPDs). In order to optimise the interface between the building and material level, the life cycle phases relevant for the creation of EPDs correspond with the modular structure applied in the building standard EN 15978 (fig. 2.33). Thus, environmental product declarations ensure the same high level of transparency with regard to the system boundaries used in making them as in the building life cycle assessment itself.

Guidelines, user manuals and planning tools

There are a number of helpful guidelines, user manuals and planning tools available in Germany, Austria and Switzerland for designing environmentally sustainable buildings.
In Germany, the Guideline for Sustainable Building [29] developed by the Federal Ministry of Transport Building and Urban Development (BMVBS) offers advice and guidance on how to design sustainable building and assess the environmental impact in accordance with the building life cycle.
The information portal "Sustainable Building" developed by the Federal Ministry for the Environment, Nature Conservation, Building and Nuclear Safety (BMUB) also offers extensive material on this subject [30], including tools for the life cycle assessment of buildings, for example information concerning the design life of building components.
The information system WECOBIS [31] offers advice on the health and environment-related aspects of building product groups; WINGIS [32], the information system for hazardous materials, provides an overview of the environmental and health compatibility of various materials and products. In Germany, WINGIS refers to the Technical Guidelines for Hazardous Substances (TRGS) and, in the EU, under the umbrella of the REACH agreement, to the Globally Harmonised System of Classification and Labelling of Chemicals (GHS).
A catalogue was published in 2006 in Austria listing the design life of technical facilities and parts; it also includes guideline values for the design life of building components and buildings [33]. The online database "baubook" developed by the Austrian Institute for Healthy and Ecological Building (IBO) offers a building component catalogue with standard structural configurations and the corresponding life cycle assessment results (including results for the global warming potential (GWP), the acidification potential (AP), the non-renewable primary energy content (PEI_{nr}) and the Austrian OI3 indicator; detailed information is available on p. 41 and in the OI3 guideline [34]).
Eco2Soft [35] is also an IBO online tool. It is used to determine the environmental properties of new builds, refurbishments and disposal processes.
The Swiss Society of Engineers and Architects (SIA) has published the recommendations SIA 112/1 [36] with general strategies for sustainable building and SIA 2032 [37] for the calculation of the embodied energy and the "embodied" greenhouse gas emissions in buildings. SIA 112/1 includes 32 criteria for sustainable building, which are assigned to the three categories social, economic and environmental compatibility. The category environmental compatibility addresses mainly energy efficiency, the use of renewable energies as well as ecology-related aspects of buildings. The recommendation SIA 2032 includes a comprehensive list of life cycle assessment results for standard building components, as well as a detailed sample calculation, which is helpful in determining the environmental properties of a building. Since 2013, SIA 2032 has functioned as the calculation basis for life cycle assessments performed according to the Swiss building label Minergie-ECO. SIA 2039 [38] helps to assess the energy demand for transportation and covered distance in accordance with the location of the building. SNARC is an SIA tool for the preliminary design phase of a project, which enables planners to make a rough estimate and compare the sustainability of buildings [39].
The electronic building component catalogue [40] was developed in Switzerland for the practical application of building life cycle assessments. By providing access to predefined standard building components, it helps to calculate the environ-

	Information for the life cycle of a building																	Supplementary information beyond the building life cycle
Life cycle stage	**Product**			**Construction process**		**Use**							**End-of-life**					**Benefits and loads**
Scenario	**A1**	**A2**	**A3**	**A4**	**A5**	**B1**	**B2**	**B3**	**B4**	**B5**	**B6**	**B7**	**C1**	**C2**	**C3**	**C4**		**D**
Type of EPD	Raw material supply	Transport	Manufacturing	Transport to construction site	Construction-installation process	Installed product in use	Maintenance	Repair	Replacement	Refurbishment	Operational energy use	Operational water use	Deconstruction/demolition	Transport	Waste processing	Disposal		Reuse, recycling and recovery potential
EPD from cradle to gate – declared unit	■	■	■	–	–	–	–	–	–	–	–	–	–	–	–	–	no RSL 3)	–
EPD from cradle to gate with added options – declared/ functional unit	■	■	■	□ 1) 2)	□ 1) 2)	□ 1) 2)	□ 1) 2)	□ 1) 2)	□ 1) 2)	□ 1) 2)	□ 1) 2)	□ 1) 2)	□ 1)	□ 1)	□ 1)	□ 1)	RSL 2) 3)	□
EPD from cradle to grave – functional unit	■	■	■	■ 1) 2)	■ 1) 2)	■ 1) 2)	■ 1) 2)	■ 1) 2)	■ 1) 2)	■ 1) 2)	■ 1) 2)	■ 1) 2)	■ 1)	■ 1)	■ 1)	■ 1)	RSL 2) 3)	□

■ mandatory □ optional 1) consideration dependent on declared scenario 2) if all scenarios are included
3) RSL = Reference Service Life: duration of use which is assumed for a building product under certain conditions (e.g. standard conditions)

2.33

mental impacts quickly and efficiently. The tool also enables dynamic modelling of individual component configurations followed by their evaluation. The basic functions are free of charge and accessible online; dynamic modelling, on the other hand, as well as the creation and storage of comprehensive construction projects can be accomplished only by using the commercially available version. The electronic building component catalogue, in particular, helps to develop a good understanding of the relationship between the selection of materials and the resultant environmental impacts at an early design stage.
The Swiss tool Lesosai [41] is also useful for preparing a building life cycle assessment according to the Minergie-ECO standard (in accordance with the guideline SIA 2032). Moreover, it can be used to calculate the energy requirements of buildings. The Swiss Eco-BKP datasheets are helpful for assessing the environmental impact of building constructions in that they support the process of selecting suitable, environmentally friendly building materials [42]. Furthermore, they provide advice and recommendations on the building biology aspects of construction products.
In the UK, the BRE Green Guide to Specifications is utilised as part of BREEAM [43]. It contains more than 1500 specifications of materials and components used in various types of building. The environmental rankings for the building elements are based on an LCA that uses BRE's Environmental Profiles Methodology 2008. Designers can compare and select materials and systems as they compile their specifications.
Another useful tool is "The UK Methodology to calculate embodied carbon of materials", published by The Royal Institution of Chartered Surveyors RICS [44]. It provides practical information on how to calculate cradle-to-gate embodied carbon emissions associated with building projects in the UK. The methodology has been developed for the application in combination with cost calculations, which are usually conducted by quantity surveyors.

Building standards and certification systems
Most building standards and certification systems for sustainable buildings or green buildings (fig. 2.35) nowadays require information that can be obtained only by performing a life cycle assessment. The introduction of EN 15978 will presumably enforce this procedure across Europe. However, the scope and level of detail in the life cycle assessment differs according to the system, since the focus of many certification systems tends to be on the energy efficiency during the operation period and issues concerning health-compatible constructions (fig. 2.36, p. 40). Whereas the German Sustainable Building Council (DGNB) requires a comprehensive building life cycle assessment according to the standards ISO 14040 and 14044, BREEAM, for example, asks only for a ranking of the relevant building components according to predefined building component catalogues and environmental databases instead of a life cycle assessment that includes the whole building. In order to receive the Minergie-ECO label used in Switzerland, only the embodied energy (according to SIA 2032) incorporated in the building components and materials is taken into account. The weighting of life cycle assessments within the overall result also differs fundamentally according to which certification system or standard was chosen. Consequently it is very difficult to directly compare the various building certification systems. The building certificates are usually completed by a qualified expert with a license for the particular scheme (e.g. DGNB auditor, BREEAM assessor or LEED Accredited Professional) at a specified fee. The costs for the certification vary according to the system: for example, obtaining a certificate according to Minergie-ECO is much more reasonable than a DGNB or LEED certificate (fig. 2.35). On account of these developments in sustainability certification, building life cycle assessments are most likely to take on greater significance. The following sections introduce the most important building certification systems and labels used in Germany, Austria and Switzerland.

2.33 Information necessary to describe the building life cycle and consider the phases relevant for the compilation of EPDs according to EN 15804:2012

BREEAM, LEED and the Code for Sustainable Homes (UK, USA)

The development of systems to assess the sustainability of buildings started in the UK and the USA during the last decade of the 20th century. The building certification systems BREEAM (UK: Building Research Establishment Environmental Assessment Method) and LEED (USA: Leadership in Energy and Environmental Design) take mainly environmental aspects into consideration with a strong focus on the energy-related performance of buildings (fig. 2.35) [45]. The evaluation of the individual criteria is based partly on qualitative, partly on quantitative evidence, and a specified number of points is then awarded for each criterion depending on the degree of fulfilment. In the case of both BREEAM and LEED, the assessment of the building's energy efficiency and the environmental impact caused by the use of construction materials is based on quantitative calculations. In the case of BREEAM, a life cycle assessment based on EN ISO 14040 and 14044 must be performed for the phase construction (with the support of the bespoke specification tool for BREEAM assessors "Green Guide to Specification") or the phases construction, maintenance/use and disposal (using the national life cycle assessment system). The assumptions are based on a building design life of sixty years; the life cycle assessment results must be submitted for at least three environmental indicators. Whereas BREEAM is already fairly advanced in the integration of life cycle assessment into its system, LEED has incorporated life cycle assessment only as a test criterion. At the moment, the LEED certification system takes into consideration the phases construction, transportation, maintenance, deconstruction and disposal, including several impact categories and indicators, such as the global warming potential (GWP), the ozone depletion potential (ODP), the acidification (AP) and eutrophication potential (EP), potential damage to respiratory organs and the primary energy consumption.
BREEAM has a scoring system with six levels for buildings: unclassified, pass, good, very good, excellent and outstanding. LEED distinguishes certification according to the ratings: certified, silver, gold and platinum. BREEAM is still used mainly in the UK, however, the system has been adapted over the years and, by launching the schemes BREEAM Europe and BREEAM DE, it now meets the demands of the European and German markets. Although most LEED-certified buildings are located in the USA, the system is, in fact, used throughout the world. Further information about BREEAM [46] and LEED [47] can be found on their respective websites .
In 2006, the UK Government established the "Code for Sustainable Homes" in order to evaluate the performance of new dwellings with regard to the categories of energy/CO_2 emissions, pollution, water, health and wellbeing, materials, management, surface water run-off, ecology and waste. According to the results achieved in these nine categories, new homes in the UK are rated with one to a maximum of six stars. Aspects of material performance are assessed by means of calculating the environmental impact, as well as assessing the responsible sourcing of materials. The two-stage assessment process (for the design and post-construction stages of buildings) is carried out by licensed assessors. More information can be found in the publications of the UK Department for Communities and Local Government [48], [49].

Minergie and the Standard for Sustainable Building in Switzerland (CH)

Minergie [50], an energy standard for the assessment of low-energy houses, was introduced on the Swiss market at about the same time as BREEAM and LEED in their respective countries. Initially, the focus of the Minergie label was also on the energy efficiency of buildings. A few years ago, Minergie introduced two new labels: the Minergie-P label for a standard comparable to that of Passive House buildings and the Minergie-A label for nearly zero-energy buildings.
Since the introduction of the Minergie-ECO standard in 2006, aspects concerning comfort, health and building ecology are assessed alongside the energy demand of a building. The Minergie-ECO label can be combined with either the Minergie-P or the Minergie-A label. Obtaining the certification with the additional ECO standard involves answering a questionnaire to assess extra criteria, such as the environmental impact, raw materials, possibilities for deconstruction, thermal comfort, noise, light and indoor air quality (fig. 2.39, p. 41). With regard to questions concerning building ecology, special attention is given to the construction materials used. Since 2013, the process of obtaining a Minergie-ECO label requires the performance of a simplified life cycle assessment, which determines the embodied energy for construction, maintenance and disposal with the help of the technical specifications SIA 2032 Embodied Energy of Buildings. In performing this assessment, a building design life of sixty years is assumed.
Due to the fact that the Minergie label has become so well established in Switzerland, it has been exported and is now also used in other countries. The costs for a certification, dependent on the size of the building, are on the average to high side.
The Sustainable Construction Network Switzerland (NNBS) introduced the Swiss Standard of Sustainable Construction (SNBS) [51] in 2013. The standard is designed in such a way that it is either based on planning tools for the construction of sustainable buildings that are already well established in Switzerland (e.g. SIA 112/1 Sustainable Building Construction, the targets of the 2000-Watt Society, the Minergie standard), or incor-

2.34

Name of the system	Certification institute, website	Focus of certification, field of application and costs	Life cycle assessment aspects considered
BREEAM (UK) Building Research Establishment Environmental Assessment Methodology	Building Research Establishment (BRE) www.breeam.org	• assessment of environmental, social and economic sustainability • all types of new and existing buildings • focus on environmental sustainability and energy efficiency • *certification costs: high*	• life cycle assessment using various tools, based on EN ISO 14040 and 14044 for the phases construction (using the tool: Green Guide to Specification) or construction, maintenance/use and disposal (using the national life cycle assessment system) • building design life: 60 years • assessment of at least three environmental indicators is required
LEED (USA) Leadership in Energy & Environmental Design	US Green Building Council www.usgbc.org/leed	• assessment of environmental, social and economic sustainability • all types of new and existing buildings (residential buildings excluded) • focus on environmental sustainability and energy efficiency • *certification costs: high*	• life cycle assessment has only been introduced as a test criterion (for the phases construction, transport, maintenance, deconstruction and disposal) • impact categories and indicators used: global warming potential (GWP), ozone depletion potential (ODP), acidification potential (AP), eutrophication potential (EP), potential damage to respiratory organs, primary energy demand
Minergie-ECO (CH)[1] Minergie	Minergie association www.minergie.ch	• assessment of user comfort and energy efficiency, including healthy and environmentally friendly construction methods • new builds and modernisations (residential buildings, office buildings, schools) • *certification costs: average to high*	• simplified life cycle assessment: assessment using the Technical Specification SIA 2032 Embodied Energy of Buildings for the construction, maintenance and disposal • building design life: 60 years • impact categories and indicators used: embodied energy
DGNB (D) ÖGNI (A) SGNI (CH)	Deutsche Gesellschaft für Nachhaltiges Bauen (DGNB) www.dgnb.de Österreichische Gesellschaft für Nachhaltige Immobilienwirtschaft (ÖGNI) www.ogni.at Schweizer Gesellschaft für Nachhaltige Immobilienwirtschaft (SGNI) www.sgni.ch	• assessment of environmental, social and economic sustainability • new builds (office buildings, industrial and commercial buildings, educational facilities, residential buildings, hotels, etc.) existing buildings (office buildings, industrial and commercial buildings, residential buildings) • all three aspects of sustainability are considered equal • *certification costs: high*	• life cycle assessment based on EN ISO 14040 and 14044 for the phases construction, maintenance, deconstruction and disposal • building design life: 50 years • impact categories and indicators used: global warming potential (GWP), ozone depletion potential (ODP), photochemical ozone creation potential (POCP), acidification potential (AP), eutrophication potential (EP), non-renewable primary energy (PE_{nr}), total primary energy demand and proportion of renewable primary energy (PE_r)
TQB (A) Total Quality Building Assessment	Österreichische Gesellschaft für nachhaltiges Bauen (ÖGNB) www.oegnb.net/tqb.htm	• assessment of environmental, social and economic sustainability • new and existing buildings (residential buildings, offices and special use buildings) • all three aspects of sustainability are weighted equally • *certification costs: comparably low*	• simplified life cycle assessment: assessment using the OI3 Index for the construction and maintenance. The disposal is determined by using the EI indicator (assessed waste volume) • the OI3 Index covers the following impact categories and indicators: global warming potential (GWP), acidification potential (AP), non-renewable primary energy (PE_{nr})

[1] certification system is not recognised by the World Green Building Council

2.35

porates them. The certification requires the performance of a simplified life cycle assessment, which includes the construction and operation phases of the building as well as all aspects concerning mobility. The standard is based on a building design life of sixty years. Two impact categories and indicators, the global warming potential (GWP) and the non-renewable primary energy demand (PE_{ne}) are used to assess the environmental impacts. Scores ranging from 1 to 6 can be achieved in the assessment system with 6 being the highest score. The assessment is performed by using qualitative and quantitative criteria from the three pillars of sustainability (ecology, economy and social responsibility). A differentiation is made between new and existing buildings. A pilot study is currently being carried out to test the practicality of the standard.

BNB, DGNB (D)

The newer certification systems, developed at the beginning of the 21st century, such as the BNB for public buildings (Assessment System for Sustainable Building), DGNB (German Sustainable Building Council) [52] and the Austrian TQB (Total Quality Building) [53] take a more holistic approach and consider all three spheres of sustainability: ecology, economy and social responsibility.

In Germany the BNB certification is mandatory for all government buildings, the DGNB label, on the other hand, is optional and can be performed on a voluntary basis. The DGNB certification system is also used outside Germany, among other places in Austria (ÖGNI), in Switzerland (SGNI) and even in China. To date, the criteria of BNB and DNGB hardly differ, since the basic concept of both certification systems was developed by the government through the German Sustainable Building Council. However, the further development of the criteria is being undertaken separately so that greater differences between the two systems may soon emerge.

The certification according to BNB and DGNB requires the performance of a life cycle assessment based on EN ISO 14040 and 14044 for the phases construction, maintenance and use, deconstruction and disposal. The assessment is based on a building design life of 50 years. The analysis of environmental impacts includes the evaluation of the

2.34 Office building in Agoura Hills (USA) 2013, ZGF Architects: new build with LEED Platinum certification

2.35 Certification systems for sustainable buildings with the most important features concerning the consideration of life cycle assessment aspects

Criteria		BREEAM	LEED	MINERGIE-ECO	DGNB	TQB
environmental aspects	environmental loads/pollution	■	■	■	■	■
	materials/resources	■	■	■	■	■
	waste	■	■	■	■	■
	water	■	■	■	■	■
economic aspects	life cycle costs	■	■		■	□
	value stability				■	□
socio-cultural aspects	safety	■			■	■
	barrier-free access				■	■
	regional and social aspects		■			■
energy	CO_2 emissions	■	■	■	■	
	energy efficiency	■	■	■	■	■
	renewable energies	■	■	■	■	■
	energy-efficient building envelope	■	■	■	■	■
	technical building services		■	■	■	■
	energy monitoring	■	■		■	■
	sub-meters and metering	■	■			■
	electrical building services	■	■	■		
health and comfort	thermal comfort	■	■	■	■	■
	indoor air quality	■	■	■	■	■
	acoustic comfort	■		■	■	■
	visual comfort	■	■	■	■	■
	occupants' extent of control	■	■		■	■
functional aspects	efficient use of space				■	
	suitability for conversions			■	■	
technical aspects	fire protection				■	■
	durability	■		■	■	■
	ease of cleaning/maintenance				■	
	resistance to weather and environmental hazards			■	■	
design/innovation	architecture				■	□
	building artwork				■	
	innovation	■	■			
processes/management	design processes	■			■	■
	site management	■	■	■	■	■
	commissioning	■	■		■	
	operation	■	□		■	■
location	micro environment	■	■		■	■
	traffic connections	■	■		■	■
	convenience for cyclists	■	■		■	
	neighbourhood	■	■		■	■
	building regulations				□	■
	suitability for extensions			■	■	
	land consumption	■			■	
	nature/landscape conservation	■	■			
	biodiversity	■	■			

□ criterion is only partly considered

2.36

2.37

following seven impact categories and indicators: global warming potential (GWP), ozone depletion potential (ODP), photochemical ozone creation potential (POCP), acidification potential (AP), eutrophication potential (EP), non-renewable primary energy demand (PE_{nr}), total primary energy demand and proportion of renewable primary energy (PE_r). The global warming potential and the non-renewable primary energy demand are weighted three times, the total primary energy demand twice and all other indicators once.
The DGNB certification system categorises the results according to three levels: bronze, silver and gold.

TQB (A)
The TQB certification system (Total Quality Building) managed by the Austrian Sustainable Building Council (ÖGNB) [54] was first published in 2002 and is now well established on the Austrian market. In the case of the TQB building certification system, the three environmental categories non-renewable primary energy demand (PE_{nr}), global warming potential (GWP) and acidification potential (AP) are assessed together in the so-called OI3 indicator (Ökoindex 3). The indicators must, in this case, be calculated by using material inventory data derived from the IBO database (Austrian Institute for Healthy and Ecological Building [55]).
The OI3 indicator provides information on the environmental impact of a single component or a whole building. In the case of a building life cycle assessment, the environmental impact of individual building components are at first calculated separately for each of the three impact categories (e.g. global warming potential). The results are then applied to 1 m² of surface area by using a linear function and finally converted into points on a scale of 0 to 100. Figure 2.38 illustrates the TQB point system. This calculation procedure is used for each of the three impact indicators required to calculate the OI3 indicator, and the points arrived at (identical weighting factor) are added together. The Guidelines for

2.36 Comparison between BREEAM, LEED, Minergie-ECO, DGNB and TQB criteria
2.37 Children's day care centre in Hannover (D) 2012, BKSP Architekten: first kindergarten in Germany with DGNB Gold certification
2.38 OI3 index: calculating the sub-indicators OI_{PEInr}, OI_{GWP} and OI_{AP}
2.39 Minergie-ECO: criteria groups, planning tools and verification procedures

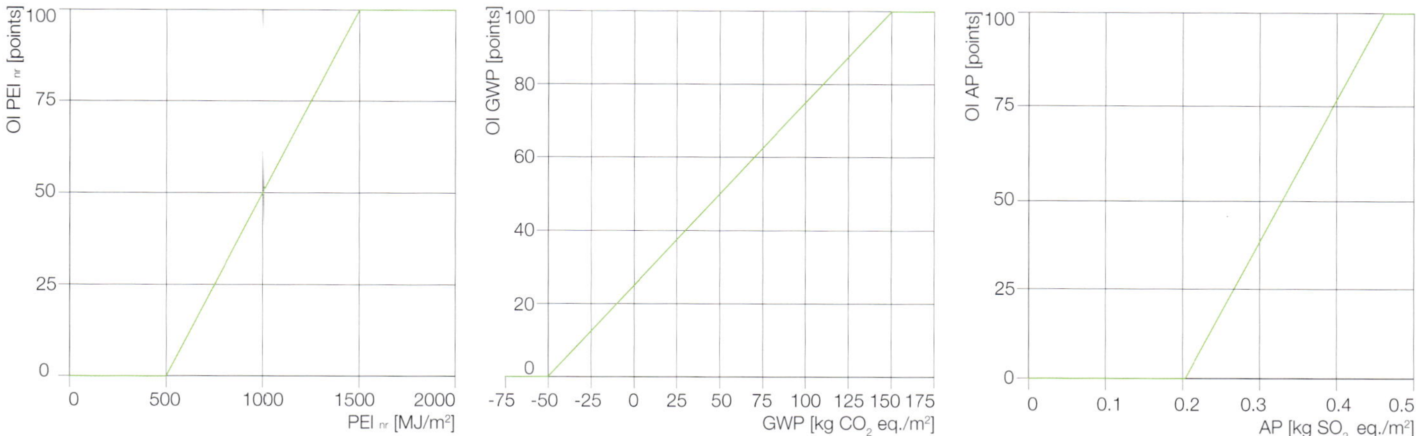

a b c
2.38

Calculating the Environmental Indicators for Buildings (Leitfaden zur Berechnung von Ökokennzahlen für Gebäude [56]) provide a detailed explanation of the procedure. There is also a free online assessment tool, which can be used to carry out the calculations necessary to obtain the TQB label. Once the project documents have been compiled using the software, the information is forwarded to ÖGNB. A nominal charge (dependent on the size of the building) must then be paid, after which ÖGNB hands the project over to an ÖGNB assessor for certification. The TQB system is fairly inexpensive in comparison to other certification systems.

HQE (F)
HQE (Haute Qualité Environnementale) is a standard for green building in France that aims at optimising indoor air quality as well as the environmental performance of buildings [57]. Originally developed in France, it is nowadays applied to buildings worldwide.

Building biology rating systems
Many building certification systems also include the assessment of pollutants. A building with, for example, a TVOC content of over 3000 μg/m³ in the indoor air will not be able to obtain a BNB or DGNB certificate.
Alongside the green building and sustainability certification systems already mentioned, there are several building biology rating systems of which two will be discussed here for illustration purposes. The Gutes Innenraumklima (GI) label (good indoor climate) was developed in Switzerland to assess the indoor air quality of new builds, refurbishments and existing buildings with regard to air pollution. The tests, in this case, may be performed only by certified institutes and organisations. The object of the measurements is to identify chemical substances (among these components like formaldehyde, which is limited to 60 μg/m³, and the TVOC content, which is limited to 1000 μg/m³), germs and particulate matter in the air supply. Existing buildings are also examined for radon and carbon dioxide. Further information concerning this label can be found on the SCERT website, which belongs to the Swiss certification body for construction products [58].
There is also a rating system for building biology-related aspects in Germany. The Health Passport issued by Sentinel Haus Institut (SHI) rates the indoor air quality according to recommendations made by the Federal Environment Agency (UBA), the World Health Organization (WHO) and the AGÖF Guidance Values.
The limit for formaldehyde is 50 μg/m³; 1000 μg/m³ is the limit for the TVOC content. The system also rates a selection of individual substances. The Sentinel Haus Institut website provides further information [59].

Databases and tools for the environmental assessment of building components and materials
Reliable life cycle inventory data is required to perform the life cycle assessment of buildings, building components and construction materials. When using life cycle inventory data, it is important to consider when and where they were compiled. Out-of-date information or considerable variations in the production processes of the examined building material can have a significant impact on the reliability and suitability of the data sets. The documentation and assessment of data quality can be carried out by using the so-called pedigree matrix (fig. 2.40) [60]. Especially when compiling and evaluating own primary data for a life cycle assessment, the matrix is an extremely helpful tool. Those wanting to draw on tried and tested life cycle inventory data will find a variety of building material databases on the Internet, such as the European reference Life Cycle Database [61] with approximately 330 data sets, the German Ökobau.dat [62] with over 700 data sets, the Austrian IBO-Ökokennzahlen [63] with approximately 500 data sets and the Swiss KBOB list for life cycle assessment data in the construction sector (Ökobilanzdaten im Baubereich) [64] with approximately 150 data sets. Another source for life cycle inventory data is the U.S. Life Cycle Inventory Database from the National Renewable Energy Laboratory NREL, which contains more than 900 processes of gate-to-gate, cradle-to-gate

	Criterion	Planning tools	Verification procedure
	Minergie requirements	SIA Standard 380/1	
	exclusion criteria		checklist
health	daylight	SIA Standard 380/4 (daylight)	(calculation)
health	noise protection	SIA Standard (noise protection)	checklist
health	indoor air climate	indoor air climate, SWKI VA 104-1	checklist
bldg. ecology	design concept	ECO-BKP	checklist
bldg. ecology	materials and construction processes	Module recycling materials, SNARC	checklist
bldg. ecology	embodied energy of building materials	Technical Specifications SIA 2032	(calculation)

2.39

and cradle-to-grave data sets, covering the energy and material flows that are associated with producing a material, component, or assembly in the U.S. [65]. In the same way as the data sets in commercial databases (e.g. Ecoinvent [66], GaBi [67]), these freely accessible data sets consist of material and energy flow data for the production of a construction material. The data is derived from various production plants and then adopted in the life cycle inventory databases either as mean values or representative single values.
The commercial databases assure greater transparency in terms of the reproducibility of the material flow calculations they are based on and are therefore frequently applied for life cycle assessments in research studies. However, the freely accessible databases are sufficiently accurate for a practical building life cycle assessment and are sometimes even based on the same data sources as the commercial databases (e.g. the KBOB list is based on Ecoinvent data).
Environmental product declarations (Type III EPDs), which are calculated according to EN 15804, are also suitable as a data source for the life cycle assessment of buildings. When using EPDs to perform a building life cycle assessment according to EN 15978, or when using a combination of product-specific EPDs with generic life cycle inventory databases, it is necessary to bear in mind that, depending on the product group (e.g. engineered timber materials, construction metals), specific conditions are defined in so called Product Declaration Rules (PCR) for the calculation of a product's environmental impact. Among other things, the rules define the functional unit or the consideration of credits deriving from recycling processes. They can differ fundamentally from one EPD to the next and from those for generic life cycle inventory databases.

Life cycle assessment software

Regarding software solutions for life cycle assessments, a distinction can be drawn between tools which are preferred in research and tools which are more practically oriented and designed especially for building life cycle assessments. The most fundamental difference is that the software for research purposes leaves more leeway for modelling and interpretation of all kinds of life cycle assessments, whereas the software for building life cycle assessments is exclusively intended for the modelling and interpretation of building life cycle assessments. The commercially available software products SimaPro [68], GaBi and Umberto [69], but also the freely accessbile software OpenLCA [70], all have a focus on research. SimaPro incorporates, among others, the Ecoinvent life cycle inventory database, whereas GaBi is based on data sets from PE INTERNATIONAL's GaBi database; Umberto, on the other hand, makes use of both databases. The free software openLCA basically features a broad range of databases. However, these have not been preinstalled and must be purchased as licenses before they can be utilized. A characteristic feature of all four programs mentioned is that they all enable the development of life cycle assessments that are not necessarily building related, which means they are suitable for a wide range of application fields.
The software products LEGEP [71] and SBS Tool [72], in contrast, were specifically developed for the life cycle assessment of buildings. Ökobau.dat is in this case used as the life cycle inventory database. The Swiss tool Lesosai [73] is also designed for the life cycle assessment of buildings. In the UK, the new ECAT Energy and Carbon Assessment Tool allows the calculation of a building's carbon footprint, taking into account the CO_2 emissions and the energy consumed throughout the whole building life cycle [74]. ECAT is an adaptation of the Swiss tool Lesosai designed to meet UK market requirements.

Criterion	Quality of data				
	high ◄——	——► average ◄——			——► low
	1	2	3	4	5
Reliability of source	verified data based on measurements	verified data partly based on assumptions or non-verified data based on measurements	non-verified data partly based on qualified estimations	qualified estimations	non-qualified estimations
Completeness	representative data from a sufficient sample of enterprises over an adequate period to even out normal fluctuations	representative data from >50% of enterprises under study over an adequate period in order to balance normal fluctuations	representative data from several (<50%) enterprises under study over an adequate period or from >50% of enterprises over a shorter period	representative data from only one of the enterprises under study or from several enterprises over a shorter period	representativeness unknown or data from a smaller number of enterprises and over a shorter period
Temporal differences	less than 3 years of difference to year of study	less than 6 years of difference to year of study	Less than 10 years of difference to year of study	less than 15 years of difference to year of study	age of data unknown or more than 15 years of difference to year of study
Geographical differences	data from area under study	average data from larger area in which the area under study is included	data from area with similar production conditions	data from area with production conditions with few similarities	data from an unknown area or very different area (North America instead of Middle East or OECD Europe instead of Russia)
Technological differences	data from enterprises, processes and materials under study	data from the processes and materials under study (identical technology) but from different enterprises	data from the processes and materials under study but different technology	data from related processes or materials	data from related processes on a laboratory scale or from other technology

2.40

	Germany	Austria	Switzerland	UK	USA
Standards	EN ISO 14040 and 14444 Life cycle assessment – Principles and framework, requirements and guidelines				
	EN 15978 and 15804 Sustainability of construction works – Assessment of environmental performance of buildings Sustainability of construction works – Environmental product declarations – Core rules for the product category of construction products				
Building standards	BNB Assessment System for Sustainable Building (federal buildings)		SNBS Swiss Stanadard of Sustainable Construction	Code for Sustainable Homes	
Building certification systems	BREEAM/LEED			BREEAM	LEED
	DGNB/ÖGNI/SGNI				
	BNB Assessment System for Sustainable Building (federal buildings)	TQB Total Quality Building	Minergie-ECO		
	SHI building certificate (Sentinel Haus Institut)		GI Gutes Innenraumklima (good indoor climate)		
Data sheets and performance guidelines	Guideline for Sustainable Building	Design life catalogue for structural installations and parts OI3 guideline indicators	2000-Watt Society SIA 112/1 Sustainable Building (building construction) SIA 2032 Embodied Energy in buildings SIA 2039 Mobility – Energy Consumption of Buildings according to their Location SNARC	BRE Green Guide to Specifications RICS Professional Information. UK Methodology to calculate embodied carbon of materials	
Planning tools	Information Portal "BMUB Sustainable Building" WECOBIS information system WINGIS information system for hazardous materials GISCODE Reference values of the UBA and federal health authorities ad hoc working group AGÖF guidance values	Baubook ECOSOFT/Eco2Soft	Eco-BKP data sheets for sustainable building Electronic building component catalogue		
Life cycle inventory database and EPDs (practice)	Ökobau.dat database	IBO reference values (Institute for Healthy and Ecological Building)	KBOB recommendations 1/2009 LCA data for building construction		U.S. LCI Database
	European Reference Life Cycle Database				
	Environmental Product Declarations (EPDs) Type III				
Life cycle inventory database (research)	GaBi database, Ecoinvent database				
LCA software for buildings (practice)	LEGEP, Lesosai			ECAT	Athena
	GaBi, SimaPro, Umberto, openLCA				
Building labels	see figure 2.15 (p. 22) and www.label-online.de				

2.41

For modelling whole building life cycle assessments in the USA, the software tool Athena Impact Estimator for Buildings is widely utilized [75]. The tool allows the development of life cycle assessments for both new builds and refurbishments. The Athena database comprises life cycle inventory data for building materials and products, as well as energy use, transport, construction and demolition processes.
The software tool EQUER is utilized by architects and engineers in France for the LCA simulation of buildings [76]. It can be used in conjunction with generic data from the Swiss Ecoinvent database as well as other life cycle inventory data for energy, water, waste, transport processes that have been collected in the context of the European REGENER project. Replacement of components at the end of their life cycle is automatically accounted for. EQUER is linked to the energy simulation tool COMFIE.
Another French tool for building life cycle assessments is the software ELODIE, developed by CSTB (Centre Scientifique et Technique du Bâtiment) [77]. It is designed to help designers in the process of assessing and optimising materials, energy use, water consumption, as well as construction and transport processes over a building's life cycle. ELODIE works with product specific material inventory data from Environmental Product declarations (EPDs) and Environmental and Health Declaration Sheets (FDES) from the French INIES database.

2.40 Quality assessment of life cycle inventory data (pedigree matrix)
2.41 Overview of tools for the assessment of buildings in terms of building biology and building ecology aspects

- Design strategies for resource-efficient buildings
- Optimisation of the material life cycle
- Optimisation of the building life cycle

Design strategies for resource-efficient buildings

Before resource efficiency can be assessed and used to develop design-based optimisation strategies, planners must take into consideration a number of indicators simultaneously. Suitable approaches can, for example, be derived from the overriding goals of efficiency, sufficiency and consistency (see Principles and fields of action, p. 14). In practice, the strategies are usually less complex; however, their effectiveness is increased if they are based on broad knowledge and an assessment of options. Material concepts are typically categorised according to planning phases and design levels (see Design phases and processes, pp. 68ff.) or in terms of components (see Environmental impacts of building components, pp. 86ff.). Many strategic approaches are, however, not related to a particular design level (fig. 1.14, p. 14), which usually means that they can be used to generate improvements on different levels. This is achieved by analysing a variety of cycles (fig. 3.1 and 3.3).
An important starting point for improvements is in this case the reduction of the development scheme as a whole. Advantages concerning the use of materials are thus achieved through:
- higher density
- a greater compactness of buildings
- a large proportion of useful floor area in relation to the built volume
- reduced soil movement

In some cases, it is even possible to reduce the primary energy input by more than 50 % in comparison to a conventionally planned building (fig. 3.2). The volume-related improvement measures are considered exhausted either when high technical requirements are placed upon a component (e.g. noise protection or facade design) or additional expenses arise in terms of operating energy (fig. 3.28, p. 54). The strategy of reduction is, by and large, independent of the implemented building materials. It is derived from the building, its use and performance during the life cycle. Depending on the type of building, different phases of the building life cycle might be particularly suited for certain improvement measures (see Optimisation of the building life cycle, pp. 57ff.).
Increased efficiency in the production and reuse of building materials can also lead to a significant improvement of the life cycle assessment. It is, for example, known that the environmental impacts of aluminium with a recycled content of 100 % are less than a tenth of those created by newly produced material.
Both approaches can either be mutually beneficial or detrimental for individual aspects of the improvement. To avoid a one-sided optimisation, it is therefore necessary to take account of both life cycles – that of the building and that of the materials. Furthermore, decisions that can clearly be assigned to the optimisation of the material life cycle must also be examined with regard to their effect on the building life cycle and vice versa.

Optimisation of the material life cycle

Regulations provide some first basic information on the material life cycle. For example, the German Closed Substance Cycle Waste Management Act (KrWG), the European Waste Framework Directive (2008/98/EG) or VDI 2243 Recycling-oriented product development include general definitions with regard to the phases of the material life cycle (fig. 3.1 and 3.3). The amendments to the German Con-

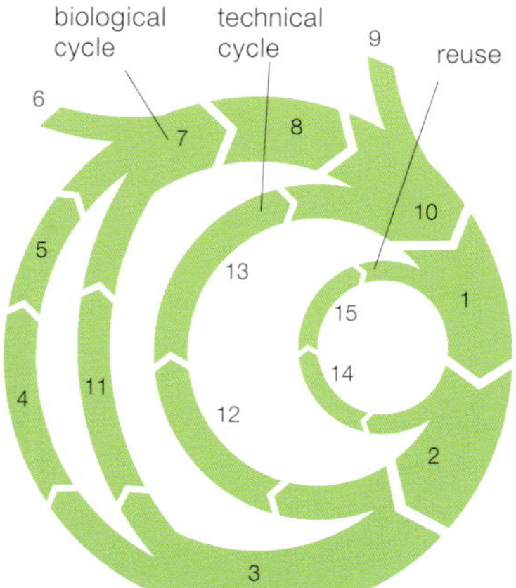

Material life cycle

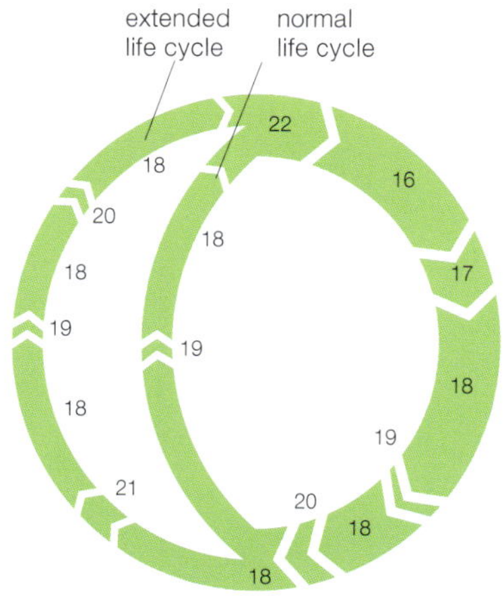

Building life cycle

1 product use
2 demolition / deconstruction / disassembly
3 separation into fractions
4 landfill
5 biological decomposition
6 environmental energy
7 material growth
8 renewable resource
9 non-renewable resource
10 building material
11 thermal recycling
12 recycling
13 secondary raw materials
14 reprocessing
15 adjustments to meet new demands
16 building/construction
17 commissioning
18 use
19 servicing / maintenance
20 repairs
21 refurbishment/conversion
22 deconstruction

3.1

struction Products Act, valid as of 1 June 2013, stipulate terms for the cyclability of building materials. Among other things, they demand that all building materials must ensure the reuse or recyclability of structural components, a long service life of the building and components, as well as the environmental sustainability of primary and secondary building materials. The aspect of resource efficiency, an important consideration for the use of materials in building, was already incorporated into the German Sustainability Strategy in 2002. The aim is to double the raw material productivity by 2020 compared with 1994 measured according to the gross domestic product [1].

Product life cycle
In terms of building material, it is possible to make improvements throughout the material's various life cycle phases. The product life cycle is divided into the phases raw material extraction, manufacturing (including packaging, sale and possibly shipment), use (including cleaning, servicing, maintenance and possibly repair) and re-use (including recycling and disposal). Depending on the calculation method chosen, the life cycle assessment may take into consideration different phases of the life cycle. In addition to specifying only the values, it has therefore become established practice to state the phase considered, or use the terms "cradle to gate" and "cradle to cradle". Cradle-to-gate" is the assessment from the "cradle", which is usually the resource extraction, to the factory gate. The use and re-use of the product is not considered in this case. Nevertheless, it is usually these cradle-to-gate assessments that are used as a basis for product assessments and the Type III Environmental Product Declarations (see Planning tools, p. 21). The cradle-to-cradle assessment, on the other hand, takes into consideration the use and re-use of products and thus projects best the product life cycle and its incorporation in the material cycle. Such assessments are generally developed by extending a cradle-to-gate assessment to include the environmental impacts associated with the use and re-use stages of the product. There is no single value for sustainability in the product life cycle. A variety of metrics are available instead, such as the life cycle costs (LCC), the primary energy input (PEI), the global warming potential (GWP) and other specifications of a life cycle assessment (see Selecting impact categories and indicators, pp. 28f.), as well as health-related measures, for example Type I Environmental Product Declarations or GIS codes. However, not one of these indicators assesses at the same time local and global environmental impacts. Even aggregate indicators, such as the OI3 indicator from Austria, measure only the global environmental impacts and have to be extended by an assessment of the pollutants.
In general, it is possible to improve a variety of aspects in the material cycle of buildings, including:

- increase of efficiency in the manufacturing processes
- use of resource-efficient alternatives
- modular and system construction methods
- materials classified as non-hazardous to health
- return of the building material to the material cycle

Efficiency increase in the manufacturing process
A product is usually created in stages involving the extraction of the raw material, transport of the resource to the production plant, the manufacturing process itself, packaging and distribution. The two stages raw material extraction and manufacturing generate the highest environmental impacts (fig. 3.5) and hence offer the greatest potential for increasing the efficiency of the manufacturing process.

Raw material extraction
Improving raw material extraction processes is generally a worthwhile investment for manufacturers. Planners are not usually in a position to implement improvement measures themselves. They do, however, have the possibility to check the efficiency of product manufacture by using so-called Environmental Product Declarations (EPD; see Databases and tools for the environmental assessment of building components and materials, p. 42). Since external and time-related aspects are also considered in the calculation of the data (e.g. national primary energy factors for electricity), up-to-date

3.1 Schematic illustration of the material and building life cycles in the construction industry
3.2 Comparison of embodied energy in Passive Houses with varying degrees of compactness
3.3 Typical development of property value and its components during the building life cycle
3.4 Development of the material input in the anthropogenic material flows, sojourn time of materials as well as the potential production of recycling waste
3.5 Average proportions of different manufacturing phases in the embodied energy of construction products in Germany

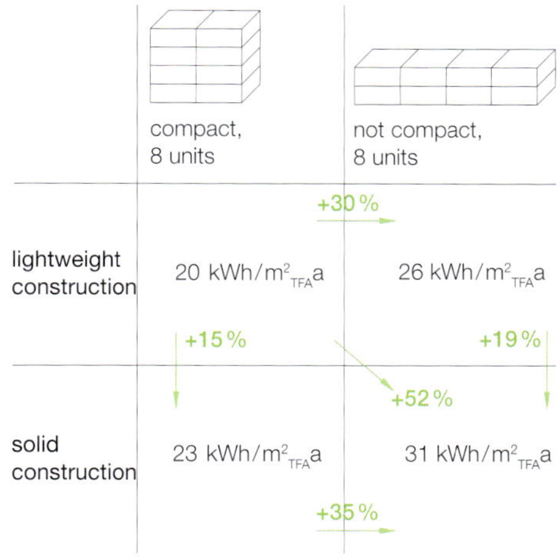

3.2

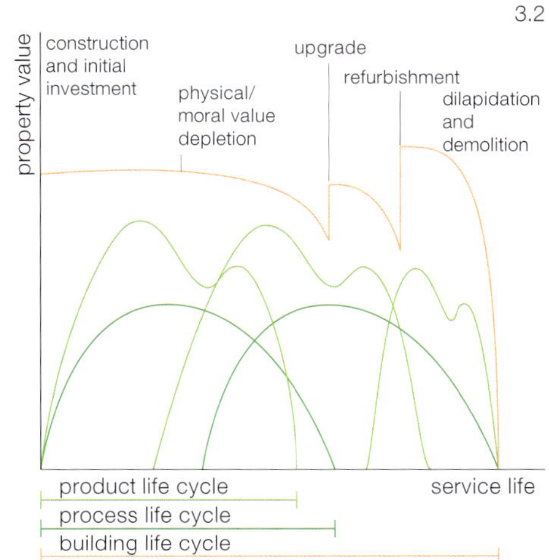

3.3

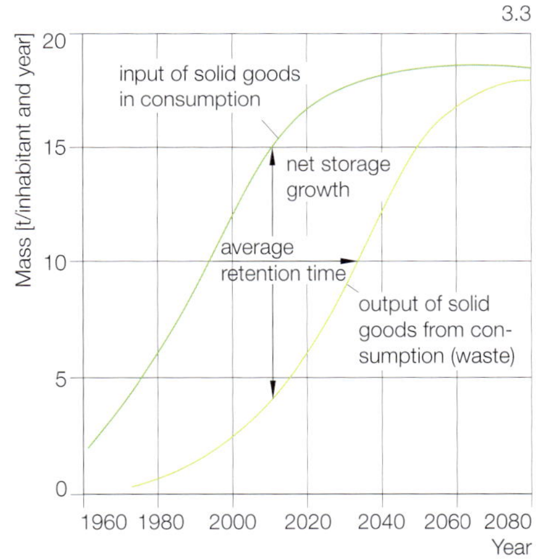

3.4

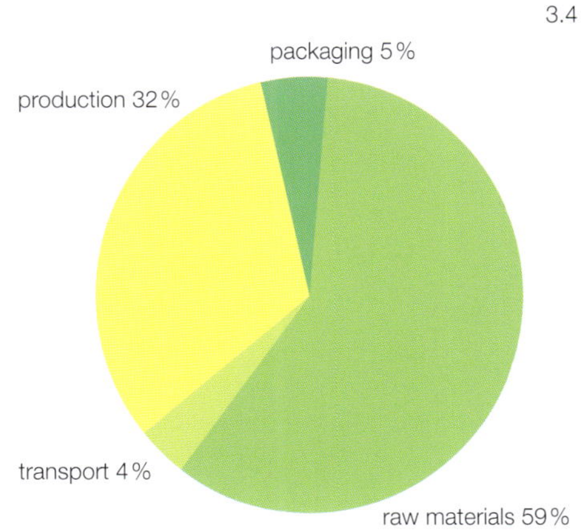

3.5

Floor beams in car park	Option 1	Option 2
type of steel	S235 JR+M acc. DIN EN 10025	S460 M acc. DIN EN 10025
section	IPE 600	IPE 500
yield point	235 N/mm²	460 N/mm²
tensile strength	360–510 N/mm²	540–720 N/mm²
height	600 mm	500 mm
weight of component[1)]	2.12 t 100 %	1.61 t 76 %
costs[1)]	100 %	83 %
total weight of floor beam	530 t	403 t

[1)] Cost and weight specifications for a ready-to-install 16-metre-long beam including camber, cleats, headed studs, flange plates and hot dip galvanising, August 2008

3.6

Cement types according to DIN EN 197-1			Main components alongside Portland cement clinker		GWP reduction
Type	**Designation**	**Notation**	**Type**	**Content [m%]**	
CEM I	Portland cement	CEM I	–	0	0 %
CEM II	Portland slag cement	CEM II/A-S CEM II/B-S	blast furnace slag sand (S)	6–20 21–35	approx. 13 % approx. 27 %
	Portland pozzolana cement	CEM II/A-P CEM II/B-P	natural pozzolans (P)	6–20 21–35	ns
	Portland fly ash cement	CEM II/A-V CEM II/B-V	fly ash rich in silic acid (VI)	6–20 21–35	ns
CEM III	blast furnace cement	CEM III/A CEM III/B CEM III/C	blast furnace slag sand (S)	36–65 66–80 81–95	approx. 47 % approx. 65 % ns
CEM IV	pozzolana cement	CEM IV/A CEM IV/B	pozzolans (D, P, Q, V)	11–35 36–55	ns
CEM V	composite cement	CEM V/A CEM V/B	blast furnace slag sand (S) and pozzolans (P, Q, V)	18–30 31–50	ns

3.7

information is essential to produce realistic results.

Substitution processes

Planners can encourage the use of marketable secondary resources (fig. 3.7/3.13–3.15). LEED and BREEAM already consider such an approach beneficial. In the case of DGNB, the use of secondary materials is projected in the improved results of the life cycle assessment. A reduced environmental impact can be achieved in particular by using regrowable resources in place of abiotic materials. Substituting wood for mineral building materials is extremely beneficial in this case as is shown by the return of wood screed, which was used mainly in the 19th century. Magnesium screed with a content of wood fibre has the advantage of being more pressure resistant, better at controlling humidity levels and warmer underfoot.

The use of scrap metal in building has grown in importance over the years. Steel is therefore the perfect material to explain the significance of substitution processes. In general, a difference is made between primary and secondary steel. Since the energy demand for the production of secondary steel made of recycled material is 47 % lower and carbon emissions can be reduced by 58 % in comparison to the blast furnace process [2], secondary steel has become an integral part of modern steel making. The relation between primary and secondary steel worldwide is approximately 55 % to 45 % [3]. Although, the recycled content varies according to the product. Reinforcing steel, for example, contains an average of around 95 % secondary material. In contrast, due to restrictions imposed by the manufacturing process, the scrap metal content of flat steel is only approximately 30 %. Thus, the planner can already reduce the environmental impact of materials by selecting products with a high secondary content.

There is further potential for resource efficiency with regard to blast furnaces and large power plants. One example is the use of so-called FGD gypsum. The waste product resulting from the flue gas desulphurisation plants of large power stations has gradually been replacing natural gypsum in the building industry since the 1980s, and, as a result, has reduced the environmental impact associated with the manufacture of gypsum products. Concerns regarding the use of FGD gypsum have been allayed step by step by introducing national regulations and quality standards. Similar processes are currently being developed for other waste products, such as fly ash and slag sand, which are, for example, used in the new concrete mixes CEM II and CEMIII (fig. 3.7; see also Office building in Krems, pp. 125ff.). With sufficient demand, planners can help these products to become established on the market.

The use of demolition waste for concrete recycling has also progressed over the last years. The improvement of the environmental impact in concrete production is only marginal though (fig. 3.9), and not applicable in each situation since the cement content has to be increased when using recycled material. However, a reduction can be achieved in the volume of demolition waste, the size of rubble tips and the areas used for gravel extraction. So, the use of recycled concrete also contributes towards landscape protection and the conservation of abiotic resources. It is for this reason that the use of recycled aggregate in concrete is now mandatory in Switzerland.

In order to shorten haul distances, gravel extraction sites are often fairly close to residential areas, which increases com-

3.6 Comparison of two slab constructions for a multi-storey car park using different types of steel
3.7 Standard types of cement (selection) and their classification including the possibility to reduce the global warming potential (GWP) by using blast furnace slag sand in place of Portland cement
3.8 Development of gravel reserves, gravel extraction and other aspects which prevent the use of gravel reserves in Germany
3.9 Comparison of cumulative energy demand (CED) between recycled and standard concrete
3.10 Comparison of the environmental impacts of residential buildings completed by using different construction methods (construction, transport, use and deconstruction)
3.11 Use of building materials in Bavarian residential building between 1979 and 2003, including the relative distribution of environmental impacts

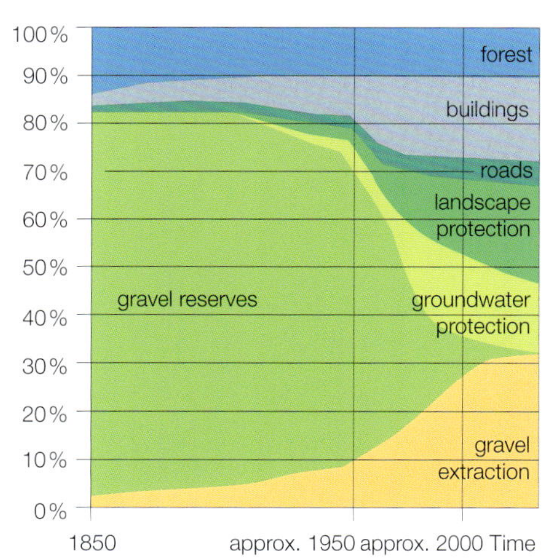

3.8

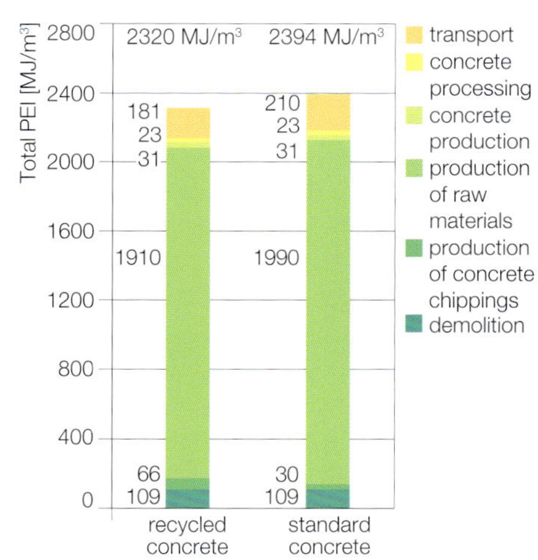

3.9

Building comparison two-storey single-family home living area approx. 120 m²; low energy standard (heat demand < 60 kWh/m²a)	**PEI primary energy non-renewable [MJ]**	**PEI primary energy renewable [MJ]**	**GWP climate gases [kg CO_2 eq.]**	**ODP ozone depletion [kg R11 eq.]**	**AP acidification [kg SO_2 eq.]**	**EP eutro-phication [kg PO_4 eq.]**	**POCP summer smog [kg C_2H_4 eq.]**
steel building	330000	110000	31000	0.00135	63	8.8	7.8
timber building	220000	260000	25000	0.00075	60	8.7	9.9
solid brick building	320000	140000	33000	0.00080	70	9.1	7.7

3.10

petition for land in these regions (fig. 3.8). The use of local demolition waste therefore also has economic advantages in these situations. The result in Germany was similar to that in Switzerland apart from the fact that the developments in Germany were influenced by cost rather than land use [4]. Recycled concrete is also available in several US American states and is becoming more common on the market.
Recycled material, either from mechanical recycling (regranulate) or feedstock reycling (monomers), can also be used for the production of plastics (fig. 3.4, p. 45). Because it is often difficult to identify the base substance of recycled material – as is the case for wood products, too – planners should obtain precise information from the manufacturers concerned.
The resource "existing building stock" is expected to gain further importance as a raw material for building over the next years. This development will no doubt encourage the creation of statutory provisions concerning the quality description and use of construction materials (e.g. Alternative Construction Products Regulation, which is currently available only as a draft).

Product optimisation
The more complex a product, the greater the opportunities for its optimisation. A differentiation must be made here between product manufacturers and companies in the construction business. Companies working in the manufacturing industry are usually dependent on the production of big batches and large quantities. They are generally not able to change their processes quickly and at short notice. Planners can therefore really only make use of new product developments in this market segment. One example in this context is the development of high-strength steel, which can increase the load-bearing capacity of a structure or reduce its weight in comparison to a conventional alternative. The Oresund Bridge (Georg Rotne, DK/SWE 2000) between Denmark and Sweden saw the installation of 82000 tons of high-strength steel with increased failure and tensile strength. In comparison to a conventional bridge construction, this innovation reduced the required amount of steel by a total of 15000 tons [5]. Since the bridge employed a microalloyed steel (i.e. a type of steel containing only very small amounts of alloying elements), the input of energy and resources per ton of steel cannot have been much higher than in the case of a conventional alternative. Thus, the resource savings almost match the material savings of 15% [6]. Depending on the function and the construction system, it is generally possible to reduce the weight and quantity of raw material required for the load-bearing structure by up to 25% (fig. 3.6).
Companies in the construction business have the necessary product-related flexibility, technical know-how and interest in innovation to enforce improvements in products. These companies frequently offer customised products. If the conditions of the project enable improvements to be carried out in cooperation with the manufacturer, the opportunity should be taken, in particular in the case of complex components or system developments (e.g. innovative facade systems). This open-mindedness gives the participants a competitive edge, which can be used to develop a unique selling point of a practice (see Holiday residence on Taylor's Island, pp. 103ff.).

Transport
Environmental impacts can also be reduced by using local products. However, the role played by transport in the total environmental impact of the building tends to be relatively minor [7]. Especially in the case of building materials with global distribution, it is important to consider that, for example, the primary energy input of a product can differ according to the country of origin. The environmental impact of steel products from Brazil or China, for instance, can be almost 30% higher than those from Central Europe [8].

Resource-efficient product alternatives
The procedure usually applied in planning practices to reduce environmental

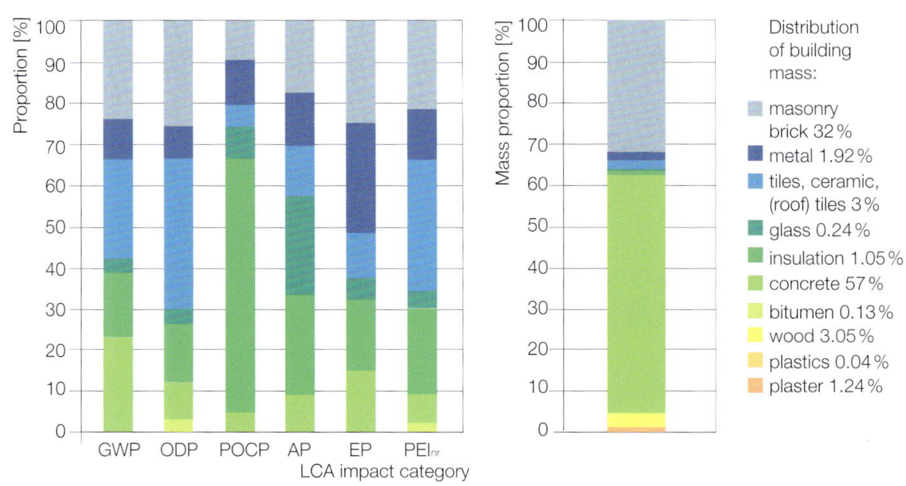

3.11

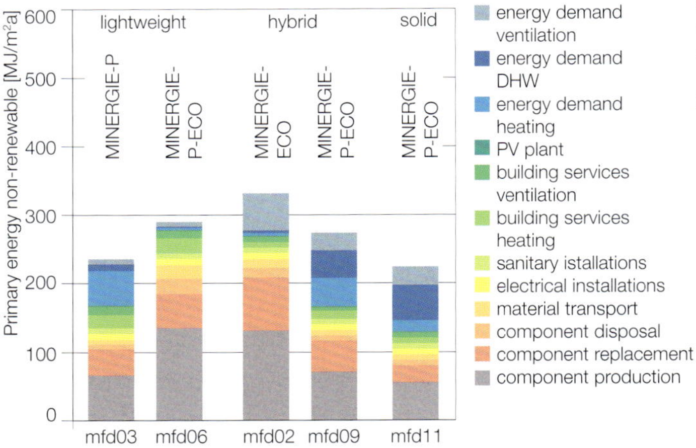

3.12

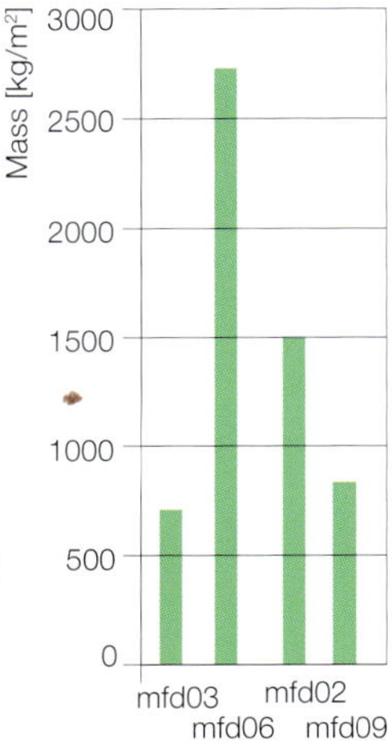

3.13

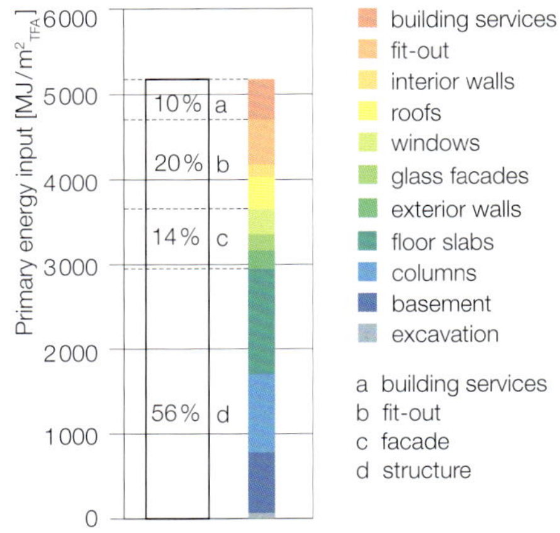

3.14

impacts is to choose an alternative building material (fig. 5.3, pp. 88f.). Since there are generally numerous alternatives and investigating all options is impractical in normal practice, it is necessary to focus on some core aspects early in the planning process (fig. 3.48, p. 60). In terms of resource-efficient product alternatives, the following fields are most suited for improvements:

- increasing the proportion of renewable materials
- optimising the load-bearing structure
- optimising structural components
- selecting products that are optimised with regard to their functional properties
- implementing modular and system construction methods

Resource efficiency through timber construction

Resource-efficient building is primarily associated with the material of the load-bearing system. Moreover, it is often believed that the greater use of renewable resources has a significant influence on the environmental impacts of a building. The fact is, however, that the primary energy demand of the load-bearing system varies only marginally for different materials. Thus, the aspect of space is more or less independent of the building material employed and associated with similar primary energy demands (fig. 3.10). The situation is different with regard to the proportion of renewable energies, which is much higher when using timber for the construction. Assuming that the thermal energy of the wood is recovered, timber constructions can usually be erected with a much lower use of fossil resources. However, the reduction of the environmental impact that can be achieved through timber construction tends to be rather low; it is usually only around 10–15% (fig. 3.15). Greater improvements in life cycle assessments can merely be achieved in the case of residential building (in particular concerning the building classes 1–3 according to the Model Building Code). So the use of timber construction is especially worth considering for homes. The potential for improvement is less pronounced in multi-storey timber constructions since these generally require elaborately engineered products, such as glulam [9], and additional measures and expenses, e.g. for fire protection.

Timber construction is much more beneficial in reducing the global warming potential than it is in lowering the primary energy input (PEI) [10]. The potential for reduction is in this case often 30–40% compared to that of a load-bearing structure made of reinforced concrete. In the life cycle assessment of timber, it is currently assumed that the CO_2 is returned to the natural carbon cycle after its useful life through thermal recycling (combustion). The wood that, in this case, is used to generate energy is substituted for fossil fuels. However, due to efficiency increases in the provision of energy (e.g. by raising the proportion of renewable energies), this substitution process is gradually starting to lose ground. It is for this reason that wood recycling should be taken more seriously. When recycled, the reduction of the environmental impact is preserved [11], and the value of the new timber products is increased by making technical advantages in the production processes accessible. In the case of, for example, the mechanical recycling of particle board, the quantity of adhesive can be reduced significantly compared to new products by incorporating "second hand" wood chips [12].

The way in which a resource is reused (e.g. thermal recycling in the case of wood or mechanical recycling in the case of metal, brick and concrete) must there-

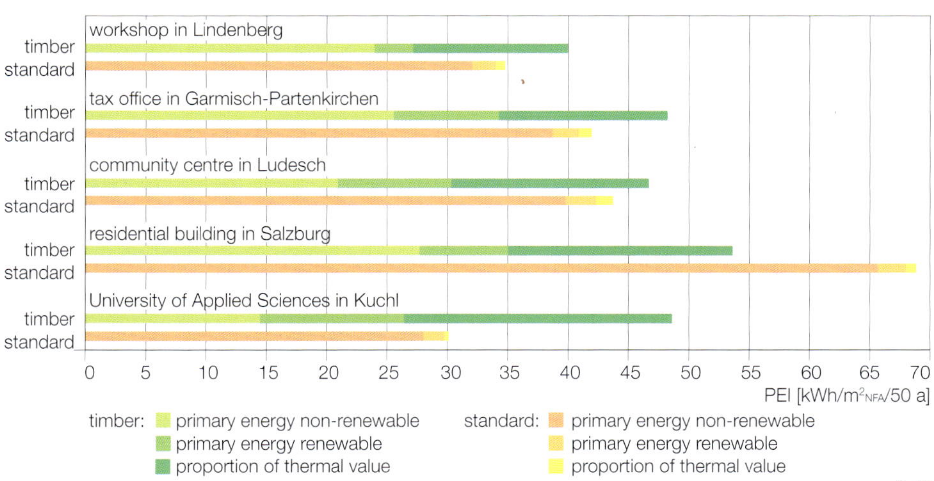

3.15

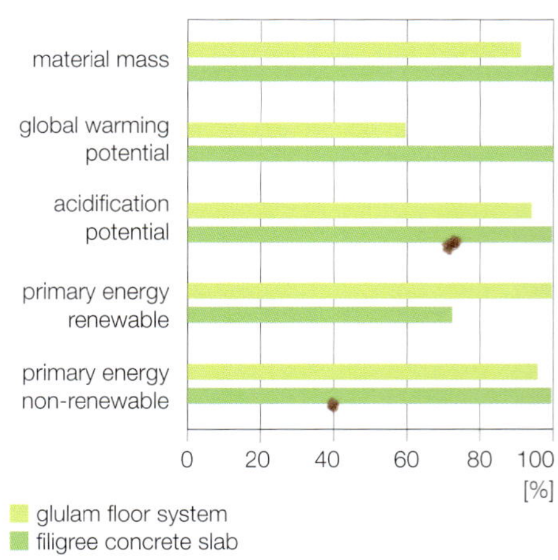

3.16

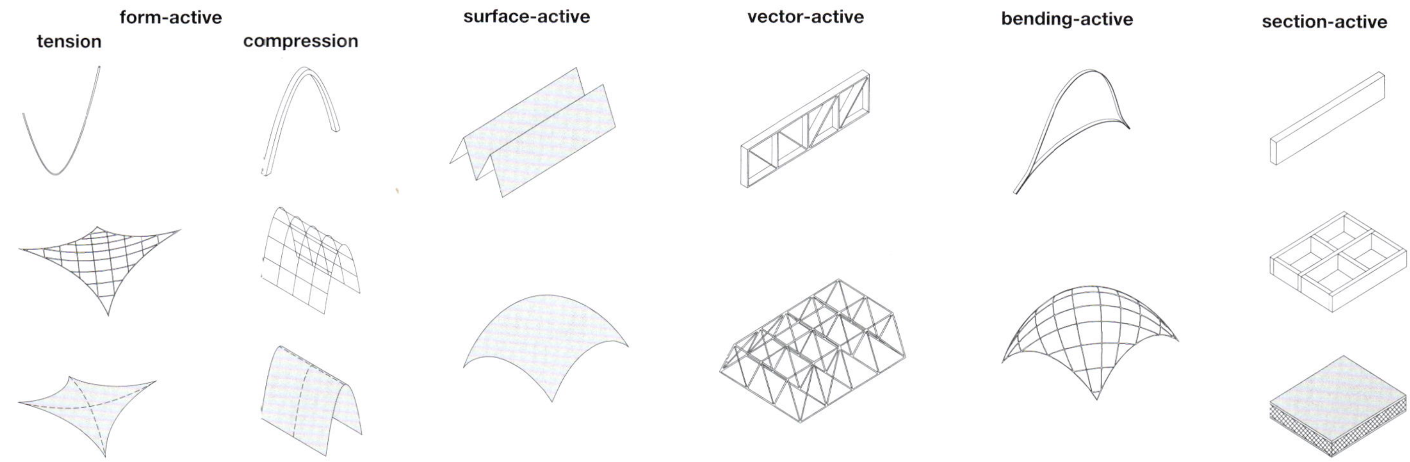

3.17

fore be taken into consideration when making comparisons for a life cycle assessment. In terms of consistency, the best medium-term solution is to make a clear distinction between the material and energy cycles.

Improving the load-bearing structure
Only approximately 10–20 % of all building products employed in a development are actually incorporated in the shell. At the same time, the shell is responsible for around 80 % of the building mass and approximately 50 % of the primary energy incorporated in the building (fig. 3.11, p. 47, 3.14) [13]. A first comparison of the constructions can therefore be performed by taking the building mass into consideration [14]. In multi-storey residential building, the mass for the development of one square metre of useful floor area can vary by a factor of five in similarly sized buildings (fig. 3.23, p. 50). The non-renewable cumulative energy demand CED_{nr} [15] for the construction, however, differs only by approximately 35 %. This supports the conclusion that lightweight constructions generally reduce the environmental impact, but that it is also possible to develop solid constructions with a low environmental impact. And the more complex the requirements, the more the environmental impacts of lightweight and solid constructions approximate: in contrast to solid constructions, lightweight interior constructions can lead to savings of around 15 %; in the case of the building envelope, the difference is around 5 % (fig. 3.24, 3.25, p. 50).
So, it is not simply possible to assess building materials in a global manner; it is rather a question of how best to achieve constructional efficiency (fig. 3.17) by providing a perfect balance of material quality and intended purpose (fig. 3.21, p. 50). This requires the performance of a technical and structural analysis of the construction design, including aspects such as critical loads, the structural system and its materials, the joining methods and self weight. The structural height, in particular, offers potential for improvement:

- Profiled surfaces
  This technique, which is perfectly suited to serial production, provides functional layers in buildings with uniaxial reinforcement. A wide range of profiled semi-finished products is available, in particular for metals and plastics. However, profiling is also implemented in timber and mineral boards. Depending on the material quality and thickness, these products can accommodate bending in the secondary axis.
- Ribbed constructions
  Ribs and stringers can be implemented as planar, one-way or two-way spanning structural components (fig. 3.20). Especially when used as part of the load-bearing structure, these elements can reduce the overall weight and enable parts to be made to measure by adjusting the reinforcing ribs to suit the particular load condition.

3.12 Comparison of primary energy input for a selection of multi-family dwellings (see also fig. 2.28, p. 33). There is no clear correlation between the type of construction and the embodied energy.
3.13 Constructed mass of the multi-family dwellings from fig. 3.12
3.14 Primary energy input according to building component groups, Eawag-Forum Chriesbach (CH) 2004, Bob Gysin + Partner BGP Architekten
3.15 Comparison of primary energy input for different buildings with timber or concrete constructions
3.16 Comparative example of the environmental impacts of a floor slab in an office building made from either timber or concrete
3.17 Examples of efficient load-bearing structures categorised according to load transfer and flow of forces
3.18 Gymnasium in Saint-Martin-en-Haut (F) 2011, Tekhnê architectes
3.19 Tram depot in Bern (CH) 2011, Penzel Valier AG
3.20 Supermarket in Graz (A) 2011, LOVE architecture and urbanism

3.18

3.19

3.20

Building material	PEI [MJ/m³]	PEI/pressure [J/kNm]	[%]	PEI/tension [J/kNm]	[%]	PEI/E modulus [J/kNm]	[%]
concrete							
C 35/40 concrete	1764	50	83 %	551	100 %	0.05	76 %
reinforced concrete (2 % steel)	4098	60	100 %	551	100 %	0.07	100 %
brick, masonry							
sand lime brick	2030	169	280 %	–	–	–	–
clay brick	1663	139	229 %	–	–	–	–
wood							
construction timber, pine,	609	72	118 %	87	16 %	0.06	80 %
glulam	3578	358	592 %	421	76 %	0.33	469 %
metals							
steel (FE 360 B)	188 400	554	916 %	554	101 %	0.89	1281 %
weather-resistant steel (WT St27-2)	204 100	454	750 %	498	90 %	0.96	1388 %
stainless steel (V2A)	411 840	824	1362 %	824	149 %	1.96	2827 %
aluminium (EN AW-7022)	753 380	1838	3038 %	1838	333 %	10.76	15 513 %
float glass	35 000	50	83 %	1167	212 %	0.50	721 %

3.21

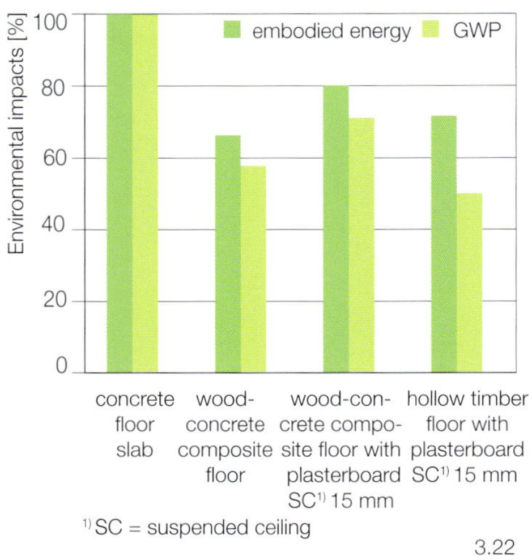

3.22

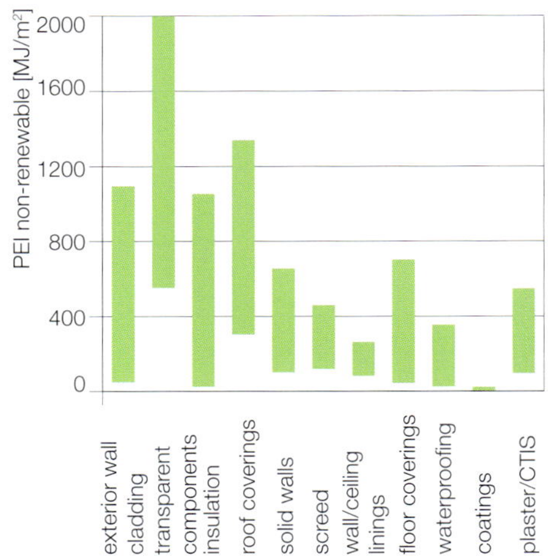

3.23

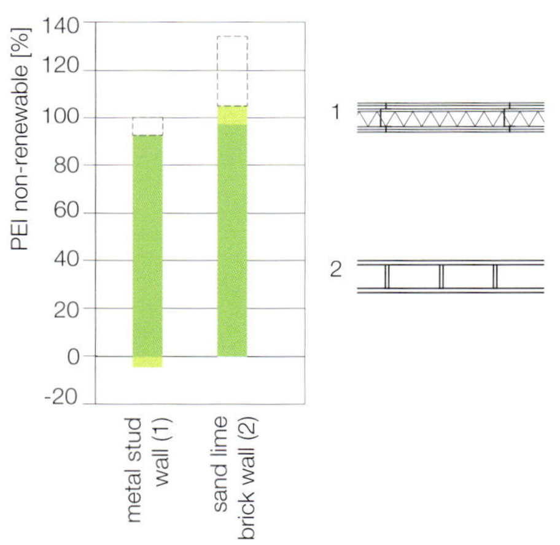

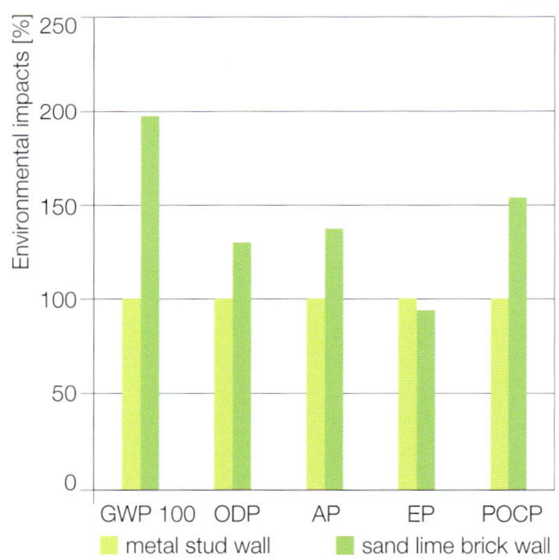

3.24

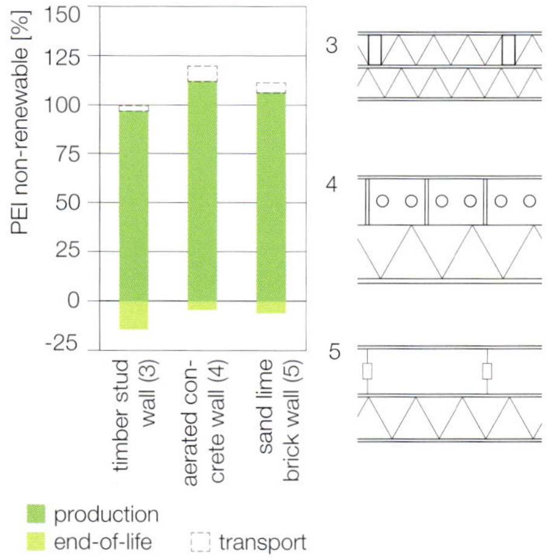

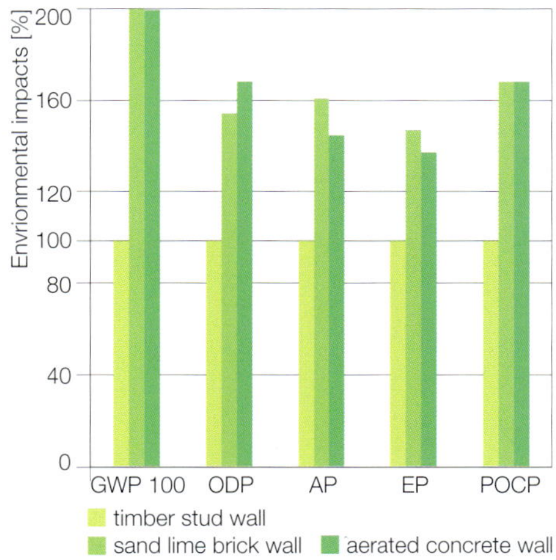

3.25

- Bar structures
  Load-bearing structures can also be resolved into tension and compression members according to the forces acting on the component (fig. 3.18, 3.19). The material efficiency can be increased considerably by separating the structural height of the load-bearing element from the thickness of the functional layer (e.g. by inserting a ceiling into a one storey-high truss).
- Sandwich constructions
  Similar to ribbed elements, sandwich constructions also allow for the development of two-way spanning elements. If the distance between the two outer load-transferring surfaces is doubled, the stiffness of the product increases 7-fold and the load-bearing capacity 3.5-fold [16]. Sandwich constructions are often made of mineral building materials, wood or metal.
- Curved panel constructions
  Three-dimensional curved surfaces obtain their rigidity through internal tension and compression forces. This structural system is frequently used as a roof structure with textile membrane and steel cable.

Material-efficient solutions can be developed by coordinating the functional, technical and structural considerations with the specific properties of the material. In the case of the structural design, the aspects tension, compression and torsion are of major significance (fig. 3.21). However, when improving individual structural elements, the question that always arises is whether the environmental impact has in fact been reduced or only "relocated". The Olympic stadium in Munich is a very noteworthy example in this regard: the lightness of the architecture could be achieved only by placing large quantities of concrete in the foundations, which naturally has a significant influence on the

3.21 Primary energy input of building materials according to different loads
3.22 Comparison of embodied energy and global warming potential of different floor slab constructions (production and disposal)
3.23 Range of non-renewable primary energy input of functional layers in buildings according to their type of use
3.24 LCA comparison between a lightweight and solid partition wall
3.25 LCA comparison between different wall constructions (U = 0.12 W/m²K; observation period 30 years, including replacement processes)
3.26 LCA comparison (production and disposal)
  a beams made from steel and GRP
  b transparent roof coverings
3.27 Office building in Remscheid (D) 2006, Architektur Contor Müller Schlüter
  a comparison of different facade constructions (global warming potential, length of use 20 a)
  b view of facade

building's environmental impact. It is only possible to develop improved structural configurations in combination with a low environmental impact in constructions where the forces acting from different directions cancel each other out. Resource efficiency assessments should therefore analyse the functional unit very carefully (see Significance of functional unit, p. 87).
The above-mentioned study [17] focuses on the environmental impacts of two very important load-bearing components: the horizontal elements and the foundations. Since both elements contribute substantially towards the distribution of loads within a structural system, the basis for building construction with reduced environmental impact is a strict structural system without laterally displaced loads.
Since buildings genera ly require several forms of load transfer, hybrid construction systems are usually beneficial in terms of saving resources (e.g. load bearing timber floor slabs; stiffening concrete core) [18]. On a component level, this is particularly noticeable in floor constructions. Wood-concrete composite floors or timber box element floor systems, for example, have a much lower environmental impact than solid concrete floor slabs with the same load-bearing capacity (fig. 3.22).

Improving structural components
Because components cf the building envelope and floor structure are responsible for large environmental impacts, it is also important to identify strategies to improve these components in terms of their functional and structural features (fig. 3.23; see Environmental impacts of building components, pp. 86ff.). The general requirements placed on the building component, such as critical load, fire protection and U-value, severely affect the

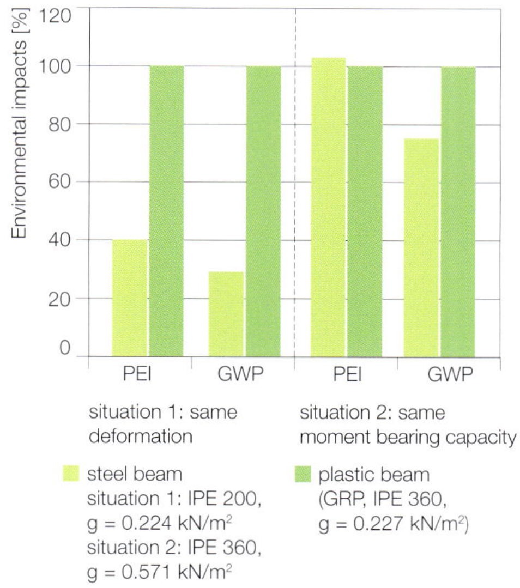

a

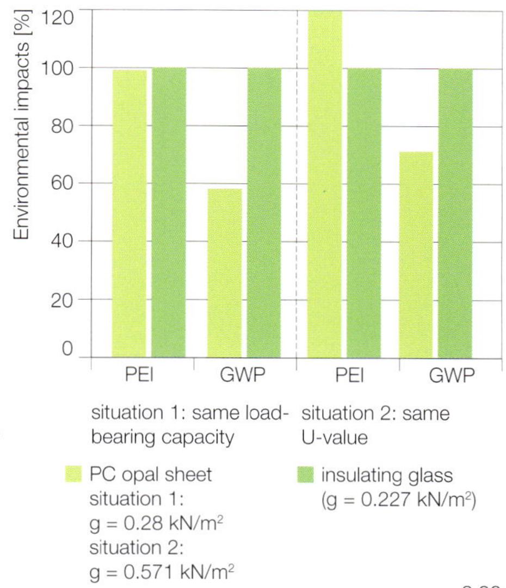

b

3.26

result and must therefore be determined in detail ahead of the assessment (fig. 3.26).
First, a product with improved construction performance is selected for the particular scheme. One example for this method is the use of dry screed board in place of wet screed. Since the structural height of cement screed is determined mainly by the bond of the generally rather brittle material, more elastic materials can deliver the same performance at lower environmental impact. Screed made of particle board, for example, contains approximately 60 % less primary energy than cement screed (see Floor systems – floor coverings, screeds and impact sound insulation, pp. 100f.).
Similar reductions, at a material level, can be achieved by using composite materials. However, improvements to the construction can cause a deterioration of the performance during the life cycle. Adding fibre to plastics, for example, increases the rigidity of the material, but reduces the possibilities for recycling it (see Return to life cycle, pp. 55ff.).

Standard products are usually oversized by manufacturers in order to offer greater versatility and, thus, reach a broader market. Nevertheless, the size of many building components could be reduced if the applied force were to be decreased. So strategies to reduce the weight per unit area, for example by introducing wider spans or longer cantilevers in concrete construction, provide greater potential for improvement (fig. 3.29).
In the field of plastics, the limits of lightweight construction are remarkable: by using sheet material with a unit weight of 170 g/m², it is possible to create a thermal separation to the exterior with a unit weight of only 0.5 kg/m². In this case, the required substructure has a much greater influence on the life cycle assessment than the plastic sheet material itself.
The same applies to the mechanical ventilation of pneumatic membrane constructions: despite being extremely efficient, the operating energy of the blower has a much greater impact on the life cycle assessment than the primary energy content of the, in comparison very durable, plastic membrane (fig. 3.28).

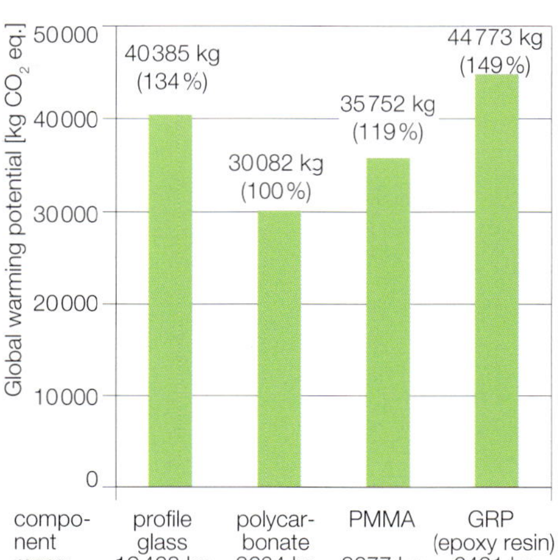

a

b

3.27

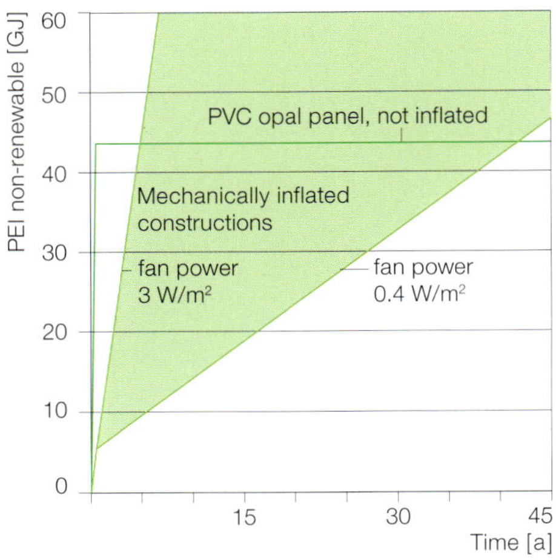

3.28

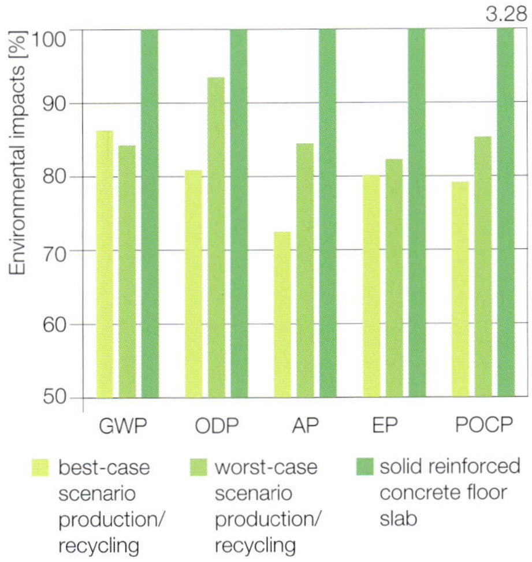

3.29

Window type (measurements 1.25 × 1.4 m)	U_w [W/m²K]	PEI_{nr} [kWh]	**GWP** [kg CO_2 eq.]
double glazing in wood frame	1.3	1882	40
double glazing in PVC frame	1.2	3678	361
triple glazing in wood frame, insulated	0.8	2277	68
triple glazing in wood/aluminium composite frame, insulated	0.8	2469	78
triple glazing in PVC frame, insulated	0.8	5456	381

3.30

3.28 Development of the primary energy demand of pneumatic constructions with mechanical inflation in comparison to conventional constructions
3.29 LCA comparison of a solid reinforced concrete floor slab with two different designs of a hollow block floor (production and disposal)
3.30 Non-renewable primary energy input and global warming potential (GWP) of different windows according to their frame materials
3.31 CO_2 emissions (positive values) and CO_2 storage potential (negative values) of various timber products (production and disposal, data taken from Ökobau.dat 2009)
3.32 Office building in Dornbirn (A) 2013, Hermann Kaufmann
a section perspective with floor slab construction
b view into office
3.33 Children's day care centre in Aarau (CH) 2012, Husistein & Partner: corridor with exposed services

Products with improved functional performance

Alongside structural improvements, it is also possible to make use of synergy effects, where one component "supports" another in a functional way. An elastic floor covering, for example, can clearly lower the transmission of noise in the floor. As a consequence, the measures for impact sound insulation can be reduced. A similar situation occurs when using autoclaved aerated concrete instead of sand lime brick as the load-bearing material in exterior walls. The lower thermal conductivity of autoclaved aerated concrete means that the thickness of insulation can be decreased while maintaining the same U-value of the wall. Thus, the environmental impact can often be reduced by taking the whole building component into consideration (fig. 3.25, p. 50). The supportive function may even make some constructional elements superfluous. This phenomenon is best illustrated by translucent facade panels made of polycarbonate (fig. 3.27, p. 51): the panel is responsible for approximately 40 % of the environmental impact caused by the functional unit "facade construction". If the panel takes on the task of transferring the loads and no longer requires a load-bearing substructure, the relative importance of the panel within the component rises; however, the environmental impact of the functional unit as a whole decreases. This would also be the case if the panel thickness had to be increased due to greater compressive and tensile stress in the facade. The maximum environmental improvement for panel materials is achieved if the product is self-supporting over several floors [19]. On a component level, this aspect is best expressed by taking a look at windows (fig. 3.30). The effect of windows on the room atmosphere and well-being of the occupants is remarkable; however, their production is also responsible for large environmental impacts. At the same time, windows affect the operating energy consumption of the building, for example due to heat gain in winter or overheating in summer. The use of windows should therefore be perfectly adjusted to ensure not only good thermal conditions but also the best solution in terms of operating energy. In the case of windows, with the same surface area and type of glass, the difference in primary energy consumption lies in the choice of the frame material. Wood and PVC frames have a lower thermal transmittance value than metal frames. Metal frames are the worst alternative in terms of the environmental impact of their production; on the other hand, they have the longest service life. Nevertheless, without taking repair and maintenance into consideration, metal frames would have to stay in a building nine times as long as a wood-framed window in order to compensate for the greater amount of energy required for the production.
In comparison to wood-framed windows, PVC windows are beneficial in terms of the simple processing techniques and the low material consumption, which in turn leads to greater cost efficiency. However, wider frames are required to compensate for the lower rigidity. Thus, the global warming potential and the primary energy input (cradle-to-gate) of a PVC-framed window is almost twice as high as that of a traditional wood-framed window. The greater proportion of frame required in the case of PVC windows generally reduces passive heat gain and the amount of daylight entering the room. The use of metal profiles to cover wooden frames for better weather resistance increases the environmental impact only marginally, since the strips of metal are very thin and light.
The same applies to an additional layer of insulation in the frame. The extra amount of primary energy required for the production of Passive House-compliant windows corresponds with the energy saved over a two-year period through reduced transmission heat loss. These figures express, from an environmental viewpoint, how significant the impact of the frame construction is in the life cycle assessment of a window assembly. At the same time, these findings conclude that highly insulated wooden frames should be used for energy reference purposes in future comparative analyses.

Modular construction systems

The use of modular construction systems is especially beneficial in situations where elusive aspects, such as quick erection times, easy maintenance, good suitability for conversion and deconstruction, are the focus of attention. The advantages of modular building systems are readily apparent and have a long tradition in building history. The projects completed by Fritz Haller in the 1960s (fig. 1.9, p. 12), which he himself referred to as "the general solution", are a good example for modular construction systems. Alongside steel construction methods, which are implemented mainly for functional buildings, halls and large office

buildings, modular timber construction systems have become established for residential buildings, schools and children's day care centres (fig. 3.33), offices (fig. 3.32) and small production buildings. In this case, the resource efficiency of a construction tends to increase in accordance with the degree of prefabrication. Since greater care must be taken in planning the details and the opportunities for introducing quality control measures are greater, off-site production reduces the tolerance required on site and leads to more slender components, fewer faults and better workmanship. Furthermore, less construction waste is produced on site due to standardised processes [20]. Prefabrication provides the opportunity to increase the proportion of mono-material batches, which in turn improves the possibilities for recycling at the end of the building's service life.
The accurate recording of built-in products by the planner and manufacturer eases maintenance and, later, the deconstruction of the building. The modular configuration of system building always requires a clear separation of constructional units (see Constructing recyclable buildings, p. 66). The separation of building services, fit-out and building envelope is particularly helpful in this case (fig. 3.33). The complex interweaving of technical elements can also lead to new functional options, as is shown by the accommodation of technical installations in the ceiling construction of an office building in Dornbirn (fig. 3.32).
It is noticeable in modular timber construction systems that the materials predominantly used have only a very low CO_2 storage capacity (e.g. structural timber, OSB board and particle board) (fig. 3.31) [21]. The in the meantime very technically-oriented perception of timber construction is on par with this very low carbon storage capacity.

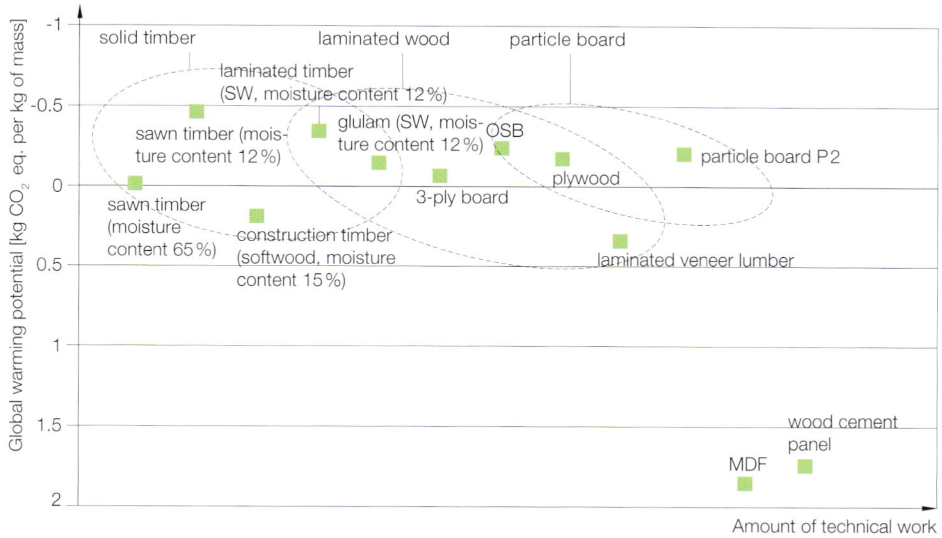

3.31

Healthy built environments
Buildings that are non-hazardous to health are created by incorporating as few pollutants as possible into the structure (see Building biology, pp. 18ff.). The reduction of natural pollutants can generally only be achieved if the building is planned in such a way that sources of pollution cannot arise or the pollutant is removed as soon as possible. The (geologically-induced) hazard caused by radon in basement rooms, for example, can be reduced by mechanical ventilation. Mould can be avoided by reducing the moisture level in the surrounding air and building components, for example by implementing moisture permeable building materials and reducing thermal bridges. In existing buildings non-hazardous materials may possibly become emitters of pollution following long-term contamination. These secondary hazards can either be caused by user-related issues (e.g. spilled liquids, cleaning detergents), or primary pollution deriving from other construction materials. A detailed survey should be performed to determine suitable measures for the remedial treatment of the building. Because these procedures are usually costly and time consuming, the aim in new builds should always be to avoid the ingress of pollutants into the building from the outset. This strategy also helps to ensure long-term maintenance of the property value. In the case of new builds, planners can avoid potential material problems by selecting suitable building products. Health risks most frequently stem from surface finishes and coatings, as well as varnishes, primers and sealants. In particular, the greater use of solvents has led to a considerable increase of pollution in buildings. Almost all hazardous substances known to be present in buildings today are contained in indirect auxiliary building materials, which make up approximately five per cent of today's total building stock.

Reduction of hazardous building materials
The first approach is to achieve a general reduction of auxiliary materials. A potential source of pollution can, for example, be avoided by using fasteners rather than adhesives when laying fitted carpets and resilient floor coverings. This measure also allows for easier replacement (see

a

b
3.32

3.33

Determination of risk factors in buildings and relevant building components

↓

Selection of building material groups with a lower potential risk

↓

Selection of materials with reduced amounts of hazardous substances (e.g. SVHC, solvents and VOC content)

↓

Assessment and documentation of the implementation of specifications on site (e.g. safety requirements)

↓

Evidence of the measures' success by taking room air measurements

3.34

Building materials assessment according to AgBB scheme

first measurement on 3rd day

- TVOC ≤ 10 mg/m³
- total of all detected carcinogens ≤ 0.01 mg/m³
- sensory test [1)]

second measurement on 28th day

- TVOC ≤ 10 mg/m³
- $\sum$ SVOC ≤ 0.1 mg/m³ [2)]
- total of all detected carcinogens ≤ 0.001 mg/m³
- assessable substances: all VOC with LCI: R ≤ 1 [3) 4)]
- non-assessable substances: total of all VOC with LCI ≤ 0.1 mg/m³ [3)]
- sensory test [1)]

1) preventative measurement; no adapted processes currently available
2) SVOC = semi volatile organic compounds
3) LCI = lowest (toxicological) concentration of interest according to AgBB scheme
4) R is the ratio between measured VOC concentration and LCI

3.35

	Standard room	DGNB conform
TVOC	2000 µg/m³	280 µg/m³
formaldehyde	14 µg/m³	6.5 µg/m³
number of measurements 50 % above AGÖF NOW value	8	5

NOW value = new building reference value (Neubauorientierungswert)

3.36

3.34 Procedure when receiving support in selecting building materials that are non-hazardous to health with regard to building biology aspects
3.35 Procedure and criteria in assessing building materials for use indoors according to AgBB scheme
3.36 Comparison of pollutant emission in two identical rooms in the case of standard work practices and implementation according to DGNB quality level 4 (occupancy profile: New office and administrative buildings 2012; time of measurement: no longer than 28 days after completion). Room fit-out: suspended metal ceiling, exposed concrete walls and lightweight glazing; terrazzo mastic asphalt screed
3.37 Hierarchical levels of recycling with illustration of definition boundaries for different guidelines
3.38 Ways of recycling and disposal of building materials including an assessment of the reuse potential in terms of resources and technical aspects

Optimising replacement processes, pp. 64ff.). At a raw material level, steel can, for example, be protected from rust by galvanising the components rather than coating them. Because the selected strategy may also have an effect on the appearance, the building material categories determined should be checked for environmental issues and potential hazardous substances at an early planning stage (fig. 5.3, pp. 88f.; www.wecobis.de).

Non-hazardous auxiliary materials
The second strategy involves selecting building and auxiliary materials that are non-hazardous to health. A number of assessment tools are available precisely for this purpose (see Tools for the ecological assessment of buildings, p. 35). Since the potential pollutant load of individual building materials can be determined only with the help of technical product and safety data sheets, this strategy is not really applicable until the later design phases. The data sheets describe procedures for handling and working with the product, provide information on ingredients and name possible hazardous compounds, including their effect during processing, use and disposal. It is most important in this case to specify the substances that the ECHA (European Chemicals Agency) lists as SVHCs (Substances of Very High Concern). Such substances have severe effects on human health and the environment (e.g. carcinogenic) and should generally be avoided.
Furthermore, all products implemented should be free of solvents. GISBAU, a system maintained by the Construction Industry Trade Association BG BAU in Germany providing information on hazardous substances, publishes so-called GISCODEs, which are very helpful in this respect. Product group codes determine products with similar health risks. GISBAU also makes recommendations on the processing of building materials during construction (see Planning tools, p. 21). The higher the number following the product group, the higher the risk to health and environment. It is not mandatory to state the codes in product brochures or data sheets. However, the GISCODE is usually provided by manufacturers on request. The level of Volatile Organic Compounds (VOC) is a further indicator, which is either stated as an emission value (e.g. in the case of floor coverings) or as an ingredient (e.g. in the case of paints and varnishes). Ecolabels or measurements of pollutants taken by the manufacturers themselves generally summarise some of these target definitions and help planners to select low-emission products. Credible ecolabels (fig. 2.15, p. 22) provide transparency on the tests that must be passed to receive the label, for example by describing the test criteria. Organisations responsible for the certification generally list certified products on their websites, which is very useful for research purposes.

Reduced pollution absorption
The third strategy is designed to prevent occupants from absorbing air pollutants. Other than being useful from an energy efficiency viewpoint, mechanical ventilation units are also beneficial in terms of health issues, since the required air exchange rate also contributes towards dissipating pollution. A further method aimed at reducing pollution absorption is to encapsulate small quantities of materials that are known to be hazardous to health. However, these measures do not generally solve the problem of pollution ingress into buildings.

Procedure during the planning process
At the raw material level, the aforementioned measures usually result in only a small variation in cost; depending on the use of the building material, it is sometimes possible to reduce costs. During the planning phase it is extremely important to accurately describe the requirements in the contract specifications [22]. This means that the requirements must be determined, at the very latest, by the time of tendering. To prevent tenderers from adding an "angst surcharge", health-related criteria should be described clearly in the contract specifications and discussed during the contract negotiations; furthermore, a contact person should be specified to deal with queries. Construction site practices must also be clarified early on, and the necessary scope of documentation must be agreed upon with the contractors. This strategy prevents additional costs from incurring during the execution phase [23], or at least keeps them at a very low level. Due to the complexity of information, verification activities tend to drive the costs up during the execution phase. Costs and effort can be reduced by repeating structural configurations and detail solutions, which in turn minimises the total number of building materials introduced in the building.
On completion of the construction work, the room air quality must then be measured to make a final check on all meas-

ures taken. The sustainability certification systems DGNB and ÖGNI, for example, request room air measurements be made for the detection of formaldehyde and VOC. If the results exceed a TVOC concentration of 3000 µg/m³ or a formaldehyde concentration of 120 µg/m³, certification can no longer be pursued. Prior assessment of the building materials according to the AgBB evaluation scheme or other ecolabels can help all project participants to stay on track (fig. 3.35). AGÖF has used previous measurements to determine a range of average values for various pollutants (AGÖF NOW (new build reference) values), which the client and planner can use to compare own results. Based on the dissipation behaviour of pollutants, it is then possible to detect whether high values will be a short or long-term hazard.

Return to life cycle

Based on life cycle thinking, the Waste Framework Directive specifies a recycling and reuse quota of 70% in Europe for the year 2020 (fig. 3.37). In Germany, these rates have so far only been met for metals, bottle glass and paper. Other examples of material recycling include the use of demolition waste to replace crushed rock, the reforming of thermoplastics, the breakdown of plastics into polymers and their repolymerisation or the production of new wood-based materials. Wood, steel and plastics could in fact be part of a closed material cycle. In Germany, however, there are rules, such as the Closed Substance Cycle and Waste Management Act (Kreislaufwirtschaftsgesetz), which are opposed to this procedure and benefit the thermal recycling of wood and plastic waste. It is for this reason that the quality of recycling should take a back seat during the planning process and attention should focus on the general reintroduction into the technical material cycle.

Recyclable constructions and mono-material construction waste are most suited for a reintroduction into the material cycle (see Constructing recyclable buildings, p. 66). Presorting waste on the construction site, according to, for example, the measures described in the DGNB certification system for a low-waste building site, is always helpful in this respect. The presorting should include mineral waste, recyclable waste, mixed construction waste, hazardous waste and asbestos-containing materials.

The training of project participants and their supervision on site by construction

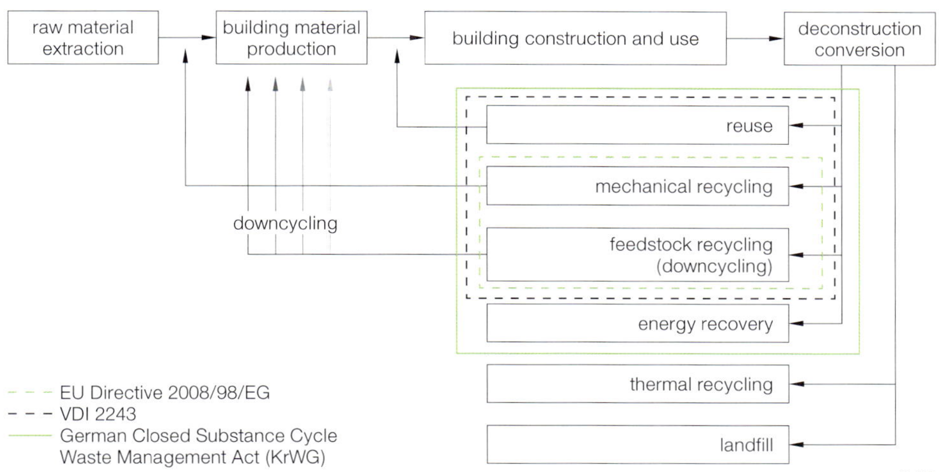

3.37

site managers encourages an orderly sorting process, and the disposal costs for pure rubble are in fact very low. Salvaged material from buildings ranges significantly in value, both in economic as well as environmental terms. The repurchase price of metal, for example, is fairly high at the moment. On the other hand, in the case of concrete rubble, the disposal costs exceed the value of the raw materials. Mineral building materials, in particular, pose a special challenge due to their high mass flow rates and rather low resource value; and it is precisely for this reason that there is a high demand for closed material cycles.

Recycling costs are dependent on the quantity of the recyclable material and its technical value, i.e. the possibility to produce higher quality goods (upcycling). In environmental assessments, a value can be assigned to the different recycling methods (fig. 3.38). Apart from the immediate reuse of a building component, common recycling methods include mechanical and feedstock recycling as well as thermal recycling. The reuse of already manufactured goods is naturally the most environmentally beneficial solution; thermal recycling, on the other hand, should be avoided since the resource is, in this case, irretrievably lost.

Reuse

The immediate reuse of building components is the most simple method to save resources at the raw material level. The fact is however that only 11% of all building components are immediately reused – a lot less than the amount of construction waste which is mechanically recycled [24]. Nevertheless, from an environmental point of view, reuse is the best solution, and can also be rather interesting from an economic perspective, such as in the case of reusing concrete components from GDR Plattenbau buildings. Depending on the expense of transportation, there is a cost saving potential of over 40% [25]. The environmental impact is generally lowest if the whole building is converted and reused. This is especially recommended for solid concrete constructions.

Opportunities to already consider reuse

	Reuse			Further treatment
	high potential	average potential	low potential	
reuse of component	component that fulfils the technical and legal requirements of a new build	component that fulfils the technical and legal requirements of an existing building	component that is still in working order, but no longer state of the art	–
mechanical recycling	comparable product in terms of technical and economic aspects	high quality raw material with high market value	high quality raw material with low market value	technically possible but economically not feasible; downcycling
thermal recycling	not responsible for any waste-specific pollutants; high calorific value	uncomplicated in large plants; average calorific value	in waste incineration plants; low calorific value	after processing
disposal (landfill)	composting and upgrading	building material debris and inert waste disposal plants	building material debris disposal plants, complicated	at landfill disposal or residual landfill; possibility of emissions

reuse potential

Quality/resource efficiency of recycling and disposal

from an environmental viewpoint ■ good ■ good to acceptable ■ acceptable □ bad recycling method

3.38

Auxiliary element	Main element (dominant material)					
	Concrete	**Steel**	**Sheet glass**	**Plaster**	**Wood (untreated)**	**PVC (foam)**
Concrete	mono material	separates easily, recycling technologies are available for steel and concrete	almost inseparable, no available recycling technologies	almost inseparable, no available recycling technologies	difficult to separate, downcycling technologies are available	difficult to separate, no available recycling technologies
Steel	separates easily, recycling technologies are available for steel and concrete	mono material	separates easily, glass is recyclable (limited use as sheet glass)	separable, recycling technologies are available for plaster and steel	separates easily, recycling technologies are available	separates, hardly any available recycling technologies
Sheet glass	difficult to separate, only downcycles	separates easily, recycling technologies are available for steel and glass	mono material	almost inseparable	separates, limited downcycling technologies are available	separates, hardly any available recycling technologies
Plaster	plaster is a hazard in concrete demolition work, only small amounts admitted due to sulphur attack	separates easily, recycling technologies are available for steel and plaster	almost inseparable, no available recycling technologies	mono material	difficult to separate, plaster disturbs mechanical recycling process and combustion	difficult to separate, no available recycling technologies
Wood (untreated)	small, very soiled wood parts are difficult to separate; large-format wood scrap uncomplicated	separates easily, recycling technologies are available for steel and wood	partially separable, wood disturbs the glass production process, downcycling is possible	difficult to separate, limited recycling technologies are available	mono material	difficult to separate, hardly any available recycling technologies
PVC (foam)	difficult to separate, if proportion of PVC is small, downcycling is possible	partially separable, PVC burns in the melting process	partially separable, PVC melts in the production process, downcycling is possible	difficult to separate, no recycling technologies are available	difficult to separate, PVC disturbs the mechanical recycling process, combustion is only possibility	mono material (technically recyclable, although seldom performed)

■ compatible, recycles well ■ limited possibilities, downcycling possible ■ incompatible, no recycling possible

3.39

during the planning process, for example in the case of temporary buildings, may even lead to new design concepts at the outset (fig. 3.42, 3.43).
It is, in this case, an advantage for the planner if the material intended for reuse is available in sufficient quantities. Standardised components, such as panels, standard beams and sections increase the stock of material. Other fields of industry are also a source for interesting products, an example here is buildings made from salvaged shipping containers (fig. 2.22, p. 27). Unfortunately, there are rarely accurate technical specifications for salvaged construction products, which often results in constraints on liability. If the product is without a manufacturer's label, the planner is responsible for providing appropriate evidence of the product's serviceability. The expense in providing the necessary product data frequently prevents the use of salvaged components. In order to avoid preparing new evidence, the component can instead be dimensioned according to the less favourable design criteria from previous specifications.
This may mean that some components are technically oversized; however, the outcome could nevertheless be interesting in terms of appearance and environmental as well as economic aspects. The example of a residential building in Enschede, with an approximately 60% proportion of reused materials, shows that the greenhouse gas emissions for the production of the load-bearing structure can be reduced by a factor of ten (fig. 3.47, p. 59).

Mechanical recycling

Mechanical recycling is the recovery of materials from waste and the production of so-called recyclates. Because this procedure creates a new product with reliable technical specifications, it is considered the traditional method of giving high-quality building materials, or materials with extremely high mass flow rates, a new lease of life.
Waste cannot be perfectly sorted (fig. 3.39). Moreover, most products are mixed with fillers and additives. On this account, recyclates rarely have the same quality as the original material. This is very evident in the case of plastics: the structure of most polymers is destroyed during recycling processes with the result that the polymer chains are shortened. Plastic products made of 100% recycled material start to differ in their properties after only three processing cycles. Significant damage generally starts to appear after five cycles, affecting all constituents of the compound (polymer chains, stabilisers, colourants, flame retardants, etc.). Only a few polymers, for example polyethylene terephthalate (PET), can be mechanically recycled without experiencing any loss of quality. Recyclates are therefore not normally used exclusively, but, depending on the intended production method, are usually mixed with new polymer materials. In injection moulding, for instance, the amount of recycled material is limited to 5% in order to maintain the quality of the polymer product [26]. Today, polymer recyclates are, for example, used in PVC window frames.
In some cases, it is even possible to improve the properties of a building material through recycling processes. Recycled wood chip, for example, (approximately 90% of the original chip mass can be recovered through recycling) binds the adhesive better than fresh wood chip and thus allows the amount of binding agents to be reduced. Furthermore, due to the fact that the recycled wood chip already has the right size for further processing, it is possible to omit a stage in the production process [27].

3.39 Compatibility of different building material groups in recycling
3.40 Compatibility of different plastics in recycling processes
3.41 Derivation of the maximum energy demand according to the Swiss concept of the 2000-Watt Society
3.42 Refurbishment of a 1960s residential building in Augsburg (D) 2013, lattkearchitekten: the energy efficiency refurbishment meeting barrier-free requirements has given the building a new lease of life

Promotion of recycling processes

Planners can encourage the development of new recycling methods not only by supporting the economic implementation of material recovery systems and collecting mono-material batches of waste on building sites, but also by adding detailed specifications for waste in tendering documents. In the case of metals, these are already largely in place; for other products, which are valuable from a resource efficiency perspective, material recovery systems will presumably be made available in the near future. PV modules, for example, will have to be returned to the manufacturer for recycling according to the scheme PV CYCLE (www.pvcycle.org) or the EU WEEE Directive (Waste Electrical and Electronic Equipment). In addition, there will be more collection points for plastics.

Concerning recycling, the potential for optimisation lies in increasing the material quality through better separation and sorting of waste. The DGNB and BNB certification systems encourage the design of deconstructable buildings (Criterion TEC 4.1.4) and the selective collection of mineral waste, recyclable materials, mixed construction waste, hazardous and asbestos-contaminated waste precisely for this purpose.

Greater detail and accuracy in the collection of construction waste can also lead to better results in the recycling process. The greater use of high-quality steel alloys, for example, has increased the need for separate collection of alloy scrap. The chances of better reuse in line with the properties of the resource are increased by making it possible to identify the material composition easily and accurately following the deconstruction of the building. Thus, labelling building components is of vital importance. Nevertheless, with regard to metals, the number of different alloys should generally be questioned carefully.

The following aspects, which can enable or improve mechanical recycling, should be taken into consideration when designing buildings [28]:

- Where possible, reversible connections, which enable the exchange of a building component, should be used (see Constructing recyclable buildings, p. 66)
- Smaller variety of building materials in order to increase the size of mono-material batches (see Material concentration and structural reduction, p. 61).
- Use of reusable mono materials. Perlite-filled insulation bricks can, for example, be recycled to produce crushed brick when no longer in use, whereas mineral wool-filled bricks are currently non-recyclable.
- In the case of inseparable constructions, the building materials should be chosen in such a way that they are compatible in the recycling process. This is generally the case if materials from the same material group are selected (e.g. cement-bound materials, fig. 3.39). In the case of polymers, however, it may be necessary to examine the compatibility of individual materials (fig. 3.40).
- In the case of inseparable constructions made of materials from different material groups, one substance must be selected as the principal component. Metal sandwich panels, for example, are usually recycled together with their bonded foam core. The combustion of the foam reduces the amount of energy required to melt the metal. However, this process leads to the irretrievable loss of the non-renewable polymer. When selecting sandwich products, the use of renewable resources should therefore be encouraged (e.g. wood or wood fibre laminated products).
- Precise documentation and/or specification. In the case of plastics, for example, the type of plastic must, according to DIN 11469, be indicated on the component itself (recycling code). Special markers in the plastic components (e.g. fluorescent colourants) also help to separate the different types of polymers more easily.
- Where possible, surface coatings should be avoided. In the case of primers and varnishes, pollutants from the coating can seep into the coated material and prevent recycling.

Main element	Additives/auxiliary elements						
	PE	PVC	PS	PC	PP	PA	PMMA
PE	■	□	□	□	■	□	□
PVC	□	■	□	□	□	□	■
PS	□	□	■	□	□	□	□
PC	□	○	□	■	□	□	■
PP	■	□	□	□	■	□	□
PA	□	□	○	□	□	■	□
PMMA	□	■	○	■	□	□	■

■ compatible
○ only compatible in small doses
□ not compatible

3.40

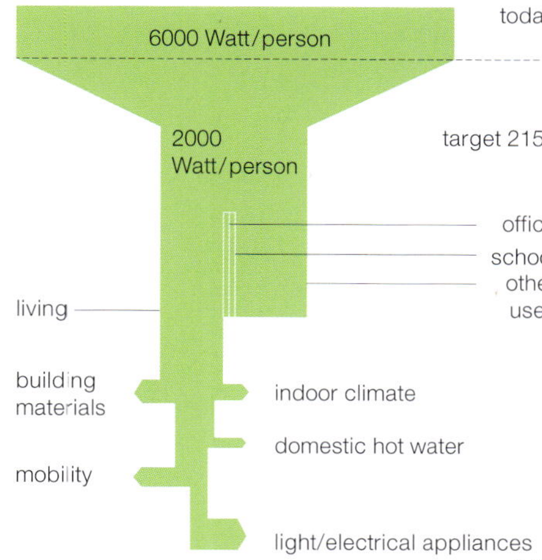

3.41

Optimisation of the building life cycle

The material life cycle already offers great potential for improvement (fig. 3.41). In many fields, however, the measures for improving the material life cycle are too abstract for planners. The design approach is much clearer when strategies refer to the building life cycle. Vari-

3.42

3.43

3.44

ous concepts, each with a different focus, have become established in this field: the cradle-to-cradle design concept [29] and the MIPS concept (material input per service unit) [30] underline the circular economy approach. The Triple Zero concept (triple zero = zero energy, zero emissions and zero waste) [31] initially ignores the construction phase, but nevertheless allows for a closed-loop assessment by returning the building to the material life cycle. The Swiss concept set out by the 2000-Watt Society is unique in that it defines separate target values for mobility, the construction and operation of the building alongside a limit for the total energy demand of buildings. This methodology makes it easier to detect the strengths and weaknesses in the design and adapt them accordingly (fig. 3.41, p. 57).

Occupancy profile as a lead indicator

The use of the building is one of the most important aspects of every design. The performance and user behaviour during the use phase have a significant impact on the construction and the selection of materials, as well as on the relation between the input of resources for the construction and operation of the building (fig. 3.45). The higher the energy input for the building operation and the more frequently energy services are required during occupancy, the more the building construction should contribute towards reducing the operating energy (fig. 3.48, p. 60). Potential changes of use and the intended duration of occupation determine the length of the observation period with regard to the use phase in the life cycle.

Many sustainability assessment systems for buildings proceed on the assumption that a change of use can be prepared for by planning ahead appropriately. If, in this case, the load-bearing structure can be retained, the environmental impact is reduced significantly as a result. In practice, however, this assumption is not generally valid. With regard to residential building, in particular, it is necessary to assess, according to the location, whether a change of use is at all realistic. The commercial relevance of the site, based on specific qualities (e.g. vicinity to the town centre, monofunctional structures or certain island positions), are important considerations in this respect. The use of buildings in suburban residential areas, for example, rarely changes.

For planning purposes, it is therefore worthwhile to categorise buildings into different occupancy profiles and use them, in accordance with the superior site qualities, as lead indicators for the development of the material concept (fig. 3.46).

Buildings with high operating energy demand and low change of use

In the case of "high energy consumers", the construction and deconstruction phases are of little significance in the life cycle of the building. Strategies which try to reduce the operating energy through use of material, on the other hand, are particularly effective in this case. Possible measures include reducing the demand for operating energy directly (e.g. by adding insulation), tapping energy sources for the building (e.g. by creating a microclimatic envelope, using air collectors or supporting the building services with process heat) or designing the energy flow in line with the demand (e.g. by introducing selective reflection measures or storage mass). The use of material is in this case usually characterised by multiple material functions (see Functional overlaps, p. 61). All five major energy services in buildings (heating, cooling, lighting, ventilation and electricity) can be optimised through the choice of material. In the case of the heat demand, optimisation is achieved, for example, by using envelope components with low transmission heat loss; in the case of cooling, through nighttime cooling of the storage mass. Solar chimneys are helpful when it comes to the ventilation of the building, and reflective surfaces are an important aspect concerning lighting. The power demand can also be reduced, for example, with the help of photovoltaic panels. Since, in the case of an office building and an observation period of 50 years, the use phase accounts for approximately 75 % of the total life cycle assessment [32], even small improvement measures suffice to significantly reduce the primary energy demand (fig. 3.48).

In buildings with a high energy demand, the building services components are replaced by more efficient ones at regular intervals. The planner can contribute towards the long-term maintenance of the building fabric by the way in which the technical elements are installed (e.g. good accessibility, simple replacement processes). Moreover, the reduction of the operating expenses through easy-to-care surfaces is also rated highly.

3.43 Temporary roof for a Pope's Mass in Freiburg (D) 2012, Werner Sobek Ingenieure
3.44 Reuse of the building membrane for bags
3.45 Contrasting developments of buildings in accordance with the frequency of changes of owners and a design adapted to these frequent changes
3.46 Possibilities for optimising building constructions in terms of their environmental impact according to their operating energy demand and the frequency of changes of owners
3.47 Single-family home with approximately 60 % proportion of reused components and building materials in Enschede (NL) 2012, 2012 Architecten
a CO_2 and primary energy demand of facade (wood from cable drums) and load-bearing structure (steel parts from a textile machine) in comparison to new build
b view of the building

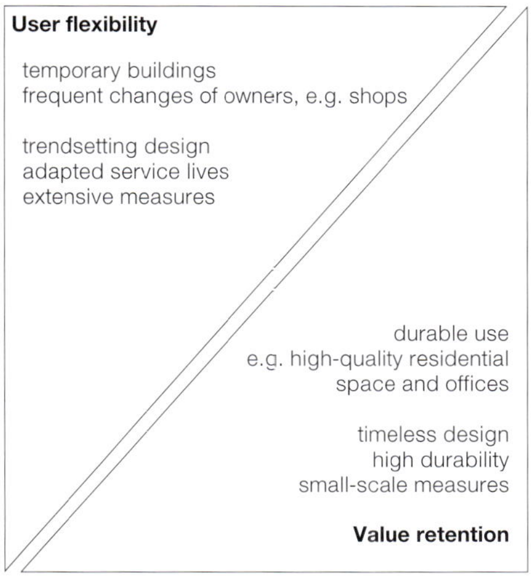

3.45

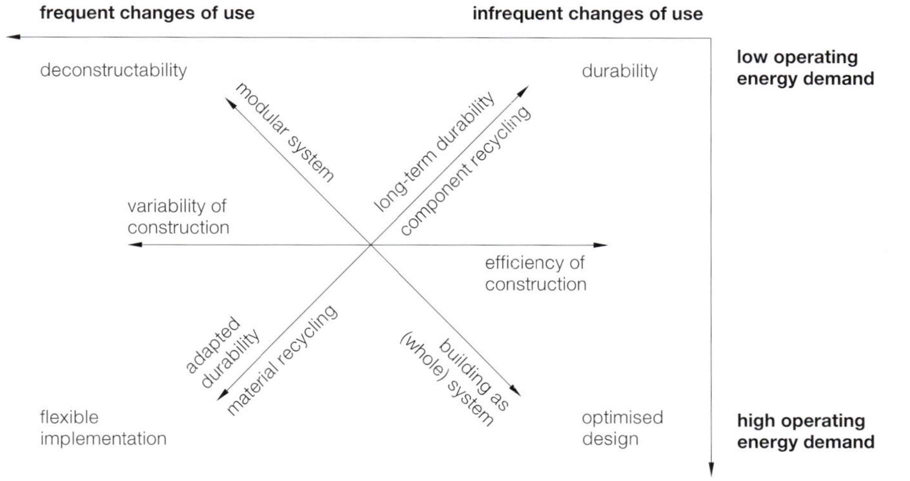

3.46

Buildings with long design lives and low operating energy demand

The significance of a component's embodied energy rises in buildings with a low energy demand and very long use phase (usually residential buildings and office buildings in upmarket areas). Figure 3.46 shows the extraordinary status of residential building, which, in accordance with current trends, will continue to gain momentum as energy efficiency rises. The Nearly Zero-Energy Standard is to become mandatory for all new builds in Europe as of 2021. At the latest from this time onwards, all new residential buildings will invest around 50 % of the total life cycle energy input in the construction.

Measures for optimising the use of material are most effective if they consider the environmental impact of components and their durability evenhandedly. Durable building materials are generally considered more environmentally beneficial than materials with low embodied energy but require frequent replacement during the service life of the building. In order to make full use of the design life of durable components, it is beneficial to choose a timeless building design. The components in very long-lasting buildings can rarely be designed in such a way that they reach the end of their service lives at the same time. It is best therefore to divide the replacement measures into smaller portions of work. As a result, buildings are able to retain their value for longer, but are less flexible when it comes to changes of use.

Buildings with short design lives

In the case of buildings and fit-outs with short design lives, the primary energy input can be improved without taking durability into consideration. Occasionally, it is also possible to neglect the environmental impacts of the building operation. These buildings include temporary structures, exhibition stand constructions, retail interiors or modular systems for use in production or office environments. Alongside reducing the environmental impacts of the production, the most important consideration in this case is feeding the resources back into the material cycle (fig. 3.43, 3.44).

The most beneficial measures for buildings with short design lives include reducing the number of building materials, selecting recyclable construction methods and producing sizable mono-material waste batches that are suitable for recycling.

Buildings with high operating energy demand and frequent changes of use

In particular when dealing with shopping centres, research and laboratory buildings, or even production plants, it can be assumed that the usage, and thus the user, will change frequently during the design life of the building. The material input for later conversions can in this case easily exceed the material input required for the original construction. Potential for improvement is provided if the input needed for change of use is kept as low as possible. Alongside reversible fit-out components, lightweight interior constructions and a neutral ceiling height (according to DGNB this should

a b

3.47

Component cycle	PEI throughout the life cycle (total building)	facade	roof	non-load-bearing construction	fit-out	building services, electricity	building services, heating	building services, sanitary
production	+	+	+	o	++	+	+	-
construction	-	o	o	+	-	-	-	-
use	+	o	++	-	-	++	++	o
maintenance	++	o	+	+	++	-	-	-
reuse	-	++	+	+	+	-	-	-

3.48

generally be greater than 2.75 m), structural reserves (e.g. concerning the dimensions of structural members or the load-bearing capacity of floor slabs) can help reduce the environmental impact of the building during its service life. The provision of spare capacity with regard to the building services, for example in pipes and duct sections, is also an important consideration for easing changes of use.

Development of material concepts

Average projects frequently show a lack of both orientation and general principles with regard to materials; however, the material concept is something that should be developed alongside the design. Ideally, its development should be in line with the project and refer to different design levels. Since most improvement measures are not related to a particular stage, many decisions can also be applied to other design levels during the course of the planning process. This approach leads to an interwoven structure of the design and material concepts, which, in actual fact, gives the overall result a more coherent feel.
An assessment matrix should be developed to help set weightings specific to the project and use of the building (fig. 3.48, 3.49). The weightings should always consider the aspects environmental impact, material performance and costs with at least one relevant criterion. The criteria must account for the total life cycle of the building [33]. It is advisable to make assumptions for all aspects at the outset of the planning process and then check and refine these during the further development (see Design phases and processes, pp. 68ff.). It is only through the examination of alternatives that credible and differentiated material concepts are conceived. The life cycle assessment of the office building LCT One in Dornbirn (fig. 3.32, p. 53) took into consideration the material performance, the environmental impacts as well as the investment costs for individual components. The aim was to clarify whether alternative configurations or materials for individual components would lead to a lower environmental impact and to identify the effect these changes would have on the costs (fig. 3.49). The results showed that, without changing the material performance, cost-neutral improvements could be made to the facade cladding, the water-bearing layer of the flat roof and the interior fit-out of a standard office.

Component	GWP improvement		Impact on costs	
roof construction on reinforced concrete roof slab	insulation	roof waterproofing	insulation	roof waterproofing
foundation (shallow foundation)	cement		cement	
walls, beams, columns	cement		cement	
floor slabs – concrete work	cement		cement	
partition walls	window glass	aluminium sections	window glass	aluminium sections
floor coverings/standard office	raised floor	carpet	raised floor	carpet
facade elements	facade cladding	insulation	facade cladding	insulation
CTIS – staircase	insulation		insulation	
CTIS – base	insulation		insulation	
CTIS – connection details	insulation		insulation	
CTIS – paint	paint		paint	

low average high

no extra costs extra costs
possibility of extra costs

3.49

As is the case for operating energy, where sustainable solutions are achieved through the combination of energy saving and energy efficiency measures, improvements to building materials cannot be brought about by a one-sided approach. Both the reduction of environmental impacts in the production and operation as well as the return of the materials to the material cycle are necessary to achieve sustainable solutions (fig. 3.50). Naturally, the reduction of the environmental impact should be the prime focus. But because feeding the materials back into the material cycle provides the stock of resources for future developments, planners are especially called upon to consider the maintenance and recyclability aspects of buildings.

Checking material concepts

Due to the effect of material at many design levels, its use is a cross-cutting issue of sustainable construction. Figure 1.14 (p. 14) is especially suited for checking the material concept. The diagram can be used to assess strategies by assigning them horizontally into efficiency and sufficiency categories. By checking the material concept at other design levels, planners are able to assess the target-oriented improvement of the project design: if the individual strategies of efficiency, sufficiency and consistency have not been fully exhausted, there is further scope for improvement in this regard.

Optimisation potential in the building life cycle

Alongside the material life cycle, which is always a relevant aspect, the assessment of the building life cycle highlights individual and thus extremely relevant improvement strategies with regard to the design. Each of the two cycles has a different impact on the various types of components. Basically, a distinction can be drawn between building materials that are a characteristic feature of the appearance and those that are not visible and thus have a more menial task in the configuration of layers.
In the case of functional materials without any significant creative input, optimisation of the material life cycle is the most effective method (see Optimisation of the material life cycle, pp. 44f.). However, for materials affecting the appearance, there is usually an environmental and considerable economic potential in optimising the use phase of the building life cycle.
The following aspects are particularly effective (fig. 3.51) in this case:

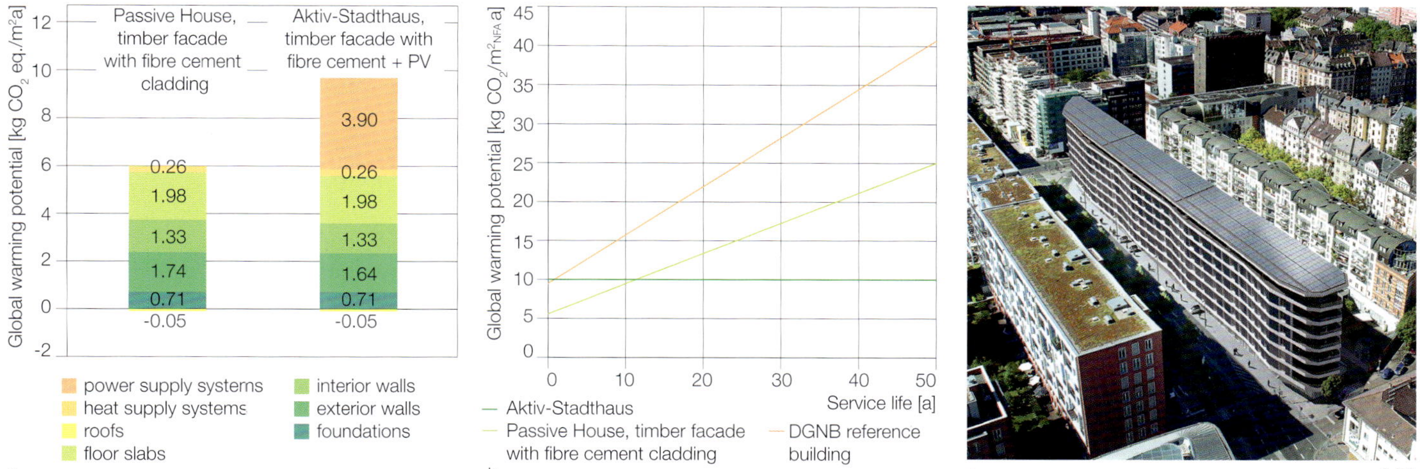

3.50

- material concentration and structural reduction
- functional overlaps
- reduced operating expenses
- reduced maintenance expenses
- optimisation of replacement processes
- optimisation of service intervals
- design for recycling

Material concentration and structural reduction

Reducing the number of building materials by concentrating on a few specific ones encourages the repetition of detail solutions. Even though the development of a single detail may require considerable time and expense, the total investment in the design is nevertheless kept within reasonable limits. The repetition of the same detail solutions increases the quality of workmanship on the building site. Moreover, due to the greater use of only a few materials, off-cuts tend to be reused, which in turn produces less trim waste. Finally, when it comes to the deconstruction of the building, the batches of mono materials are larger resulting in more economic recycling processes.
Structural reduction, on the other hand, describes the general minimisation of connection details and thus the reduced expenditure for construction work. Dispensing with covered roof gutters, for instance, generally reduces the material input. Structural reduction tends to always mitigate the environmental impact of the component manufacturing process. Simplified component geometries and the reduction of joints ease maintenance and service processes in the use phase and consequently lower costs (see Resource-efficient product alternatives, pp. 47ff.). Material concentration and structural reduction strategies are especially effective in the case of small-scale, unitised materials with recurring jointing methods. Masonry construction is a historical archetype perfectly expressing these strategies. However, the effect is also relevant on a component level: in particular, in the case of roof constructions, the joints and detailing (structural connections, corner details, guttering, etc.) often have a greater impact on the life cycle assessment than the functional layer itself [34]. Thus, a smaller number of joints is beneficial in terms of the total building life cycle assessment.

Functional overlaps

Whenever a single building component fulfils several functions simultaneously, the environmental impact is lessened. Unlike, for example, bituminous screed, terrazzo screed offers a much more durable surface finish. If the number of layers in a component can be reduced by implementing this methodology, advantages are achieved through greater energy and economic efficiency (fig. 3.57, p. 63). Facades and surface finishes provide the greatest potential for such measures (fig. 3.56, 3.58, p. 63). Both of these areas are, of course, distinguished by high functional requirements. Particularly in the case of facades, a layer does not even have to be omitted to reduce the environmental impact. A measurable benefit can already be identified if building materials, in addition to their constructional function, contribute towards lowering the operating energy demand. Examples include roofing membranes with integrated thin-film photovoltaic modules or sheet metal roofing equipped with brackets for fixing solar panels. These systems manage without additional metal substructures for the PV modules and avoid using a component that is elaborate from an environmental viewpoint. Transparent facade surface areas are especially effective multifunctional building components. Among other

Aspect of material optimisation	SFH	MFD	office/administration	laboratories	educational bldgs	commercial bldgs
material concentration and structural reduction	■■■	■■	■■	■■	■■	■■
functional overlaps	■■	■■	■■■	■■■	■■	■■
reduction of operating expenses	■■	■■	■■■	■■■	■■■	■■■
reduction of maintenance expenses	■■	■■	■■■	■■■	■■■	■■■
increase of durability	■■■	■■■	■■	□	■■	□
optimisation of replacement processes	■■■	■■	■■	□	■■■	■■
optimisation of service intervals	■■■	■■■	■■■	□	■■■	■■
design for recycling	□	■■	■■■	■■■	■■	■■■

■■■ high ■■ average □ low relevance

3.51

3.48 Relevance of different life cycle phases with regard to the primary energy demand of buildings and building components as well as the strength of their influence at different design phases
3.49 Office building in Dornbirn (A) 2013, Hermann Kaufmann: identification of potentials for improving building components and their impact on the investment costs
3.50 Aktiv-Stadthaus (energy plus building) in Frankfurt/M. (D) 2015, HHS Planer + Architekten
a global warming potential for facade construction in comparison to a Passive House facade
b development of the global warming potential in comparison to a Passive House and the DGNB reference building. The environmental expenses for building the energy plus building are paid back after less than ten years.
c aerial view (photomontage)
3.51 Impact assessment of various life-cycle-related optimisation concepts according to different building types

things, they affect the building's thermal balance, the lighting conditions, the air exchange facilities as well as air humidity. These building components are even able to generate electricity, for example by using glazing with integrated shading devices made of PV cells.
It goes without saying that multifunctionality increases the expense of a component. If, for example, an adjustable shading device set between the panes of a window cannot be replaced without exchanging the whole glazing unit, the expense for the component rises significantly during the life cycle, possibly even exceeding the savings achieved in construction and operating energy. Detailed research has in fact revealed that a lower degree of technology, i.e. less technical equipment per square metre of floor area, leads to an overall reduction of life cycle costs (fig. 3.52) [35]. Thus, it is generally not feasible to combine functions, if the service life of the corresponding components differs too significantly.
There is no set definition for evaluating such complex integral material performance issues, for example in the life cycle assessment. A decision concerning if and when optimum results are obtained must be made in each individual situation, possibly by using structural and dynamic simulation technology. Furthermore, the increase of individualised, purpose-made building components (customised production), means that it is easier to take into consideration basic parameters, for example the impact of the microclimate or the geometry of existing buildings (see Phase 1: Project brief/feasibility study, pp. 71ff.).

Reduced operating expenditures

The requirements concerning cleanliness and hygiene, long-term value maintenance, wear behaviour (sound reduction, slip resistance of floor coverings, etc.) and appearance are fundamental for the operating expenses of a building. The ease of cleaning has a big influence at the raw material level. The conclusion that can be drawn from a study on the life cycle of a floor covering shows that the environmental impact during the use phase is only a minor concern in terms of the component life cycle [36]. Thus, the aspect of cleaning is one of the few fields in building where expenditure and environmental impact differ in their development.
The impact of cleaning on the life cycle costs, however, is much more significant: the cleaning costs of buildings in Germany frequently exceed the heating costs. The follow-on costs for servicing and maintenance of a component can also exceed the construction costs by far (fig. 3.54). It is for this reason that the ease of cleaning is often a consideration in sustainability certification systems. Alongside technical facilities, floor coverings, windows and doors, interior walls and finishes result in high maintenance costs. A design based on low cleaning expenses tries to prevent dust from accumulating (e.g. by installing filters in ventilation systems) and dirt being brought in from outside (e.g. by using mats and grids in the entrance zones). A length of approximately ten steps reduces the dirt accumulation by approximately 80%. An economic design also means selecting surface materials which are easy to clean with mechanical equipment. Thus, smooth, jointless and hard-wearing surfaces are highly recommended features in an easy-to-clean building (fig. 3.57). A clear separation of surfaces which require frequent and less frequent cleaning is also beneficial in this respect. Colours and patterns can also have a positive effect: dirt is easily visible on plain, light-coloured and cold materials; less visible, though, on earth-coloured and patterned surfaces.

Coatings and coverings intended to reduce the effort and expense of cleaning are technically beneficial in the short term. However, they are usually not very durable and are difficult to separate from their base material. This may mean that the low operation costs are accompanied by higher costs for maintenance, repair and deconstruction work.

Easy-care floor coverings

The aspects of cleaning are best explained by taking a closer look at floor coverings since the annual cleaning costs can be reduced by up to 30% by fitting an easy-care floor covering (fig. 3.53).
In terms of cleaning, hard natural and artificial stone flooring is the best choice with regard to environmental aspects. Its durability is also beneficial in economic terms. Ceramic floor tiles are also easy to clean; however, the appearance of the tiles usually deteriorates over time due to wear and tear.
Resilient floor coverings rarely lead to higher operating costs than hard floor coverings in offices, in particular. However, the sound-absorbing properties reduce noise in work environments. Linoleum and natural rubber floor coverings are particularly environmentally friendly in this case. Carpets can be cleaned efficiently using vacuum cleaners. Low durability and the necessity for thorough cleaning in high-traffic zones is, however, a disadvantage. The care of wooden floors is more costly than that of resilient floor coverings. On the other hand, they can be sanded down several times, depending on the thickness of the wear surface, and therefore have a longer service life. The higher investment costs for floor coverings usually correspond with greater durability. If the longer life span is made use of by establishing clearly defined room zones, lower life cycle costs are ensured.

3.52 Relationship between use of technology and building life cycle costs
3.53 Amount of cleaning required by different floor coverings according to the Guideline for Sustainable Building
3.54 Life cycle and investment cost per year according to components
3.55 Cleaning costs for different facade finishes according to the Guideline for Sustainable Building (ns = not specified)
3.56 Signal cabin in Basel (CH) 1998, Herzog & de Meuron: functional overlap of sun shading system and weather protection in the facade
3.57 Office building in Stuttgart (D) 2012, Blocher Blocher Partner: functional overlap of surface finish and load transfer at floor level
3.58 Refurbishment of a gymnasium in Berlin (D) 2011, ludloff+ludloff Architekten: functional overlap of ceiling finish and sun shading system

3.52

Floor surface material	Amount of cleaning [%]	Intensive cleaning [%]
polished granite (reference area)	100	100
concrete floor tiles	102	105
resin-bonded stone	102	100
natural stone, polished	102	100
tiles, glazed	110	125
tiles, unglazed	120	135
natural stone, rough	120	125
linoleum	105	130
PVC	105	130
smooth rubber flooring	120	115
studded rubber flooring	150	150
sealed wooden floor	120	– [1]
carpet	90–140 [2]	200

[1] sanded and resealed
[2] average value: 110

3.53

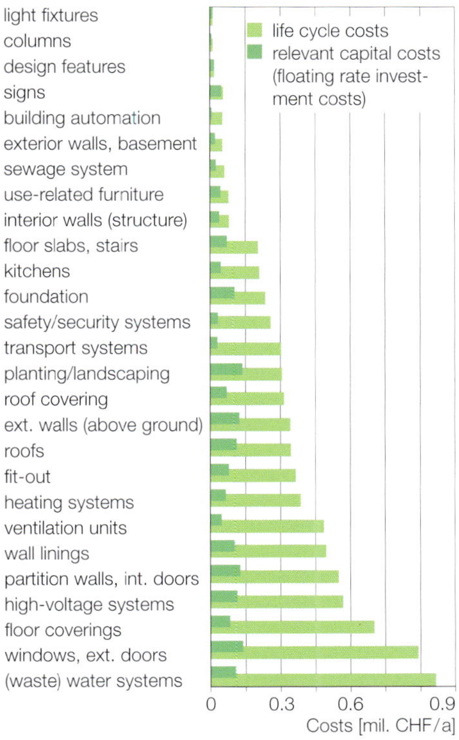

3.54

Facade material	2-storey building cleaning cycle [a]	2-storey building index[1] [%]	10-storey building cleaning cycle [a]	10-storey building index[1] [%]
aluminium cladding				
anodised surface finish (polished)	2	700	1	1600
strip-coated surface finish	2	310	2	400
sheet-coated surface finish	2	310	2	400
copper cladding	ns	ns	ns	ns
zinc cladding	3	470	ns	ns
enamelled sheet steel finish	1	310	310	400
reconstituted stone cladding with open or sealed joints	20	100	20	100
glass cladding				
rear side enamelled	1	440	1	240
rear side enamelled and metal oxide coated	0.25	1750	0.25	960
concrete cladding with substructure	12	680	12	1280
large format precast concrete elements	12	680	12	1280
facing brickwork, double-leaf masonry wall	20	420	20	620
wood or wood-based cladding[2]				
solid timber, full cover sheathing	5	170	–	–
solid timber sheathing, heartwood, untreated	10	20	–	–
facade panels made from wood-based products	10	100	–	–
fibre cement panels				
large format	2	310	2	200
small format	10	380	ns	ns

[1] in comparison to natural stone (= 100 %)
[2] according to information provided by the German Society for Wood Research (DGfH)

3.55

Easy-care facades
In the case of planar facade materials, enamelled glass elements are the most costly and difficult to clean. Timber cladding, on the other hand, is usually easy to clean with the help of high-pressure cleaners. The expectations of the observer are also beneficial when it comes to wood. A slight amount of soiling and natural fading is more acceptable in this case than it is for other building materials. This allows the number of cleaning cycles to be reduced. Windows and doors, in particular, are the facade elements that require the most intensive cleaning (fig. 3.55). Good access for cleaners is thus essential, and, when dealing with high-rise buildings with large glazed areas, suspended platforms may have to be provided. Hydrophilic or hydrophobic organic coatings can further reduce the cleaning requirements. However, such coatings are sensitive to scratching, and, according to current technology standards, very difficult to renew once damaged. Furthermore, the coatings require special treatment concerning the use of cleaning methods and detergents, which in turn increases the costs.
With composite thermal insulation systems there is a danger of algae formation. To prevent this from happening, biocides are added to the final coat of plaster or to the facade paint of some composite thermal insulation systems. According to the EU Biocide Directive 98/8/EG [37], the substances used must be listed in Annex I. Nevertheless, there is always a danger that the active ingredients may elutriate. Their use should therefore be questioned very carefully in sensitive situations, such as children's day care centres.

Reduction of maintenance expenditures
In order to reduce the environmental impacts during the use phase, planners can influence the likelihood of having to exchange certain building components and their ageing process (fig. 3.60, p. 65).

Ageing, durability and service life
Durability is calculated as a theoretical indicator and describes the period during which a building material can maintain its function in a specified context of use. In accordance with the building use and weather conditions, durability is usually determined as a period with a mean value. The mean value describes the durability in normal design and application conditions; the higher value refers to optimised conditions (fig. 3.59, p. 64). The indicators are either determined theoretically by analysing cases of

3.56

3.57

3.58

damage or practically by performing field tests. They are used as reference values in the planning phase; however, the actual service life is always dependent on the specific conditions of use [38]. Since the results of studies tend to differ fundamentally for building materials, it is always useful to compare results from several sources (fig. 3.62). It is also important to consider the types and intensities of use assumed for the studies.

On the whole, the service life of building components has decreased continuously over the last 50 years [39]. Among other things, this is due to the shorter service lives of fitted materials, the liability of constructions for repair, high wear and tear due to intensive use as well as more aggressive environmental conditions [40]. Planners can estimate the service life of a selected component on the basis of the conditions of use, the influencing factors, standard technical implementation, the predetermined quality of workmanship and the proposed measures concerning maintenance and repair (fig. 3.61, 3.63) [41]. The results of the German research project "Tools for the qualitative estimation of material and component service life" are, among other things, useful as a reference for standard constructions [42]. The factors of relevance for the building components have been compiled and weighted for a variety of conditions. However, replacements are not always induced by material-related defects. Components are frequently replaced because of regulatory, technical, safety or aesthetical reasons or because the building undergoes a functional change (fig. 3.65, p. 66) [43]. Alterations to directives and regulations, as well as technological progress, cannot easily be foreseen. EU directives give general guidance to Member States. Planners can therefore use them to identify basic objectives (e.g. with regard to the energy efficiency performance of buildings, building services and/or the rights of persons with disabilities) and design future-proof buildings accordingly. The ageing performance should also be considered in this context since the decisions made at the design stage have a considerable impact on the long-term use of a building. Alongside building components, the layouts of a building, the facade design or the way the building is embedded in its surroundings may also no longer meet today's needs.

Building components with a high-level of creative potential, an aesthetically pleasing ageing process and reduced visual wear and tear contribute towards a long building service life [44]. Ideally, building components are designed in such a way that only single elements need to be replaced without affecting the design of the whole building.

Optimising replacement processes

Building components must be replaced at the end of their service life. In general, buildings consist of a hierarchical structure of elements, layers and components, which are, among other things, dependent on one another due to immediate connections and other constructional constraints. Especially when the service life of components differs, it must be possible to replace defective parts without impairing or damaging others. Classification according to similar servicing, repair and replacement cycles is beneficial in this respect:

- Material unit
  A material unit is a manufactured, ready-to-use resource, which does not have to be separated further (e.g. concrete, wood, plastics, glass, metal). The

Component	**Service life** from – to	average
concrete foundation	80–150	100
exterior walls/columns:		
concrete, reinforced, exposed	60–80	70
natural stone, exposed	60–250	80
brick, clinker, exposed	80–150	90
concrete, concrete block, brick, sand lime, faced	100–150	120
light-weight concrete, faced	80–120	100
pointing, exposed brickwork	30–40	35
steel	60–100	80
softwood, exposed	40–50	45
softwood, faced; hardwood, exposed	60–80	70
hardwood, faced	80–120	100
interior walls/columns:		
concrete, natural stone, brick, clinker, sand lime	100–150	120
light-weight concrete	80–120	100
steel	80–100	90
softwood	50–80	70
hardwood	80–150	100
roofs, roof framework:		
concrete	80–150	100
steel	60–100	80
timber roof framework	80–150	120
glulam trusses	40–80	50
nailed trusses	30–50	30
wall, parapet copings, window cills, outside:		
natural stone	60–150	80
clinker	80–150	90
concrete, precast elements, ceramic, tiles, artificial stone	60–80	70
copper sheet	40–100	50
aluminium, steel, galvanised, fibre concrete	30–50	40
PVC	15–30	20
zinc sheet, cement render	20–30	25

Component	**Service life** from – to	average
waterproofing measures against non-pressing water	30–60	40
exterior coat:		
lime paint	6–8	7
synthetic dispersion	10–25	20
mineral paint	10–25	15
oil paint and synthetic resin	5–20	8
impregnation on brick	15–25	20
impregnation on wood	10–20	15
PVC coating on concrete	15–30	20
external rendering:		
cement render, lime cement	20–50	40
PVC render	25–35	30
CTIS	25–45	30
cladding mounted on substructure:		
natural stone, slate, artificial stone panels	60–100	80
copper sheet	70–100	80
fibre cement panels, lead sheet	40–60	55
aluminium	50–100	60
zinc sheet; steel sheet, galvanised	30–60	45
PVC	30–50	40
glass	40–70	50
stainless steel substructure	80–120	100
steel substructure	30–60	45
timber substructure	30–50	35
sun shading devices, exterior:		
light metal, fixed	50–100	60
aluminium, adjustable or PVC	20–30	25
awnings	10–20	15

Component	**Service life** from – to	average
floor configurations:		
floors under floor covering (bonded screed and screed on separating layer)	60–100	80
screed as the final wearing course (cement, granolithic screed and mastic asphalt screed)	40–60	50
floating screed	25–50	30
dynamic timber floor	40–50	45
floor coverings:		
natural stone hard	80–150	100
natural stone soft, concrete floor tiles, artificial stone	60–100	70
hardwood, ceramics	50–70	60
softwood	30–50	40
PVC, linoleum	15–25	20
textile	8–20	10
sealing, varnish	8–10	8
impregnation, oil, wax	3–5	4
flat roof sealing:		
without protective layer	15–30	20
with protective layer (gravel, planting)	20–40	30
roof drainage, integrated:		
roof water inlet made from stainless steel, PVC, cast	25–50	40
parapet gutter, zinc sheet, PVC	20–30	25
roof covering of pitched roofs:		
zinc sheet	25–40	35
corrugated fibre cement panels, small-format fibre cement panels	30–50	40
roof tiles, concrete tiles	40–60	50
slate tiles	60–100	70
copper	40–100	50

3.59

product does not necessarily have to be in working order for recycling. Thus, the unit (e.g. a pane of glass or roof tile) can be damaged when removed.

- Functional unit (component)
  Functional units generally involve a combination of building materials (e.g. vapour barrier, substructure, insulation glazing). Monolithic components, consisting of a single material only, are an exception in this case; the recycling of these is particularly effective.
- Utilisation unit (assembly)
  Utilisation units involve one or more components. They fulfil several functions simultaneously and are designed for a specific use (e.g. thermal envelope, windows including glass, frame and handle; floor configurations).
- Technical/constructional unit
  Technical and constructional units consist of several assemblies and combine to form the structure of the building. DGNB uses categories such as technical building services, non-structural elements, non-load-bearing framework elements and load-bearing framework elements [45]. Alternatively, the units can be categorised according to DIN 276 (level 2) or according to the key aspects of a building (e.g. components adjoining exterior space, components adjoining interior and exterior space; components adjoining interior space; building services inside; building services outside).

If access on a small scale is not provided, replacement processes usually affect whole assemblies at one time [46]. By making it more simple to separate and disconnect material configurations, planners can reduce the interference in the units requiring replacement (fig. 3.69, p. 67). This is best achieved by positioning the durable layers, such as the load-bearing structure, on the inside of a utilisation unit.
However, it is not always possible to arrange layers according to their design lives. Insulation layers, for example, tend to be less durable than the water-bearing exterior layer of a facade or roof. They should therefore remain easily accessible. Detachable connections provide opportunity for repair or, if necessary, replacement of these layers (fig. 3.70, p. 67). For some layers, there are to date no reliable service life data, such as is the case for bonded vapour or wind barriers. Furthermore, roof insulation, for example, cannot usually be exchanged without damaging the roofing sheet. The only helpful measure in the case of connected or bonded layers is therefore to choose products with similar design lives in order to ensure that their replacement becomes necessary at the same time.
Secondly, high-maintenance elements and building services components, in particular, must remain accessible at all times. This is generally the case if they form an independent unit, such as, for example, exposed wires and pipes. Clustering lines in shafts, integrating them in a system of conduits or introducing a modular structure of building services with maintenance and control facilities in separate room zones ensure the simple exchange or retrofitting of new technology lines. The design life of technical building services is frequently overestimated and the fact that retrofitting may be required within only a few years is often disregarded. DGNB recommends using only 80 % of the shaft and conduit capacity to enable future alterations.

Optimising maintenance cycles

There are various strategies concerning maintenance, all of which have a signifi-

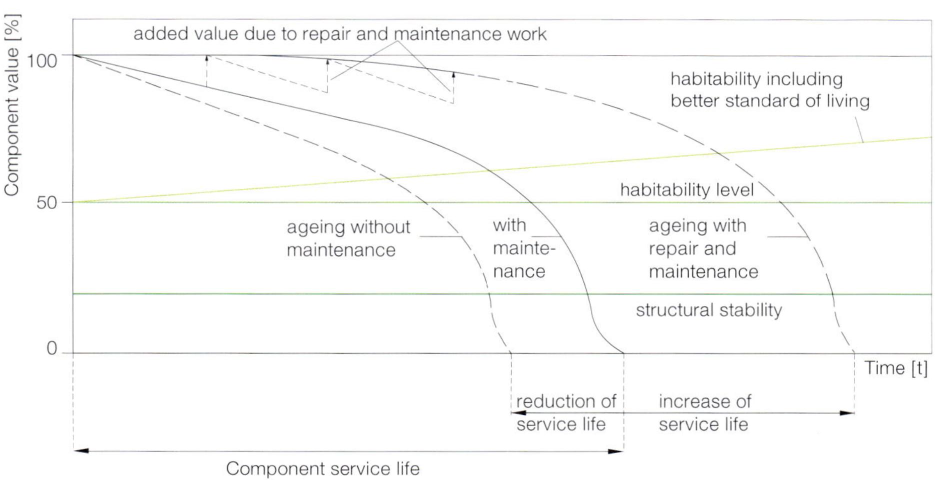

3.60

Impacts on components	
Classification according to origin	
impacts from outside	• solar radiation • precipitation • wind • temperature-based impacts
impacts from inside	• impacts through building use • impacts through defective use
Classification according to impact levels	
biogenic impacts	
chemical impacts	
physical impacts	
material-specific wear and tear performance	

3.61

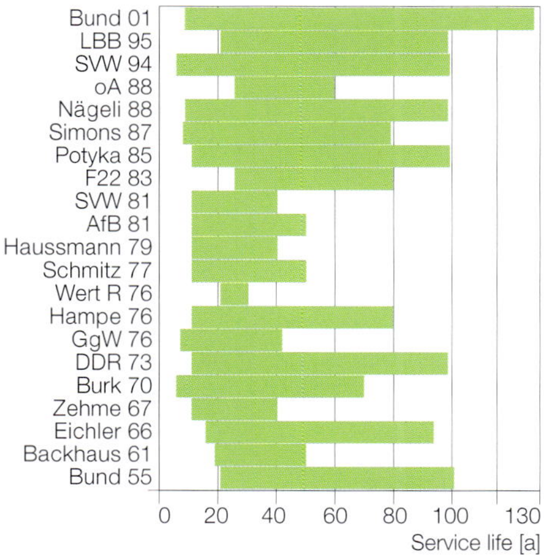

3.62

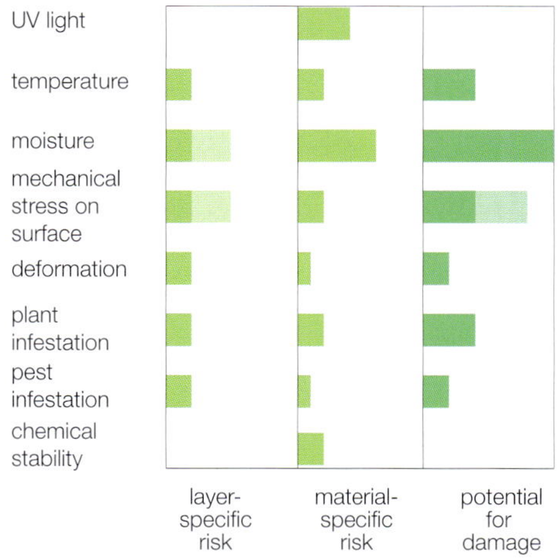

3.63

3.59 Service life of different components according to the Guideline for Sustainable Building
3.60 Development of a component's service life in accordance with repair and maintenance
3.61 Exemplary factors influencing the life cycle of a component
3.62 Comparison of data from different sources (publication years 1955–2011) regarding the service life of floor coverings
3.63 Evaluation of factors influencing the durability of composite thermal insulation systems. There is a definite potential for damage if two factors are given: a force acting on the respective layer and the vulnerability of the respective material to the imposed force (material specific risk).

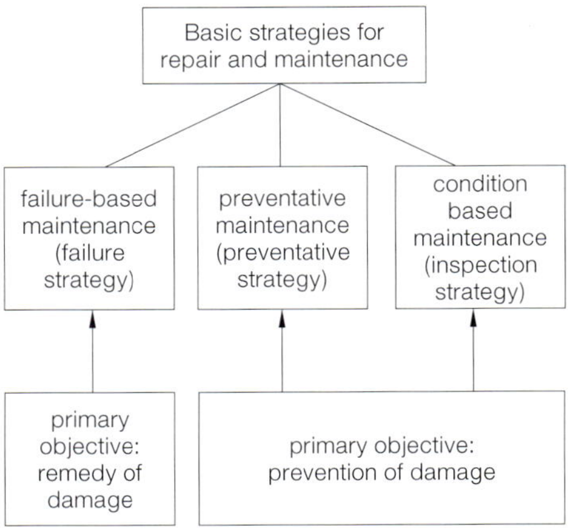

3.64

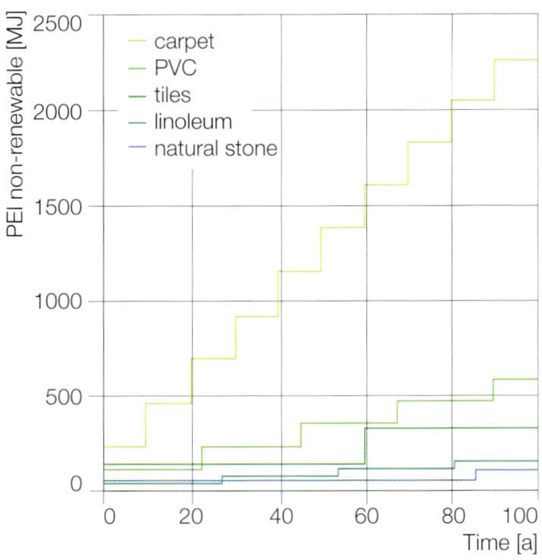

3.65

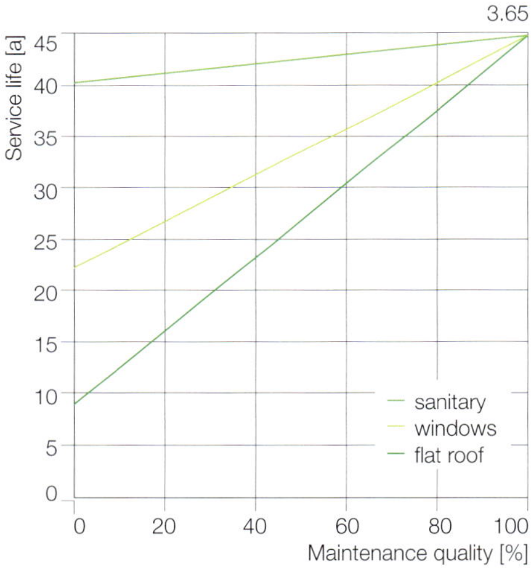

3.66

Component		**Possible reduction of service life**
solid structure		0–10 %
other structures		10 %
roof covering	• steep roof	70 %
	• flat roof	80 %
facades	• conventional render	10 %
	• composite system	30 %
	• wood	50 %
windows,	• wood	50 %
shutters	• metal, PVC	10 %
electrical installations		0 %
heating		0 %
other building services		20 %
sanitary		10 %
fit-out		0 %

3.67

cant impact on the service life of components and the measures required for their repair and replacement (fig. 3.64).
Preventative maintenance is designed to avoid the consequences of failure before it actually occurs through servicing (e.g. tests, measurements and adjustments). Servicing, which is usually costly, is performed at regular intervals, the length of which is either based on time (in the case of regular use) or on the intensity of use. Preventative maintenance is usually applied to high-cost building services components.
Condition-based maintenance monitors the performance (e.g. CO_2 measurements in the output air of heating systems) or wear and tear (e.g. the frictional wear of a floor covering). The component is exchanged as soon as the device fails to meet a minimum threshold value, or – in the case of components with minor importance – once a fault is actually detected. Condition-based maintenance does not usually include any preventative measures; as a result, however, the service life of the component drops (fig. 3.66, 3.67).
Planning can influence matters and arrange for different layers of materials to reach their performance limits at the same time. This makes maintenance easier to plan, technically as well as economically. If replacement is not required for every utilisation unit individually, but simultaneously for whole assembly units, maintenance measures can be planned and performed with greater flexibility (fig. 3.68). Replacement measures can either be carried out on a large-scale as a single package or on a small-scale involving several smaller packages [47]:

- combined measures:
  The long service life of building materials is rarely made use of in buildings with varied functions, increasing user requirements or a high-level of technical detail. Maintenance work is therefore usually designed to adapt the building to these new requirements by performing extensive conversions. In this case, it is beneficial if all building materials contained within a unit reach the end of their service life at the same time. Extensive wear and tear of building components or assemblies also has an effect on the operating efficiency and market value of the property. It tends to be cyclical, which can, for example, also have an effect on the composition of tenants. A "low to average service life" of assemblies has the effect that the operating efficiency and market value fluctuates quite considerably; however, it also allows for alteration work to be performed to meet these new requirements at an early stage. This strategy is best pursued in the case of, for example, the interior fit-out of shop premisses, where the durability of building materials can be chosen to correspond with the length of the lease.
- small-scale, long-term measures:
  The longer the expected use phase of a building and the more constant its use, the more important the consideration of the use phase. Long service lives help to reduce the environmental impacts of building materials. This is especially relevant in the case of residential building with high-quality fit-out.
  Because durable building materials rarely reach the end of their service lives at the same time, it is sensible to organise retrofit and replacement measures in smaller packages. A time lapse in replacement cycles involving small-scale units has the effect of minimising the embodied energy and thus reducing the environmental impacts. The value of the building remains consistent providing the owner with a steady rate of return. However, the replacement cycles, which tend to be performed at short notice as a result of this strategy, reduce the flexibility of building use.
- small-scale, medium term measures:
  A slightly shorter service life together with smaller-scale maintenance measures still allows moderate changes to be made to the building at the same time as increasing the property value. The shorter the service life, the more important the recovery of the material's embodied energy in the life cycle of a building.

Constructing recyclable buildings

If, despite providing a user flexible design, a building cannot be given a new lease of life, it has to be deconstructed. The aim in this case should be to return all components to the material life cycle (see Return to life cycle, pp. 55ff.). Introducing improved maintenance cycles for replacements is already an important step towards better recycling (see Optimising replacement processes, p. 64) since the tasks involved require a clear definition of recyclable units. The bigger the scheme, the higher the probability of producing significant recycling fractions. The smaller the unit of recyclable material (ideally this should be a material unit), the more likely it is to achieve a high-quality recycling process.

Assembly and disassembly processes are normally identical in reverse and are thus dependent on one another [48]. Connections that can be undone without any major difficulties are fundamental for this approach (fig. 3.68). Force-locking connections (e.g. screws) are in this case better than bonded connections (e.g. glued or welded). The reduction of joints as well as the number of different connection methods is a further advantage. The undoing of connections should take priority in the case of building components which either form a separate utilisation unit or technical/constructional unit (see Optimising replacement processes, pp. 64f.). The closer a material moves towards the raw material level, the less important it is to provide for deconstruction without damaging the parts. On the other hand, it is more important, in the case of mechanical recycling, to consider the compatibility of materials and bonding agents (fig. 3.39, p. 56; 3.40, p. 57). Since properties usually undergo a long period of use between planning and deconstruction, planners must ensure that connections can still be undone after years of being in place. Moreover, materials should be labelled adequately in order to return them to their material life cycle after deconstruction. The long-term transparency of the scheme is facilitated by supplementing the documents with a summary of the reuse/recycling concept, including all the important building information, such as the interdependencies of utilisation units, possibilities for extending functional layers, the implemented raw materials with their corresponding mass fractions, as well as any possible hazardous compounds or pollutants.

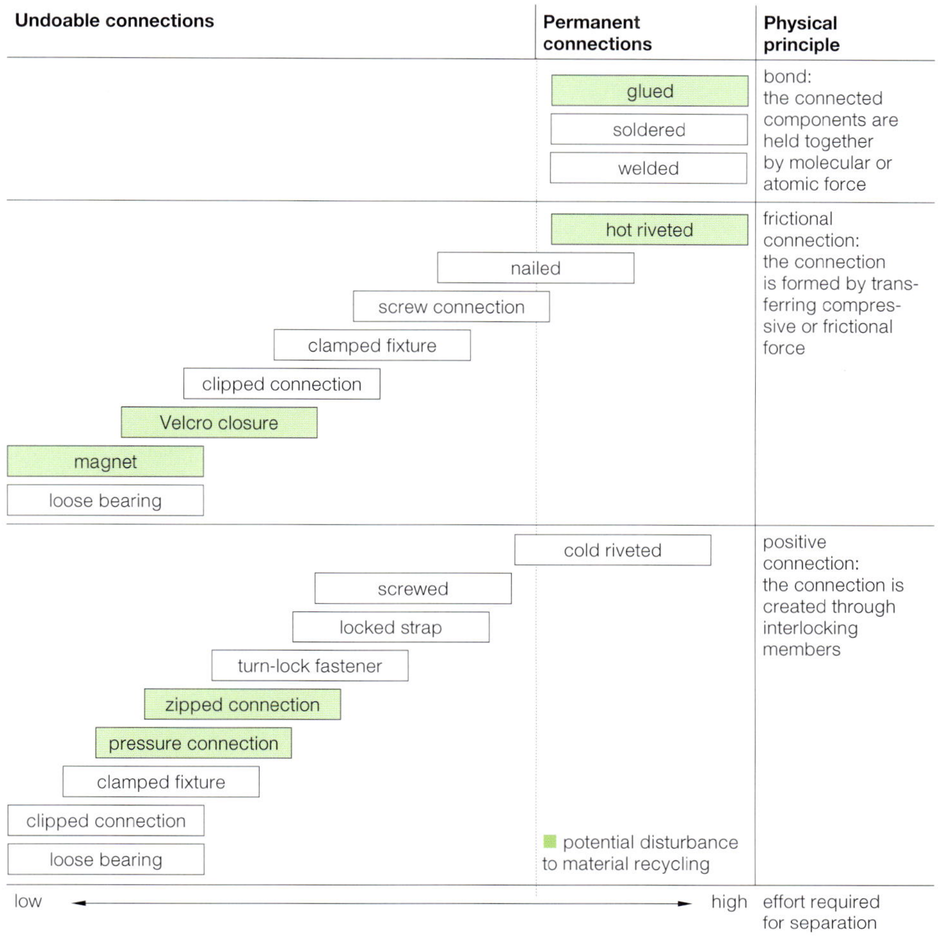

3.68

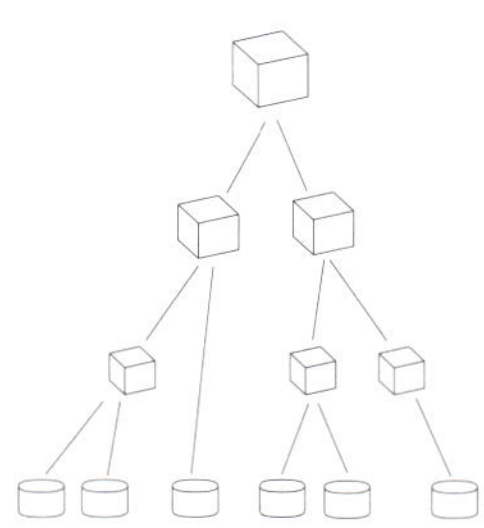

	Undoability	Recyclability
technical and constructional units	easily undoable	separable connections
utilisation unit	undoable	separable connections
functional unit (component)	damaged when undone	separable or fully recyclable
material	separable	if possible connections should be made from same material

3.69

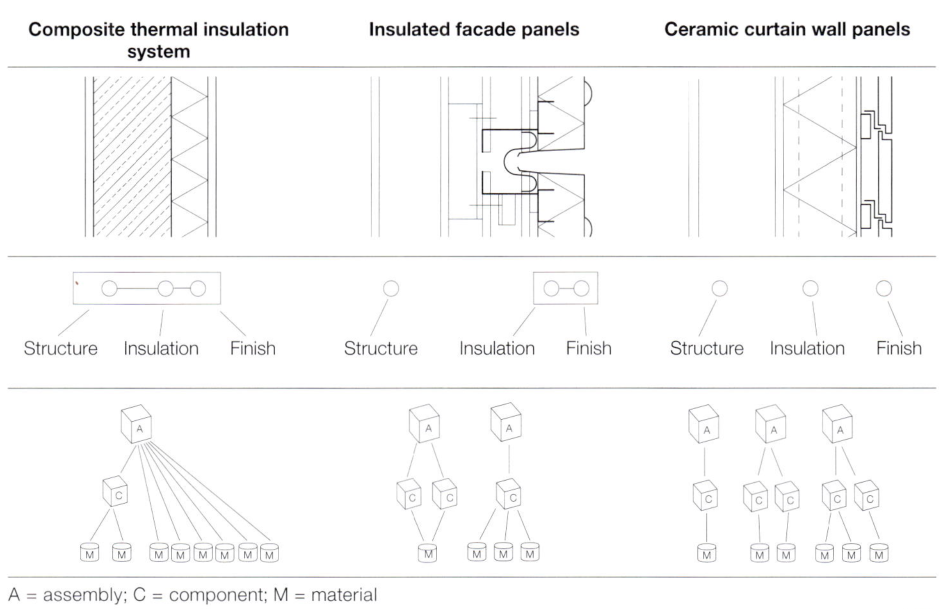

3.70

3.64 Strategies and targets of repair and maintenance work
3.65 Theoretical development of the primary energy input based on the example of floor coverings
3.66 Service life of components depending on the quality of maintenance performance
3.67 Reduction of the service life of different components without the performance of any maintenance work
3.68 Assessment of the undoability of connections
3.69 Requirements concerning the undoability of connections and the recyclability of components and materials in order to achieve a recyclable building design
3.70 Exemplary illustration of different facade constructions. The structural relations between assemblies, components and materials has a fundamental impact on the recyclability of facade constructions.

Optimisation as a process

The aim of this section is to assign the essential and most useful processes for optimising the construction in terms of building biology and building ecology factors to the respective project design phases. In this case, the phases do not correspond to those established by the German HOAI or the RIBA Plan of Work, but are based on the standard sequence of events in building development (fig. 4.1). The six phases cover the entire process of planning and operating a building.
To this day, it is often difficult to make a clear statement about the final phase of the building life cycle – deconstruction – since predictions for periods of 50 to 100 years are so uncertain that sensitivity analyses lack any real meaning. This said, there is no doubt that the disassembly and recycling of building components and construction materials plays a very important role in the assessment of environmental impacts. It is for this reason that the general principles mentioned in the chapter "Strategies for material use in the construction process" (pp. 44ff.) must guide the decision making process throughout the design phase.
These are:

- in the building life cycle (conformity of designated use):
  - adapt the material input to the intended use
  - adapt the durability of building materials and constructions to the intended use
  - incorporate efficiency-increasing construction methods
  - incorporate facilities for changes of use
  - make use of separable constructions
- in the material life cycle (use of resource-efficient and environmentally friendly building materials):
  - use permanently available resources
  - implement building materials with a low primary energy input (embodied energy) and low environmental impacts, in particular with regard to greenhouse gases (GWP)
  - substitute recycled materials and industrial waste for primary resources
  - optimise the construction of selected building components
  - use non-toxic, low-emission products
  - prepare for reuse and recycling by: ensuring that layers and building materials can be separated into mono materials; avoid hybrid and composite materials; use building materials which can be recycled with little energy and raw material input.

In order to meet the high standards implied by a resource-efficient construction method, the performance of particular planning tasks is usually brought forward to earlier design phases. This is firstly based on a need to conduct analyses fundamental to the project brief (e.g. subsoil investigation, site contamination, medium and long-term requirements); secondly, a high degree of structural detail is necessary to make a sound judgement on the construction in the context of design competitions and preliminary studies (e.g. detail sections, concepts for building services, energy supply or service shafts, building process management).
Today, the primary purpose of building process management is to ensure effective organisation of increasingly complex processes as well as the mitigation of program cost and avoidance of scheduling problems. Based on the additional requirements that sustainable building imposes on the selection of materials and their connection, all conditions and risks must be determined at an early stage, and effective and thorough exchange of information among project participants is essential. The customary ways of compensating for cost overruns and missed deadlines, for example by adapting quality specifications during the design and construction process or switching the sequence of construction trades, are limited in this case. In concrete construction, for example, longer curing periods must be taken into account if sulphate slag cement is used to reduce the global warming potential (see Comparisons between design options and components, p. 73). Cold spells in winter can severely hamper and delay concrete placement processes. For environmental reasons, additives frequently mixed in to accelerate the curing process and the use of heater blowers to help dry out the building should be avoided. Thus, in order to minimise the risk of adverse climatic conditions and cost fluctuations, sufficient contingency time should be allowed for when determining the project scope. The possibilities to control risk factors such as these during the construction process are limited.
Extensive use of prefabricated elements in construction places greater demand on coordination and requires a more detailed definition of interfaces in the design process. A holistic approach is needed when establishing the configuration, shape, construction and appearance of the building and building components. This necessitates the early involvement of consultants and specialists (integrated planning approach). In many situations, especially with regard to large schemes, it makes sense to bring specialised energy and environmental consultants into the

4.1 Overview of planning phases and optimisation potentials in the planning process
4.2 Phase-related suitability of tools

Phase	1 Project brief/ feasibility study	2 Competition/ concept design	3 Developed design/ planning application	4 Procurement/ execution drawings	5 Construction	6 Handover/ use
Service phases according to HOAI (D)	1	2	3; 4	5; 6	7; 8; 9	–
Service phases according to SIA 102 (CH)	11; 21; 22	31	32; 33	41; 51	41; 52; 53	–
Work stages according to RIBA Plan of Work 2013 (UK)	1	2	2; 3	4; 5	6; 7	–
Basic principles and considerations	• cetermine basic conditions and requirements • clarify long-term use requirements • research into regulations and constraints • assess and evaluate existing building stock • set objectives	• determine strategies and develop basic concepts • recognise interdependencies, contradictions and synergies • draw comparisons between variants and components	• review and detail assumptions made in preliminary design • check conformity with building codes and budget category limits	• further development of construction design with regard to detail and product selection • optimise joint and detail configurations • incorporate sustainability aspects in tender documents	• optimise construction site operations • monitor and ensure quality on site	• requirements for optimal building use • observe interdependencies of life cycle costs and environmental impacts during operation
Relevant aspects and measures	• urban design and exterior space • volume and scale	• topography and exterior space • (load-bearing) structure and building envelope • building services concept • infrastructure and mobility	• comparison of building materials and products • requirements and exclusion criteria • preparation of (simplified) LCAs • optimisation of key components	• special building material and product requirements, product selection • procurement criteria	• product requirements and specifications • quality monitoring and assurance • construction sequences	• cleaning, servicing, maintenance and operation instructions • as-built drawings and calculations • building owner's manual

4.1

Tools	Bldg. biology	Bldg. ecology	Planning phase	Language EN	Language FR	Free	License	Description	Link
BNB target agreement/ BNB pre-check system	■	■	1–2			■		tools for the BNB assessment system	www.nachhaltigesbauen.de
Snarc		■	1–2		■	■		scheme for the assessment of sustainability in competition designs	www.eco-bau.ch
SIA 2040 tool Energy Efficiency Path		■	1–3		■	■		Excel calculation of 2000-Watt buildings	www.energytools.ch
SIA 2040 tool for the calculation of 2000-Watt sites		■	1–3		■	■		Excel calculation of 2000-Watt sites	www.2000watt.ch
Bewertungssystem Nachhaltiges Bauen (BNB)	■	■	2–5	■ [1]		■		assessment system for the comprehensive evaluation of sustainable office buildings	www.nachhaltigesbauen.de
Minergie-ECO checklist	■	■	2–5		■	■		assessment system for building ecology and health-related issues in development schemes	www.minergie.ch
Eco-Devis	■	■	2–4		■	■		illustration of materials that are interesting in terms of environmental aspects according to the Swiss building cost planning scheme (BKP)	www.eco-bau.ch
Electronic building component catalogue		■	2–4 (5)		■	■	■ [3]	component catalogue for the determination of U-values and environmental parameters	www.bauteilkatalog.ch
SBS Building Sustainability		■	2–5	■		□	■	online tool for the environmental assessment of buildings	www.sbs-onlinetool.com
TQB tool	■	■	2–5	■			■	online tool for the comprehensive assessment of buildings according to ÖGNB	www.oegnb.net/en/
GaBi SimaPro Umberto OpenLCA		■	3–5	■			■	analysis software for life cycle assessments	www.gabi-software.com www.simapro.com www.umberto.de/en/ www.openlca.org
WINGIS	■		3–5	■	■	■		hazardous materials information system published by the Berufsgenossenschaft der Bauwirtschaft	www.wingis-online.de/ wingisonline/Default.aspx
Eco-BKP	■	■	4		■	■		guidelines for environmentally friendly building according to the Swiss building cost planning scheme (BKP)	www.eco-bau.ch
Athena EcoCalculator		■	2–3	■		■		free Excel-based LCA tool that provides quick LCA results for more than 400 common building assemblies - fast but limited in design options	www.athenasmi.org/tools/ ecoCalculator/index.html
Athena Impact Estimator		■	2–4	■			■	whole building analysis tool that allows professionals to compare alternate design and construction scenarios by modelling their own custom assembly and envelope configurations	www.athenasmi.org/tools/ ecoCalculator/index.html
EeB Guide Project Tool		■	2–3	■	■	■		website with guidance, training materials and policy notes on how to conduct LCA studies	www.eebguide.eu
BEES Tool		■	2–4	■		■		LCA tool incorporating both environmental and economic performance of buildings	www.nist.gov/el/economics/BEESSoftware.cfm
Methodology to calculate embodied carbon of materials		■	2	■		■ [4]		information for the calculation of embodied carbon in buildings and their components	www.rics.org/ch/
Bath Inventory of Carbon and Energy (ICE)		■		■		■		database with embodied energy/embodied carbon data for over 200 building products and materials	www.circularecology.com

■ full applicability □ limited applicability [1] only available in English [2] publication must be purchased [3] extended scope of functions
[4] only available to RICS members

4.2

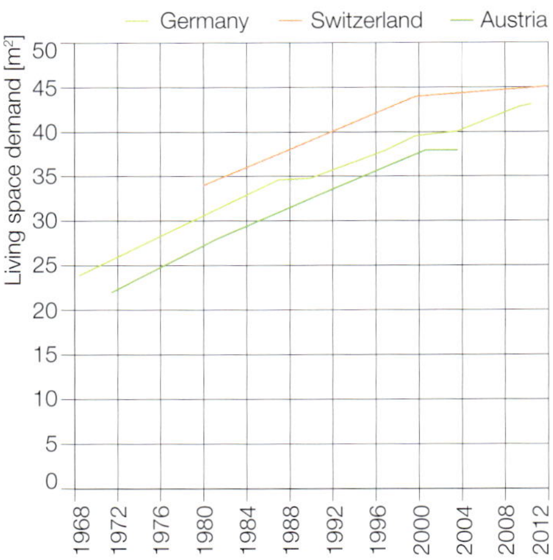

4.3

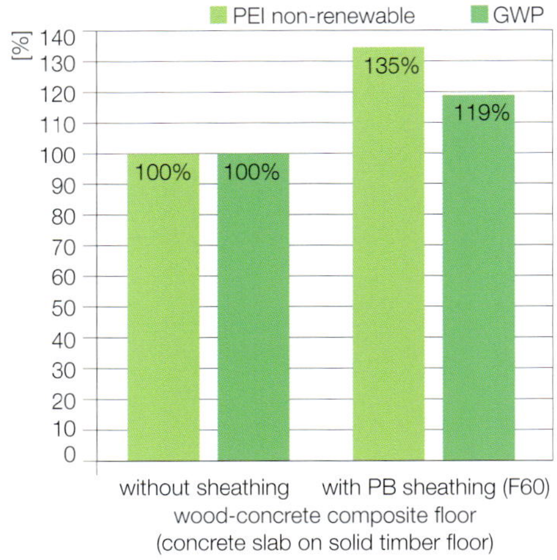

4.4

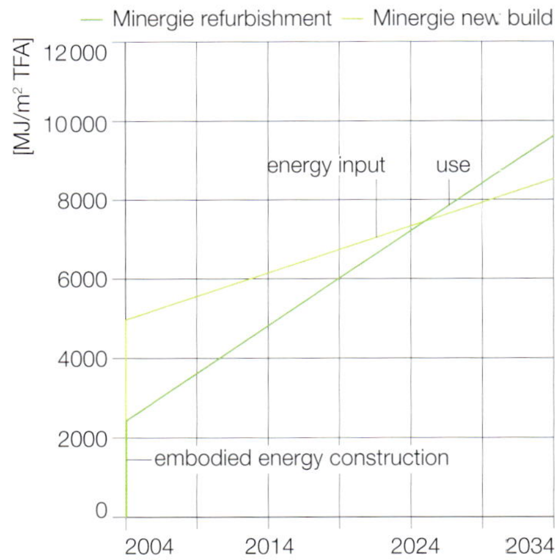

4.5

project team. The greater amount of work involved in the early design phases of a project may well need to be taken into account in contracts and could possibly lead to alterations in the official scales of fees. This approach has already been taken in some pilot projects, such as the development of Masdar City in the United Arab Emirates. The fees for the first three planning phases, according to the RIBA Plan of Work [1] (Appraisal, Design Brief and Concept Design), are approximately 15 % higher than those of comparable projects. The differing conditions and requirements should therefore be taken into consideration in the project preparation work and contract design. Some tasks exceeding those of standard practice may have to be reimbursed separately; this also applies to design tasks that are brought forward.
Achieving sustainability objectives generally means going beyond the performance of contractual obligations while remaining in compliance with standards and the recognised rules of engineering. Clarity concerning required and useful additional measures can be achieved early on if the design team, acting together, establishes necessary objectives (e.g. by using the assessment tool "Haus der Zukunft" (House of the future), fig. 4.6 and 4.7). In normal circumstances, it is neither useful nor necessary to go beyond the specifications set out in standards and codes. The optimisation of individual aspects should not take priority in the planning process, rather a comprehensive analysis of relevant subjects and matters resulting from greater awareness. As is already the case for some towns and communities, in the medium term the fulfilment of sustainability objectives will be inherent to the planning process. Taking public buildings in Zurich, for example, the planning and certification according to Minergie-P-Eco is considered an integral part of an architect's typical work activities and is not specifically reimbursed.

4.3 Living space demand per person in Germany, Austria and Switzerland since 1968
4.4 Comparison of environmental impacts between wood-concrete composite floor with and without plasterboard (production and end-of-life; per m²)
4.5 Energy life cycle comparison (incl. embodied energy) of a refurbishment and new build over a 30-year period
4.6 Assessment criteria and levels, House of the Future, HTA Luzern (CH) 2006: The research project was used as an opportunity to develop a tool for the holistic assessment of buildings and the definition of objectives among planners, clients and occupants.
4.7 Interdependencies and synergies of design objectives, House of the Future, HTA Luzern
4.8 Küppersbusch estate, Gelsenkirchen (D) 1996, Szyszkowitz Kowalski. A noise bund made from rubble was built to block out the noise from the railway line. The lenticular-shaped park in the centre of the property is designed as a rainwater retention and infiltration basin.

Structure of the chapter

The six design phases described in this chapter are:
- 1 Project brief/feasibility study
- 2 Competition/concept design
- 3 Developed design/planning application
- 4 Procurement/execution drawings
- 5 Construction
- 6 Handover/use

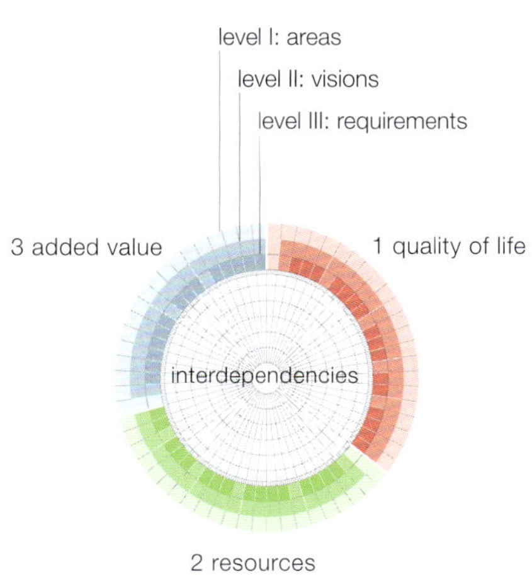

4.6

As a rule, the same questions are asked at each stage:
- basic principles and considerations: what are the opportunities in the corresponding design phase to influence the outcome and which considerations and assessments have to be made to meet the objectives? Which approaches and principles can be followed?
- steps and measures: which measures ensure that aspects of building ecology and building biology are best accounted for (step-by-step approach to sustainable development)?
- instruments and tools: which tools and techniques are most suited for establishing a basis in the decision-making process? How are these best incorporated into the design process at reasonable cost? Which synergies are likely to be achieved through the application of specific tools?

The following six subchapters consider the basic principles and considerations as well as the specific design issues and measures for each of the planning stages. The suitability of the individual techniques and tools for a certain design phase is illustrated in figure 4.2 (p. 69). An overview of measures to improve

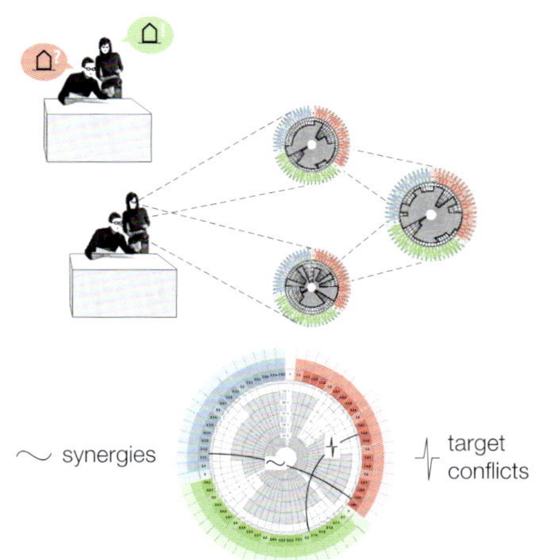

4.7

building, material and process-related matters according to a particular stage is presented in figure 4.27 (p. 82–85).
The planning practices and applicable rules and regulations vary considerably from one country to the next. Unless otherwise stated, the recommendations in the following sections apply to the circumstances in Germany and Switzerland.

Phase 1: Project brief/feasibility study

Stage 1 includes all measures and considerations which are undertaken before the actual design is commenced (clarification of the project brief, determination of project objectives, structural survey, site analysis, feasibility studies, etc.).

Basic conditions and requirements

When establishing the conditions and requirements, all parameters must be examined very closely. The greatest potential for leverage often lies in standards and building codes, and they should not simply be taken for granted. Current fire safety standards for multi-storey timber construction, for example, are the result of the efforts of planners and clients who were not willing to accept former regulations. The tightening of regulations and building codes over the last decade has not only led to a better quality of workmanship but also increased safety standards. Most specifications (e.g. minimum sizes and heights of residential units or requirements concerning technical or structural features) tend to limit scope when it comes to optimisation of buildings. Moreover, our increasing demand for more space and a higher standard of fit-out (fig. 4.3) conflicts with the aim of minimising resource consumption. The greatest potential for reduction, and at the same time the easiest to achieve, resides in questioning the status quo and consciously excluding extremely resource-intensive building components and materials.

Long-term use requirements

An appropriate use of available resources is the basis for an efficient design. It is for this reason, and in order to avoid improvement measures being determined by a shotgun approach, that the short, medium and long-term interests and requirements of building operators and users should be assessed in detail (e.g. with the help of the Minergie-ECO checklist, criterion GN01 or the BNB profile 3.2.3; see Optimisation of the building life cycle, pp. 57ff.).

Parameters and constraints

Building regulations and constraints are frequently the cause for negative environmental impacts. The requirement for non-flammable surfaces, for example, demands that ceilings and walls are sheathed with gypsum plasterboard or gypsum fibreboard, which increases the primary energy input (PEI) of the construction considerably (fig. 4.4). The obligation to provide too many car parking spaces on inner-city sites increases the size of the sub-ground structure, which is generally responsible for a large proportion of a building's environmental impacts. The consequences of the obligation to connect to district heating, which makes the use of solar energy unprofitable or possibly even worthless, are comparable.
The specifications in development plans concerning permissible density, building height and volume can also be questioned if considered necessary. By purposely exceeding the specifications concerning volume, it is often possible to reduce the site coverage or increase the structural density to a more appropriate level. However, in order to obtain an official permit, detailed studies must usually be provided concerning the impairments to surrounding properties, resulting from the changes made to the development plan.

Assessment and evaluation of existing building stock

The analysis and evaluation of the existing building stock in terms of its risks and potential is a key task when establishing the design brief. In the case of existing properties, studies should include an assessment of the structure as well as the ways and means of dealing with the local ecosystem or contaminated ground.
Due to the high PEI and GWP of a primary construction, retention of building stock is often favoured over removal (see Single-family home in Hamburg, pp. 109ff. and Lower secondary school in Langenzersdorf, pp. 133ff.). However, this approach assumes that the existing structure largely meets the requirements of the planned occupancy profile (see Occupancy profile as a lead indicator, p. 58). If the analysis reveals that, as a result of retaining the building, space efficiency is much lower, flexibility of use is reduced dramatically or resource consumption for the operation of the building is much higher, the pros and cons must be weighed even more carefully. In particular, in the case of buildings with a very high energy demand, such as laboratories, hospitals or swimming pools, the construction should take a back seat in the overall assessment. The construction of a new build is then usually the more sensible decision from an environmental perspective unless, of course, the structure is worth retaining in terms of cultural heritage (fig. 4.5). In the case of residential and office buildings, it is usually worthwhile carrying out a detailed study. This especially applies if development of a new building would result in only marginal improvement to the structural density on the site (fig. 1.2, p. 9 and 3.51, p. 61). Furthermore, the retention and further development of the existing building stock is usually the better solution from a financial viewpoint. A moderate increase of rent is all that is then required to finance the construction work. Also, in terms of social compatibility within the neighbourhood, a new building might be viewed less favourably.

Objectives

The key aspects of the design and contradictions therein are identified more easily if the specifications concerning design objectives and quality standards are in place at an early design stage. During the course of compiling a detailed scope statement, clients and planners should therefore produce a list of objectives together, including aspects concerning conservation of environment and resources. Documents published by BNB (objectives definition overview according to BNB) or the Swiss SIA 112/1 standard might be useful in this context as a kind of template. The Swiss system "Modules for the future home" (Module for das Haus der Zukunft) was also developed according to the SIA 112/1 standard. Among other things, it provides the opportunity to identify and illustrate possible objectives

4.8

and synergies in an interactive dialogue between clients and planners (fig 4.6 and 4.7).

Urban design and exteriors

When reflecting on the urban design and the exteriors, the site should be examined for possible contamination and pollution. It is also recommended to record flora and fauna. Contaminated ground or a number of trees worth retaining can, for example, induce a change in the arrangement of volumes or the topographical design of the site (fig. 4.8, p. 69). Aspects of land use often play an important role when it comes to developing the urban design concept. Considerations should involve the proportion of sealed surface areas in the same way as the proportion of covered areas. Simple studies concerning volume and overshadowing can be extremely helpful at this early stage when assessing the density and proportion of sealed surfaces that is tolerable from an urban design perspective (fig. 4.10). On inner-city sites, in particular, great importance is attached to the seepage quality of the exterior surface finishes.

Volume and scale

It is also important to strive for a high utilisation factor and space efficiency with regard to the building itself. Attention should, in this case, focus not only on the structural density but also on a high utilisation ratio. The expected number of residents or work spaces is in actual fact more meaningful than the net floor area. The level of utilisation is usually also influenced by building legislation and typological features (orientation, mix of residential units, useful building depth, length of escape routes, etc.). Compact structures with a minimised building envelope surface area and a perfect wall-to-window ratio provide the best conditions in moderate climates to balance the varied requirements of sustainable building. If the lengths of a cube are reduced, the shape remains the same, however, the ratio of surface area to volume (A/V ratio), or in other words the surface area to gross floor area, is increased significantly. Consequently the embodied energy per square metre of floor area also rises in the case of similar material configurations. The same situation applies if the shape of the building is less compact, despite retaining the same area of floor space, (fig. 4.12). Nevertheless, there is also a limit to the degree of compactness. Not only is the amount of daylight reduced in very compact buildings, but there is often a lack of "soft factors", which are responsible for the quality of space and wellbeing (e.g. the quality of access and communication zones, the scale and opportun ties for creating niches).
The distance to neighbouring buildings, the use and height of the building itself influence the fire prevention requirements with regard to the construction and building envelope. This is an interesting aspect in that inflammable facade cladding and constructions with a low fire rating tend to have lower environmental impacts.

Phase 2: Competition / concept design

Phase 2 involves analysing the basic requirements, clarifying the objectives, developing a (preliminary) design concept, collaborating with authorities in order to assess the likelihood of receiving planning permission, and preparing a cost estimate.

Strategies and basic design concepts

The process of developing resource-efficient buildings does not differ greatly from that of other design strategies. The main difference lies in the timely determination of all parameters and aspects concerning building ecology and building biology (fig. 4.28, pp. 82f.) as well as a consistent consideration thereof in all design phases. The design process should therefore be unbiased as to the

4.9

4.10

4.9 Concept study of LifeCycle Tower, Hermann Kaufmann ZT GmbH. Perimeter beams made from reinforced concrete interrupt the glulam pillars in each storey and prevent the vertical spread of fire.
4.10 Studies to understand the degree of overshadowing caused by densification measures
4.11 Comparison of the primary energy demand per resident in a residential estate, including best and worst case scenarios
4.12 Building envelope factors and the embodied energy of model buildings
4.13 Fehlmann estate, Winterthur (CH) 2010, Bob Gysin + Partner BGP Architekten. The trees are retained in the inner-city park and used to enhance the qualities of the location for the development of new apartments.

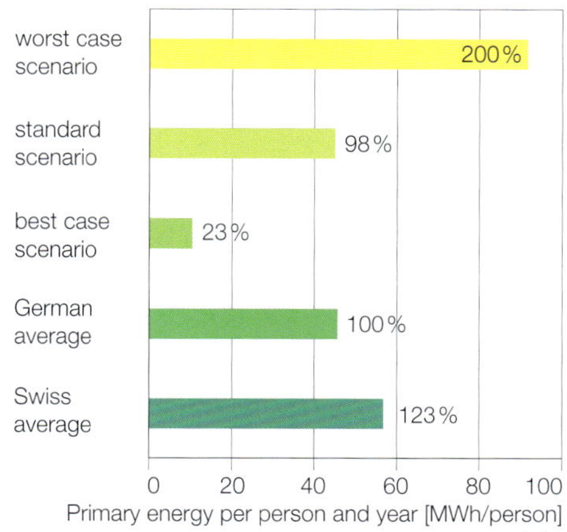

4.11

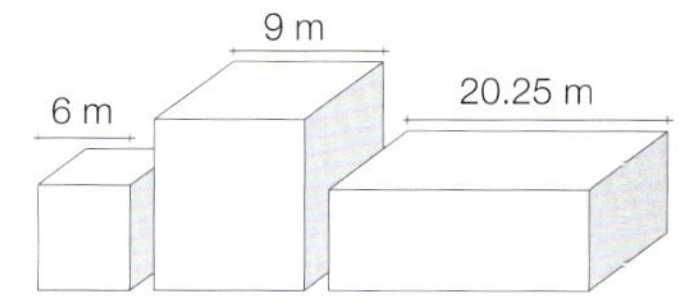

	6 m cube	9 m cube	cuboid
A/V ratio	1 m^{-1}	0.666 m^{-1}	0.765 m^{-1}
floor area [m^2]	76 m^2	243 m^2	243 m^2
embodied energy [MJ/m$^2_{FA}$]	5000	2311	2831

4.12

result and, from the outset, pay careful attention to the selection and application of suitable methods and tools (fig. 4.2, p. 69).
Issues and parameters relevant to the design are best identified by analysing the specific considerations and requirements. These can vary considerably according to the task at hand. In the case of low buildings, for example, the basement levels and the foundation play a decisive role in the energy input of the construction, whereas in higher buildings the efficiency of the load-bearing structure and an assessment of the fire protection requirements carry greater weight (fig. 4.9). Flexible use, the concept of the building services and the design of the facade are decisive factors in office buildings. In residential buildings, which are characterised by long use phases, greater importance is attached to a space-efficient and neutral design of the floor plans as well as a suitable standard with regard to fit-out and technical installations (see Optimisation of the building life cycle, pp. 57ff.). Thus, in order to identify a suitable approach and the most relevant issues, a thorough analysis of the use, type and context of the building concerned must be made. The principles and comparisons illustrated in the chapters "Strategies for material use in the construction process" (pp. 44ff.) and "Environmental impacts of building components" (pp. 86ff.) provide some important considerations in this regard.

Interdependencies, contradictions and synergies
The basic principle concerning an efficient use of resources "as much as necessary, as little as possible" is based on detailed knowledge of the interdependencies characteristic of design and development processes. The relations between objectives, requirements and demands should therefore be determined at the beginning of the design phase in order to identify synergies and contradictions. Multifunctional building components and measures fulfilling several functions simultaneously are potential levers for the design (see Functional overlaps, p. 61). Contradictions must be made transparent to the design team and the client to allow for a deliberate prioritising of objectives and requirements (fig. 4.7, p. 70).

Comparisons between design options and components
Simple tools can already be used at early design and planning stages to draw comparisons between design options (e.g. SIA 2040 tool, fig. 4.2, p. 69). The tools add quantitative data to the predominantly qualitative assessment methods, thus providing opportunity for verification. Alongside an approximate determination of GWP and PEI on a building component level, the performance of a sensitivity analysis or a best case/worst case scenario may be helpful (fig. 4.11) to assess the effectiveness and the consequences of specific measures. In the case of a component comparison, it may be useful to calculate not only the mean value, but also the degree of fluctuation, both up and down. For example, by using sulphate slag cement in conventional reinforced concrete ceiling slabs, it is possible to reduce the global warming potential by up to 65 %, whereas the GWP for a timber floor structure can rise by up to 400 % if the floor element is sheathed with fire protection panels on the underside and finished with mastic asphalt screed instead of dry screed made of gypsum fibreboard on top (fig. 3.7, p. 46; fig. 4.4, p. 70; fig. 4,20, p. 78).

Topography and exteriors
The way of dealing with topography, in particular in the case of sloping sites, can have a significant influence on the environmental impacts. Deep cuts into the slope produce large quantities of excavated material, which must be removed and disposed of. Slope stabilisation measures, as well as greater surface areas in contact with the ground, increase the need for elaborate concrete and waterproofing work, which would be largely unnecessary if the building were raised and set on piers. However, the proportion of built elements below ground and the method of foundation (pier, point or strip footings, flat foundation) also have a considerable impact on the GWP and PEI in the case of level sites (see Single-family home in Hamburg, pp. 109 ff.).
When it comes to the exterior design, the proportion of sealed surface areas, the selection of materials and the way in which the roof and exterior areas are used play an important role. In particular in densely built-up neighbourhoods, great importance is attached to outdoor areas and adapting their design and use requirements to the existing trees and plants, as well as the other ecological qualities of the site (fig. 4.13). If it is not possible to prevent the sealing of existing green areas, compensatory measures should be sought. In the case of developments with large areas of green, the approach to local water cycles should be considered in addition to the infiltration of precipitation on site (e.g. planning of a reed bed sewage system for the processing of grey water, incorporation of a local rainwater infiltration system in the exterior design, fig. 4.14, p. 74).

(Load-bearing) structure and building envelope
The long-term use requirements are fundamental for the design of the load-bearing structure (flexibility, utilisation cycles, suitability for conversions). And, depending on the location and the type of use, there may be large discrepancies. In the case of laboratory and office buildings, it makes sense to establish a clear separation between structure and fit-out, whereas, in the case of residential buildings, it is at first necessary to determine realistic conversion scenarios and the amount of effort required for their imple-

4.13

mentation. If the residential building is located in a residential area, the likelihood of it being changed into an office building is fairly low. Alongside planning a flexible load-bearing structure, the objective should be to achieve an uninterrupted transfer of vertical loads in order to minimise the consumption of resources and prevent the accumulation of additional costs.
The use of protruding and setback elements, including large cantilevered constructions, should be weighed very carefully against the additional structural effort and expense as well as the larger surface areas enclosing the heated volume. If required, a more sculptural appearance can be created by dividing the volume into zones that are intelligent from an energy efficiency point of view (fig. 4.15).
In accordance with the orientation and depth of the building, the position of windows and the window-to-wall ratio influence the amount of daylight penetrating the building and thus the demand for artificial lighting and mechanical ventilation. The same applies to the type and control system of sun shading devices and the choice of facade cladding. The embodied energy is largely circumstantial in the case of these parameters. Not so, however, when it comes to the choice of frame material (PVC, steel, aluminium, wood-aluminium, wood, etc.) and facade material, where embodied energy plays a quite significant role (see Transparent facades, pp. 94f.).

Building services concept

The effect of the building services concept on the building's environmental impact is also quite significant. The wiring as well as the position and layout of service shafts in the interior influence the area requirement and the building volume but also the measures required for fire prevention. In buildings with mechanical ventilation systems, the positioning of the plant room and the layout of ducts for the supply and extraction of air have a fundamental impact on the structure.
The first thoughts concerning the arrangement and size of volumes should take into consideration the use of the building envelope or ambient heat for the generation of energy in the same way as the possibilities for rainwater or grey water harvesting. The way in which the horizontal cables and ducts are laid (incorporated in floor slabs, suspended ceilings or raised floors, or a visible installation) has an impact on not only the ease of maintenance work and the suitability for conversions but also on the storey height and the thickness of components (see Lower secondary school in Langenzersdorf, pp. 133ff.). It is also important to understand that a high degree of technical sophistication usually also involves a greater need for servicing and maintenance work.

Infrastructure and mobility

Over the last years, quite a few cities, such as Zurich, Freiburg, Trier and Basel, have accumulated positive experiences from the development of mobility concepts, which are able to reduce the mobility-induced environmental impacts of buildings. The actual demand for car parking in inner-city areas or locations easily accessed by public transport is frequently well below what is specified in statutory requirements. A decrease in the number of car parking spaces usually allows the size of basement structures and the area of sealed surfaces to be reduced. For this reason the development of a mobility concept that includes structural and organisational measures to control mobility behaviour has become a fundamental component of resource-efficient building.
In Zurich, for example, a special permit can be obtained for "housing with low car use" if the mobility concept satisfactorily demonstrates the appropriateness of the planned residential scheme. The requirements include, on the one hand, the fulfilment of various site criteria (e.g. the vicinity to schools, day care centres, public transport, provision of local amenities and services, etc.) and, on the other hand, the introduction of effective compensatory measures (e.g. more parking spaces and facilities for bicycles and motorbikes, incentives and parking spaces for car-sharing vehicles, deposit facilities for home supply services, rental concepts and terms in the tenancy agreements to provide special fare concessions or free travel on public transport). In order to stimulate residents to become more environmentally friendly in their mobility behaviour, there should be an adequate supply of paths and cycle stands at a suitable distance and a priority on pedestrian access to buildings and exterior facilities. If there are no guidelines or examples for the development of a mobility concept in the city or community concerned, it may be worthwhile investigating into the actual car parking situation in the immediate vicinity of the planned development. The results will ideally give some indication as to whether the current regulations are still appropriate for the requirements and whether further clarification is necessary and beneficial.

Phase 3: Developed design / planning application

Phase 3 involves the completion of the design concept including the definition of all components, the cost estimation/calculation and the preparation of the building permission application with the aim of obtaining planning approval.

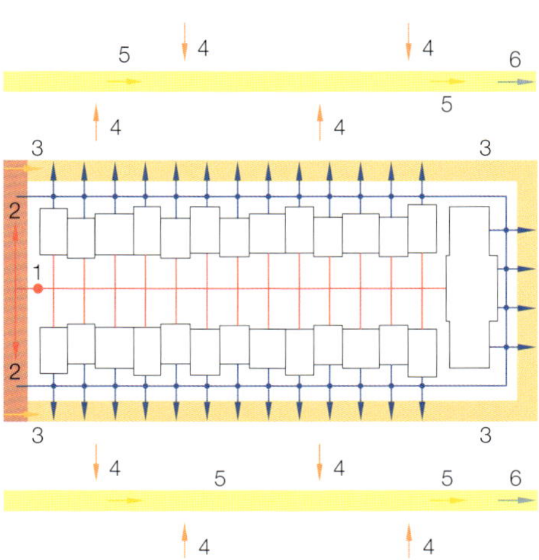

1 multi-compartment septic tank (mechanical pretreatment)
2 reed bed sewage system (main treatment (90 %), foil covered)
3 2nd treatment process (5 % clarification)/inlet of roof/surface water run-off (band of reeds or willows)
4 overflow to 3rd treatment process
5 3rd treatment process (5 % clarification, reed and willow planting)
6 outflow into existing trench system

grey water 100 % (1st treatment process)
rainwater/grey water 10 % (2nd treatment process)
rainwater/grey water 5 % (3rd treatment process)
rainwater/grey water 0 %
water pipeline with connection for each DU (e.g. garden irrigation)

4.14

4.14 Feasibility study for a residential estate at IBA Hamburg (D) 2013, HHS Planer + Architekten. Incorporation of grey water and wastewater use in the exterior design concept.
4.15 Refurbishment of Witikon care centre (CH) 2010, BGP Architekten. Energy efficiency zoning of floor plan in a care centre for senior citizens with an active solar facade system.
4.16 Ecological comparison of two functional units. In the case of a flat roof using a gravel-covered warm roof system (U-value 0.1 W/m²K), the global warming potential (GWP) can be reduced by 65 % according to the type of insulation and waterproofing materials used.
4.17 Köschenrüti residential estate, Zürich (CH) 2014, Bob Gysin + Partner BGP Architekten. Installation of a prefabricated sanitary unit made from lightweight concrete.

4.15

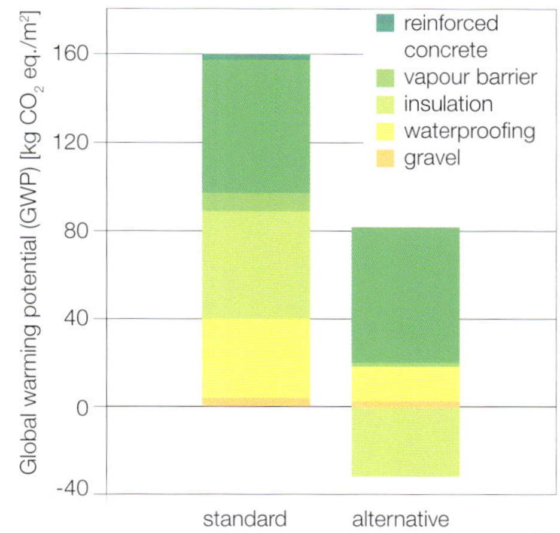

4.16

Review and specification of assumptions made during preliminary design phase

The selection of materials has far-reaching consequences on the environmental impacts of a building. The various, slightly simplified, assumptions made during the course of the preliminary design are usually based on standard materials and component configurations. Drawing conclusions about the expected environmental impacts is therefore difficult and such assumptions are really only intended to form a basis for comparison between different systems and concepts based on mean values. It is not until the exact configuration of layers is determined that it becomes clear whether a component meets or even exceeds assumptions made earlier. Even in the case of components with identical technical and functional requirements, significant differences can exist in the ecological and biological properties (fig. 4.16). For example, in a flat roof system for a gravel-covered warm roof with a U-value of 0.1 W/m²K, the GWP can be reduced by up to 65 % depending on the choice of insulation and waterproofing materials (standard plus roof: 230 kg CO_2 eq./m² – improved warm roof, gravel covered: 80 kg CO_2 eq./m²). The same holds true for the cladding of ventilated facade systems (see Mixed residential and commercial building in Zurich, pp. 117ff.), floor coverings and interior wall constructions. The assumptions made in the preliminary design phase should therefore be reviewed and questioned carefully during the development of the final design. Sometimes a detailed analysis reveals that the originally defined parameters cannot be met for project-specific reasons (such as increased soundproofing or noise protection requirements, greater atmospheric influences, aspects concerning the operation or maintenance of the building) or that it may even be possible to exceed them by making creative or constructional alterations. In other cases, it might make sense to fall back on previously rejected component configurations and materials. On this account all components with a surface area or volume that adds up to more than 20 % of the total component area or volume should undergo a detailed examination and comparison with regard to, for example, embodied energy, durability, susceptibility to wear and tear and maintenance friendliness.

In the case of highly prefabricated building components (sanitary units, facade elements, modular elements, etc.), or even the whole building (see Holiday residence on Taylor's Island, pp. 103ff.), it may even be necessary to bring forward certain aspects of the production information and detail design. Close attention must be paid to the planning of construction sequences, including the interfaces of different trades. The use of prefabricated elements frequently leads to shorter construction periods and lower costs (see Modular construction systems, pp. 52ff.). However, a high degree of prefabrication also requires the adjustment of planning sequences. For the production of a sanitary unit, for example, the surface finishes, colour scheme and sanitary equipment must be selected early in the execution planning phase (fig. 4.17). When prefabricating facade or floor elements, the planning of all technical installations, if these are to be accommodated in the components, must also be coordinated and completed at an earlier design stage. As a consequence, the amount of coordination and detail planning required during the design phase increases significantly.

Conformity with building codes and budget category limits

Alongside the structural design and moisture protection, fire prevention and soundproofing requirements have a considerable impact on the construction's demand for resources. These requirements can often be satisfied by making use of special construction techniques and implementing resource-efficient methods. However, special solutions often require a detailed evaluation involving appropriate authorities, specialist planners and possibly also testing institutes with regard to their acceptability. Creative and technically sophisticated solutions frequently fail due to regional or even local differences in building regulations or a lack of inspection certificates. Particularly in the case of large schemes, it may be wise or even necessary to perform case-by-case reviews or fire prevention tests, which require sufficient notice and time to prepare. Hence, these procedures must be planned and coordinated in good time – at the latest during the planning application processes.

Because most cost estimates are prepared using either the building volume or area method, innovative solutions are

4.17

often difficult to evaluate. When preparing a preliminary cost estimate, it is therefore important to examine all key components in terms of their economic factors. This approach, however, usually requires a high level of detail as well as information concerning the planned construction sequences. Especially when dealing with new construction methods and innovative building materials, not all those involved in planning may have the same level of experience and knowledge as would be the case for a standard construction; furthermore, there may only be a limited range of companies available and qualified to execute the work. Thus, experienced specialists and companies should be involved early on in the planning process, especially with regard to questions concerning the technical implementation on site (fig. 4.19, p. 77).

Building material and product comparisons

Alongside the creative and functional requirements, the expected environmental impacts and costs (including cleaning and maintenance) are also important considerations when it comes to selecting materials. The comparison of different structural configurations (fig. 4.18) helps to evaluate alternative solutions and visualise the corresponding advantages and disadvantages. It is important, in this case, to examine not only those elements that are most important from the viewpoint of quantity but also those building materials and components regarded as critical in terms of building biology (sealants, varnishes, solvents, etc., fig. 2.9, p. 19)
In addition to the load-bearing structure and the facade, particular attention should be paid to the detailed description of building components in the chapter "Environmental impacts of building components" (pp. 86ff.).

Requirements and exclusion criteria in the selection of building materials

Before performing a quantitative assessment of environmental impacts for specific building components, it is worthwhile to determine exclusion criteria concerning building biology and environmental aspects. The specifications provided by the relevant certificates and labels are generally useful in this respect (fig. 2.15, p. 22; fig. 2.35, p. 39). The BNB criterion "Risks for the local environment" [2], for example, includes advice on the selection of materials and products, as well as a list of substances which should be avoided. The BREEAM criterion Hea 02 also includes a list with corresponding requirements concerning the use of surface materials.
In addition to the determined objectives, it is useful to create requirement profiles for the most important building components and surfaces. Alongside specifications concerning use, susceptibility to wear and tear, maintenance and cleaning, the profiles should include information on environmental properties. It makes sense, for example, that the requirements regarding indoor air quality and surface finishes for day care centres and schools are more stringent than those for retail or storage facilities. The conflicting aims that often arise in the definition of requirements should ideally be discussed openly before the detail planning stage commences.

Development of a (simplified) life cycle assessment

It is essential to perform a quantitative assessment of the environmental impacts during the design phase in order to make a credible statement on the environmental impacts of a building. The objectives and requirements of the project are particularly important for the scope of the calcu-

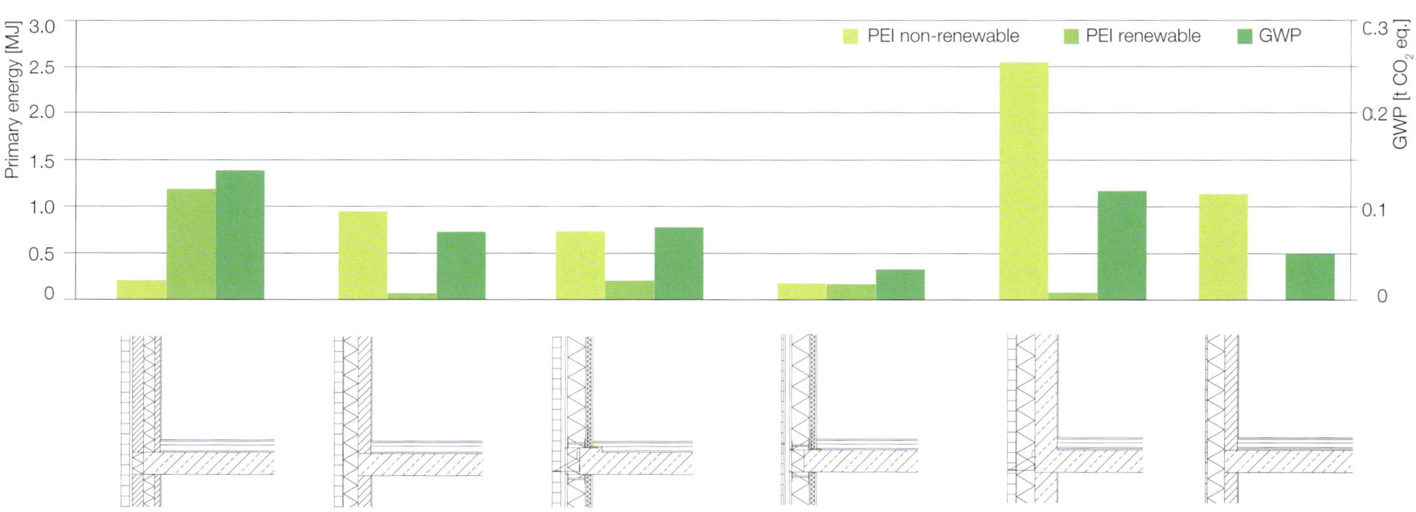

Description	**wood-cement brickwork + clinker facing**	**hollow brick + mineral wool + clinker facing**	**2-layer timber exterior wall + wood-clinker facing**	**2-layer timber exterior wall + thin-tile wood-clinker facing**	**concrete facade + cavity insulation + clinker facing**	**sand lime masonry wall + CTIS + thin tile masonry facing**
Configuration of layers	11.5 cm clinker facing brick 4 cm cavity 37.5 cm wood-cement brick 1.5 cm clay plaster total thickness: 54.5 cm	11.5 cm clinker facing brick 1 cm cavity 20 cm mineral wool (WLG 035) 17.5 cm hollow brick (λ 0.09 W/mK) 1.5 cm clay plaster total thickness: 51.5 cm	11.5 cm clinker facing brick 6 cm cavity 3 cm hydrophobic wood fibreboard 30 cm timber I beam/ cellulose insulation 2 cm structural board 2.5 cm clay building board total thickness: 54.5 cm	5.5 cm thin brick tiles on backing 6 cm aluminium substructure/cavity 3 cm hydrophobic wood fibreboard 30 cm timber I beam/ cellulose insulation 2 cm structural board 2.5 cm clay building board total thickness: 48.5 cm	11.5 cm clinker facing brick (with bracket fixtures) 1 cm cavity 25 cm cavity insulation (EPS, WLG 035) 30 cm reinforced concrete 1.5 cm plaster total thickness: 54.5 cm	2.5 cm clinker tiles 24 cm composite thermal insulation system (EPS, WLG 035) 17.5 cm sand lime brick (SG 2.0) 1.5 cm clay plaster total thickness: 45.5 cm

4.18

lations and the choice of an appropriate tool. The results are essential to balance the improvement potentials in the following planning phases. This is why the calculations should not be performed at the end of the design phase, but at an earlier stage in order to allow the findings to be incorporated in the planning application and tender documents.
If the aim is to obtain a building certificate, the calculations are also helpful for risk assessment purposes. Early analyses give some indication as to whether the project specifications are attainable with the measures planned. Several certification systems (e.g. DGNB/BNB) recommend performing a first life cycle assessment (LCA) during the design stage, which should also involve energy-related aspects. The design stage is therefore also a convenient time for establishing the life cycle costs (LCC).
In most cases, the calculations are performed by energy and sustainability specialists using complex and highly efficient tools (fig. 4.2, p. 69).
Even if the objective agreement does not specifically include the performance of a life cycle assessment, the development of the final design should nevertheless be used to carry out calculations for the most important components and materials. The results should provide opportunity to decide whether the intended construction is an improvement over a standard construction. Variation studies are a tried and tested method to compare different configurations of the same component with a reference component. Here it is important to take into consideration the interdependencies, which derive from the respective component variations. They may affect not only other components (e.g. when comparing load-bearing and non-load-bearing facade or partition wall configurations) but also the operation and maintenance of the building (e.g. the quicker deterioration of facade cladding if wood is used rather than fibre cement or glass fibre concrete).
Simple and inexpensive tools, some are also available free of charge, are usually suitable for carrying out variation studies (fig. 4.2, p. 69).
The aim of the comparison should be to determine the relative best option for the respective project and not to reach absolute target values. The tool should therefore always be chosen according to the size of the project, the later use of the results and the probable fields of application in future projects.

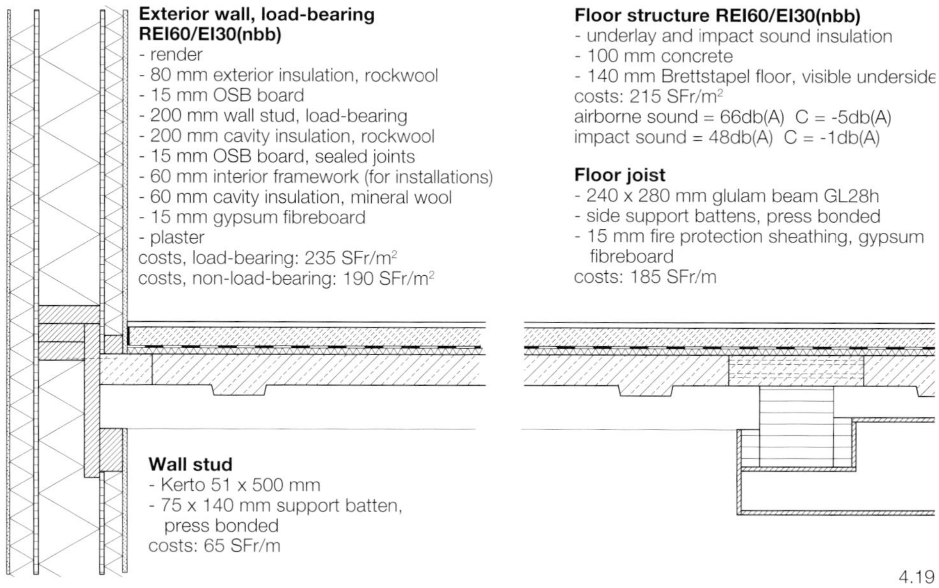

4.19

Optimisation of key components

A comparative life cycle assessment of functional units or on a component level should always be performed in such a way that it is possible to derive clear statements with regard to the further design phases. The comparison of, for example, different cavity facade systems reveals that the substructure, in particular if it is made of aluminium or stainless steel, contributes most significantly to the GWP and PEI (see Mixed residential and commercial building in Zurich, pp. 117ff.). One way of improving the exterior facade cladding could therefore be to minimise the necessary substructure by using lighter panels and reducing the distance to the skin, or by using larger, more rigid panels which would allow the space between the vertical supports to be increased.
The early planning of key details in all standard components and elements is a basic requirement for performing component-related improvement processes. In order to make clear statements at this design stage, planners, especially those with little experience in developing life cycle assessments, may find it easier to perform the tasks in several iteration steps. For this reason they should start performing calculations at an early design stage.

Phase 4: Procurement/execution drawings

In the fourth phase, the approved design is processed in such a way that the scheme can be developed. Bills of quantities and a performance description are prepared as a basis for the tender documents.
Since the processes and regulations for this phase vary significantly from one country to the next, the focus here is on a few general aspects.
The following paragraphs are based mainly on the situations in Germany and Switzerland.

Development of the construction design with regard to detail and product selection

Depending on the degree of prefabrication, the joint design principles for elements and component layers should be finalised at the very latest during the procurement and construction design phase. The construction details determine the theoretical service life of a component and its individual layers. The aim should be to provide components with a service life appropriate to the construction task. If components have a short life span, the construction should allow for easy replacement – without making it necessary to dispose of parts unaffected.
By selecting products manufactured according to sustainable manufacturing and processing techniques, i.e. products that are among the most environmentally friendly in their category, the building materials industry is encouraged to continuously develop more ecological manu-

4.18 Elbtorquartier Hamburg (D) 2013, Bob Gysin + Partner BGP Architekten. Comparison of primary energy input (PEI) and global warming potential (GWP) of different exterior wall configurations
4.19 Hardturm residential estate, Zürich (CH) Bob Gysin + Partner BGP Architekten (in planning). Construction design planned by timber engineer with specifications on costs and sound insulation of individual components

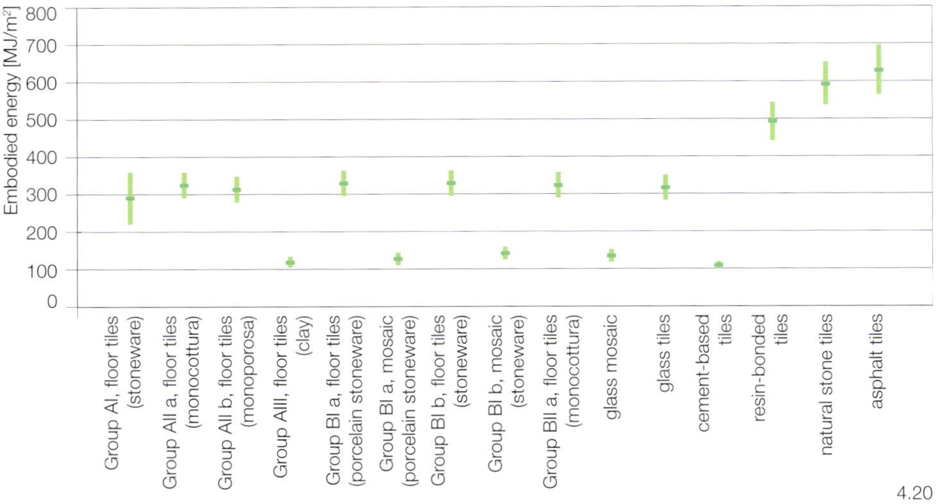

4.20

facturing principles. The requirements for building materials (good availability, regional accessibility and production, resource-efficient and low-pollutant manufacturing techniques, etc.) should be specified in the tender documents by stating the relevant certificates and labels (Blue Angel, FSC, etc.; fig. 2.15, p. 22). As a result, it is not only possible to ensure the technical and visual comparability of products but also equivalent environmental standards.
Thus, when selecting building materials, planners should enquire into the manufacturing process and possibly also whether a product certification has been obtained, which assesses the degree of improvement of the material and energy cycles resulting from the production process (e.g. Cradle-to-Cradle certificate). However, planners and clients can also influence the environmental impacts of selected products beyond the criteria assessed in the various labels. In the case of tile floor coverings, for example, alongside the decision concerning the source material (clay, stoneware, porcelain stoneware, natural stone, asphalt), the choice of tile format has the largest impact on the consumption of resources for a square metre of flooring. Producing large-format tiles requires a much greater amount of material and energy than making small-format mosaic tiles due to, in part, the much lower wastage (fig. 4.20).

4.20 Comparison between the embodied energy of different tile flooring products (specifications of product groups for ceramic floor coverings according to EN 14411)
4.21 Multi-unit dwelling in Bennau (CH) 2009, Grab Architekten. Visible installation of cables and ducts in apartment hallway
4.22 Blower-door test to determine the airtightness of the building envelope
4.23 Pollutant detection in rooms using two different systems

Optimisation of detail and joint configurations
In order to ensure a long service life, lower maintenance and repair expenses as well as a non-destructive deconstruction of the building, attention must be paid to the configuration of details and joints.
The aim should be to use finishes and materials that age with dignity and require little effort when it comes to retouching the surfaces. Furthermore, the details should be designed in such a way that elements are protected from weathering and mechanical damage (e.g. protrusions and roofs on the exterior, hard-wearing roomline products, such as skirting boards, etc.). The use of openable connections (screws, clamps, dowels and nails, see Constructing recyclable buildings, pp. 66ff. and Holiday residence on Taylor's Island, pp. 103ff.) is indispensable for a simple and straightforward deconstruction and replacement of parts. Composite materials and fully bonded layers should be avoided in order to prevent more durable layers from being damaged when replacing surfaces and components with shorter service lives. For cleaning, servicing and maintenance purposes, it is important to provide good accessibility to components and technical installations (fig. 4.21).

Incorporation of sustainability aspects in tender documents
The incorporation of sustainability aspects in the tender documents is of prime importance to ensure that the specifications made during the design phase are actually implemented on site. Furthermore, the integration of environmental criteria into the description of works is designed to ensure fair and transparent competition among bidders. Alongside information concerning the selected building materials and products (e.g. VOC limits, GISCODES, heavy metal contents), the tender documents should also include specifications concerning the optimisation of construction processes. In detail this means information about the reduction of waste, noise and dust, as well as a lower consumption of resources and pollution caused by construction operations. These measures are designed to reduce environmental impacts both on a global (energy, resources, waste) and local scale (noise, soil conservation). At the same time, they are designed to increase health and safety for all persons working on the construction site (noise, dust).

Special building material and product requirements, product selection
The preliminaries of the tender documents should make special reference to building ecology and building biology. Ideally, there should be sections containing information on the certificates and labels that are being aimed for. The use of "prohibited" additives and production methods must be specified (in accordance with the provisions of the label), as well as the product's place of origin for selected materials (e.g. local wood products, maximum distance to concrete plant). If bills of quantities are used for tendering purposes, the corresponding requirements must also be referred to in the individual items (FSC certification, grey EPS, PVC and halogen-free electrical installations, etc.). Special attention should be paid to the finishing of surfaces (paint, varnishes and primers; oil paint, transparent coatings, impregnating agents) since these are mainly responsible for the content of formaldehyde and VOC emissions in indoor air. The choice usually requires the balancing of good durability, low maintenance costs and the environmental requirements of the surface finishes.

Contract award criteria
In the case of a design and construct contract, the award criteria should not be based on price alone. Instead, the most economically advantageous tender should be favoured by including the life cycle costs in the assessment (see Phase 6, p. 80). When specifying the award criteria and the order of priority, an emphasis should be placed on ecological and health-related aspects in cases where technical-functional requirements are equal. According to the Act Against Restraints of Competition (Gesetz

gegen Wettbewerbsbeschränkungen, GWB), in Germany contracts valued above the EU threshold are permitted to specify further requirements involving social, environmental or innovative aspects if these have a direct relation to the subject matter of the contract and arise from the description of the service to be rendered. There is also the possibility to request details of the environmental management procedures from the bidder when executing the job, e.g. an EMAS certificate (Eco-Management and Audit Scheme). In order to determine the most important criteria, the ecological performance of a service should be defined in the Additional Technical Terms of Contract in the preliminaries of the tender documents. The classification of pollutants established by the Assessment System Sustainable Building (Bewertungssystem Nachhaltiges Bauen, BNB) can be used as a basis in this context. The list contains various performance levels for a number of different product applications and uses. Up to BNB performance level 4, the environmental material requirements can usually be implemented at no or very little extra cost.
Alongside incorporating the Additional Technical Terms of Contract in the preliminaries of the tender documents, it has proven beneficial to check the bills of quantities to determine whether specific demands have a negative impact on the product implemented at an item level (e.g. solvent-containing adhesives), and, if necessary, remove it from the list accordingly. It also makes sense, in particular in the case of bidders with little experience in fulfilling environmental requirements, to name products that satisfy the specifications in addition to requesting quotations.

Before awarding the contract, it is worth arranging a meeting with selected contractors to clarify any technical issues and point out the environmental and health-related aspects specific to the project. This strategy avoids misunderstandings arising during advanced construction stages. The contract award is considered the official authorisation to implement the contract in accordance with the respective environmental requirements. In order to maintain the same level of quality throughout the construction phase, the tenderer should follow up the contract award by providing a material list. This should be checked for conformity with the specified environmental requirements and displayed at the building site.

Phase 5: Construction

Phase 5 involves the development of a cost plan on completion of the planning stage and the site supervision and management work during the construction phase.

Optimisation of construction site operations

The specifications for environmentally improved construction site operations must already be defined in the tender documents. Requirements that have an effect on scheduling should be considered even earlier, in the design phase. Alongside the reduction of waste, noise and dust, soil protection as well as a minimisation of resource consumption and pollutant emissions are among the most important measures that contribute to environmentally improved construction site operations. Taking measurements for quality assurance purposes during the construction phase (see pictures below) is a fundamental requirement to ensure that the environmental objectives determined in the target agreement and project design are actually met. In addition, project superintendents and site managers should continuously review the working drawings and monitor the execution of works on site.

On-site quality monitoring

Measurements for quality assurance purposes taken during the construction phase are essential for meeting the environmental objectives determined in the target agreement and project design. It goes without saying that more stringent requirements with regard to the thermal protection and energy consumption of buildings require a higher quality of workmanship. In practice, however, this is often opposed by rising cost and time pressure.
The documentation of the building materials and products used, including the corresponding material safety data sheets, is above all designed to ensure a smooth and resource-efficient operation of the building. The availability of detailed information is particularly important in the case of conversions and, eventually, the deconstruction of the building.

Product requirements and specifications

The documentation of the building materials and products used, including the corresponding material safety data sheets, is designed to ensure a smooth and resource-efficient operation of the building. Details on the building materials used are particularly important for conversion and deconstruction work. Furthermore, in the event of damage, this information makes it far easier to draw conclusions about the cause of the problem.

4.21

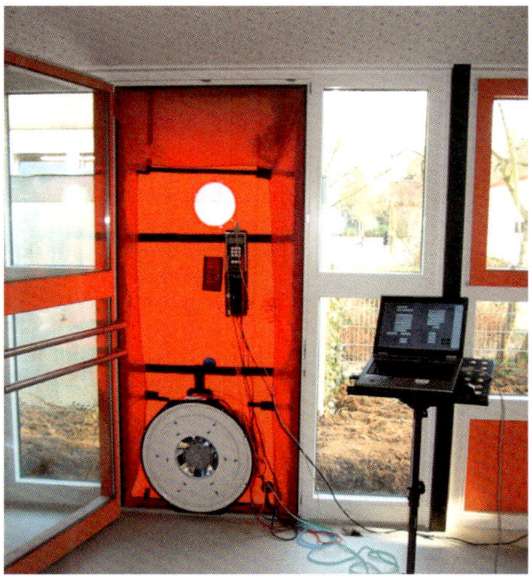

4.22

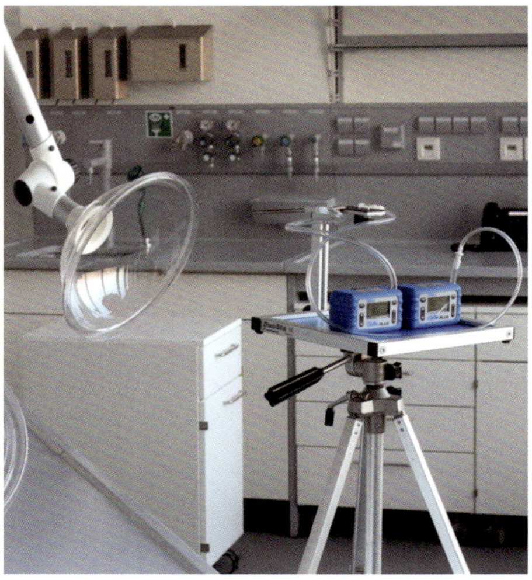

4.23

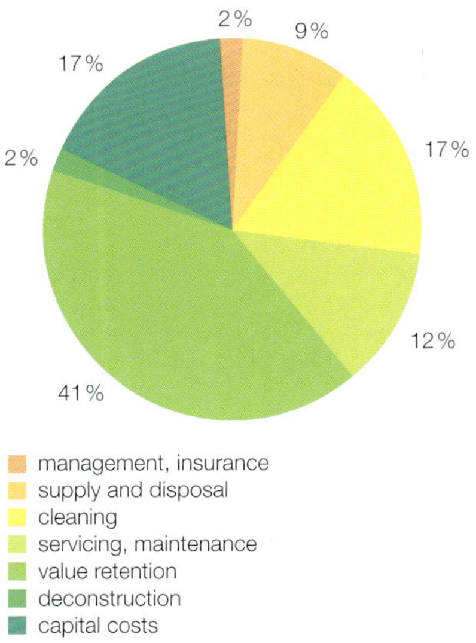

4.24

The documentation of the building materials used should be amended and reviewed continuously throughout the construction phase. The aim is to produce a comprehensive collection of all material and product safety data sheets so that materials and products can be traced at a later date.

Quality assurance and control

Measurements are a fundamental tool for checking the quality of workmanship on site. The tests, most of which are performed on completion of the project, include, for example, blower-door tests, pollution and acoustic measurements. Individual measurements, such as noise protection measurements of the facade or in rooms, can and should be performed before completion of the finishing work in order to provide easier access when remedying defects. Blower-door tests (fig. 4.22) are also often performed as soon as the building envelope has been made airtight (with windows installed, a continuous airtightness layer in place, fully plastered interior walls and all building services installations fitted, however, without interior sheathing). Unfortunately the costs are higher at this stage than on project completion due to the greater effort required to seal and close up service pipes and ducts; on the other hand, it is much easier at this stage to remove and remedy any defects. In any event, it is recommended that a second blower-door test should be performed on final approval in order to detect any hidden defects, such as leaky sockets or broken siphons. The costs in larger buildings can be reduced by selecting random fire compartments and testing them. Sometimes conveying the message that an airtightness test will be performed is enough to put contractors on their toes.

The pollutant load indoors is generally measured within 28 days of completion and before the building is occupied. More than anything, though, the measurements are intended for documentary purposes and to check the quality of the construction. In the case of DGNB or BNB certificates, the air pollution is a make-or-break criterion, which decides whether a building is permitted to enter the certification procedure or not (fig. 4.23, p. 79; see Healthy built environments, pp. 53f.).

Construction processes

The specifications concerning the construction processes are determined in the procurement documents and are binding for all participating contractors. They are, on the one hand, designed to reduce the production of waste and to ensure the correct separation of materials on site, which is achieved by training all participants and checking waste collection points at regular intervals, and, on the other hand, to introduce measures for the minimisation of noise, for example, by implementing noise protection facilities, using low-noise tools and machines and adhering to quiet hours (fig. 4.26). Soil protection policies are intended to prevent damage to the ground, both mechanical (by reducing excavation and soil storage on site; preventing soil compaction and disturbance of soil strata) as well as chemical (through protection policies to avoid soil and groundwater contamination).

In order to cut down on the consumption of resources during the construction phase, environmental requirements should be determined for building site logistics and construction site operations. For example, only vehicles with the highest emission classes should be used for the transportation of building products and excavated material. If at all possible, transportation distance for excavated soil as well as for the delivery of concrete for the main works should be limited. Especially in the case of development schemes requiring extensive excavation work, the number of trips needed to dispose of the soil is very high. By putting appropriate policies in place, the total distance of kilometres can, in some cases, be reduced by a six-digit figure (fig. 4.25; see Office building in Krems, pp. 125ff.).

Ideally, the building shell should dry naturally, rather than by using a heating system. This can be achieved by allowing a period of at least 30 days, during which the building is aired before it is taken into operation. The 30-day period actually provides the perfect opportunity to perform indoor air measurements.

Phase 6: Handover/use

Phase 6 describes the handover and documentation of the completed building; furthermore the operation of the development throughout the total life cycle up until deconstruction.

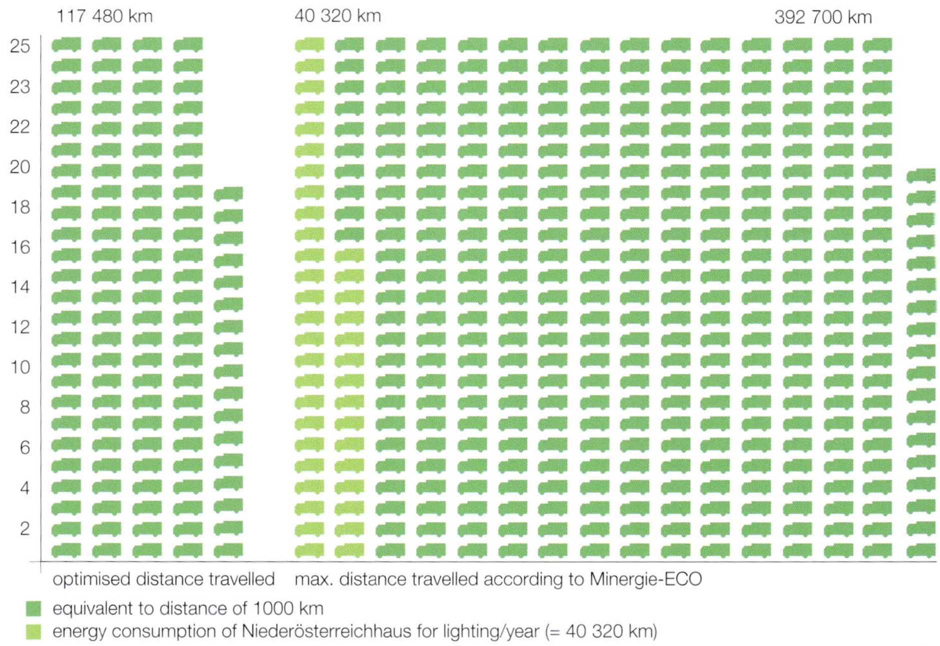

4.25

Requirements for optimal building use

The interface between the construction and the use phase of the building is generally marked by the coordinated handover to the client after final acceptance of the completed building. Due to the continuously rising requirements, the more complex structural configurations and the higher level of technical detail in buildings, the absence of defects alone is no longer sufficient to allow the optimal operation of the development. In order to operate, clean and maintain the building in an orderly fashion, the complete information deriving from the design process must be handed over to the person in charge. This information should not only include instructions on how best to clean surfaces and ducts but also operating manuals for building services installations. Furthermore, comprehensive information concerning constructional details and the materials used must be made available to ensure that maintenance and repair tasks can be carried out in a satisfactory manner.

Interdependencies of life cycle costs and environmental impacts during operation

A detailed analysis of the life cycle costs would exceed the scope of this book. Although high energy costs generally have a negative impact on operating costs, there is no real direct causal relationship between the economic operation of a building and its total environmental impact. Even a resource-efficient building can be operated inefficiently. Nevertheless, there are some interdependencies between these two aspects that must be taken into consideration.

High operation and maintenance costs can have a similar impact on the service life of a building as a faulty or inadequate design that is unable to meet the long-term requirements of the building users. In both cases it can prove necessary to introduce maintenance and upgrade measures before the complete building or a certain component has actually reached the end of its potential design life, or to discontinue operation of the building and possibly even remove it. The number of indoor swimming pools that have had to close over the last years due to energy and maintenance costs that could no longer be met is only one example of these circumstances. Uneconomic operation can, however, also necessitate early repair and maintenance measures in office and laboratory buildings, or even their complete removal.

Similar situations can occur on a component level if sufficient consideration is not given to the long-term protection and usability of the components during the design and construction phase. According to a selection of buildings in Zurich, figure 3.54 (p. 63) illustrates which components are most affected by life cycle costs. The average allocation of life cycle costs is then presented in figure 4.24.

The target-oriented implementation of the repair and maintenance strategies described in the chapter "Strategies for material use in the construction process" (pp. 66f.) has the most significant impact on the service life of components. Simply checking the sealing membranes in buildings at regular intervals prevents damage to the insulation layers and load-bearing structure. These procedures, however, require good accessibility to the different layers (see Strategies for material use in the construction process, pp. 44ff.).

Cleaning, servicing, maintenance and operation instructions

The preparation of a manual by the planner with advice on how to clean, maintain, service and repair components is intended to allow for an efficient operation of the building. The overall aim is to reduce the costs during the use phase and extend the maintenance cycles in order to achieve a reduction of the life cycle costs and the resource consumption.

As-built drawings and calculations

The adaptation of the working and detail drawings to reflect what has actually been built on site is a fundamental requirement for the operation of the building, including possible modernisation and refurbishment measures. Information concerning the exact configuration of layers and construction of details is absolutely essential not only in the event of damage and for planning conversions but also to obviate the need for sounding tests. In order to compare the actually measured energy consumption with the calculations made during the design phase, all calculated results should be reviewed and possibly updated on completion of the construction work.

Building owner's manual

The compilation of a building owner's manual with instructions for the efficient and proper operation of building services should nowadays be an integral part of planning services. Numerous studies have shown that the actual energy consumption of a building is very much dependent on how well occupants understand how to operate the building and, in particular, the technical installations. The city of Frankfurt has determined that energy consumption can be reduced by approximately 20 % by performing operational improvements and introducing energy monitoring systems. Moreover, a better understanding of the building's functional principles generally leads to greater user satisfaction.

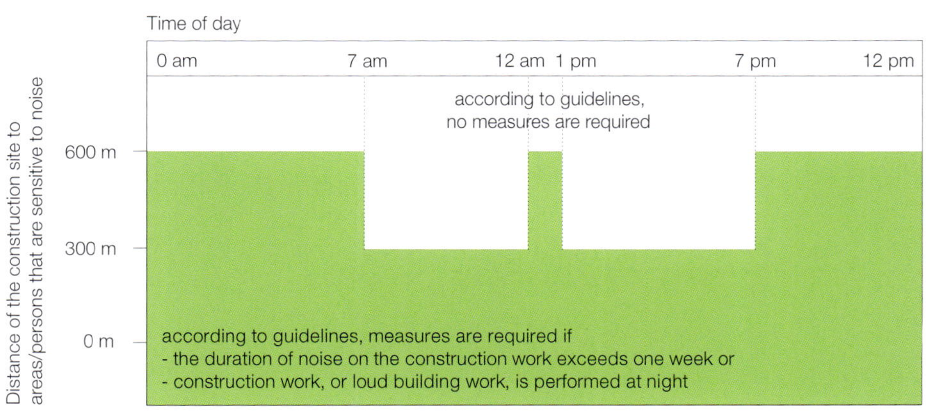

4.26

4.24 Annual life cycle costs of municipal buildings in Zurich according to cost groups
4.25 Niederösterreichhaus in Krems (A) 2011, AllesWirdGut Architekten: kilometres covered by lorries for the transportation of excavated material and for the main works (see pp. 125ff.)
4.26 Quick test to assess noise protection measures on building sites according to the Swiss Guidelines on Building Noise
4.27 Phase-related relevance of design topics (see following pages)

	Criterion	Subcriterion	Impact level: Impact	Impact level: Performance	Planning phase 1	2	3	4	5	6	Objective of the measure
G	**Building concept**										
G01	Site and existing building stock	contaminated land and pollutants	positive impact	positive impact	implement	implement	implement	implement	implement	observe	long-term and environmentally sustainable solution concerning the cleanup of contaminated and polluted ground with the aim of reducing hazards to persons and environment
G02		existing building stock	positive impact	positive impact	implement	implement	observe	observe	observe		reduction of costs and environmental impacts by reusing existing building stock in full or in part
G03		microclimate	positive impact	positive impact	implement	implement	implement	observe	observe	observe	improvement of microclimate, greater biodiversity, preservation of water cycles
G04	Use	space efficiency	positive impact	slight negative impact	implement	implement	implement	observe			minimal use of space per person at comparable quality
G05		surface sealing	positive impact	slight negative impact	implement	implement	observe				improvement of microclimate and biodiversity, maximisation of usable exterior areas
G06		car parking	positive impact	slight negative impact	implement	implement	implement				maximisation of usable exterior areas and reduction of environmental impacts, improvement of microclimate and biodiversity
G08		allocation of uses	positive impact	positive impact	observe	implement	implement				minimisation of structural and technical measures as compensation for an unfavourable allocation of uses
G09		flexibility of use	positive impact	slight negative impact	implement	implement	implement	observe			flexibility of use in terms of the life cycle and phases
G10		suitability for extensions	positive impact	slight negative impact	implement	implement	observe				long-term use, adaptable layouts to meet future space demands
G11	Volume	volume above ground	positive impact	positive impact	observe	implement	implement				reduction of energy and resource consumption throughout the entire life cycle
G12		volume below ground	positive impact	negative impact	observe	implement	implement				improvement of microclimate and biodiversity, reduction of environmental impacts through construction
G13	Load-bearing structure and interior finishes	foundation	positive impact	slight negative impact	observe	implement	implement	observe			reduction of environmental impacts through construction
G14		load-bearing and non-load-bearing components	positive impact	negative impact		implement	implement	observe			high flexibility of use, long-term use (incl. conversions)
G15		vertical load transfer	positive impact	positive impact		implement	implement	observe			reduction of environmental impacts through construction
G16		horizontal load transfer	positive impact	positive impact		implement	implement	observe			reduction of environmental impacts through construction
G17	Building envelope	facade	positive impact	positive impact		implement	implement	observe			lower environmental impacts produced through the construction of the building, improvement of thermal comfort
G18		roof	positive impact	slight positive impact		implement	implement	observe			energy generation, optimisation of the microclimate, collection and use of rainwater from roof surfaces
G19		insulation and waterproofing	positive impact	positive impact		implement	observe	observe	implement		reduction of energy and resource consumption throughout the entire building life cycle
G20	Technical installations	decentralised/ centralised	positive impact	positive impact		implement	implement	implement			reduction of energy and resource consumption throughout the entire building life cycle, space-efficient design
G21		separation of layers building services	positive impact	slight negative impact		implement	implement	implement	observe		high flexibility of use, long-term use possibly through conversion and non-destructive deconstruction of technical building services
M	**Materials**										
M01	Environmental impacts	life cycle assessment	positive impact	slight negative impact	implement	implement	implement	implement	observe	observe	reduction of environmental impacts throughout the entire life cycle of building components
M06		chemical wood preservatives	positive impact	positive impact			implement	implement	implement	observe	reduction of health hazards to occupants through chemical wood preservatives
M07		biocides	positive impact	positive impact			implement	implement	implement	observe	reduction of health hazards to occupants through biocides
M08		organic solvents indoors	positive impact	positive impact			implement	implement	implement	observe	reduction of formaldehyde emissions indoors
M09		PU foams	positive impact	positive impact			observe	implement	implement	observe	reduction of possible emissions caused by the use of PU foams indoors
M10		heavy metals	positive impact	slight positive impact		observe	implement	implement	implement	observe	reduction of groundwater pollution caused by the wash-out of heavy metals from sheet metal surfaces
M11	Resource consumption	primary energy non-renewable	positive impact	slight negative impact	implement	implement	implement	implement	observe	observe	reduction of consumption of fossil energy carriers
M12		primary energy renewable	positive impact	slight negative impact	implement	implement	implement	implement	observe	observe	reduction of primary energy demand
M13		proportion of renewable energies	positive impact	slight negative impact	observe	implement	implement	implement	observe	observe	increased proportion of renewable energies generated on site in the total primary energy demand
M14		timber/sustainable material sources	positive impact	slight negative impact			observe	implement	implement	observe	protection of tropical, subtropical and boreal forests from deforestation, support the sustainable management of wood resources
M15		water utilisation	positive impact	slight negative impact		observe	implement	implement	implement	observe	reduction of effort and expense for the supply and extraction of water, minimisation of disturbance to natural water cycle

implement
observe
positive impact
slight positive impact
negative impact
slight negative impact

Measures	Reference buildings (pp. 102 ff.) TI 103	HA 109	ZU 117	KR 125	LA 133	Sources
contamination analysis and measures to remove and dispose of contaminated material (incl. tests for radon contamination) are performed in advance						DGNB ST 57
detailed examination of existing properties with regard to suitability for planned use in terms of technical, structural as well as spatial aspects		●			●	BREEAM Wst 02 LEED MR 1.1; 1.2
minimise sealed surface areas, prevent lowering of groundwater table, provide versatile use of exterior space	●					DGNB ST 6; ST 14; ST 15 BREEAM LE 02; LE 03; LE 04; POL 03 LEED SS 5.1; 5.2; 7.1
space-efficient layouts, minimisation of service and circulation areas	●	●			●	DGNB ST 27
minimise footprint of building, reduce sealed surface areas, avoid building below open exterior space	●					DGNB ST 15 BREEAM Mat 02 LEED SS 5.1; 5.2; 7.1
reduction of car parking spaces at basement and ground floor level by providing alternative transportation services						LEED SS 4.3; SS 4.4
demand-oriented arrangement of uses in layout and section (lighting, orientation, service and utility rooms, load-bearing capacity and span lengths, room sizes, etc.)			●	●		
development of a short-term, medium-term and long-term use strategy as a basis for creating a concept for conversions	●					DGNB ST 27
provision of opportunities for extensions and reserves for further development to cater for future requirements	●					
optimisation of the A / V ratio by providing a compact, but well lit and heated volume	●			●	●	
minimisation of structures below ground	●	●	●			
reduce the amount of excavated material and size of foundations as well as the weight of the building	●	●				
separate the primary structure from the secondary structure and finishes; assess the differences between short-term and long-term use	●	●	●			DGNB ST 27; ST 42
continuous vertical load-bearing structures	●		●	●		
short spans, minimum slab thickness, suitable selection of materials	●		●			
high flexibility of use, perfect amount of window surface area, reduced component thickness	●		●		●	BREEAM Hea 01; Mat 04
make use of roof surface areas for energy generation, rainwater harvesting, stabilisation or optimisation of the microclimate		●	●	●		DGNB ST 14
minimisation of the requirements for fire protection and waterproofing, continuous insulation plane with as few projections and setbacks as possible in order to minimise the insulated surface area and the use of elaborate building envelope details		●		●		
short cable, pipe and duct runs, good accessibility and retrofitability, high efficiency, minimisation of space for vertical and horizontal distribution systems	●		●	●	●	DGNB ST 28
avoid setting cables, pipes and ducts into concrete slabs and screed, good accessibility and retrofitability for all service lines and technical installations	●		●		●	DGNB ST 28
avoid using building materials with high environmental impacts; use materials, which minimise the environmental impacts (GWP, ODP, POCP, AP and EP) produced during the operation of the building		●	●	●	●	DGNB ST 1; ST 2; ST 3; ST 4; ST 5 BREEAM Mat 01; LEED EA P3
avoid the use of chemical wood preservatives in heated indoor areas		●	●	●	●	DGNB ST 6 LEED IEQ 4.4
avoid the use of biocides or coating compounds treated with biocides in indoor areas (paint and plaster)		●	●	●	●	DGNB ST 6 LEED IEQ 4.2
avoid using engineered timber or timber products with UF or MUF bonding agents, adhesives based on formaldehyde and solvent dilutable products		●	●	●	●	DGNB ST 6; BREEAM Hea 02; LEED IEQ 4.4
avoid using PU sealants and foams for joining, sealing or filling cavities			●			
avoid the use of materials containing lead, cadmium or chrome VI; avoid using large exposed areas of blank copper, titanium or galvanised steel without installing a suitable metal filter		●		●		DGNB ST 6
avoid using building materials with a high non-renewable primary energy input; select materials that minimise the primary energy input (non-renewable) during the operation of the building	●	●	●	●	●	DGNB ST 10 BREEAM Ene 01; Ene 05; Ene 06; Ene 07; Ene 08 LEED MR 3; MR 4
avoid using building materials with a high non-renewable primary energy input; select materials that minimise the primary energy input during the operation of the building	●	●	●	●	●	DGNB ST 11 LEED MR 6
generation of renewable energy in and on the building		●	●	●	●	DGNB ST 11 BREEAM Ene 04 LEED EA 2
avoid using timber and timber products from outside Europe without an FSC, PEFC or comparable label		●	●	●	●	DGNB ST 8 BREEAM Mat 03 LEED MR 7
reduce the consumption of water; ensure a responsible use of grey water and wastewater, make provisions for rainwater harvesting		●		●		DGNB ST 14 BREEAM Hea 04; Wat 01; Wat 04 LEED WE P1; WE 1; WE 2; WE 3

DGNB: criterion analogous to DGNB performance profiles, valid as of 2012 BREEAM: criterion analogous to BREEAM New Construction, version 2.0, valid as of 10/2012
LEED: criterion analogous to LEED 2009 New Construction and Major Renovations, valid as of 10/2013

4.27

	Criterion	Subcriterion	Impact level: Impact	Impact level: Performance	Planning phase 1	2	3	4	5	6	Objective of the measure
M16	Durability	weather resistance facade	positive impact	positive impact		observe	implement	implement	observe	observe	long service life of facade, windows and fixed shading devices
M17	Durability	durability surface finishes	positive impact	positive impact		observe	implement	implement	observe	observe	long service life and good resistance to wear and tear of wall, ceiling and floor finishes with the aim of reducing the replacement cycles
M18	Cleaning, servicing and maintenance	load-bearing structure	positive impact	positive impact		observe	implement	implement	observe	implement	simple implementation of maintenance and repair work with regard to load-bearing structure
M19		non-load-bearing structure outside	positive impact	positive impact		observe	implement	implement	observe	implement	simple and easy cleaning, servicing and maintenance processes with regard to facade, windows and exterior doors
M20		non-load-bearing structure inside	positive impact	positive impact		observe	implement	implement	observe	implement	simple and easy cleaning and maintenance processes with regard to floor coverings and interior glass surfaces
M21	Deconstruction, separation and reuse	deconstruction structure	positive impact	slight negative impact		observe	implement	implement	observe	implement	reduction of landfill waste, raw materials and production energy by ensuring the deconstruction of the structure into mono materials
M22		deconstruction fit-out	positive impact	slight negative impact		observe	implement	implement	observe	implement	reduction of landfill waste, raw materials and production energy, reduction of effort and expense for conversions by ensuring a simple deconstruction of interior fit-out into mono materials
M23		recyclability of building materials	positive impact	slight negative impact		observe	implement	implement	observe	implement	reuse and recyclability of building materials in the same or lower quality product cycles with the aim of reducing resource consumption as well as the volume of waste
M24	Indoor climate	thermal comfort in summer	slight negative impact	positive impact		implement	implement	observe	observe	observe	provision of comfortable indoor climate in summer, reduction of energy consumption, increase productivity in work environments
M25		thermal comfort in winter	slight negative impact	positive impact		implement	implement	observe	observe	observe	provision of comfortable indoor climate in winter, reduction of energy consumption, increase productivity in work environments
M26		pollutants in existing building components	positive impact	positive impact	implement	implement			implement		low pollution of indoor air by allergens and other pollutants, professional disposal of polluted building components
M27		pollutants in indoor air	slight positive impact	positive impact		observe	implement	implement	implement	observe	provision of good air quality indoors in terms of hygiene-related aspects
M28		electromagnetic radiation	slight positive impact	positive impact		observe	implement	implement	implement	observe	low immission through ionising and non-ionising radiation
B	**Construction processes**										
B01	Project preparation	use concept/demand analysis	positive impact	positive impact	implement	observe					development of need-based and appropriate design concept
B02		building regulations	positive impact	positive impact	implement	implement	implement	observe	observe		reduction of requirements and, as a consequence thereof, the resulting constructional measures
B03		target definition	positive impact	positive impact	implement	implement	observe	observe			early determination of design objectives and quality standards, including the ensuing synergies and contradictions
B04	Integral planning	planning team	positive impact	positive impact	implement	implement	implement	observe	observe		optimisation of the design and the planning process by developing innovative and project-specific concepts
B05		alternative solutions	positive impact	positive impact	observe	implement	implement	implement	observe		development and clear presentation of the solution most suited to the specific construction task
B06	Construction site	removal and site preparation	positive impact	slight negative impact	implement	implement			observe		removal and return of the building materials to the material cycle, preservation of microclimate and environmental qualities
B07		heating of building shell	positive impact	slight negative impact			observe	implement	implement		reduction of energy and resource consumption during construction operations
B08		waste on building site	positive impact	slight positive impact				implement	implement		reduction of waste volume, in particular non-reusable construction waste (rubble, excavated material, packaging, etc.)
B09		construction sequences	positive impact	slight negative impact			observe	implement	implement		reduction of resource consumption and emissions during construction operations
B10		noise on building site	positive impact	slight negative impact				implement	implement		prevention of all unnecessary noise deriving from building operations for the health benefit of all participants and residents
B11		dust on building site	positive impact	slight positive impact				implement	implement		prevention of formation of dust on the construction site for the health benefit of all participants and residents
B12		soil and ground protection	positive impact	slight negative impact			observe	implement	implement		prevention of mechanical and chemical damage to the ground and groundwater through contamination, compaction and mixing of strata
B13	Quality assurance	documentation	positive impact	positive impact				observe	implement	implement	preparation of as-built documents in the form of a manual with the most important building parameters as a basis for future construction measures and monitoring procedures
B14		measurements	positive impact	positive impact				observe	implement	implement	quality assurance and assessment of achievements as a fundamental requirement to meet the environmental objectives determined in target agreement and design concept
B15		handover	positive impact	positive impact				observe	implement	implement	reduction of operation costs, extension of replacement cycles

implement
observe
positive impact
slight positive impact
negative impact
slight negative impact

Measures	Reference buildings (pp 102 ff.) TI 103	HA 109	ZU 117	KR 125	LA 133	Sources
selection of highly weather-resistant materials (e.g. fibre cement, glass, corrosion-resistant metals, etc.) for the facade and either PVC, aluminium or wood-aluminium frames for the windows; sufficient protection from the weather (depth of roof overhangs and protrusions at least 0.2 x height of the affected component)	■		■			BREEAM Mat 05
selection of highly resistant surface materials (surface hardness, repairability, etc.)					■	DGNB ST 40
easy access to components of the load-bearing structure in need of maintenance or repair (e.g. corrosion, protection against moisture, fire protection, pest infestation, etc.)	■		■		■	DGNB ST 40
ensure accessibility of exterior glass surfaces by using either no or only very simple tools; provide structural protection to opaque exterior surfaces to prevent soiling; use dirt-repellant surfaces and materials that age well	■		■			DGNB ST 40
select floor coverings with dust and dirt tolerant designs, fix skirting boards, use entrance mats to prevent dirt and dust being carried into building; easy-to-clean floors without interruptions (radiators, standing lamps, etc.) or recesses; ensure easy access to interior glass surfaces				■	■	DGNB ST 40
avoid using composite materials, which prevent the sorting into mono materials; it must be possible to deconstruct all implemented building materials using processes that are available today	■		■			DGNB ST 42
use of undoable, mechanical connectors to ensure the replacement, strengthening or recyclability of parts without damaging adjoining building components	■	■			■	DGNB ST 42
avoid using difficult-to-recycle insulation materials (EPS, XPS, composite panels, wood-cement particle board, cellulose with borate, etc.), floor coverings (PU, epoxy resin, wood-based tiles, PVC, rubber/natural rubber), windows, pipes, flat roof waterproofing membranes (rubber/natural rubber) and facade cladding materials (cement-bonded particle board)	■	■	■		■	
limit operative temperature in summer and avoid all forms of draughts; avoid asymmetric radiation; maintain recommended level of relative humidity	■	■	■	■	■	DGNB ST 19 BREEAM Hea 03 LEED IEQ 6.1; 6.2
limit operative temperature in winter and avoid all forms of draughts; avoid asymmetric radiation; maintain recommended level of relative humidity	■	■	■	■	■	DGNB ST 18 BREEAM Hea 03
preliminary tests for asbestos, PCB (joint sealants) and PCP (wood preservative) performed by professionals for the deconstruction of buildings; disposal of all polluted materials in technically correct manner		■			■	
avoid use of products with biocides, formaldehydes and chemical wood preservatives indoors; use of respirable fibres only in areas that are sealed off from outside air; ensure a sufficient supply of fresh air to rooms indoors		■	■	■	■	DGNB ST 20 BREEAM Hea 02 LEED IEQ 3.1; 3.2; 4.1; 4.2; 4.3
plan for non-ionising radiation, positioning of all main cables outside the main use areas, introduction of service cables in one position, earthing concept, if necessary relocation of cables			■			
determination of needs and requirements by developing a utilisation concept/needs analysis in cooperation with the client/occupants	■	■	■	■	■	DGNB ST 43 BREEAM Man 01 LEED EA P1
assessment of the appropriateness and meaningfulness of statutory requirements and regulatory leeway, development of alternative concepts			■	■		
definition and balancing of design objectives and quality standards; consideration of environmental aspects		■	■	■		DGNB ST 43 BREEAM Man 01; Man 02
involve professionals for the most important areas of the design; incorporation of management and administrative aspects in the planning process		■	■	■	■	DGNB ST 44; ST 45 LEED EA P1
development, analysis and assessment of alternative solutions in accordance with the depth of detail of the corresponding phase throughout the development of the design (phase-oriented planning)		■	■	■	■	DGNB ST 45 LEED EA 1; EA 4
orderly removal of existing structures (concept with specifications concerning reuse, recycling and disposal); prevent the clearing of trees, alternatively provide measures for replacement (same number)					■	
refrain from heating the building shell to speed up the drying process before completing the insulation of the building envelope						BREEAM Man 03
avoid the production of waste on the construction site and provide for high-quality and non-hazardous recycling of unavoidable waste through training and waste separation			■	■		DGNB ST 48 BREEAM Man 03; Wst 01 LEED MR 2
use building machines and transport vehicles with the highest emission classes; limit the distance for the disposal of excavated material and delivery of concrete as much as possible			■	■		BREEAM Man 03
adherence to noise and vibration ordinances, observation of quiet hours, use of low-noise tools					■	DGNB ST 48
use of machines and other facilities to prevent the formation and removal of dust					■	DGNB ST 48 LEED SS P1
development of a soil protection concept to prevent damage to the ground, either mechanical (reduction of excavated material, on-site soil storage; prevention of soil compaction and disturbance of soil strata) or chemical (by protection policies to avoid soil and groundwater contamination)	■					DGNB ST 48
documentation of the implemented building materials and products, including the provision of all corresponding product data sheets; only use products that are delivered in their original packaging				■	■	DGNB ST 50 LEED EA P1
measurements of TVOC, formaldehyde, CO_2 and possibly also the radon concentration and non-ionising radiation indoors; observe a 30-day airing period before commissioning the building				■	■	DGNB ST 50 BREEAM Man 01; Ene 02
provision of cleaning, servicing, maintenance and repair instructions; development of as-built drawings and calculations; preparation of building owner's manual		■		■	■	DGNB ST 47

DGNB: criterion analogous to DGNB performance profiles, valid as of 2012 BREEAM: criterion analogous to BREEAM New Construction, version 2.0, valid as of 10/2012
LEED: criterion analogous to LEED 2009 New Construction and Major Renovations, valid as of 10/2013

4.27

- Components in the building biological and building ecological assessment
- Floor constructions
- Opaque facades
- Transparent facades
- Roofs
- Load-bearing and non-load-bearing interior walls
- Floor systems – floor coverings, screeds and impact sound insulation

Components in the building biological and building ecological assessment

Most constructional improvements in everyday business life are played out on a building component (functional unit) and assembly (several building components) level. This is simply the area that provides the greatest potential for the optimisation of building biology and building ecology-related aspects. Alterations at this level are usually of little aesthetic interest since functional (and not visible) properties tend to be most relevant for the life cycle assessment of building components.
The limits of an assessment based purely on building biology or purely on building ecology considerations are clearly shown in building component comparisons. Since only a small proportion of building materials contains significant amounts of pollutants, only a small quantity of materials must be examined in terms of the health-related impact. However, it is often the case that building materials suspected of being a biological hazard are excluded from a life cycle assessment because they fall below the selected cut-off criterion (e.g. 1 % of the environmental impacts, see Life cycle impact assessment, p. 32). The most significant materials in terms of pollutant content are surface finishes, joints and connections between individual component layers, whereas the large and voluminous components with the greatest potential for ecological optimisation tend to be irrelevant in terms of their biological impact. The frequently stated contradiction between building biology and building ecology-based optimisation is therefore of no consequence. In fact these two fields of consideration complement one another and only when examined simultaneously provide a comprehensive ecological picture (fig. 5.4, p. 89).
There are very few components for which both building biology and building ecology requirements are substantial at the same time. The typical issues concerning their assessment is best explained by taking a look at waterproofing membranes for flat roofs. Plastic membranes can match bitumen membranes in terms of their technical performance but have much lower environmental impacts. So waterproof sheeting made from PVC is beneficial from a building ecology viewpoint (fig. 5.21, p. 97). The situation concerning building biology is an entirely different matter altogether since the plasticizers contained in the membranes wash out over time and leach into groundwater. Thus, from a holistic ecological point of view, PVC membranes are not recommended. When taking building ecology and building biology considerations into account at the same time, configurations using membranes with a reduced amount of plasticizers (VAE, EVA) are the better solution for standard situations. There are even membranes without any plasticizers on the market (e.g. made from EPDM). However, these have the ecological disadvantage that their environmental impact is almost twice as high as that of EVA membranes.

Flexibility of use	Building characteristics
high	• repetitive, modular structure • skeleton construction consisting of flat slabs and pillars • building depth of approximately 13.50–16.00 m allowing the creation of mixed and three-aisle office layouts • uniform ceiling height of at least 3.50 m • primary grid is a multiple of secondary grid • fit-out grid of approximately 1.15–1.35 m • easily accessible building services lines in central shafts • modular partition wall and facade systems
average	• building depth of 16.00–22.00 m providing the perfect degree of user flexibility at average effort and expense (structural measures: skylights in uppermost storey, optimised space conditions by improving artificial light and ventilation) • load-bearing interior walls can be changed (partial removal and addition of columns in replacement) • fit-out grid of 1.35–1.50 m (not perfect in terms of space-saving layout)
low	• building depth < 11.50 m not allowing any kind of reversible office layouts • building depth > 22.00 m requiring extensive structural measures (light wells, larger windows, skylights in uppermost storey) • load-bearing corridor walls or cross-wall construction • no uniform ceiling height or ceiling heights < 3.00 m • fit-out grid > 1.50 m • load-bearing elements prevent a flexible layout of building services lines • exterior sun shading devices available only for certain rooms/areas

Assessment parameters
structure • ceiling height • building depth and primary grid • structural system • access to building → horizontal and vertical access routes → position/size of fire compartments
building envelope • facade → type/system of facade
spatial fit-out • partition walls → use structure and number of rooms → position and quality of partition walls • floor structure → type/system of floor • ceiling structure → type/system of ceiling
technical fit-out • building services → media technical provisions → quality of lighting → technical installations

5.1

Significance of functional unit

In addition to building biology and building ecology criteria, building comparisons are often subject to overriding requirements, such as fire protection, noise abatement, as well as winter and summer thermal protection. It is therefore important to ensure that the selection and definition of the determined functional unit is performed accurately by taking not only the functional requirements but also the "soft factors" into consideration (see Life cycle assessment of buildings, pp. 27ff.). Among other factors, these include:

- possibilities to perform compensatory measures
- functional connection of building components
- stand-by capacities and additional functional services to increase user flexibility and suitability for conversions

It is particularly important on a component level to take the intersections between the individual components into consideration. Sometimes overriding requirements can be satisfied by other components, rather than the one currently being considered, or even by implementing compensatory measures. The more important the examined component is for the overall performance of the building (e.g. the load-bearing structure) the more can usually be achieved through compensatory measures with regard to other issues. One example in this respect is timber construction: instead of sheathing the load-bearing timber components with gypsum plasterboard, the construction can be left bare and complemented by adding a sprinkler system [1].
The effects on other components must also be taken into consideration when performing a life cycle assessment. A simple example for this issue is the height of the floor construction, which can either increase or decrease the facade surface area (fig. 5.2).
By performing suitable functional links, it is often possible to reduce the environmental impacts of building components. Even though a clear separation of functional layers simplifies the allocation of different building component elements and their corresponding performance in a life cycle assessment, it is not always beneficial for reducing the environmental impacts. For discussions with clients, it has therefore proven successful to state the added value of each component option not illustrated in the life cycle assessment. Greater user flexibility or extra technical capacity, in particular, increase investment costs considerably. The aim is, by weighing the different options, to find a balance between extra costs and possibly long-term advantages during the use phase of the building [2]. Added benefits provided by individual options can only be considered in a comparison of components by extending the life cycle assessment boundary. It makes sense therefore to create an overview of the corresponding links and interdependencies before performing a detailed analysis of individual components. The aim should be to estimate the value and consequences of dependencies and check them by taking alternative component configurations into consideration.

Component description

The following pages provide an overview of possible implementation options for building components that are most relevant from a building biology point of view, such as plasters and paints, wood products and engineered timber, insulation and windows (fig. 5.3, pp. 88ff.). The chapter is then completed with an examination of various building components with regard to the most important assessment parameters. The following components have been examined:

- floor constructions
- opaque facades
- transparent facades
- flat/pitched roofs
- interior walls, load-bearing and non-load-bearing
- floor systems – floor coverings, screed and impact sound insulation

At first, each component is examined according to properties affecting the product's service life. The most frequently occurring functional links, which influence the functional unit, are illustrated in the following. The main emphasis is on the assessment of environmental impacts arising during the life cycle of the component. This aspect is supplemented by an illustration of the most significant potential for biological and ecological improvements.
The life cycle assessments presented were calculated according to the assessment rules for the DGNB/BNB system. They are based on building material data sheets as well as parameters concerning reuse and recycling derived from the German database ökobau.dat and are based on a service life of 50 years. In the case of recycling processes, methods were chosen that are standard practice today for that particular building material. The service lives of the selected building components were also established according to data from the BNB system. The calculations also take into consideration possible replacements of components or layers that become necessary during the service life. The service life of these layers is stated separately.
The configurations of components are not always identical in terms of their technical requirements. The aim was far more to illustrate the potential for selected improvement strategies.
In general, the components can be allocated to one of three different categories:

- components which require operating energy
- components whose environmental impact is determined by high servicing and maintenance costs due to frequent replacement processes
- components which are predominately characterised by their manufacturing energy

The facts and figures presented here are intended only as reference values. They should generally be adjusted to the specific project and, if need be, product data should be obtained from other sources, such as Environmental Product Declarations (EPDs). Comparisons can, of course, always be performed by using freely available tools (fig. 4.2, p. 69). Furthermore, before applying the results to other countries, it should be checked whether the assumptions made for the country in question are also applicable, or which changes might be evoked by certain parameters (e.g. different data sources or service lives).

5.1 Influence of different building features on the flexibility of use and assessment parameters for the evaluation of building flexibility
5.2 Influence of different floor constructions on the building facade

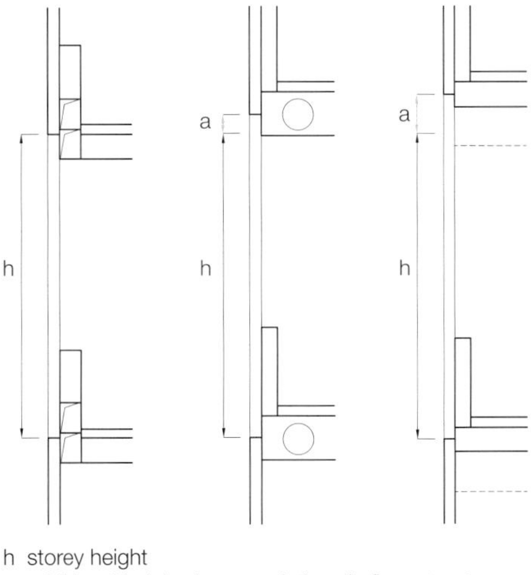

h storey height
a additional height due to variations in floor structure

5.2

Ecologically not recommended materials	Ecologically acceptable building materials	Ecologically good building materials
Insulation materials		
insulation materials (floors)		
XPS board (HCFC foamed)	EPS perimeter panel (HCFC free) foam glass slab (bonded with bitumen adhesive) XPS board (HCFC free)	foam glass granulate foam glass slabs (loosely laid)
insulation materials (inverted roof)		
XPS board (HCFC foamed)	EPS perimeter panel (HCFC free) XPS board (HCFC free)	
insulation materials (flat roof)		
polyurethane board XPS board (HCFC foamed or with metal foil laminate)	EPS panel (EPS W) mineral wool insulation board (MW-WD) XPS board (HCFC free) foam glass slab (bonded with bitumen adhesive)	wood fibreboard cork board foam glass slabs (loosely laid)
insulation materials (over rafters)		
polyurethane board	EPS panel (EPS W) mineral wool insulation board (MW-WD)	wood fibreboard
insulation materials (composite thermal insulation system)		
mineral wool insulation board (MW-PT) if there are no requirements concerning fire protection or diffusibility	EPS panel (EPS F) mineral wool insulation board (MW-PT) if there are requirements concerning fire protection and diffusibility	hemp insulation wood fibreboard cork board mineral foam board
insulation materials (cavity facade)		
	mineral wool insulation board (MW-WF)	flax insulation hemp insulation wood fibreboard sheep's wool insulation cellulose board
insulation materials (between battens and rafters)		
EPS panel (EPS W)	mineral wool insulation board and felt (MW-W)	flax insulation hemp insulation wood fibreboard sheep's wool insulation loose cellulose cellulose board
insulation materials (impact sound insulation below screed)		
mineral wool insulation (MW-T) polyurethane board	EPS panel (EPS T) mineral wool insulation board (MW-T, airtight installation, meeting highest requirements in timber construction)	wood fibreboard cork board
insulation materials (thermal insulation below screed)		
polyurethane board XPS board (HCFC foamed)	EPS panel (EPS W) mineral wool insulation board (MW-T, airtight installation) XPS board (CO_2 foamed)	expanded clay expanded clay pellets cork board foam glass slabs (situations with higher technical requirements)
insulation materials (insulation for heating, ventilation and sanitary equipment)		
mineral wool insulation (so long as there are no requirements concerning fire protection) polyurethane board	mineral wool insulation board (if required for fire protection purposes)	sheep's wool insulation

Ecologically not recommended materials	Ecologically acceptable building materials	Ecologically good building materials
Plasters and paints		
dry liners		
gypsum plasterboard composite	gypsum plasterboard gypsum fibreboard	clay building board timber sheathing
plaster		
synthetic resin plaster synthetic resin plaster (containing solvents)	silicate plaster lime cement plaster gypsum plaster (up to a moisture level W1)	lime cement plaster (open to diffusion) lime plaster clay plaster
facade render		
synthetic resin dispersion render synthetic resin render synthetic resin render (containing solvents)	silicone resin render cement render	silicate render lime cement render cement render in plinth areas (high hydraulic) lime render
render for composite thermal insulation system		
thin-coat synthetic resin plaster	thin-coat silicone resin plaster	thin-coat silicate render thin-coat lime cement plaster thick-layer lime cement plaster
thermal insulation render		
	thermal insulation render with EPS additives thermal insulation render with perlite	thermal insulation render with aerogel
facade paint		
silicone resin paint synthetic resin dispersion paint		dispersion silicate paint silicate paint
finishes for non-mineral surfaces		
solvent-containing coatings acid hardening fixers		water-based, low-VOC coatings oils and waxes from renewable resources (on wood)
interior wall paint		
acrylic and synthetic resin dispersion paint latex paint	latex paint, low emission acrylic and synthetic resin dispersion paint, low emission dispersion silicate paint silicate paint distemper paint lime dispersion paint	natural resin dispersion paint powder distemper casein paint lime paint
interior wall paint with high requirements concerning moisture protection		
wall paint with fungicide additive		silicate dispersion paint silicate paint lime dispersion paint lime paint
Wood and engineered timber products		
wood and engineered timber products (interior fit-out)		
particle board (synthetic resin bonded with high emissions) OSB flat-pressed board (with high emissions) plywood panel	5-ply solid wood panel particle board (cement bonded) particle board (synthetic resin bonded) OSB flat-pressed board high-density fibreboard (dry process)	medium-dense fibreboard (MDF) light wood wool panel 3-ply solid wood panel softwood scaffold panel solid timber (tongue and groove) single-ply solid wood panel
wood and engineered timber products (exterior cladding)		
light wood wool panel (composite with insulation materials) wood fibre panel (cement bonded)	OSB flat-pressed board particle board	high-density fibreboard medium-dense fibreboard, open to diffusion softwood scaffold panel
wood and engineered timber products (furniture)		
plywood panel	medium-dense fibreboard particle board (synthetic resin bonded)	high-density fibreboard (uncoated) 3-ply solid wood panel single-ply solid wood panel

5.3 Ecological assessment of building materials according to their area of use

5.4 Building components, layers and joints that are relevant for a building biology assessment with a focus on indoor pollutants (left) and a building ecology assessment (right)

Ecologically not recommended materials	Ecologically acceptable building materials	Ecologically good building materials
Proofing membranes		
vapour barriers		
aluminium foil bitumen membrane with aluminium lining PVC sheet plastic composite sheets	bitumen membrane polyolefin sheet moisture adaptive vapour barriers	kraft paper moisture diffusing constructions (without vapour barrier)
separating membranes (e.g. in floor structures)		
	polyolefin sheet plastic composite sheets	kraft paper
primers		
bitumen compound with solvent base hot bitumen compound solvent-based primers	bitumen compound with solvent base solvent-free synthetic resin	solvent-free synthetic resin primer with dispersion base
building components with ground contact – horizontal		
bitumen membrane (fully bonded) plastic waterproofing membrane (fully bonded) hot bitumen compound	ECB membrane (mechanically fixed)	PIB membrane (mechanically fixed)
building components with ground contact – vertical		
bitumen compound with solvent base bitumen membrane (fully bonded) plastic waterproofing membrane (halogen free, hot glued) asphalt mastic	bitumen compound with solvent base	sealing slurry water-repellent render
roof membranes		
bitumen membrane (weldable bitumen sheet or laid in hot bitumen) CSM waterproofing membrane (chlorine-sulphurised polyethylene) plastic waterproofing membrane (halogen free, bonded) PVC waterproofing membranes	bitumen membrane (self-adhesive waterproofing membrane) bitumen membrane (mechanically fixed) plastic waterproofing membrane (halogen-free, mechanically fixed)	polyolefin sheet (mechanically fixed) PIB membrane (mechanically fixed)

Ecologically not recommended materials	Ecologically acceptable building materials	Ecologically good building materials
Floor coverings		
floor coverings for damp rooms, entrance areas, etc.		
PVC flooring synthetic resin bonded artificial stone porcelain stoneware tiles, polished epoxy resin flooring (PU/EP)	ceramic tiles, porcelain stoneware tiles	ceramic tiles (abrasion class 4/5 according to ISO 10545) artificial stone flooring terrazzo natural stone flooring rubber floor covering
floor coverings for kindergartens and schools		
laminate flooring PVC flooring epoxy resin flooring (PU/EP)	(natural) rubber floor covering	wood floor, oiled, low emission linoleum floor covering
floor coverings (high wear and tear)		
synthetic stone flooring (synthetic resin bonded) synthetic carpet PVC flooring laminate	linoleum (natural) rubber floor covering porcelain stoneware tiles, polished	artificial stone flooring or terrazzo (with recycled content) ceramic tiles (abrasion class 4/5 according to ISO 10545) parquet flooring (oiled) mosaic parquet (oiled)
floor coverings (low wear and tear)		
polyolefin covering PVC flooring cork floors with PVC coating	synthetic carpet (low-emission) (natural) rubber floor covering cork parquet (fully bonded) ready-to-lay cork parquet	parquet flooring (oiled) mosaic parquet (oiled) multi-layer parquet flooring linoleum floor covering natural fibre carpet (low-emission)
Windows		
windows		
aluminium windows windows with thick, heavy metal-containing coating PVC windows	aluminium windows (if very exposed or high fire protection requirements) wood windows	wood-aluminium windows wood window, made from certified wood wood window (if structural wood protection is provided)

5.3

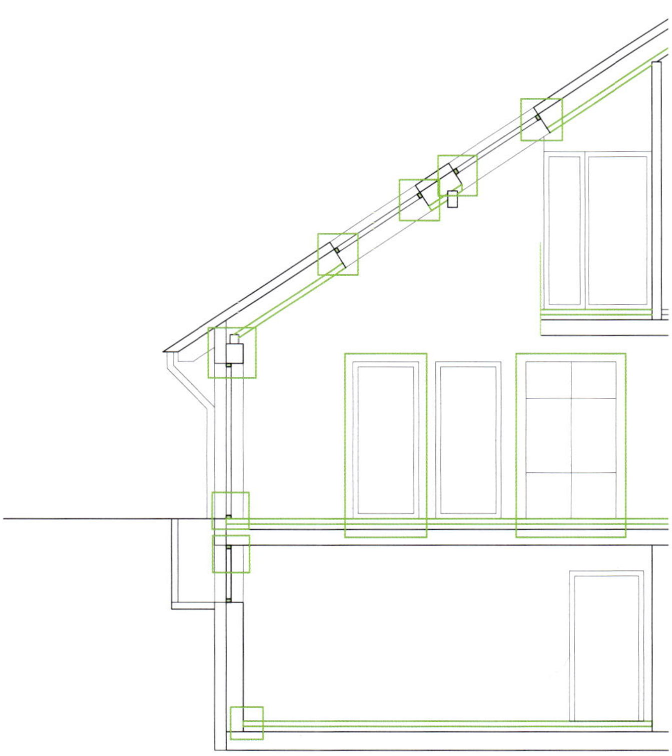

Building biology assessment

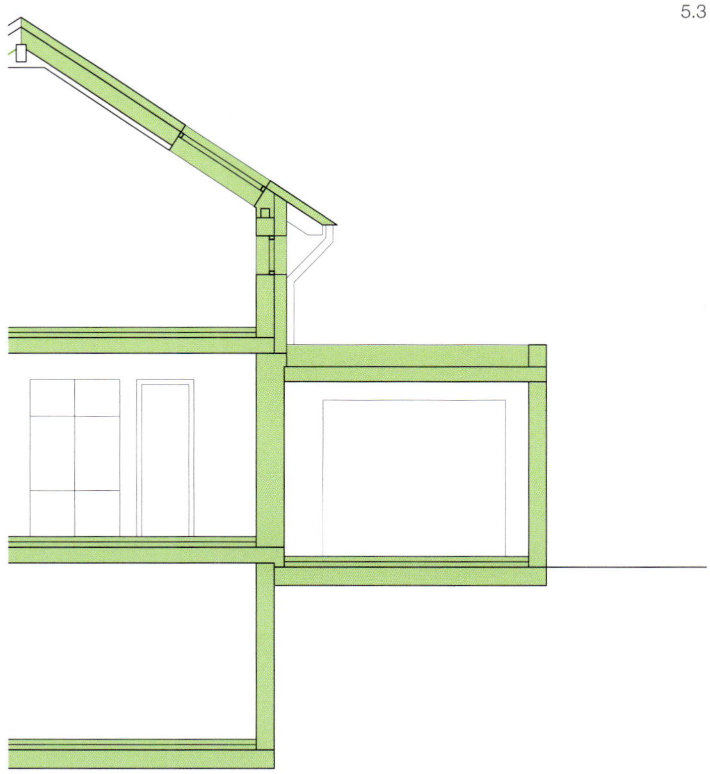

Building ecology assessment

5.4

Floor constructions

Floor structures tend to have a significant influence on the environmental impacts of building constructions. Even though the primary energy input per square metre is only 330–1390 MJ/m² in the case of standard configurations [3], floors are important elements in terms of area and volume (fig. 5.6). In the case of reinforced concrete buildings, the floor elements make up some 45–55 % of the total concrete mass [4]. Their protected position within the building means that they usually have long service lives. Depending on the type of construction, the load-bearing element can last up to 80 years or more. The service life is really only shortened in the case of constructional problems, damage to waterproofing membranes or other forms of destruction [5]. The type of load transfer has a significant influence on the environmental impacts of the load-bearing structure. If possible, the loads should be transferred directly without any major displacements. In terms of flexible use and suitability for conversions, it is beneficial to provide the imposed load and span length with a certain degree of leeway. Too much, however, has a negative impact on the component's life cycle assessment.

Optimisation factors

interaction of load-bearing element and floor construction	++
reduction of span lengths	++
reserve load capacity	-
optimisation of structural height	++
material of the tension zone	+++
reduction of dead load	+
reduction of soundproofing requirements	+
reduction of fire protection requirements	++
in the case of increased fire protection requirements:	+
reduction of gypsum plasterboard thickness	+
reduction of metal use	+
reduction of insulation inlay	

5.5

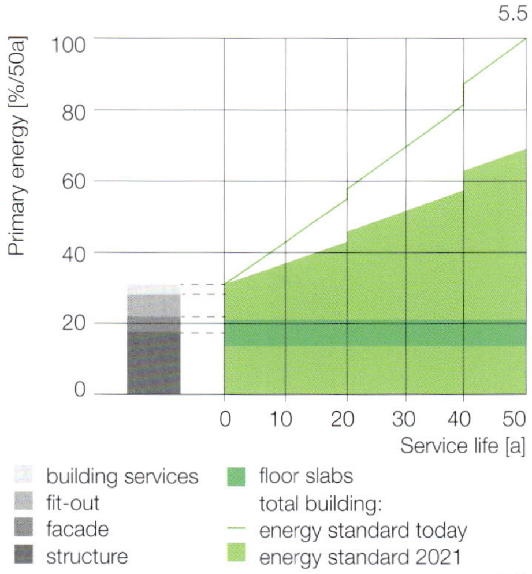

5.6

Alongside their load-bearing function, floor structures must also be designed to meet noise and fire protection requirements. On this account they usually consist of a load-bearing element and surfacing materials. Floor coverings are dealt with separately in this chapter (see pp. 100f.).
Floor structures with exposed ceilings can function as a thermal buffer and help provide a better indoor climate. If they are incorporated in the energy concept accordingly and subjected to night-time ventilation, the mass is able to contribute towards the cooling of the building.

Available load-bearing structures

In addition to the standard flat slab made of reinforced concrete, there are a number of other floor constructions. From an environmental point of view, they can be divided into two categories: constructions made of predominantly mineral substances and timber constructions.
In the case of mineral constructions, the environmental impacts can be reduced by up to 30 % when compared to a standard flat slab. The greatest improvements can be achieved by increasing the structural height (e.g. by using slab-and-beam floor systems) or by implementing resource-saving blast-furnace cement (see Office building in Krems, pp. 125ff.). The savings achieved by reducing the mass of concrete elements tend to be lower. For example, the primary energy input decreases by approximately 10 % when using hollow core slabs. Hollow floors with plastic void formers, such as bubble decks, can reduce the primary energy input by approximately 15–20 % in particular in the case of long spans [6]. A change of material in the tension zone of the floor structure (e.g. timber-concrete composite floor systems on timber beams or profiled steel sheet-concrete composite floors) can also lead to a reduction of the environmental impact; however, these solutions must first be considered according to their fire protection requirements. Traditional concrete constructions can also be improved by prestressing the structural members: prestressed precast concrete slabs reduce the cumulative energy demand by around 13 %; the global warming potential, however, is very similar to that of a standard in-situ concrete floor slab [7].
In the case of precast concrete constructions, the transportation of the elements also plays a fundamental role in the assessment. Depending on the basis of the assessment (global warming potential or primary energy input), prestressed precast concrete floor slabs only fare better than an in-situ concrete floor slab up to a distance of approximately 250–350 km between the concrete plant and the construction site [8].
The environmental impacts of timber constructions are even lower. The primary energy input for load-bearing timber floors can actually fall below zero. The best results can be achieved by solid timber floor structures, but hollow timber and timber-concrete composite floors, which all feature a solid timber panel to provide tensile reinforcement, also produce good results (fig. 5.7). Brettstapel panels are not quite as good due to the large proportion of iron (nails), which requires a large amount of manufacturing energy [9].

Suspended ceilings

From a primary energy point of view, plaster, gypsum plasterboard and gypsum fibreboard are the most beneficial ceiling materials. Engineered timber products with little processing or cement-bonded wood wool panels are also a good solution. Due to the greater quantity of material, suspended ceilings require a higher primary energy input than ceiling finishes that are directly applied or mounted to the underside of the floor slab. The type of substructure also has a significant influence. Timber substructures are most beneficial in this case. The primary energy input is higher when using metal substructures [11], with galvanised steel leading to the best results.
The use of fire protection layers also has a significant impact. Constructions that are able to meet fire protection requirements without an additional layer of mineral wool tend to have lower environmental impacts than those with insulation.
It goes without saying that the ecological benefits of using a load-bearing timber structure are reduced considerably by having to add suspended ceilings for fire protection purposes. In the case of a structurally optimised solid timber-concrete composite floor with an F90 rating, the suspended ceiling has a higher environmental impact than the saving made using timber instead of a standard concrete flat slab (fig. 5.7).

5.5 Ecological optimisation potential of floor slabs and ceiling finishes
5.6 Primary energy input of a typical non-residential building (incl. operating energy) throughout the life cycle and the embodied energy of floor slabs
5.7 Life cycle assessment figures for various floor structures over a 50-year period
5.8 Life cycle assessment figures for various suspended ceiling systems over a 50-year period

Floor constructions [1 m² of floor] production, maintenance and deconstruction observation period: 50 a	**PEI** primary energy non-renewable [MJ]	**PEI** primary energy renewable [MJ]	**GWP** climate gases [kg CO_2 eq.]	**ODP** ozone depletion [kg R11 eq.]	**AP** acidification [kg SO_2 eq.]	**EP** eutrophication [kg PO_4 eq.]	**POCP** summer smog [kg C_2H_4 eq.]
1 reinforced concrete flat slab	501	40	63.7	$1.4 E^{-6}$	0.122	0.0165	0.0114
concrete (20 cm; steel reinforcement 2 %); plaster (0.5 cm)							
2 slab-and-beam floor	359	27	47.6	$1.1 E^{-6}$	0.090	0.0124	0.0064
concrete (12 cm, steel reinforcement 1 %) on 15 % of floor surface area; concrete beams (20 cm, steel reinforcement 5 %)							
3 hollow concrete floor slab	452	33	63.0	$1,5 E^{-6}$	0.118	0.0165	0,0108
concrete (30 cm, steel reinforcement 1.5 %)							
4 hollow block floor	526	56	59.2	$1.3 E^{-6}$	0.113	0.0150	0.0102
concrete (12 cm, steel reinforcement 1 %); concrete beams 15 % (20 cm, steel reinforcement 5 %); vertically perforated brick 85 % (20 cm)							
5 profiled steel sheet-concrete composite floor	451	30	55.0	$1.3 E^{-6}$	0.116	0.0145	0.0120
concrete (16 cm, steel reinforcement 2 %); steel sheet (0.07 cm)							
6 timber beam floor	-158	740	-17.6	$-4.1 E^{-7}$	0.078	0.0139	0.0060
OSB panel (1.9 cm); timber beams (20 cm) on 11 % of surface area, mineral wool infill (20 cm); OSB panel (1.9 cm); gypsum plasterboard (1.25 cm)							
7 hollow box floor	-276	745	-20.4	$-6.6 E^{-7}$	0.071	0.0130	0.0055
OSB panel (2.4 cm); timber beams (18 cm) on 8% of surface area, mineral wool infill (18 cm); OSB panel (1.9 cm)							
8 solid timber floor	-348	1911	-20.9	$-2.3 E^{-6}$	0.209	0.0365	0.0114
glulam (18 cm)							
9 timber-concrete composite floor (concrete on solid timber panel)	-137	1534	15.3	$-1.7 E^{-6}$	0.284	-0.0126	0.0177
concrete (10 cm, stainless steel reinforcement 0.5 %); glulam (14 cm)							
10 timber-concrete composite floor (concrete panel on glulam beams)	378	324	44.1	$6.6 E^{-7}$	0.257	-0.0173	0.0158
concrete (10 cm, stainless steel reinforcement 0.5 %); glulam beams (14 cm) on 20 % of surface area; timber battens (2.4 cm)							
11 reinforced concrete slab with slag cement (approx. 80 %)	371	40	24.4	$1.7 E^{-7}$	0.070	0.0098	0.0060
concrete CEM IIIb (20 cm, steel reinforcement 2 %)							

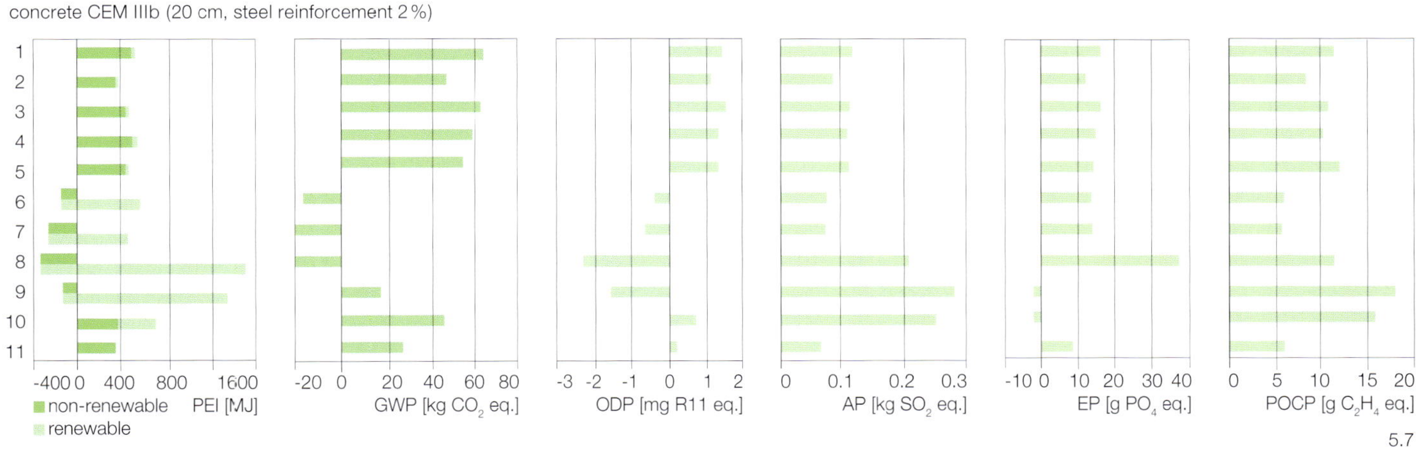

5.7

Ceiling finishes [1 m² of floor] production, maintenance and deconstruction observation period: 50 a	**PEI** primary energy non-renewable [MJ]	**PEI** primary energy renewable [MJ]	**GWP** climate gases [kg CO_2 eq.]	**ODP** ozone depletion [kg R11 eq.]	**AP** acidification [kg SO_2 eq.]	**EP** eutrophication [kg PO_4 eq.]	**POCP** summer smog [kg C_2H_4 eq.]
12 timber substructure F30	48	69	3.6	$-1.2 E^{-7}$	0.011	0.0025	0.0013
2 × gypsum plasterboard, fire protection insulation (1.25 cm); 2 × timber battens (3.6 × 5.6 cm); connectors, galvanised steel							
13 metal substructure F30	72	4	4.8	$4.9 E^{-8}$	0.013	0.0017	0.0017
2 × gypsum plasterboard, fire protection insulation (1.25 cm); metal hat profile (3.6 cm); connectors, galvanised steel							
14 metal substructure F60	134	7	9.0	$8.5 E^{-8}$	0.024	0.0032	0.0031
2 × gypsum plasterboard, fire protection insulation (1.25 cm); 2 × CD 60/27 steel sheet (0.6 mm); connectors, galvanised steel							
15 metal substructure F90	189	10	12.4	$8.8 E^{-8}$	0.030	0.0046	0.0038
gypsum plasterboard, fire protection insulation (2.5 cm); gypsum plasterboard, fire protection insulation (1.8 cm); 2× CD 60/27 steel sheet (0.6 mm); connectors, galvanised steel							

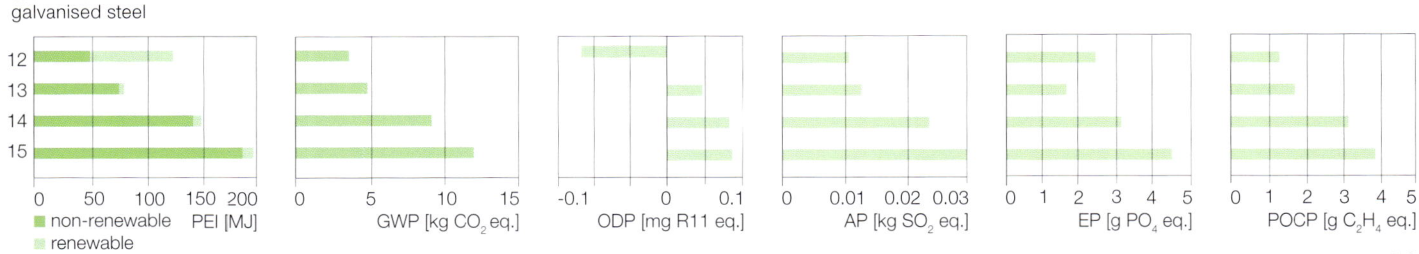

5.8

Opaque facades

The exterior cladding, the layer of insulation, the load-bearing construction and the interior finish are all components of the opaque facade. According to the constructional, economic and creative conditions, the environmental impact of facades can vary by a factor of ten (e.g. exterior cladding: 290–2890 MJ/m²) [11]. The component is subject to weathering, and, in addition, deformation through mechanical stress and strain [12].
The higher and less compact a building is, the greater the significance of the facade within the overall system. Therefore the building's degree of compactness offers potential for substantial savings (see Volume and scale, p. 72). However, in terms of the total building life cycle, the quality of the insulation is fundamental for the environmental impacts of opaque facades (fig. 5.10). Even in the case of high quality insulation and elaborate facade constructions, the heat loss through the component tends to exceed the energy input for the construction by far. The insulation materials, when considered alone, definitely have a positive influence throughout the building life cycle. In the worst case, the primary energy payback time is just below eleven years (foam glass or rockwool with a high density; refurbishments; U-value of the existing structure: 0.6 W/m²K; U-value after the upgrade: 0.1 W/m²K) [13].
Soundproofing and fire protection requirements also have an impact on the life cycle assessment. Since noise protection generally requires the input of mass, for facades the ecological advantages of lightweight constructions tend to be limited. Naturally, the environmental impacts increase further if additional elaborate measures are required, for example, to prevent the vertical spread of fire.

Optimisation factors

A/V and FSI ratio	+
thermal optimisation	+++
weather protection of component	+
fire and noise protection	+
joints and detail design	++
durability	+++
reversible facade constructions	++
insulation material	+
material of the load-bearing structure	+
constructional integration of insulation	++
weight reduction of cladding	+++
safe, non-toxic interior finishes	+++

5.9

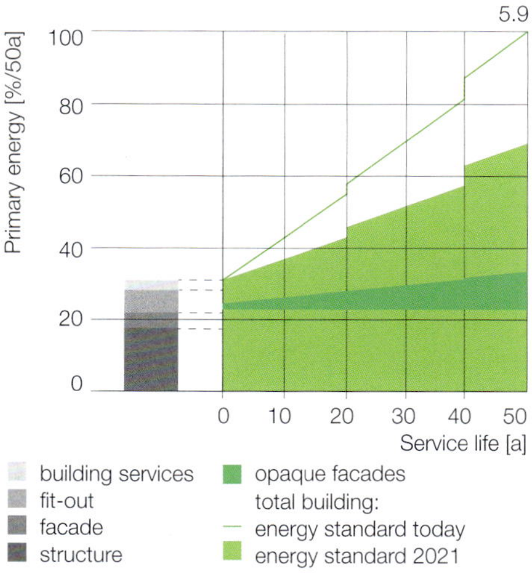

5.10

Load-bearing components

The lowest environmental impacts for the component are generally achieved if timber can be used for the load-bearing structure of the facade (fig. 5.12). The primary energy input of solid timber walls is particularly low, however the results are less favourable for other impact categories. Timber panel constructions perform best in all categories.
In the case of mineral building materials, easily manufactured, heavy and load-bearing materials, such as sand lime brick and concrete, are most beneficial. However, the functional separation of insulation and load-bearing structure in the case of mineral materials does not always lead to ecological benefits. An exterior wall construction with perlite filled perforated bricks, for example, has lower environmental impacts than a standard sand lime brick wall with a composite thermal insulation system. A rendered exterior wall made of aerated concrete blocks is beneficial from an environmental point of view so long as no extra layers of insulation are added.

Constructional integration of insulation

The constructional integration of insulation and weather protection has a significant influence on the durability of facades and thus also on the environmental impacts. In terms of finishes, lime-cement render, (hydraulic) lime render and silicate render fare well, as does cement render in plinth areas [14].
Ventilated cavity facades with light cladding are much more beneficial over a 50-year period than facades with a composite thermal insulation system. The substructure for mounting the exterior skin provides a further opportunity for improvement. Due to their lower environmental impacts, timber substructures should be preferred to metal constructions (fig. 5.11). If a large proportion of metal is required to transfer the load of the exterior skin (e.g. in the case of a rear-ventilated brick face), the load transfer can become a driving force for the environmental impacts of the facade (Abb. 5.12).
There is generally always scope for improvement in the number and design of joint details, e.g. rain gutters, windows and corners. These details tend to use large quantities of material even if this is not always necessary [15].

Insulation

The layer of insulation includes both the insulation material itself and the way it is fixed to the structural component (e.g. adhesive or mechanical fixings). The primary energy input can vary by a factor of ten for materials with identical insulation properties [16]. The requirements for facade insulation materials (e.g. the λ value) are generally fairly low, which means that materials with good life cycle assessment results can be chosen.
Today there is a large range of renewable insulation materials on the market, such as hemp, flax, wool, cork, cellulose and wood fibre insulation boards. Mineral alternatives include mineral foam boards, foam glass (without bitumen coating) and foam glass gravel. Since these insulation materials are extremely durable, the whole facade construction should be designed for a similarly long service life. Mineral wool insulation boards (MW-PT) are a good alternative from an environmental point of view if the facade has to deal with stricter requirements with regard to fire protection and diffusion. Foamed plastics (their environmental impact is very much dependent on the density of the material used), however, should be avoided for environmental reasons. The only exceptions include, for example, EPS or EXP foamed without (partially) halogenated compounds for below ground use, which necessitates a certain degree of pressure resistance [17]. The DGNB/BNB system also recommends using cellular plastic foams manufactured without the use of halogenated compounds. In Switzerland, on the other hand, the Minergie-ECO certificate forbids the use of foamed plastic insulation in buildings.

Interior wall finishes

Low-emission products should be used for wall finishes inside (see Load-bearing and non-load-bearing interior walls, pp. 98f.).

Cladding for exterior wall [1 m² of wall (U-value 0.2 W/m²K)] production, maintenance and deconstruction observation period: 50 a	**PEI** primary energy non-renewable [MJ]	**PEI** primary energy renewable [MJ]	**GWP** climate gases [kg CO_2 eq.]	**ODP** ozone depletion [kg R11 eq.]	**AP** acidification [kg SO_2 eq.]	**EP** eutrophication [kg PO_4 eq.]	**POCP** summer smog [kg C_2H_4 eq.]
1 sand lime brick with CTIS[1]	1056	40	70.7	$1.2\,E^{-6}$	0.165	0.019	0.122
gypsum plaster (1 cm); sand lime brick with thin-bed mortar (15 cm); CTIS incl. dowels and render (16 cm)[1]							
2 sand lime brick with ventilated timber facade[2]	376	734	33.1	$4.4\,E^{-7}$	0.125	0.022	0.009
gypsum plaster (1 cm); sanc lime brick with thin-bed mortar (15 cm); timber studs (18 cm); mineral wool (18 cm); PE sheet; battens (5.4 cm); larch cladding (2.4 cm)[2]							
3 sand lime with fibre cement panels on timber substructure	557	296	44.5	$1.2\,E^{-7}$	0.136	0.019	0.011
gypsum plaster (1 cm); sand lime brick with thin-bed mortar (15 cm); timber studs (18 cm); mineral wool (18 cm); PE sheet; battens (5.4 cm); fibre cement panels (1.2 cm)							
4 sand lime with fibre cement panels on aluminium substructure	606	129	61.6	$2.3\,E^{-6}$	0.115	-0.050	0.016
gypsum plaster (1 cm), sand lime brick with thin-bed mortar (15 cm); aluminium substructure (18 cm); mineral wool (16 cm); PE sheet; fibre cement panels (1.2 cm)							

replacement cycles: [1] CTIS 40 a; [2] timber cladding 30 a (all other materials: 50 a)

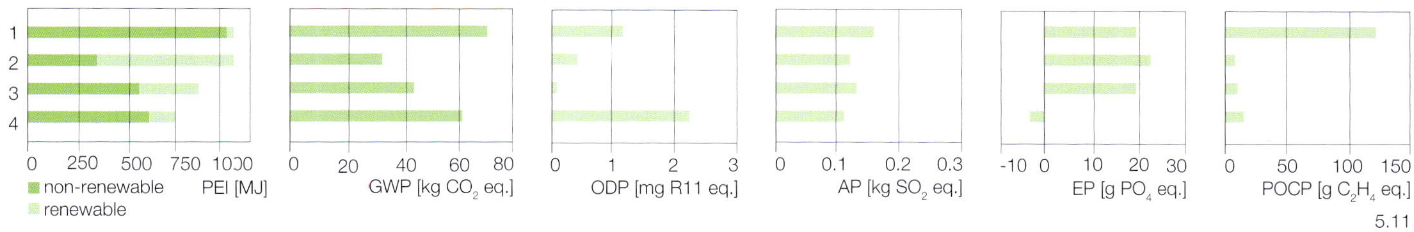

5.11

Opaque exterior wall [1 m² of wall (U-value 0.2 W/m²K)] production, maintenance and deconstruction observation period: 50 a	**PEI** non-renew. [MJ]	**PEI** renew. [MJ]	**GWP** [kg CO_2 eq.]	**ODP** [kg R11 eq.]	**AP** [kg SO_2 eq.]	**EP** [kg PO_4 eq.]	**POCP** [kg C_2H_4 eq.]
5 cavity wall with solid timber and wood fibreboard (37.1 cm)[1]	-525	3141	-34.7	$-4.6\,E^{-6}$	0.204	0.0333	0.0160
structural solid timber (18 cm); wood fibreboard (14 cm); protective membrane (0.03 cm); timber battens (2.4 cm); timber cladding (2.4 cm) [1]							
6 reinforced concrete wall with CTIS (36 cm)[2]	1286	55	100.1	$2.6\,E^{-6}$	0.261	0.0294	0.1313
gypsum plaster (1 cm); reinforced concrete wall (20 cm, with 2 % reinforcement); CTIS incl. dowels and render (16 cm)[2]							
7 sand lime brick with CTIS (31 cm)[2]	1056	40	70.7	$1.2\,E^{-6}$	0.165	0.0190	0.1222
gypsum plaster (1 cm); sand lime brick (15 cm, with thin-bed mortar); CTIS incl. dowels and render (16 cm)[2]							
8 vertically perforated brick with perlite infill (52 cm)[3]	872	173	67.0	$6.2\,E^{-7}$	0.115	0.0177	0.0111
gypsum plaster (1 cm); vertically perforated brick (47 cm, with thin-bed mortar); standard render (1.5 cm)[3]							
9 vertically perforated brick with mineral wool and cavity	1281	91	81.6	$5.0\,E^{-7}$	0.209	0.0276	0.0061
gypsum plaster (1 cm); vertically perforated brick (24 cm, with thin-bed mortar); mineral wool (16 cm); facing brick (SF) with metal wall ties and studs (11.5 cm)							
10 timber wall panel with mineral wool, rendered (30 cm)[3]	343	475	0.0	$5.8\,E^{-7}$	0.103	0.0171	0.0071
gypsum plasterboard (1.25 cm); OSB panel (1.9 cm); timber studs with mineral wool (18 cm); lathing board (1.9 cm); standard render (1.5 cm)[3]							
11 timber I section wall, mineral wool, rendered (29 cm)[3]	465	477	-0.6	$9.3\,E^{-7}$	0.114	0.0186	0.0089
gypsum plasterboard (1.25 cm); OSB panel (1.9 cm); timber I section with mineral wool (17 cm); lathing board (1.9 cm); standard render (1.5 cm)[3]							
12 timber panel wall with cellulose, rendered (30 cm)[3]	328	742	10.0	$3.6\,E^{-7}$	0.145	0.0512	0.0132
gypsum plasterboard (1.25 cm); OSB panel (1.9 cm); timber studs with cellulose (18 cm); lathing board (2 cm); standard render (1.5 cm)[3]							
13 steel sandwich panel mit mineral wool (U-value 0.3 W/m²K)	586	27	40.2	$1.6\,E^{-6}$	0.182	0.0185	0.0150
steel sandwich panel (14 cm); mineral wool (18 cm); hat profile (0.1 cm); corrugated sheet metal (0.02 cm)							
14 additional data: post in interior [per m]	224	18	28.5	$6.4\,E^{-7}$	0.55	0.0074	0.0051
concrete C35/42 (30 × 30 cm, 2 % steel)							

replacement cycles: [1] timber cladding 30 a; [2] CTIS 40 a; [3] render 45 a (all other materials: 50 a)

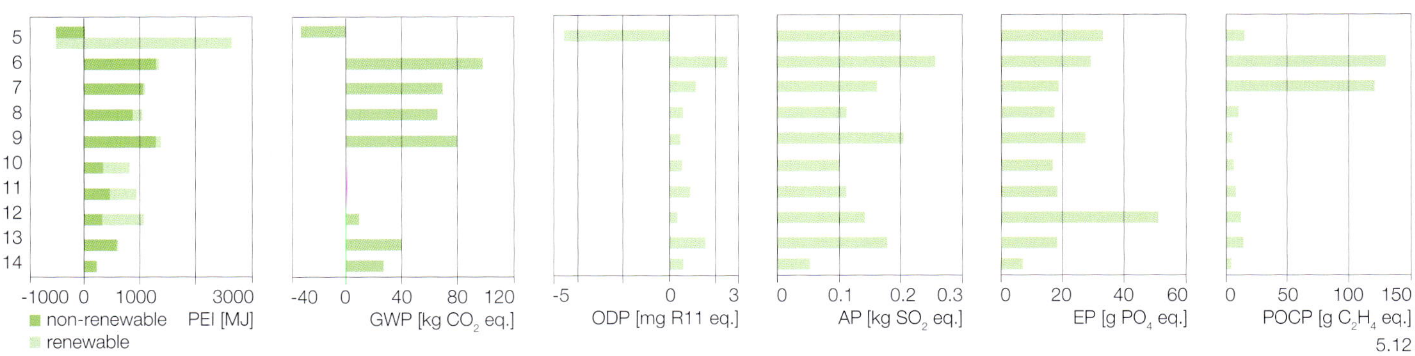

5.12

5.9 Ecological optimisation potential of opaque facade constructions

5.10 Primary energy consumption of a typical non-residential building (including operating energy) and embodied energy for opaque facades

5.11 Life cycle assessment figures for opaque facades made of sand lime brick (U-value 0.2 W/m²K) with different solutions concerning the insulation

5.12 Life cycle assessment figures for opaque facades (U value 0.2 W/m²K – exception steel panels: U value 0.3 W/m²K) including additional data for interior posts and framed glazing

Transparent facades

Transparent facades, consisting of glazing units and frames, are the components which, in terms of surface area, require the highest primary energy input (fig. 3.23, p. 50) [18]. Their use should therefore ideally be determined according to operational energy aspects, such as an improved supply of daylight or the utilisation of solar heat.
Since the transmission heat loss of a window can exceed the primary energy input within only a few years, the thermal quality of windows should be particularly good. The extra costs involved in insulating the frames is nominal from an environmental viewpoint (fig. 5.17). Because insulated frames also help reduce the formation of condensation on the inner faces, their use is presumably also responsible for longer service lives of windows.

Glazing unit

The material of transparent components tends to have only a minor impact on the life cycle assessment of buildings. The production of an insulated double glazed unit (432.7 MJ/m²) requires a similar

Optimisation factors

optimisation in terms of operating energy, in particular:	+++
thermal protection (U-value)	+++
solar heat gain (g-value)	++
use of daylight (τ-value)	++
reduction of soundproofing requirements	+
proportion and material of frame	+++
service life	++
weather protection (for wooden frames)	++
proportion of opening sashes	++
safe, non-toxic coating of frame	++
thermal optimisation	++
optimisation of deconstruction processes	+

5.14

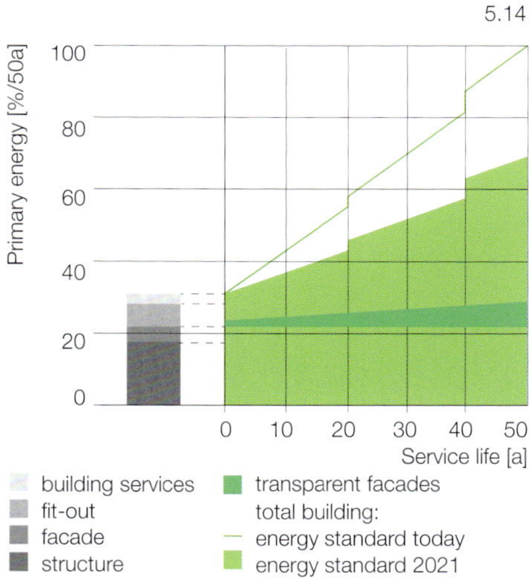

5.15

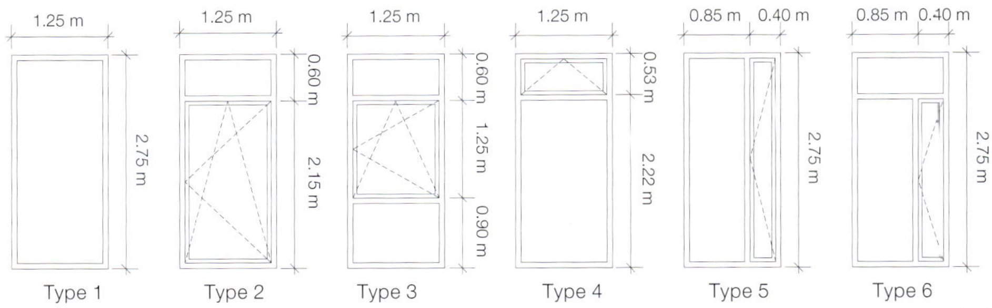

5.13

amount of primary energy as a twin-wall polycarbonate panel (32 mm, 3.9 kg/m²: 472.3 MJ/m²) [19]. A greater glass weight, which is, for example, needed to produce large-format windows, or a larger number of panes, however, have a significant influence on the environmental impacts. Additional tempering or the use of plastic films inside double or triple glazed units have a similar effect. This is, for example, the case for sound-insulating glass or railings made of safety glass. To date, there is no proven data for these particular issues; nevertheless, it is a fact that all of these aspects have a significant influence on the environmental impacts of the glazing unit.

Window frame materials

Since self-bearing glass constructions are rare, the frame or substructure of the glazing unit is of major importance. The frame materials tend to have a greater influence on the life cycle assessment than the glass itself. Most frames are currently made of wood, wood-aluminium composite constructions, aluminium or plastics (usually PVC). Frames made of polypropylene, polyethylene or polyurethane are also available on the market.
In comparison, natural timber frames fare particularly well (fig. 5.16) [20]. Even an increase of recycling from approximately 35 to 85 % in the case of aluminium, and 2 to 70 % in the case of PVC, has no effect on the environmental advantage of wooden-framed windows [21]. However, the gap between frame constructions made of wood and wood-aluminium is starting to close. In particular in the case of thermally-efficient frames, the difference between the environmental impacts of wood and wood-aluminium composite frames is only very slight (fig. 5.17).
Since environmental impacts tend to affect the service life of windows, the durability of the frame material is particularly significant in the case of wooden frames. Woods with a low resistance (e.g. spruce, pine, Douglas fir and larch) have service lives of only 40 years; woods with a higher resistance (e.g. oak and robinia), on the other hand, reach life spans of up to 60 years [22]. Since chemical treatment is not required in the case of these timbers, durable, hard-wearing wood should be used for timber-frame windows. Regular maintenance is an important aspect with regard to the service life of wood-frame windows.
The frames and their coatings are to a large part responsible for the emissions of windows to indoor air. It is for this reason that, in particular on the inside, careful attention should be paid to the use of biocide-free coatings with a low solvent and VOC concentration (e.g. RAL-UZ 12 a) [23].

Glass facades

In the case of fully glazed facades, systems using a timber load-bearing structure achieve the best results. The environmental impacts of modular glazing systems with a steel substructure are lower than systems with an aluminium substructure. According to the design of the facade, the environmental impacts of office facades can vary by almost 100 % (fig. 5.13, 5.18). The proportion of frame is particularly relevant in this respect: the less the better – especially in the case of opening sashes. A reduction in the number and size of openings naturally also decreases the need for primary energy-intensive window seals.

5.13 Different window design options for an office building facade. The calculations in figure 5.18 are based on these window configurations.
5.14 Ecological optimisation potentials of transparent facades
5.15 Primary energy consumption of a typical non-residential building (including operating energy) throughout the life cycle and the embodied energy of transparent facades
5.16 Life cycle assessment figures for a window (format 1.25 × 1.4 m) according to the frame material
5.17 Life cycle assessment figures for a window (format 1.25 × 1.4 m) according to the thermal properties of the frame
5.18 Life cycle assessment figures for a modular glazing system measuring 1,25 × 2,75 m in accordance with the facade arrangement

Windows with different frame materials [1.25 m × 1.4 m] production, maintenance and deconstruction observation period: 50 a	**PEI** primary energy non-renewable [MJ]	**PEI** primary energy renewable [MJ]	**GWP** climate gases [kg CO_2 eq.]	**ODP** ozone depletion [kg R11 eq.]	**AP** acidification [kg SO_2 eq.]	**EP** eutrophication [kg PO_4 eq.]	**POCP** summer smog [kg C_2H_4 eq.]
1 aluminium frame with double glazing	2885	310	209.1	$2.1\ E^{-6}$	1.04	-0.28	0.079
insulated double glazing; aluminium frame, thermally isolated (U_w-value: 1.4 W/m²K; g-value: 0.6); window seals; tilt-and-turn hardware; handle							
2 wooden frame with double glazing[1)]	1882	1166	40.0	$4.0\ E^{-8}$	0.28	0.06	0.133
insulated double glazing; hard wood frame (U_w-value: 1.3 W/m²K; g-value: 0.6)[1)]; window seals; tilt-and-turn hardware; handle; coating							
3 PVC frame with double glazing[2)]	3678	61	360.8	$1.7\ E^{-6}$	1.00	0.11	0.127
insulated double glazing; PVC frame (U_w-value: 1.3 W/m²K; g-value: 0.6)[2)]; window seals; tilt-and-turn hardware; handle							
4 wood-aluminium composite frame; double glazing	2009	1212	57.5	$-1.5\ E^{-6}$	0.33	0.06	0.125
insulated double glazing; wood-aluminium composite frame (U_w-value: 1.3 W/m²K; g-value: 0.6); window seals; tilt-and-turn hardware; handle							

replacement cycles: [1)] frame coating 8 a; [2)] frame 40 a (all other materials: 50 a)

5.16

Windows with different thermal properties [1.25 m × 1.4 m] production, maintenance and deconstruction observation period: 50 a	**PEI** nicht ern. [MJ]	**PEI** erneuerbar [MJ]	**GWP** [kg CO_2 eq]	**ODP** [kg R11 eq]	**AP** [kg SO_2 eq]	**EP** [kg PO_4 eq]	**POCP** [kg C_2H_4 eq]
4 wood-aluminium composite frame with double glazing	2009	1212	57.5	$-1.5\ E^{-6}$	0.33	0.06	0.125
insulated double glazing; wood-aluminium composite frame (U_w-value: 1.3 W/m²K; g-value: 0.6); window seals; tilt-and-turn hardware; handle; coating							
5 wood-aluminium composite frame with triple glazing	2440	1232	76.0	$-1.0\ E^{-6}$	0.46	0.08	0.135
insulated triple glazing; wood-aluminium composite frame (U_w-value: 0.95 W/m²K; g-value: 0.5); window seals; tilt-and-turn hardware; handle; coating							
6 wood-aluminium composite frame, insulated; triple glazing	2469	1223	78.1	$-1.2\ E^{-6}$	0.47	0.08	0.136
insulated triple glazing; wood-aluminium composite frame, EPS frame insulation (U_w = 0.8 W/m²K; g-value: 0.5); window seals; tilt-and-turn hardware; handle							

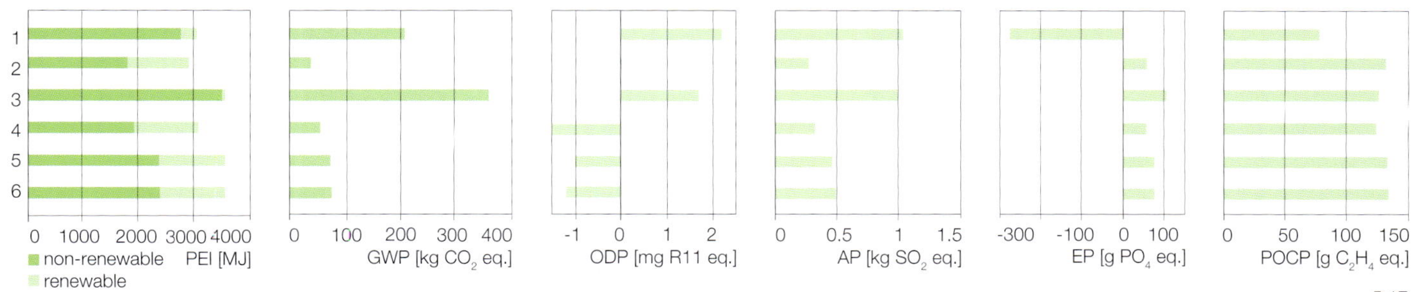

5.17

Windows with different designs [1.25 m × 2.75 m] (compare fig. 5.13) production, maintenance and deconstruction observation period: 50 a	**PEI** non-renew. [MJ]	**PEI** renew. [MJ]	**GWP** [kg CO_2 eq.]	**ODP** [kg R11 eq.]	**AP** [kg SO_2 eq.]	**EP** [kg PO_4 eq.]	**POCP** [kg C_2H_4 eq.]
Type 1 – wood-aluminium composite frame	2139	900	93.8	$-7.8\ E^{-7}$	0.63	0.099	0.11
insulated double glazing; wood-aluminium composite frame (U_w-value: 1.3 W/m²K; g-value: 0.6)							
Type 2 – wood-aluminium composite frame	3193	1784	100.0	$-7.8\ E^{-8}$	0.61	0.100	0.19
insulated double glazing; wood-aluminium composite frame (U_w-value: 1.3 W/m²K; g-value: 0.6); window seals; tilt-and-turn hardware; handle							
Type 3 – wood-aluminium composite frame	3034	1710	93.4	$-5.1\ E^{-7}$	0.65	0.102	0.18
insulated double glazing; wood-aluminium composite frame (U_w-value: 1.3 W/m²K; g-value: 0.6); window seals; tilt-and-turn hardware; handle							
Type 4 – wood-aluminium composite frame	2736	1390	97.8	$-5.3\ E^{-7}$	0.67	0.102	0.15
insulated double glazing; wood-aluminium composite frame (U_w-value: 1.3 W/m²K; g-value: 0.6): window seals; tilt hardware; handle							
Type 5 – wood-aluminium composite frame	3208	1884	92.1	$-6.3\ E^{-7}$	0.63	0.103	0.20
insulated double glazing; wood-aluminium composite frame (U_w-value: 1.3 W/m²K; g-value: 0.6); window seals; turn hardware; handle							
Type 6 – wood-aluminium composite frame	3129	1860	90.2	$-5.8\ E^{-7}$	0.66	0.102	0.19
insulated double glazing; wood-aluminium composite frame (U_w-value: 1.3 W/m²K; g-value: 0.6); window seals; turn hardware; handle							

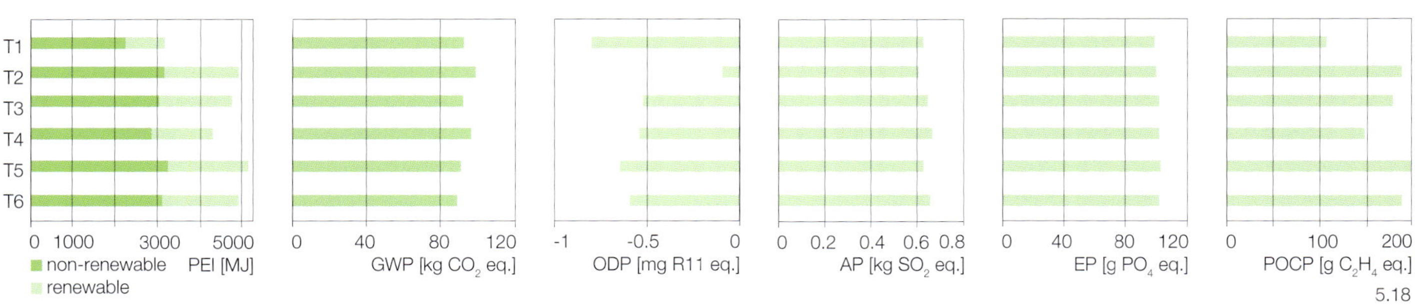

5.18

Roofs

Roofs consist of the roof covering (roof tiles or waterproofing membrane), the insulation and the necessary substructure. Since roofs are part of the building envelope, they are roughly as energy intensive as facades; as a rule their primary energy input (PEI) is approximately 10% higher than that of facades (580–3460 MJ/m²) [24].
The aspects that place the greatest burden on the component are protection against weather and moisture [25]. Deformation caused by temperature changes is a further relevant issue in the case of flat roofs. Due to the requirements of weather protection, the roof covering is subject to shorter replacement cycles than the rest of the roof construction (fig. 5.21). Flat roof waterproofing membranes are particularly susceptible to faulty design and installation issues, which are often difficult to find after completion. Consequently, when damage does occur, large areas are generally affected. Component layers which are easy to repair and replace therefore contribute towards a lower environmental impact of flat roofs (fig. 5.19). The soft factor "roof shape" has a significant impact on the expense and effort required for the construction of roof details. The shapes and connection details of roofs with simple geometries are less expensive and elaborate [26]. Close attention must always be paid to thermal bridges at roof outlets, ventilation pipes, flat roof drains and any other form of intersection.

Optimisation factors

simple roof design	++
thermal optimisation	+++
weather protection	++
insulation material	++
waterproofing membrane material	++
reduction of penetrations	++
maintenance and repair work of roof covering without causing damage to insulation	++
adjustment of replacement cycles between insulation and waterproofing membrane	+

5.19

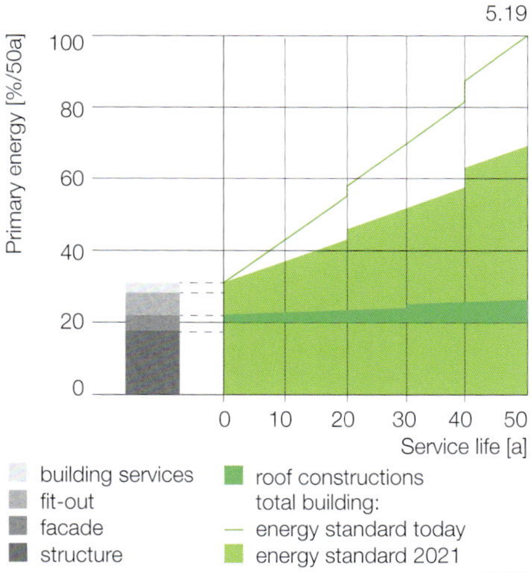

5.20

Types of construction

The requirements of the insulation material are very low in the case of pitched roofs. In fact, the considerations that apply to the roof insulation are similar to those for facades (see pp. 88f. and pp. 92f.).
Alongside the insulation, the roof covering has the most significant influence on the environmental impacts of pitched roofs. Timber, slate and fibre cement panels are the most recommended materials in terms of environmental issues. Metal sheet is also a good alternative provided the long service life is actually made use of. However, rainwater eventually causes the metal to wash out and leach into the environment. This is why roof runoff should pass through a heavy metal filter [27].
Flat roofs can be completed as cold, warm or inverted constructions. Cold roofs, in particular those made of timber, feature the lowest environmental impacts. They require only a third, or up to a half, of the non-renewable primary energy of warm roofs [28]. However, cold roofs can only be used in very particular situations. Inverted and warm roofs are therefore the most commonly used constructions. Because with inverted roofs the insulation is not protected by the waterproofing membrane, an adjustment factor of 0.05 W/m²K has to be considered when calculating the U-value according to DIN 4108. Thus, in order to achieve the same U-value as a warm roof, the component requires a greater amount of insulation and, as a result, approximately 15% more primary energy. If, as is standard practice today, a light, water-repellent membrane made of PE fibre is inserted above the insulation in the inverted roof, the adjustment factor is reduced to approximately 0.03 W/m²K. The adjustment factor can be omitted by adding an impermeable waterproofing membrane. Consequently the primary energy input of the inverted roof is only approximately 1% higher than that of a warm roof, but it offers better conditions for maintenance and repair (fig. 5.22).

Insulation

The main contributor to the environmental impacts of roofs is the insulation. From an environmental viewpoint, wood fibre panels and cork insulation boards are most suited to warm roofs. However, the more standard EPS and mineral wool insulation is almost just as good. In the case of inverted roofs, foamed glass or extruded polystyrene (XPS) boards are most suitable due to their water resistance [29]; their environmental impact is only marginally higher. Bitumen-coated cellular glass boards are not nearly as good. CFC-foamed XPS has a negative effect on the global warming potential. CO_2-foamed XPS boards are a better alternative in this respect.

Waterproofing

In order to reduce the primary energy input of waterproofing membranes, the bitumen content should be minimised. Bituminous waterproofing membranes, sometimes with a metal inlay, require almost as much primary energy for their production as a reinforced concrete floor slab [30]. Metal reinforced and polymer modified bituminous waterproofing membranes have extremely high environmental impacts. EVA, PVC and EPDM membranes achieve the same results at a much lower primary energy input. The reduced material thickness is particularly beneficial in these materials. The quantity of plasticizers is a further criterion when it comes to choosing waterproofing membranes: even in the case of membranes with a low leaching potential, large amounts of plasticizers are released into the environment [31]. PVC has the largest proportion of plasticizers, whereas EPDM and polyolefin are free of plasticizers. EVA and VAE both contain small amounts of plasticizers.

Fixtures

Flat roofs can be fitted by using adhesives, mechanical fixtures or adding weight. The type of fixture has only a minor impact on the primary energy input of roofs; values around 0.5–5 MJ/m² are typical in this context [32]. Styrene butadiene glue should be used when fixing EPDM membranes as the amount of emissions is lower than is the case for PUR adhesives [33]. Mechanical fixtures and a layer of gravel are the worst solution from a primary energy input point of view. However, they offer clear advantages when it comes to maintenance and deconstruction.

5.19 Ecological optimisation potentials of roofs
5.20 Primary energy consumption of a typical non-residential building (including operating energy) and embodied energy of the roof construction
5.21 Life cycle assessment figures for roofs and various roof coverings over a 50-year period
5.22 Life cycle assessment figures for various flat roof configurations over a 50-year period

Roof coverings and waterproofing membranes [1 m² of roof] production, maintenance and deconstruction observation period: 50 a **a) flat roofs:**	**PEI** primary energy non-renewable [MJ]	**PEI** primary energy renewable [MJ]	**GWP** climate gases [kg CO_2 eq.]	**ODP** ozone depletion [kg R11 eq.]	**AP** acidification [kg SO_2 eq.]	**EP** eutrophication [kg PO_4 eq.]	**POCP** summer smog [kg C_2H_4 eq.]
1 bitumen waterproofing membrane	1047	269	-0.6	1.1 E^{-6}	0.077	0.009	0.0145
gravel (5 cm); bitumen cap sheet (0.5 cm); bitumen base sheet (0.4 cm); OSB board (1.9 cm)							
2 EVA membrane	256	265	-14.5	4.9 E^{-7}	0.027	0.004	0.0037
gravel (5 cm); EVA sheet (0.15 cm); polyester fleece (0.5 cm); OSB board (1.9 cm)							
3 PVC membrane	301	270	5.5	6.4 E^{-7}	0.096	0.009	0.0080
gravel (5 cm); PVC sheet (0.18 cm); polyester fleece (0.5 cm); OSB board (1.9 cm)							
4 EPDM membrane	482	269	-6.2	5.0 E^{-7}	0.039	0.018	0.0088
gravel (5 cm); EPDM membrane (0.114 cm); polyester fleece (0.5 cm); OSB board (1.9 cm)							
5 in addition: extensive green roof system	707	21	22.3	1.2 E^{-7}	0.066	0.005	0.0273
soil (8 cm); filter fabric PE-HD (0.1 cm); expanded clay aggregate filter (3 cm); XPS drainage panel (3 cm); root barrier, polyester fleece (1.5 cm)							
b) low and high-pitched roofs:							
6 pantile roof tiles	210	118	19.0	-7.5 E^{-6}	0.041	-0.007	0.0059
ceramic pantile roof tiles with 2.5% aluminium snowguard; battens and counterbattens (2 × 5.4 cm); roofing membrane; screws							
7 concrete roof tiles	246	105	-0.1	7.8 E^{-7}	0.038	0.004	0.0037
concrete roof tiles incl. 2.5% customised cast aluminium components (2.5 cm); battens and counterbattens (2 × 5.4 cm); roofing membrane; screws							
8 titanium zinc sheet	150	310	-13.4	4.1 E^{-1}	0.018	0.004	0.0032
double lock standing seam titanium zinc sheet (0.07 cm); stainless steel fixtures; PP fleece (0.8 cm); OSB board (1.9 cm); battens (5.4 cm); screws							
9 copper sheet	-115	313	-16.0	4.1 E^{-1}	0.004	0.003	0.0024
standing seam copper sheet (0.07 cm); stainless steel fixtures; PP fleece (0.8 cm); OSB board (1.9 cm); battens (5.4 cm); screws							
10 fibre cement panels	47	170	16.6	8.2 E^{-7}	0.051	0.005	0.0051
fibre cement panels (0.8 cm); battens and counterbattens (2 x 5.4 cm); nails; PE roofing membrane							
11 slate roof shingles	90	152	13.6	2.1 E^{-7}	0.109	0.016	0.0118
slate roof shingles (0.8 cm); battens and counterbattens (2 × 5.4 cm); nails; PE roofing membrane							
12 wooden roof shingles	-145	412	-8.0	-6.4 E^{-7}	0.018	0.003	0.0065
wooden shingles (2.1 cm); battens and counterbattens (3.6 × 5.4 cm); nails; PE roofing membrane							

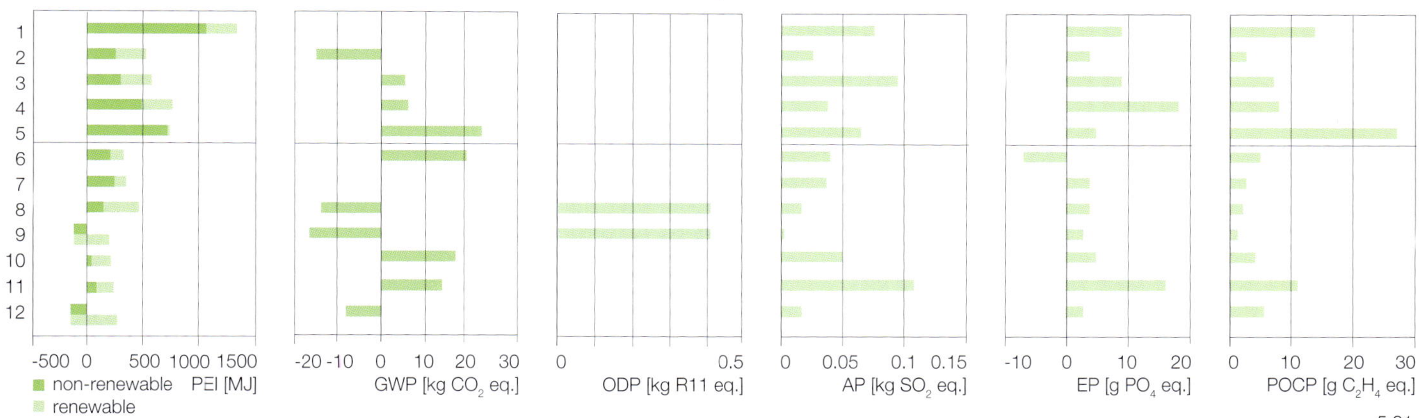

5.21

Flat roof configurations [1 m² of flat roof (U = 0.20 W/m²K)] production, maintenance and deconstruction observation period: 50 a	**PEI** non-renew. [MJ]	**PEI** renew. [MJ]	**GWP** [kg CO_2 eq.]	**ODP** [kg R11 eq.]	**AP** [kg SO_2 eq.]	**EP** [kg PO_4 eq.]	**POCP** [kg C_2H_4 eq.]
13 warm roof	1336	47	91.4	2.0 E^{-6}	0.177	0.034	0.1258
gravel (5 cm); EPDM membrane, polyester fleece (0.12 cm); EPS insulation (16.5 cm); reinforced concrete slab (20 cm with 2% reinforcement)							
14 traditional inverted roof (ΔU = 0.05 W/m²K)	1539	48	98.2	2.2 E^{-6}	0.192	0.035	0.1642
gravel (5 cm); EPS insulation (22 cm); EPDM membrane, polyester fleece (0.12 cm); reinforced concrete slab (20 cm with 2% reinforcement)							
15 inverted roof with separating membrane (ΔU = 0.03 W/m²K)	1463	48	95.5	2.1 E^{-6}	0.186	0.034	0.1469
gravel (5 cm); foil sheet, EPS insulation (19.5 cm); EPDM membrane, polyester fleece (0.12 cm); reinforced concrete slab (20 cm with 2% reinforcement)							
16 inverted roof with waterproofing (ΔU = 0 W/m²K)	1353	48	91.8	2.0 E^{-6}	0.178	0.034	0.1259
gravel (5 cm); bonded sheet, EPS insulation (16.5 cm); EPDM membrane, polyester fleece (0.12 cm); reinforced concrete slab (20 cm with 2% reinforcement)							

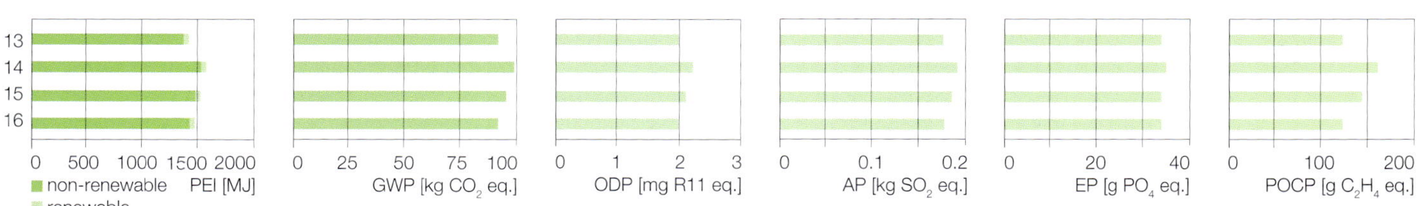

5.22

Load-bearing and non-load-bearing interior walls

A life cycle assessment of interior walls includes the structure and the surface finishes. In general, interior walls contribute only marginally to the environmental impacts of buildings (fig. 5.24).
The bearing structure of interior walls is primarily affected by moisture and temperature changes as well as deformation in the building. The surfaces, on the other hand, are subject to mechanical forces and occasionally also UV radiation [34]. Solid partition walls, in particular, make an important contribution to summer thermal protection. Furthermore, the coatings of interior wall surfaces can impair the indoor air quality significantly (fig. 5.23). The soundproofing requirements of partition walls have a considerable impact on the life cycle assessment; possibly even more so than the load-bearing capacity of the interior wall. According to DIN 4109, the sound insulation of a wall is dependent mainly on the mass of the component. It goes without saying that interior walls are themselves a load on the load-bearing structure. In comparison to solid partition walls, lightweight construction reduces the material consumption and the primary energy input of the primary structure by approximately 7–12 % [35]. A further important aspect is flexibility of use, which a light fit-out is more likely to ensure than solid construction.

Wall construction
Depending on the soundproofing requirements, the primary energy input of non-load-bearing light walls is generally approximately 15–35 % lower than that of non-load-bearing solid walls. Light partition walls also fare better than solid walls if they have to be supplemented by load-bearing columns (fig. 5.12, p. 93). Mixed construction methods with light panelling only on one side combine the advantages of both systems (fig. 5.24).

Lightweight construction
Lightweight constructions, using either timber or metal stud frames, contain less embodied energy than solid walls. They can also be replaced more easily and can better accommodate technical installations. The total primary energy input tends to be lower in the case of metal stud frames; timber stud frames, on the other hand, contain less non-renewable primary energy [36]. When optimising stud partition walls, the effort and expense involved in multi-layered gypsum plasterboard is usually higher than that of a thicker wall construction (fig. 5.8, p. 91). A further potential for saving resources lies in the choice of insulation. Natural insulation materials, in particular, such as cork or wood fibre panels, have a positive influence on the environmental impacts of interior walls [37].
In the case of interior walls made with timber stud frames, the sheathing on both sides must be decoupled from the structure to avoid noise transmission. This is best achieved by, for example, adding counterbattens to the vertical studs. This only has a negligible effect on the environmental impact.

Solid walls and mixed construction methods
The primary energy consumption of solid wall constructions is determined mainly by the load-bearing material. Concrete and sand lime brick have a low environmental impact, whereas aerated concrete and masonry brick have a higher primary energy input. Particularly in the case of high soundproofing requirements, mixed and composite constructions, combining solid and lightweight construction methods, are suited to reduce the environmental impact of the construction (fig. 5.25). From a life cycle assessment point of view, it is therefore beneficial to use the walls with higher soundproofing requirements as load-bearing interior walls (e.g. walls between dwelling units, corridor walls in the case of a cellular office layouts).

Wall sheathing
The primary energy input of traditional wall sheathing materials varies less than that of other components. Common materials, such as mineral plaster, engineered timber panels or plasterboard, are beneficial from an environmental point of view, as is the use of clay building board [38]. Bracket-mounted panelling with decorative features, on the other hand, is problematic. The perceived value of the material usually corresponds with the primary energy input, and the environmental impacts tend to be high. For example, veneer plywood sheathing on both sides of a wall has a higher environmental impact than the wall itself. The effect is intensified by using a metal substructure (e.g. in the case of natural stone cladding panels). The use of a timber substructure, in place of aluminium or steel, is the more environmentally friendly solution [39].

Indoor air quality
Due to their large surface area, interior walls have a significant impact on the quality of indoor air. Primers, trowel-applied coatings, surface finishes and possibly also surface sealers are important considerations in this context. Mineral wall constructions are at an advantage since, as a compound with mineral plaster and paint, they form a recyclable unit and at the same time produce very low emissions. However, mineral paints (e.g. silicate or lime paints) or low-pollutant natural resin, distemper or casein paint can also be applied to lightweight walls. Even among the widespread acrylic and synthetic resin paints, there are low-emission products with Type I environmental product declarations, e.g. Blue Angel designated low-emission paints (RAL-UZ 102).
The service life of wall finishes can be extended by adding protective elements in mechanically stressed and highly frequented areas (e.g. handrails, kick boards, skirting boards). These measures postpone the need for a new coat of paint, thus helping to prevent a further input of pollutants.

Optimisation factors

choice of wall construction	++
synthesis of noise protection and load-bearing structure	+
suitability for conversion and deconstruction	++
accessibility of technical installations	+
protection of the component against mechanical damage	++
environmental impact and service life of sheathing materials	+++
safe, non-toxic surface finishes	+++

5.23

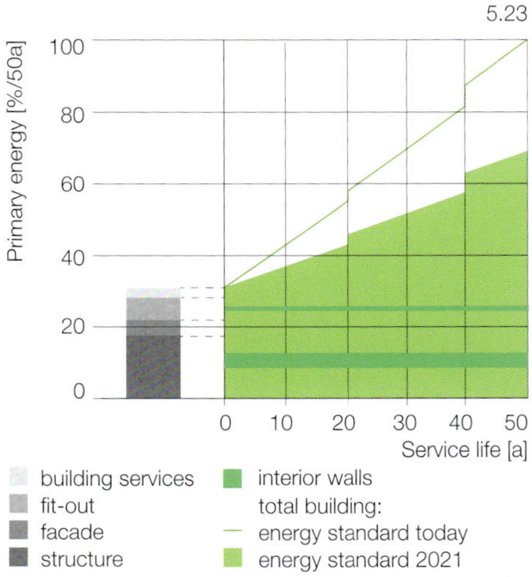

5.24

5.22 Ecological optimisation potentials of load-bearing and non-load-bearing interior walls
5.23 Primary energy consumption of a typical non-residential building (including operating energy) and embodied energy of interior walls
5.24 Life cycle assessment figures for various interior wall configuration over a 50-year period

Load-bearing interior walls [1 m² of interior wall; 52 dB noise reduction] production, maintenance and deconstruction observation period: 50 a	**PEI** primary energy non-renewable [MJ]	**PEI** primary energy renewable [MJ]	**GWP** climate gases [kg CO_2 eq.]	**ODP** ozone depletion [kg R11 eq.]	**AP** acidifi-cation [kg SO_2 eq.]	**EP** eutro-phication [kg PO_4 eq.]	**POCP** summer smog [kg C_2H_4 eq.]
1 solid sand lime brick wall; 380 kg; 52 db (32 cm) (solid sand lime brick wa l; 490 kg; 55 db)	493 (602)	42 (52)	58.8 (72.6)	3.0 E^{-8} (3.6 E^{-8})	0.050 (0.061)	0.0105 (0.0129)	0.0045 (0.0055)
gypsum plaster (1 cm); sard lime brick wall (30 cm); thin bed mortar, gypsum plaster (1 cm)							
2 solid clay brick wall; 380 kg; 52 db (26 cm) (solid clay brick wall; 490 kg; 55 db)	630 (773)	109 (135)	48.2 (59.2)	7.9 E^{-7} (9.9 E^{-7})	0.084 (0.103)	0.0115 (0.0141)	0.0063 (0.0077)
gypsum plaster (1 cm); solid brick (24 cm); thin bed mortar, gypsum plaster (1 cm)							
3 solid concrete wall; 1 % reinforcement; 52 db (23 cm) (solid concrete wall; 1 % reinforcement; 55 db)	310 (412)	20 (27)	44.1 (57.3)	1.1 E^{-6} (1.4 E^{-8})	0.082 (0.105)	0.0120 (0.0154)	0.0074 (0.0096)
gypsum plaster (1 cm); concrete (21 cm); reinforcement; gypsum plaster (1 cm)							

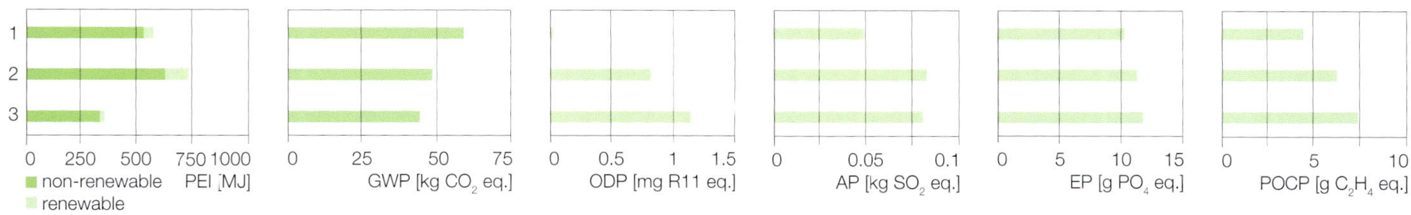

Non-load-bearing interior walls [1 m² of interior wall] production, maintenance and deconstruction observation period: 50 a	**PEI** primary energy non-renewable [MJ]	**PEI** primary energy renewable [MJ]	**GWP** climate gases [kg CO_2 eq.]	**ODP** ozone depletion [kg R11 eq.]	**AP** acidifi-cation [kg SO_2 eq.]	**EP** eutro-phication [kg PO_4 eq.]	**POCP** summer smog [kg C_2H_4 eq.]
4 light partition wall; steel studs CW 75-06; 52 db (12.5 cm) (light partition wall; steel studs CW 75-06; 55 db)	260 (340)	16 (20)	16.0 (20.8)	7.4 E^{-7} (1.1 E^{-6})	0.052 (0.065)	0.0075 (0.0096)	0.0044 (0.0057)
2 × gypsum plasterboard (2.5 cm); mineral wool insulation (6 cm); steel studs (7.5 cm); 2 × gypsum plasterboard (2.5 cm)							
5 light partition wall; steel studs CW 100-06; 55 db (15 cm)	265	16	16.3	7.5 E^{-7}	0.053	0.0076	0.0046
2 × gypsum plasterboard (2.5 cm); mineral wool insulation (6 cm); steel studs (10 cm); 2 × gypsum plasterboard (2.5 cm)							
6 light partition wall; 38 db (8.5 cm)	116	71	7.3	6.4 E^{-8}	0.025	0.0041	0.0020
gypsum plasterboard (1.25 cm); mineral wool insulation (4 cm); timber studs (6 cm); gypsum plasterboard (1.25 cm)							
7 light partition wall; 44 db (12 cm)	105	113	6.4	1.6 E^{-7}	0.033	0.0054	0.0024
gypsum plasterboard (1.25 cm); mineral wool insulation (6 cm); timber studs (8 cm); counterbattens (2.4 cm); gypsum plasterboard (1.25 cm)							
8 aerated concrete wal with sheathing; 52 db (30.25 cm)	603	126	78.4	-6.3 E^{-8}	0.141	0.0168	0.0165
gypsum plaster (1 cm); aerated concrete P6 (20 cm); timber studs (8 cm) with mineral wool infill (6 cm); gypsum plasterboard (1.25 cm)							
9 solid sand lime brick with woodwool board; 52 db (25.5 cm) (solid sand lime brick with woodwool board; 55 db) (32.5 cm)	151 (276)	190 (201)	46.0 (61.8)	-3.0 E^{-7} (-3.0 E^{-7})	0.046 (0.058)	0.0096 (0.0123)	0.0035 (0.0045)
gypsum plaster (1 cm); sand lime brick (13 cm at 52 db/20 cm at 55 dB); timber studs (8 cm); hard wood fibreboard (2.5 cm); gypsum plaster (1 cm)							
10 solid sand lime brick wall; 115 kg; 38 db (10 cm)	166	13	17.5	1.1 E^{-8}	0.017	0.0032	0.0017
gypsum plaster (1 cm) sand lime brick in thin bed mortar (8 cm); gypsum plaster (1 cm)							
11 solid clay brick wal; 85 kg; 34 db (13.5 cm)	153	21	11.2	1.3 E^{-7}	0.020	0.0026	0.0016
gypsum plaster (1 cm); clay brick in thin bed mortar (11.5 cm); gypsum plaster (1 cm)							

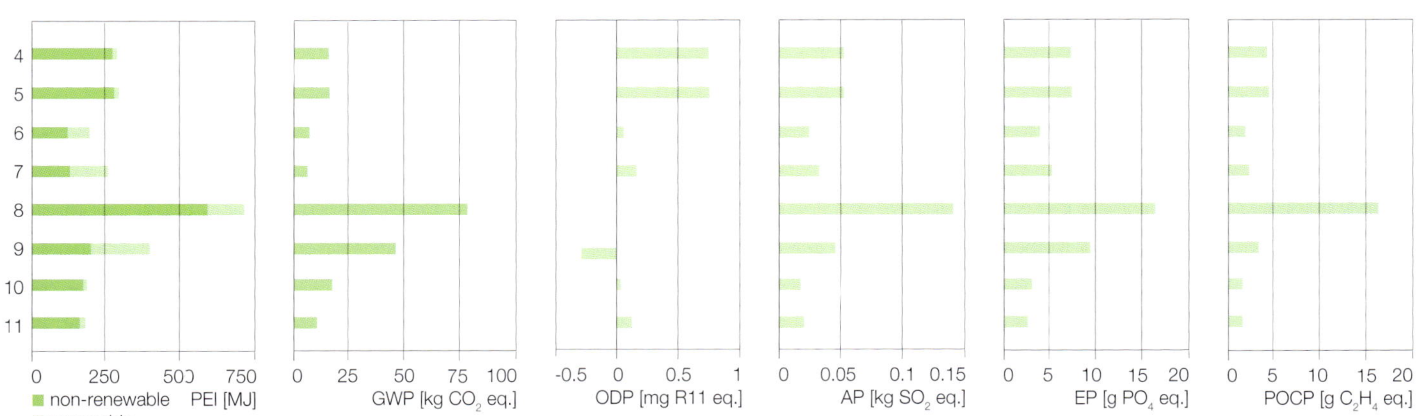

5.25

Floor systems – floor coverings, screed and impact sound insulation

Floor systems are the components in a building subjected to the most wear and tear. Numerous requirements come together in floors. The type and intensity of use, the required soundproofing, the incorporation of heating systems (e.g. underfloor heating) as well as the accommodation of cables and pipes have a significant influence on the floor system and hence the environmental impacts. For instance, more primary energy is usually required to produce floating screed than bonded screed [40]. Specific material properties may also have an effect on the floor system, and thus the environmental impacts: mastic asphalt screed or stone wood screed, for example, are beneficial when it comes to impact sound insulation due to their greater elasticity. Among the factors with an influence on floors are deformation (for impact sound insulation), mechanical forces (e.g. abrasion of floor coverings) and moisture. There is a close connection between the replacement cycles of the wearing surface [41], the load-distributing layer and soundproofing: if, for example, the impact sound insulation has a shorter service life than the screed or the floor covering, the replacement cycles can be the cause for much greater (unnecessary) environmental impacts.

Optimisation factors

limit to necessary layers only	++
material of wearing surface	+++
fastening of wearing surface	+
material for impact sound insulation	+
material of separating membrane	++
replacement of individual layers	++
suitability of surface for cleaning	++
durability of wearing surface	+++
health aspects	+++
reduction of mechanical damage	++
reduction of cleaning cycles	+++

5.26

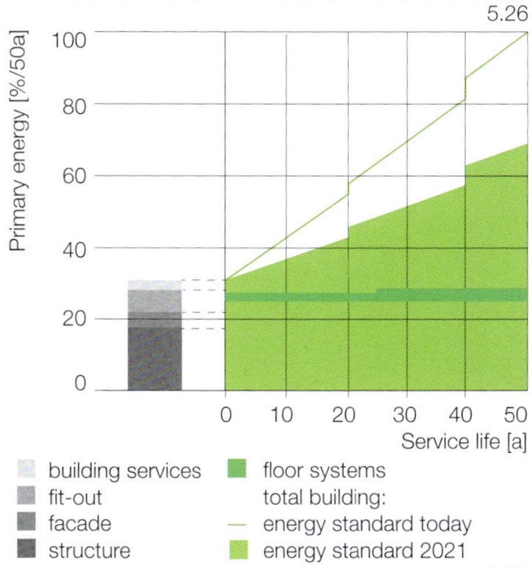

5.27

Functional layers

Alongside the wearing surface, the screed and the impact sound insulation, floor systems frequently feature screeding compounds, separating sheets or primers. Screeding compounds (e.g. fire-dried sand, light concrete not modified by synthetic resin) and primers play only a marginal role in the life cycle assessment of floors. In the case of primers, it is important to make sure that solvent-free products are used [42]. However, as regards the separating membrane between the screed and the impact sound insulation, there is considerable potential for optimisation. Kraft paper and plastic foil made from recycled waste are most beneficial in this case. The latter enables an almost 20% reduction of primary energy consumption in the screed and impact sound insulation layer in comparison to newly produced PE foils [43]. Due to its high density, mineral wool is not really suitable as a soundproofing material. Cork and wood fibre insulation boards, as well as EPS, can reduce the environmental impacts of the screed and insulation layer by up to 10% in comparison to a solution using mineral wool. Emissions and environment-damaging substances, such as fire protection compounds, must be taken into account when using plastic foams.

Screed

Under normal circumstances, the choice of screed only has a marginal influence on the primary energy consumption of the floor system [44]. Among the standard types of screed, cement screed has the lowest primary energy input; mastic asphalt screed produces the lowest global warming potential. Depending on the primary products and the implementation of the material, the fairly unusual stone wood screed can also be beneficial from an environmental viewpoint [45]. Plastic fibres (nylon, polyester) are more suitable for reinforced screed with a primary energy input approximately 3 to 20-times lower than that of steel fibres or reinforcement nets. Joints are, from an environment point of view, best made using synthetic resin-modified mortar [46]. The comparison of different floor systems shows that the reduction of mass is a fundamental issue in terms of environmental impacts. Dry screed made from gypsum fibre or gypsum plasterboard results in environmental impacts 50–60% lower than those of mastic asphalt screed. If it is possible to use timber products, such as OSB board, as is the case in small single-family homes, the outcome may even be a negative global warming potential (fig. 5.28).
Cement screed, mastic asphalt and OSB board can function as both the bearing and wearing surface (fig. 0.1, p. 7). This solution, without a typical floor covering, improves the life cycle assessment considerably. Thin seal coats have only a marginal effect on the life cycle assessment as can be seen in this example of cement screed: even a polyurethane resin coating with a thickness of 100 μm has a primary energy input of only approximately 20 MJ/m^2, which is around 6% of the primary energy input for screed and impact sound insulation together.
It is almost impossible to find products for sealing floors that are free of solvents. Nevertheless, the aim should be to find products with a low GIS code and low VOC content [47].

Floor coverings

The choice of floor covering is usually governed by creative aspects and the intended cleaning processes. The wearing surface itself and the corresponding service life have the most significant influence on the life cycle assessment (fig. 5.29) since wearing surfaces with short service lives quickly add up to high environmental impacts. Because the adhesives of floor coverings also contribute to the environmental impacts, fitting carpets and resilient flooring without the use of adhesives is beneficial both in terms of environmental impacts as well as the component's suitability for deconstruction. Laminate (possibly also ready-to-lay parquet) can also be installed without glue, which has the effect that it is easier to remove and the floor covering can even be reused. Nevertheless, there are ecological optimisation potentials for glue, too. Mineral adhesives are better due to the fact that the emissions to indoor air are lower. A similar combination of low environmental impact and reduced emissions also applies to low-pollutant acrylic dispersion glue (e.g. according to the Emicode EC1 and EC1^{plus} labels) [48].

5.26 Ecological optimisation potentials of floor systems
5.27 Primary energy consumption of a typical non-residential building (including operating energy) and embodied energy of floor structures
5.28 Life cycle assessment figures for various screeds over a 50-year period
5.29 Life cycle assessment figures for various floor coverings over a 50-year period

Screeds [1 m² of screed] production, maintenance and deconstruction observation period: 50 a	**PEI** primary energy non-renewable [MJ]	**PEI** primary energy renewable [MJ]	**GWP** climate gases [kg CO_2 eq.]	**ODP** ozone depletion [kg R11 eq.]	**AP** acidification [kg SO_2 eq.]	**EP** eutrophication [kg PO_4 eq.]	**POCP** summer smog [kg C_2H_4 eq.]
1 cement screed (d = 7.5 cm)	300	9	23.5	5.3 E^{-7}	0.055	0.0088	0.0055
cement screed (5.5 cm); PE separating foil (0.01 cm); mineral wool impact sound insulation 25-5 (2 cm)							
2 anhydrite screed (d = 6 cm)	310	15	16.3	2.2 E^{-8}	0.097	0.0117	0.0044
anhydrite screed (4.0 cm); PE separating foil (0.01 cm); mineral wool impact sound insulation 25-5 (2 cm)							
3 mastic asphalt (d = 5.25 cm)	365	16	9.2	2.3 E^{-8}	0.032	0.0045	0.0133
mastic asphalt (3.0 cm); ribbed cardboard (0.25 cm); mineral wool impact sound insulation 25-5 (2 cm)							
4 OSB board (d = 5.2 cm)	230	445	-26.7	8.3 E^{-7}	0.050	0.0077	0.0054
OSB 2 × 16 mm (3.2 cm); mineral wool impact sound insulation 25-5 (2 cm)							
5 gypsum plasterboard (d = 4.5 cm)	145	8	8.9	9.4 E^{-9}	0.025	0.0046	0.0019
dry screed board 2 × 12.5 mm (2.5 cm); mineral wool impact sound insulation 25-5 (2 cm)							
6 gypsum fibreboard (d = 4.5 cm)	120	6	7.5	8.6 E^{-9}	0.022	0.0036	0.0016
gypsum fibre board (2.5 cm); mineral wool impact sound insulation 25-5 (2 cm)							

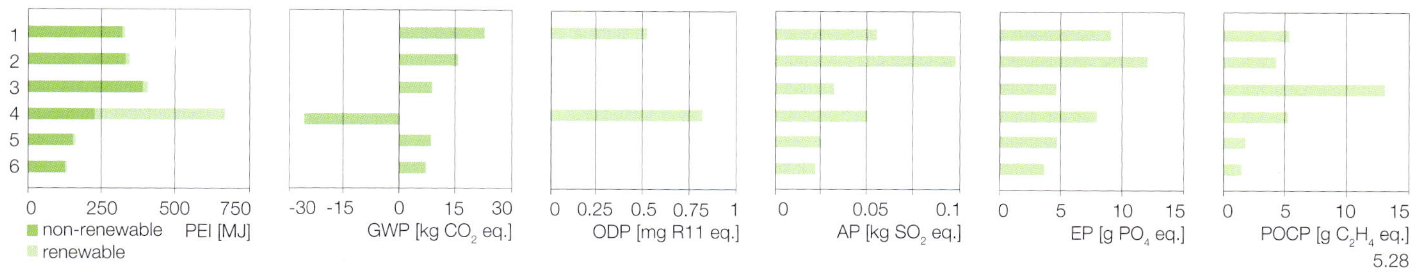

5.28

Floor coverings [1 m² of floor covering] production, maintenance and deconstruction observation period: 50 a	**PEI** non-renew. [MJ]	**PEI** renew. [MJ]	**GWP** [kg CO_2 eq.]	**ODP** [kg R11 eq.]	**AP** [kg SO_2 eq.]	**EP** [kg PO_4 eq.]	**POCP** [kg C_2H_4 eq.]
7 natural stone	172	13	13.6	1.5 E^{-7}	0.166	0.016	0.0103
limestone floor tiles 30.5 × 30.5 cm (1 cm); grouting, mortar group II, 2% of surface area (0.9 cm); thin bed mortar (0.3 cm)							
8 stoneware tile flooring	96	4	6.8	6.2 E^{-9}	0.012	0.001	0.0010
stoneware tiles 30 × 60 cm (0.8 cm); grouting, mortar group II, 2% of surface area (0.7 cm); thin bed mortar (0.3 cm)							
9 ready-to-lay parquet, floating[1)2)]	161	638	-5.2	-2.9 E^{-7}	0.065	0.009	0.0086
parquet sealant[1)]; ready-to-lay parquet 1.25 cm[2)] (2.5 mm oak wearing surface, 10 mm laminated timber core); PE foil							
10 parquet flooring, glued[3)]	87	612	-8.0	-3.1 E^{-7}	0.072	0.009	0.0137
heating oil[3)]; oak wearing surface (2.25 cm); acrylate dispersion							
11 laminate[4)]	259	671	-16.2	9.5 E^{-7}	0.120	0.033	0.0279
laminate with melamine resin coating[4)], MDF base (0.8 cm); PE foam underlay[4)]							
12 linoleum[5)]	178	144	7.3	1.1 E^{-6}	0.116	0.022	0.0059
rolled linoleum flooring (0.25 cm)[5)]; acrylate dispersion (0.4 kg)							
13 natural rubber[6)]	984	13	54.5	1.5 E^{-6}	0.271	0.016	0.0169
rolled natural rubber flooring (0.2 cm)[6)]; acrylate dispersion (0.4 kg)							
14 PVC flooring[7)]	1630	44	93.7	3.8 E^{-6}	0.437	0.030	0.0314
rolled PVC flooring (0.225 cm)[7)]; wearing surface 0.07 cm with glass reinforcement; acrylate dispersion (0.4 kg)							
15 PU coating[8)]	1106	13	45.8	2.1 E^{-6}	0.168	0.014	0.0195
polyurethane coating (0.25 cm)[8)]							
16 needle-punched carpet[9)]	1036	20	78.7	2.4 E^{-6}	0.202	0.035	0.0238
needle-punched carpet (2 cm)[9)]; acrylate dispersion (0.4 kg)							

replacement cycles: [1)] parquet varnish 10 a; [2)] parquet 40 a; [3)] heating oil 5 a; [4)] laminate + PE foil 20 a; [5)] linoleum 25 a; [6)] natural rubber 25 a; [7)] PVC 20 a; [8)] PU 30 a; [9)] carpet 10 a; all other materials 50 a)

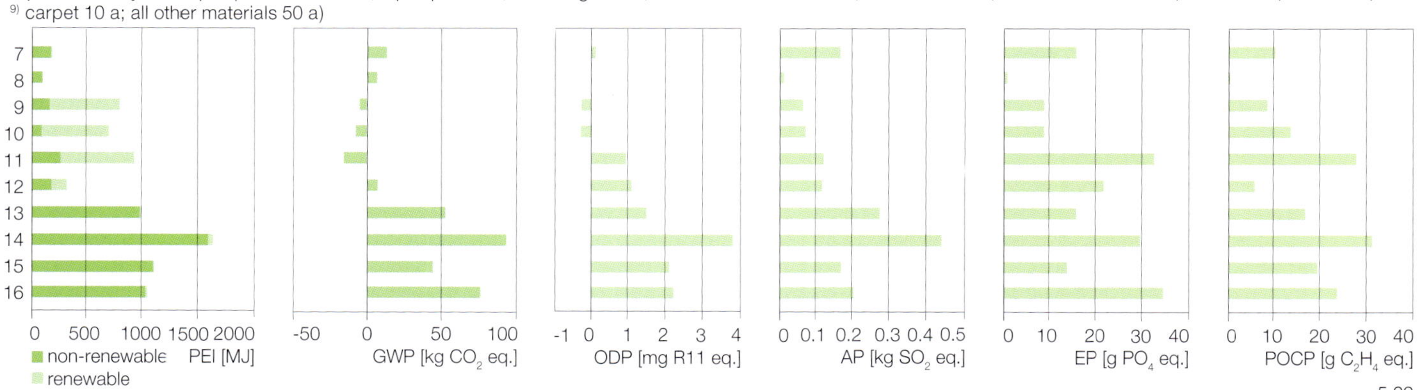

5.29

- Holiday residence on Taylor's Island (USA)
- Refurbishment and conversion of single-family home in Hamburg (D)
- Mixed residential and commercial building in Zurich (CH)
- Office building in Krems (A)
- Lower secondary school in Langenzersdorf (A)

Introduction

The previous chapters explored individual topics and criteria relevant for sustainable construction and explained the adjustments which have to be made during the course of a design process to optimise the environmental impact of construction details. In order to identify the "perfect" strategies and concepts for the project concerned, it is also important to fully understand the complex results of improving the ecological aspects of a design.
Reference buildings are particularly suited to this task. The following schemes highlight that, subject to the underlying circumstances, the use and objective of the building, totally different strategies can bring about equally successful results. Moreover, the reference buildings illustrate that, in the case of similar conditions, widely different approaches can lead to comparable results in terms of environmental impact. For, sustainable construction is not restricted to a single material or type of construction, but assesses and chooses from a large range of possibilities.
The selection of projects provides not only an insight into this creative and structural diversity but also into a large range of typologies and locations (fig. 6.1). Alongside small and large-scale residential buildings, the selection also includes an office building and a school. Refurbishments and extensions are assessed in the same way as new builds. The construction principles range from traditional brick and concrete structures, timber frameworks and solid timber structures to steel frame constructions. And last but not least, the example buildings show that traditional aesthetic values, such as transparency and honesty, are not necessarily evidence of an extremely sustainable design. The load-bearing structure of a building can either be used as a design feature, as is the case for the single-family home on Taylor's Island, or merely to fulfil its inherent purpose and later be concealed by cladding, as is the case for the mixed residential and commercial building in Zurich. No matter which approach is opted for, it is rarely possible to make a clear distinction between the degree of sustainability achieved by these constructions.

Page	Project	Typology						Old/new		Type of construction					Brief description of construction
		Multi-unit apartment block	Residential building	Office building	Educational building	Commercial building	Special use building	New build	Existing building stock	Timber frame structure	Solid timber structure	Light solid structure	Heavy solid structure	Metal frame structure	
p. 103	Holiday residence on Taylor's Island (USA)		■					■						■	• modular aluminium frame structure • prefabricated timber balloon frame components used as infill elements in walls and floors • dismantable construction and joining principles
p. 109	Refurbishment and conversion of single-family home in Hamburg (D)		■						■	■		■			• energy efficiency upgrade and extension to existing solid structure • new partition walls using lightweight construction method • extension built as a timber frame structure with fully-glazed facades and rear-ventilated fibre cement cladding
p. 117	Mixed residential and commercial building in Zurich (CH)	■				■		■			■		■		• timber/concrete hybrid building • basement and ground floor built as reinforced concrete skeleton construction • upper storeys built using hollow timber floor elements and solid timber walls with rear-ventilated glass fibre concrete cladding
p. 125	Office building in Krems (A)			■				■					■		• solid, low-CO_2 reinforced concrete construction with large proportion of blast furnace slag cement • load-bearing concrete facade with composite thermal insulation system
p. 133	Lower secondary school in Langenzersdorf (A)				■				■	■		■			• refurbishment and conversion of existing solid structure • minimum interference in existing building stock • new build as timber frame structure with rear-ventilated wood and fibre cement cladding

6.1

Holiday residence on Taylor's Island

What happens to buildings at the end of their service life? Like most products, they are generally disposed of as waste. Those building products and materials used that are not identified, separated or sorted are usually irretrievably lost. Only a small proportion of materials is reused, and those then tend to depreciate in value (downcycle) or be incinerated (thermal recovery). Thus, the building sector is responsible for approximately 60 % of global waste production. [1]

Design to Dissemble

The Loblolly House was developed as a prototype for a "deconstructable" building. The aim was that the individual components can be assembled quickly and easily, but also dismantled without causing any destruction (see Strategies for material use in the construction process, pp. 55f.). The elements are joined using mainly reversible connection systems in order to allow for easy separation, sorting and reuse of the components and materials. This construction method allows several problems to be addressed simultaneously:

First, the consumption of resources is minimised by enabling the reuse of building materials. The deposits for abiotic resources, in particular metals, have been depleted to such a degree that there are already higher concentrations of the valuable resources in landfills than in the ores that are still stored in the ground.

The second aspect is that the energy consumption for the development of new buildings is reduced considerably by recycling raw materials and reusing components since the largest proportion of the components' embodied energy derives from the mining and production of these resources.

The third point concerns the alleviation of the waste problem: waste disposal sites take up large areas of valuable space and continue to contaminate the ground and water throughout the world with noxious substances which gradually leach out of the stored waste.

Project description

Taylor's Island is a peninsula off the coast of Maryland, a large part of which is designated as a nature preservation area. The wooded, approximately 45-metre-wide site covering a total area of almost 11,000 m², is located on the eastern side of Chesapeake Bay. Almost 300 m in length, it is situated between the main road and the sea shore. The view from the building opens up to the west across the sea, whereas the rear faces onto a dense forest. In response to these very different situations, Kieran Timerberlake developed floor plans using a single-corridor concept. Thus all living rooms face west and are fully glazed. The other three facades are closed except for a few nar-

Project participants
Client: Stephen Kieran, Philadelphia
Architects: Kieran Timberlake Architects, Philadelphia

Building parameters
Location: Taylor's Island, Maryland (USA)
Design period: 2005–2007
Construction period: 2006/07
Use: holiday residence
Plot: 11,103 m²
Built surface area: 149.5 m² (raised)
Gross floor area (GFA): 298.5 m²
Useful floor area (UFA): 189.3 m²
Treated floor area: 189.3 m²
Volume: 825 m³

Objective
Zero waste (deconstruction with no leftover remnants of the building structure as well as high quality recycling at the end of the life cycle)

Energy parameters
A/V ratio: 0.87
Space heat demand: 59 kWh/m²a
Primary energy value Q_p (DHW, heating and auxiliary power): 79 kWh/m²a

U-values
Exterior wall: 0.18 W/m²K
Roof: 0.092 W/m²K
Raised floor: 0.092 W/m²K
Window: 1.1 W/m²K

6.1 Overview of presented buildings
6.2 Holiday residence on Taylor's Island (USA), Kieran Timberlake 2007. View from the south

6.2

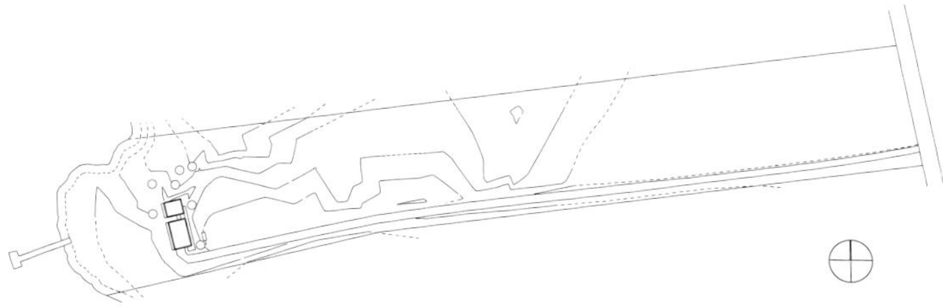

6.3

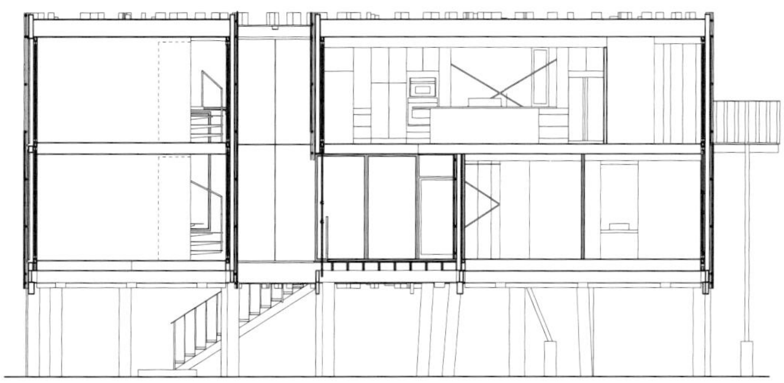

6.4

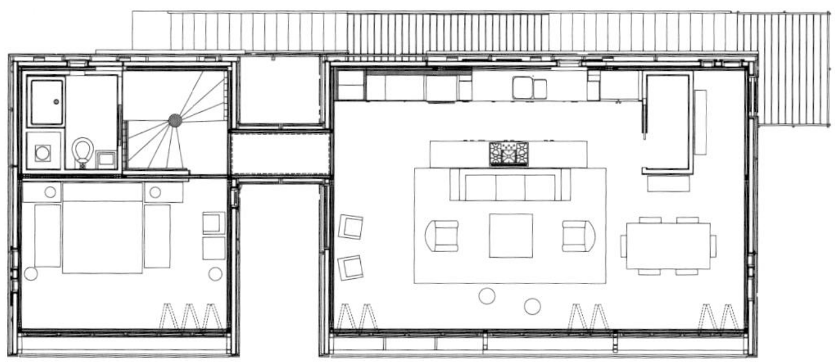

6.5

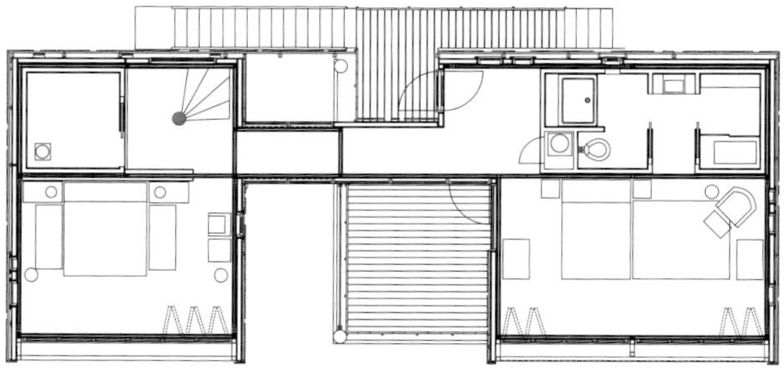

6.6

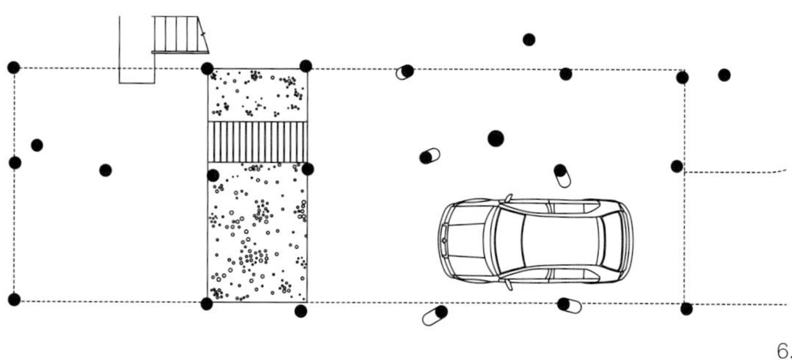

6.7

6.3 Site plan, not to scale
6.4 Longitudinal section, scale 1:250
6.5 Second floor plan, scale 1:250
6.6 First floor plan, scale 1:250
6.7 Ground floor plan, scale 1:250

6.8 Working principle of west facade (solar shading devices/thermal buffer)
6.9 View of the rear east-facing facade with stairs to living area
6.10 Bedrooms on first floor

row floor-to-ceiling windows which allow for a particular view out.
The raised two-storey structure is accessed via an exterior single-run stairway. It is positioned alongside the rear facade and takes residents and visitors up to the top floor. So the building is actually entered on the second floor which accommodates the living and dining area. A spiral staircase in the interior leads down to the first floor where space is provided for two bedrooms with en-suite bathrooms.
A narrow setback divides the volume into two parts with a fully glazed bridge forming the only connection between the two. The space beneath the building protects the residential areas above from tidal flooding, which occurs frequently here; it also functions as a covered space for the family car. There is a small bamboo garden below the setback in the facade which is adjoined by a covered terrace on the first floor. The small outdoor area is therefore on a level with the tips of the bamboo grove and protected from the sun and rain. The functional areas form a spine at the back of the building, including the bathrooms, a utility room, storage space and the open-plan kitchen facing the living room.

Facade and energy concept

There is a strong interdependence between the energy concept and the building design. The rooms are heated and cooled mainly through the west facade (fig. 6.8), which is designed to control the energy input according to demand. The inner layer is made up of glass elements, the outer one of aluminium frames which are filled with polycarbonate panels. The entire glass facade can be fully opened by folding the elements away horizontally. The outer layer, on the other hand, is opened and folded vertically in order to cater for different weather conditions.
On hot days, the panels can be raised fully, creating protruding elements that prevent direct radiation from the high-standing summer sun and the resulting problem of overheating in the interior. The rooms can be cross ventilated by opening up the inner glass facade to exploit the cool sea breezes (fig. 6.10). On cooler days, the residents can fully close both the inner and outer layers of the facade with the effect that the cavity between the two is heated by solar radiation penetrating the outermost translucent layer. During longer periods in winter, when the house tends not to be used, the

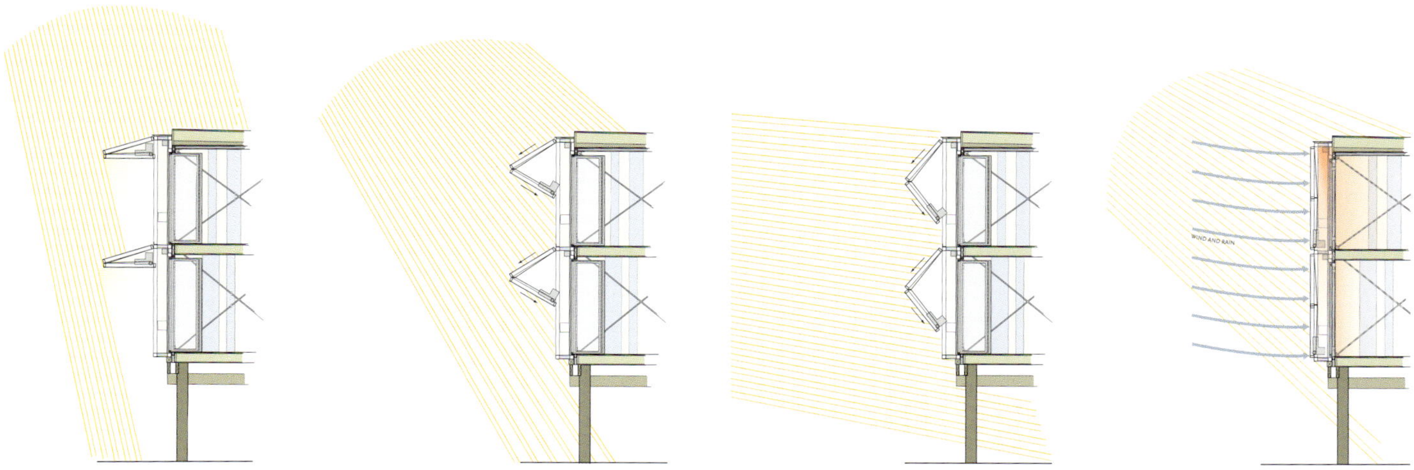

6.8

polycarbonate panels function as a weather shield.
These passive measures are supported by a few simple technical systems. The living rooms are equipped with ceiling fans to increase the air circulation on hot summer days. A split refrigeration system can be switched on if required and a gas boiler is used to heat the rooms during the spring and autumn months. The building envelope and the rooms inside are equipped with sensors to measure temperature and solar radiation. The working principle of the facade can be monitored by assessing the temperature profiles outside, inside and in the cavity between the facade layers in different conditions and at different positions of the panels. The monitoring of the facade is intended to provide greater understanding for the future about how best to operate the two-layered construction and the means of moving the panels automatically.
The north, east and west sides of the building are finished with rear-ventilated cedar wood cladding. The design of the building envelope is perfectly adapted to its setting. Due to the random arrangement of timber panels, the building visibly adopts the character of the tall pines and blends in well with the surrounding landscape (fig. 6.9).

Construction and material specifications
Because the building is positioned on a slightly remote and unspoilt piece of land not far from a nature preservation area, the architects sought a construction which would impair the surrounding landscape as little as possible. So they developed a structure based on principles that are well-established in the American building industry (structural metal framework and timber stud structure). The construction of the Loblolly House consists of an aluminium framework set on a number of timber piles. The pressure impregnated pine piles were driven into the ground to a depth of between 6 and 9 m. When the building is dismantled, the timber piles can simply be left in the ground without causing any negative environmental impact. Two additional hollow piles were added to the structural supports to accommodate the technical supply lines for the building.
A bearing structure made of wood-based panels is positioned above the load-bearing timber construction to form a perfectly level surface between the timber and aluminium structures and provide for a certain degree of tolerance between the two structural systems. The load-bearing aluminium framework is clad with prefabricated solid timber panels on the exterior. The panels were produced by joining squared timber members with wood-based panels. All power cables and heating pipes were fitted into the elements before arriving on site. The only outstanding work to be completed on site was to connect up the lines. The floors are also made of timber frame elements. However, these have been clad with plywood on the underside as a ceiling

6.9

6.10

6.11

finish and solid bamboo up above as the floor surface. Due to the large amount of installation work involved in the wet rooms, the kitchen and bathroom zones were separated into two units and delivered to the building site as fully pre-constructed modules ready to be connected. All building services systems including all connections were incorporated in these units. Their good working order was checked in the workshop so that all pre-installed heating pipes only had to be connected on site.
The heat is distributed and transferred using a panel heating system that is incorporated in the wall and floor elements. As a result the total construction work only took ten weeks (six for the prefabrication off site and four weeks for the assembly on site).

Design and construction process

In contrast to the industrial production processes in other countries, construction work on US-American building sites has hardly progressed in the last decades. As a result the country's construction industry has been experiencing stagnation in productivity for more than 40 years (fig. 6.12). Whereas, for example, in the automobile industry, prefabricated components are joined together with pinpoint precision and incredible speed, most building components and materials are not made to measure until arriving on site, where they are then cut and joined, and sometimes even produced, at great expense.
Kieran Timberlake's aim is to improve construction processes to meet the standards in automotive manufacturing and thus make the construction of buildings cheaper and faster. Alongside economic advantages, these changes could bring about ecological benefits, such as a lower consumption of raw materials by using more efficient production processes, as well as less noise and pollutant emissions on the building site. Moreover, the mechanical joining of elements also helps to make the processes of deconstruction much easier. Individual layers and components can be dismantled and replaced as soon as they become worn or whenever requirements change.
The Loblolly House was developed as a prototype for the application of industrial production processes in the building industry. In contrast to a life cycle assessment, which primarily focuses on the quantification of material flows, the architects concentrated on simple ways to

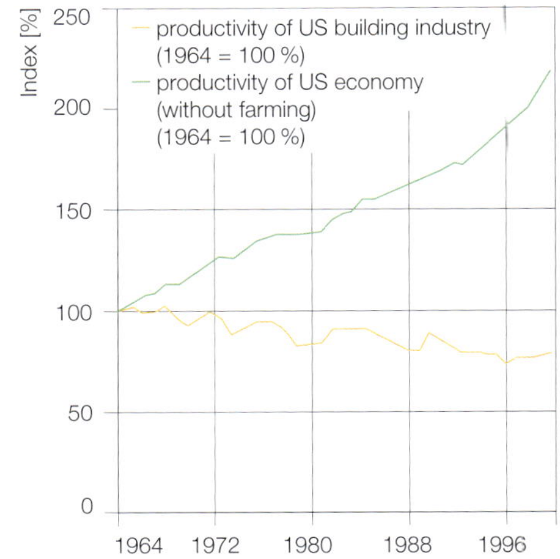

6.12

assemble and disassemble the individual building materials. In the case of the modular framework of extruded aluminium sections, all connections are reversible using bolts, screws and fasteners exclusively (fig. 6.13 and 6.14). When it comes to the end-of-life deconstruction, the entire building can be dismantled into individual components, which can then either be reused or recycled (fig. 6.15, p. 108). The architects have already once completed the deconstruction process of a temporary prototype design, the so-called Cellophane House, which was erected for a useful life phase of only six months.
The use of aluminium, which, due to its high primary energy content, is critical as a "one-time use" item, has many advantages when used in deconstructable buildings: it is light and extremely durable, even without a surface coating, which in turn makes recycling easier. The possibility to reuse entire building components is also increased if uncoated members are used, simply because their surface is not damaged to the same degree through assembly, use and dismantling; thus, "natural" aluminium is in many ways better suited to this type of construction.

Environmental impact

The values listed as primary energy input (PEI) in figure 6.16 (p. 108) express the energy encapsulated in the components used, not however the energy that can be regained through further use. In the case of some components (aluminium sections, timber beams and panels), it is possible to retrieve almost the total amount of embodied energy by reintroducing the elements into a new life cycle. Only the comparably small amount of energy required for the deconstruction and transportation of the material would then have to be taken into consideration.

The most likely fate of all components and materials that cannot be reused directly would be recycling. Most of the timber and wood-based panels can be shredded and used to produce new wood-based products. The alternative would be thermal use. In the case of timber with minimum processing requirements, this would mean low emissions of carbon dioxide throughout the total life cycle of the product. All other materials accumulated during the deconstruction, such as old and worn plastics (PET, PVC and PC) and composite materials (e.g. fibre glass) can, if at all, be used only as a low-quality supplement for the production of new plastics. To this date, coated glass is not specified as being recyclable.
On closer consideration, it becomes apparent that the possibilities to reuse, at an equal standard, the components and materials retrieved during the deconstruction of a building are limited (see Reuse, pp. 55f.). This issue, however, is subject to the prevailing production processes in the building industry and the range of materials available on the market, and can be influenced only marginally by design or construction measures. Establishing a circular economy in the construction business will only become possible by employing materials that can be reused with little energy input and minimum emissions. On the other hand, one of the basic requirements for dismantling individual building components and materials is the development of construction principles which allow for simple and quick separation in the deconstruction phase. This is the only way to ensure the purity of recycled materials necessary for the production of new high-quality building components at reasonable expense.

Prototype for life cycle-oriented design and construction processes

As a model residential building, the Loblolly House is an important milestone in the establishment of life cycle-oriented design and construction processes. From a building typology viewpoint, its modular system is best suited for detached two to three-storey buildings. The measurements of the building can be perfectly adapted to the load-bearing capacity, available dimensions and room sizes. In the meantime, the architects have further developed the prototype in cooperation with a modular prefab home builder (LivingHomes, Santa Monica) to a sellable series of individualised single and multi-unit dwellings. Due to the high degree of prefabrication, less than 30 % of all components have to be joined on site; in comparable projects this proportion is usually around 90 %. As a consequence, the total construction period can be reduced to approximately five months.

Conclusion

Based on the high rate of prefabricated processes and the reversible connections of building components on site, the Loblolly House achieves a new technological standard in the building industry. The construction can be completed within a shorter period of time, at higher quality and, in the case of mass production, at lower cost. The reversible connections, in particular, which facilitate the separation of the materials, reduce the impact on the environment and obviate the need to use new resources. This shift in paradigm is based on a changing understanding of discipline: the building was not developed as a static item, but as an integrated production process. It is an approach that could fill the gap between building industry and architecture, which seem to be further apart in the USA than in Europe. Kieran Timberlake have used the modified construction principles to introduce a superior design, similar to what Charles and Ray Eames did in their Case Study Houses 60 years ago.
According to architects and planners, this is precisely where greater potential lies: it will only be possible to give sustainable design the impetus it so desperately needs to become an overriding factor if architects can succeed in further developing sustainable construction principles as part of an overall superior design approach.

6.13

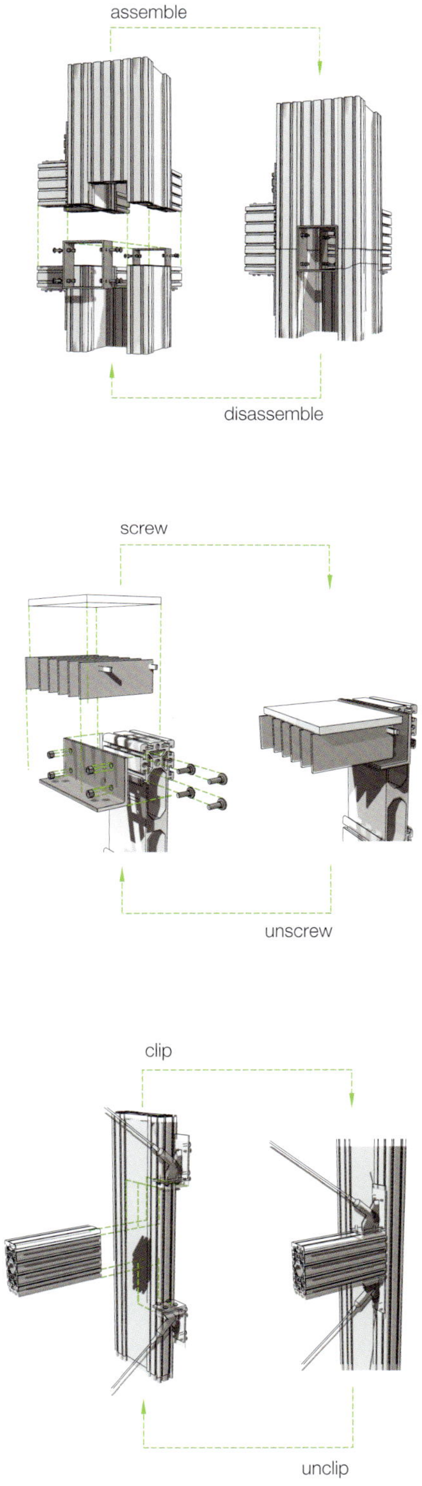

6.14

6.11 Sequence of construction processes
6.12 Comparison between productivity development in the US building industry and in the US economy as a whole (farming excluded) from 1964 to 2003
6.13 Corner detail of the aluminium frame with diagonal bracing to resist wind loads
6.14 The sequence of steps in assembling and disassembling the aluminium framework

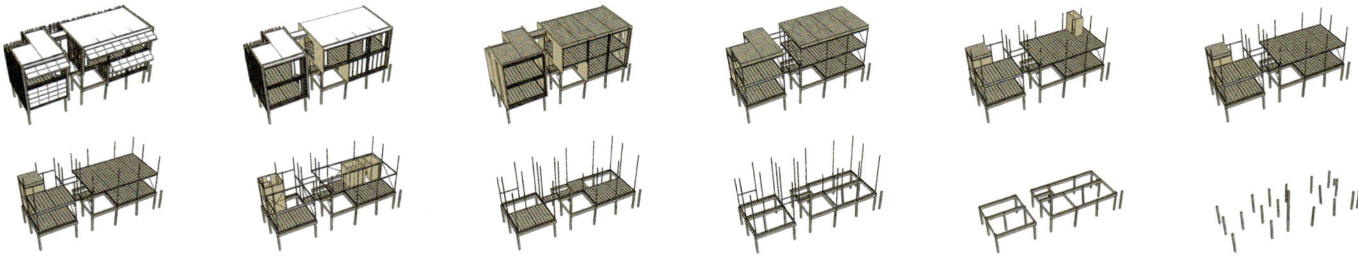

Instructions for step-by-step deconstruction of building

1. Deconstruction of the exterior stairway.
2. Removal of timber cladding on the east, north and south facades by releasing the clip connections between the panels and substructure.
3. Deconstruction of timber frame elements in exterior walls (not containing any technical installations). This is achieved by unscrewing the bolts between the elements and the aluminium structure.
4. Removal of all technical installations from the ducts integrated in roof and floor slabs.
5. Deconstruction of timber frame elements in the roof: removing the waterproofing membrane and XPS insulation; opening the bolts between the elements and the aluminium structure.
6. Deconstruction of the prefabricated sanitary unit on second floor (bathroom): opening the bolted connections to three aluminium joists at the north-east corner; loading the whole sanitary unit onto a truck with the help of a crane.
7. Deconstruction of the circular steel stair inside: opening the bolted connections and loading the whole stair element onto a truck with the help of a crane.
8. Deconstruction of the prefabricated sanitary units on first floor (guest bathroom and kitchen): opening the bolted connections to three aluminium joists at the north-east corner; loading both sanitary units onto a truck with the help of a crane.
9. Removal of the foldable sun shading devices in the west facade: opening all bolted connections to the steel substructure.
10. Deconstruction of the foldable glazing elements in the west facade: opening all bolted connections to the steel substructure.
11. Deconstruction of the steel tube construction in the west facade together with all U-shaped connectors. This is achieved by releasing the bolts to the primary load-bearing structure.
12. Deconstruction of all floor elements including the incorporated technical installations. This is achieved by releasing the bolts to the primary load-bearing structure.
13. Deconstruction of the primary load-bearing structure (aluminium framework) by opening all bolted connections.
14. Deconstruction of the horizontal timber base beneath the first floor.
15. Deconstruction (as far as possible) of the foundation piles: sawing off the parts protruding from the ground.
16. All remaining elements are packed and loaded onto two trucks and removed.

6.15

Elements, materials and their environmental impact

Element	Stairs	Facade cladding	Roof elements	Glazing west facade	Wall elements	Floor elements	Primary load-bearing structure	Foundation
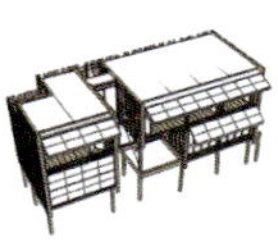		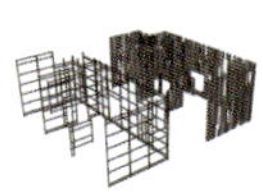		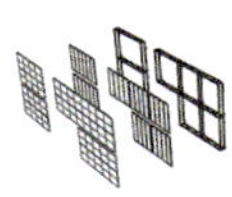		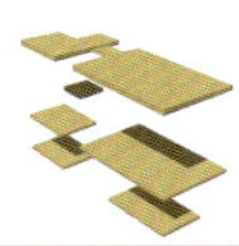	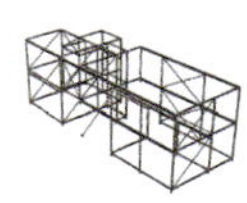	
Material	a) steel	a) pine wood	a) EPDM membrane b) XPS insulation c) plywood d) timber beams e) mineral wool infill insulation	a) steel frame b) acrylic glass panels c) foldable glazing in aluminium frame	a) glass b) birch LVL c) PU spray insulation d) fibre cement panels e) timber posts	a) mineral wool insulation b) bamboo plywood c) pine wood d) birch LVL e) timber beams	a) aluminium beams b) steel connectors	a) timber piles b) timber base frame
Weight [kg]	a) 900 kg steel	a) 1314 kg pine wood	a) 141 kg EPDM b) 114 kg XPS c) 3527 kg plywood d) 714 kg mineral wool e) 646 kg timber beams	a) 900 kg steel b) 621 kg acrylic glass c) 10141 kg foldable glazing	a) 1298 kg glass b) 5606 kg birch plywood c) 1216 kg PU d) 324 kg fibre cement e) 3026 kg timber	a) 1036 kg mineral wool b) 1116 kg bamboo c) 108 kg pine wood d) 1349 kg birch LVL e) 1293 kg timber beams	a) 3878 kg aluminium b) 450 kg steel	a) 5172 kg timber piles b) 2313 kg timber beams
Energy content [kWh]	a) 5645 kWh	a) 1321 kWh	a) not calculated b) 4076 kWh c) 12245 kWh d) 5729 kWh e) 650 kWh	a) 5645 kWh b) 15803 kWh c) 39442 kWh	a) 5049 kWh b) 19462 kWh c) 446 kWh d) 856 kWh e) 3044 kWh	a) 8345 kWh b) 465 kWh c) 108 kWh d) 46782 kWh e) 1300 kWh	a) 205851 kWh b) 2823 kWh	a) 5201 kWh b) 2326 kWh
Global warming potential [kg CO_2 eq.]	a) 1723 kg	a) –1524 kg	a) not calculated b) 2377 kg c) –1963 kg d) 1109 kg e) –750 kg	a) 1723 kg b) 4423 kg c) 8112 kg	a) 1038 kg b) –4708 kg c) 52325 kg d) not calculated e) –3510 kg	a) 1616 kg b) –1295 kg c) pine wood d) –1133 kg a) –1500 kg	a) 46531 kg a) 862 kg	a) –5999 kg b) –2683 kg
Reusable materials	a) steel	a) pine wood	c) plywood d) timber beams e) mineral wool	a) steel frame b) acrylic glass panels c) foldable glazing	a) glass b) birch LVL c) PU spray insulation d) fibre cement panels e) timber posts	a) mineral wool insulation b) bamboo plywood c) pine wood d) birch LVL e) timber beams	a) aluminium beams b) steel connectors	b) timber base frame
Recyclable materials			a) EPDM membrane b) XPS insulation					a) timber piles

6.16

Refurbishment and conversion of single-family home in Hamburg

As of 1 January 2021, all new buildings developed in Europe must have a net energy demand of almost zero. This requirement is manifested in the European Performance of Building Directive (EPBD); however, the precise definition of "almost zero" is still awaited. The LichtAktiv Haus approaches the methodology with an experimental focus and found a platform at the symposium "Building the City Anew" (Stadt neu bauen), which took place in the context of the International Building Exhibition IBA in Wilhelmsburg, Hamburg. Approximately 50 architectural, economic and cultural projects, each with model character, have been completed there since 2006. The intention of the LichtAktiv Haus is to focus on the subjects suburban change, the quality of life in small dwelling units and the energy saving potential of refurbishments.

Project description

The project is based on an unrefurbished semi-detached house completed in 1954 with a built surface area of 8 × 8 m and an extension which was formerly used as a stable. This type of building offered residents a modest degree of comfort after the Second World War and enabled them to be self-sufficient by growing fruit and vegetables in the large garden behind the house [2]. The interior, on the other hand, was cramped and, with the very low ceilings, hardly met the requirements of today's living standards [3]. Furthermore, the home was in no way able to measure up to current energy standards. This is generally the case for approximately half of Germany's building stock [4]. Despite all of these shortcomings, the semi was retained, refurbished and extended by a timber-framed new build, which increases the available floor area by approximately 60 % (fig. 6.17). The extension accommodates the living and dining area, the kitchen, an entrance area and utility room. The more private bedrooms are located in the old part of the building.
The main idea was that the house blend into the streetscape, but also to reinterpret the vegetable and fruit garden as a means of energy conservation and food production. The result of these considerations was to fully cover the energy demand with local renewable sources without putting any constraints on quality of living, flexibility, provision of daylight or window ventilation. The approach was developed during the course of a student competition in the module Design and Energy-Efficient Building at Technische Universität Darmstadt. The award-winning design was finally developed together

Project participants
Client: Velux Deutschland GmbH, Hamburg
Concept: Katharina Fey (TU Darmstadt)
Project design: Technische Universität Darmstadt, Chair of Design and Energy-Efficient Building
Construction design: Ostermann Architekten, Hamburg
Energy concept: HL-Technik, Munich
Light concept: Prof. Peter Andres PLDA, Hamburg
Structure: TSB-Ingenieure, Darmstadt

Building parameters
Location: Hamburg, Germany
Use: residential - conversion and extension of semi-detached house
Design period: 2009/10
Construction period: 2010
Living area: 132 m^2
Net floor area: 229 m^2
Treated floor area: 172 m^2
Envelope surface area: 581 m^2
Heated volume: 643 m^3
Window surface area: 102 m^2
Property value: €460000

Energy parameters according to EnEV (2009)
Primary energy demand: 47.2 kWh/m^2a
Maximum value (EnEV): 137.6 kWh/m^2a
Deviation to EnEV requirements: 65.7 %
Final energy electricity: 18.2 kWh/m^2a
Space heat demand: 71.4 kWh/m^2a
DHW demand: 12 kWh/m^2a
Standard heat load: 7954 W
Output photovoltaics: 75 m^2/ 8.8 kW_p
(performance factor: 13.5 %)
Solar thermal collectors: 19.8 m^2
PEI non-renewable (50 a): 68.5 $MJ/(m^2_{NFA} \cdot a)$
GWP (50 a): 4.1 kg CO_2 eq./$(m^2_{NFA} \cdot a)$

6.15 Single-family home on Taylor's Island (USA) 2007, Kieran Timberlake. Instructions for deconstruction
6.16 Structure, environmental impact and recyclability of building materials used
6.17 Single-family home in Hamburg (D) 2010, Technische Universität Darmstadt, Chair of Design and Energy-Efficient Building. View from southwest

6.17

with an interdisciplinary planning team including architects, building services engineers and light designers.

Construction and material specifications

The original construction of sand lime brick still dominates the appearance of the old building. The exterior wall surfaces were merely upgraded by fitting a mineral-based composite thermal insulation system (fig. 6.29, p. 113). New screed and a light parquet floor were added to the original reinforced concrete ground slab and the timber beam first floor. A decision was made to dismantle the original roof structure and replace it with a new rafter roof as the old structure was contaminated with wood preservatives and quite a few timber members had in any case to be removed to install new rooflights. Light grey fibre cement tiles now cover the roof in order to reduce overheating through solar radiation in summer. The solid interior partition walls were left in place wherever possible. All new partition walls are drywalls with metal studs and gypsum board sheathing.
The extension was built using a timber stud structure with mineral wool-filled cavities (fig. 6.32 and 6.34, p. 115). The end walls have been clad with fibre cement panels to match the colour hues of the old building. The longer sides of the extension feature a mix of windows and opaque surfaces; the latter are in fact elements of single-pane safety glass in aluminium frames. This skin is continued along the entire length of the building and thus also incorporates the carport at one end and the terrace at the other end of the new build. The mono-pitched roof of the extension as well as the flat roof of the connecting element are made of timber beams. In order to mount the solar thermal collectors and photovoltaic panels, the mono-pitched roof has an aluminium substructure. Hence, the modules are a means of supplying energy and also weather protection, and, as a result, obviate the need for an additional roof covering (see Functional overlaps, pp. 61f.).
The new ground slab extends throughout the entire new build (including the carport and terrace). The slab beneath the living areas and the connecting element is completed as a reinforced concrete base with foam glass insulation and EPS, and finished with cement screed. The latter, which is in fact the final floor finish, accommodates an underfloor heating system. The interior partition walls in the extension are made of timber studs lined with gypsum board.
The ground slab in the carport has been finished with concrete paving stones laid in a gravel bed. At the other end of the new build, however, the screed finish of the living room is continued out onto the terrace. Translucent glass-glass photovoltaic modules have been used above these two outside areas to provide protection from rain and sun, but also as an additional source of energy.
Wood-aluminium windows have been fitted both in the old and new parts of the single-family home. The vertical surfaces are triple glazed; the roof windows double glazed.

Energy concept

The project's design motto "home made" was fulfilled by providing a combination of passive measures in the old and new parts of the building to reduce the energy demand and active measures in the new build to make use of renewable and local energy sources.
The passive measures generally apply to the quality of the building envelope.

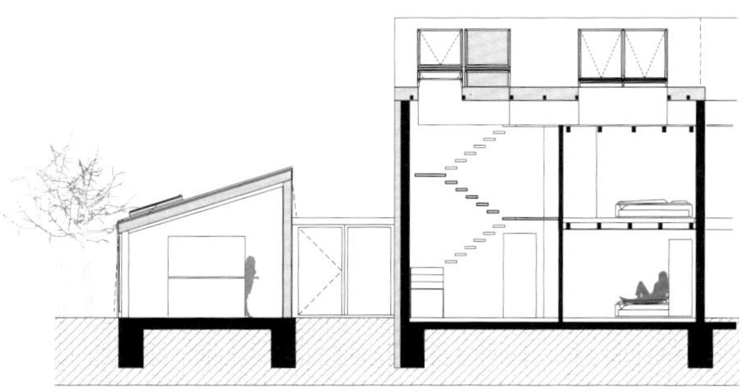

6.18

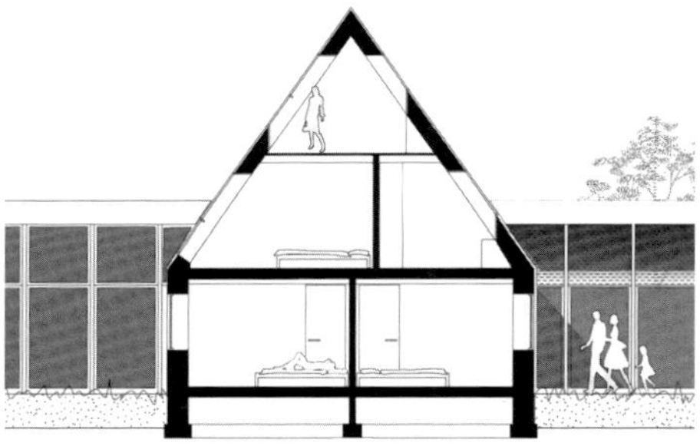

6.19

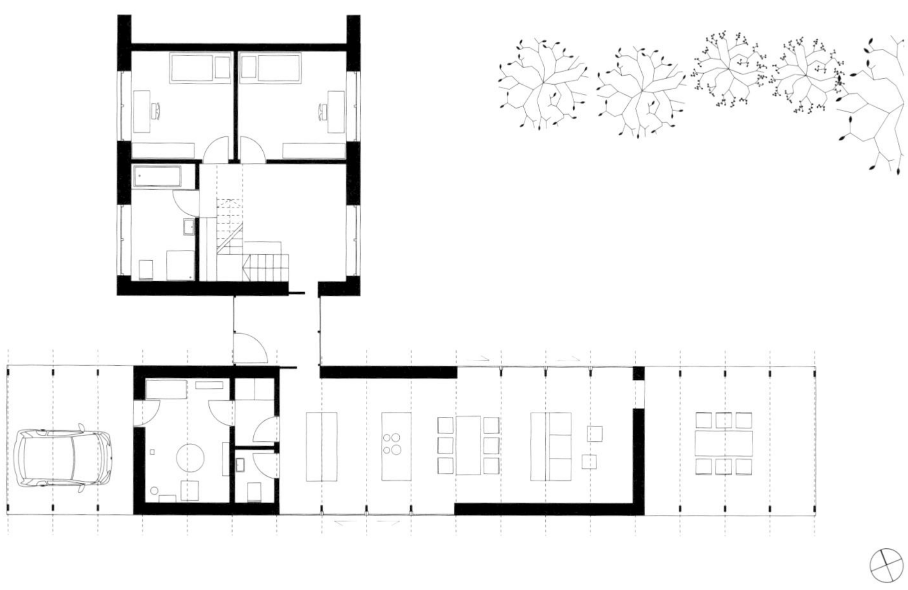

6.20

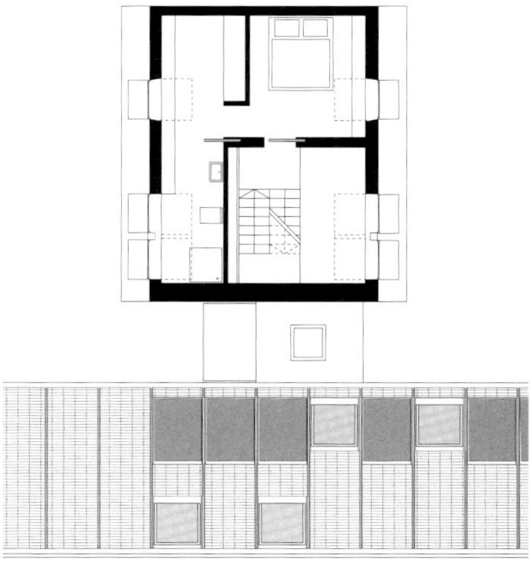

6.21

Transmission heat loss has been reduced by insulating the exterior walls; the greater airtightness is responsible for a much lower space heating demand. These modernisation measures reduced the total final energy demand for production of domestic hot water, space heating, building services and domestic power from 293.6 kWh/m²a to 108.5 kWh/m²a [5]. The measures were enhanced by a daylighting design (fig. 6.24), which was produced parallel to the first sketches and constituted a distinct feature of the integrated planning process [6]. In contrast to the original dwelling with a total window surface area of only 18 m², the completed project now has openings with an area of approximately 90 m²; almost 60 m² are part of the new build [7]. The cramped layout of the main access area was opened up to create a vertical daylight shaft (fig. 6.25). This multi-storey space receives daylight from above and functions as the building's main communication zone. Due to the large proportion of window surface area, the average daylight factor is now approximately 5 % in both parts of the building; in some areas, it even reaches almost 10 %. As a comparison: the German Sustainable Building Council (Deutsche Gesellschaft Nachhaltiges Bauen – DGNB) already awards the highest possible number of points in the category "New residential buildings 2012" to a situation where 50 % of the living area is supplied with a daylight factor of 2 % [8].

In the old part of the single-family home, a large proportion of the new window surface area is incorporated in the saddle roof (fig. 6.23). This solution ensures a more even distribution of daylight. The heat gain, on the other hand, is much higher than in the case of vertical windows, simply because rooflights admit light from almost all angles and let a large proportion of global radiation into the building. Nevertheless, the solid construction of the old building is able to absorb the solar heat gain during the day and dissipate the heat to the cooler room air at night. So the solid sand lime walls are, in fact, a heat store. In order to assist the removal of warm air from the interior, the windows have been positioned at different levels in the facade and roof. This window arrangement increases the natural stack effect.

The extension, in contrast, has only a very small proportion of roof glazing (fig. 6.22). The reaction time and degree of response to overheating is more pronounced than in the older building, and the solar heat gain is transmitted to the interior space almost immediately. The process has been slowed marginally by activating the screed as thermal mass.

The positions of the openings in the older and newer parts were determined according to thermodynamic simulations performed during the design phase. In addition, all windows have been equipped with automatically controlled solar shading and anti-glare protection devices to avoid overheating.

6.18 Longitudinal section (existing building and extension), scale 1:250
6.19 Section through existing building, scale 1:250
6.20 Ground floor plan, scale 1:250
6.21 First floor plan (excerpt), scale 1:250
6.22 Energy and climate concept of extension
6.23 Energy and climate concept of existing building
1 solar energy input through rooflights
2 natural ventilation (stack effect)
3 photovoltaics
4 solar thermal collectors (for DHW and underfloor heating system)
5 rain water harvesting
6.24 Daylight simulation
6.25 Vertical daylight shaft (open stairwell) in refurbished part of building

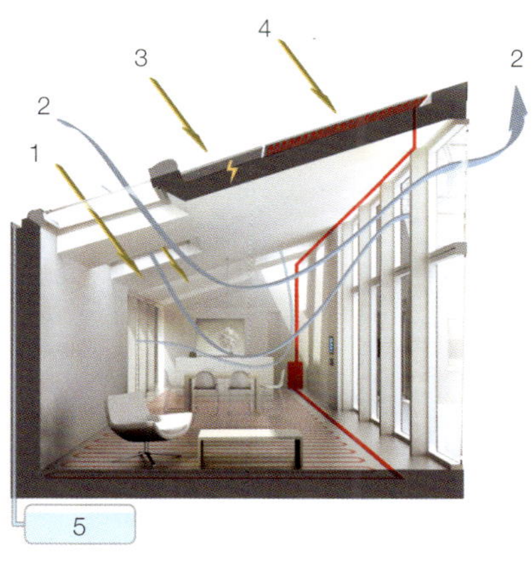

6.22

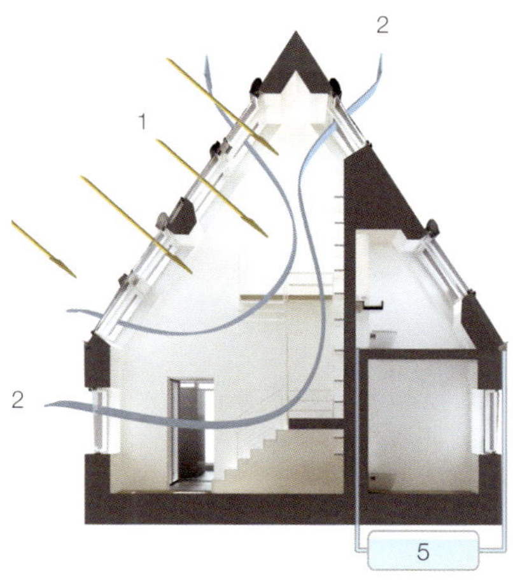

6.23

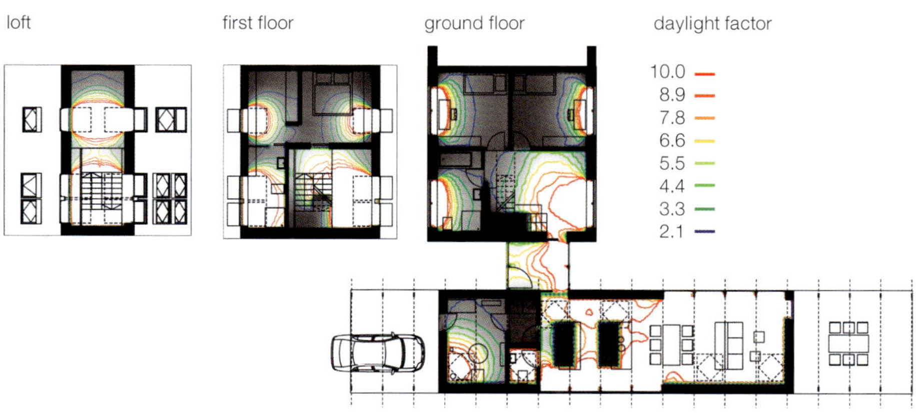

6.24

6.25

Alongside passive measures, the building envelope also features active energy-saving systems. The new extension, for example, is a small local power station that supplies the residents with heat and power. Roof-integrated solar thermal collectors and photovoltaic panels have been used as visible elements in the architectural design. The solar thermal collector plant, covering an area of 19.8 m², generates heat and domestic hot water in connection with an air-to-water heat pump. The system incorporates a large hot water tank with a capacity of 940 l for the provision of hot water in both the new and old part of the dwelling and to feed the underfloor heating system. The power needed to operate the building services systems (auxiliary power including heat pump, and domestic power including lighting) is generated by the photovoltaic plant covering an area of 75 m². The polycrystalline cells in the roof covering and the translucent glass-glass modules above the terrace and carport are designed to produce approximately 7000 kWh of electricity per year; any excess power is fed into the local grid [9]. In order to reduce ventilation heat loss as well as improve the climate and comfort conditions inside, all windows have been equipped with state-of-the-art sensor technology. The sensors are used to record and monitor the temperature, air humidity and concentration of CO_2 and VOC inside. All windows are controlled automatically to maintain the minimum air exchange and the indoor climate in accordance with the readings taken by the sensors. In comparison to a mechanical air handling unit, this solution makes do without any elaborately fitted air ducts. The sensor technology is also responsible for operating the sun shading and anti-glare devices. Alongside controlling the indoor temperature in summer, the sun shading devices are used to improve the thermal insulation properties of the building envelope in cold winter nights and thus reduce transmission heat loss through windows. Thanks to the refurbishment, the annual final energy demand of the building has been reduced by almost 65%. The primary energy demand currently lies at 47.2 kWh/m²a and thus undercuts the threshold value of the EnEV 2009 by 65.7%.

Design process and first experiences

During the design phase, the planning team closely examined the approach to the existing building by comparing three possible modernisation options, each with a different budgetary solution (fig. 6.26). The "basic modernisation" involved only an energy efficiency upgrade of the building envelope. The structure of the building was to a large part retained. The floor plan was given a more spacious and modern feel by opening up the walls in a few carefully chosen places.
The option "extended modernisation" involved a total overhaul of the building, which meant removing everything down to the bare walls. The aim was to totally strip the old house and upgrade the building envelope. A small timber-framed construction was added to the original building as an extension.
The solution "Aktivhaus modernisation" is more or less comparable with the project that was eventually carried out in Hamburg-Wilhelmsburg.
On completion of the refurbishment and after an exhibition period within the context of the IBA, the project entered a two-year test phase with a test family. The study was conducted by an interdisciplinary research team including architects, sociologists, building services and solar engineers using a monitoring programme. Sensors and meters recorded the family's energy and water consumption, the room

a b c 6.26

	Basic modernisation	Extended modernisation	Aktivhaus modernisation
Building envelope	refurbished	refurbished	refurbished
Building structure	openings in the layout	fully stripped	fully stripped
Roof	upgraded + rooflights	upgraded + rooflights	new rafter roof + rooflights
Building services	oil condensing boiler, radiators, solar thermal collectors + DHW tank	air-to-water heat pump, solar thermal collectors, buffer storage tank, underfloor heating, DHW tank	air-to-water heat pump, solar thermal collectors + PV buffer storage tank, underfloor heating, DHW tank
Extension	retained + glazed ridge	small timber frame structure	large timber frame structure
Space	2–3 persons	3–4 persons	4 persons
Energy demand + CO_2 emissions (added to the unrefurbished building)	−50%	energy −60%, CO_2 −70%	energy −65%
Costs (gross)	€140000	€274000	€460000

6.27

6.26 Design alternatives (floor plans, scale 1:500):
a basic modernisation
b extended modernisation
c Aktivhaus modernisation (completed design)
6.27 Comparison of design options
6.28 Roof gallery in refurbished part of the existing building
6.29 Section through facade/roof of existing building, scale 1:50
1 Roof:
fibre cement roof covering, light grey
40/60 mm battens
30/50 mm counter battens
roofing membrane (s_d = approx. 0.15 m)
35 mm wood fibre insulation panels
100/220 mm rafter with mineral wool insulation infill (WLG 035)
15 mm OSB panel as vapour barrier airtight-sealed joints
12.5 mm gypsum board
2 Window:
triple glazing in wood/aluminium frame
3 Exterior wall:
10 mm mineral render
200 mm mineral wool insulation
240 mm original masonry wall
10 mm plaster finish

6.28

temperature, daylight factor, indoor air quality, the performance of automatic control systems and requirements for manual operation.
Alongside these quantifiable figures, the study also took into account the residents' personal experience of living in the building by means of interviews, questionnaires and keeping an online diary. The sociologists, in particular, are hoping to use this information to identify factors that quantify the sense of wellbeing in buildings, an aspect which, from a scientific point of view, is still beyond the knowledge of present-day research.
Experience from the first year has shown that the approach to resource conservation is in line with the standard of living. The yield from the photovoltaic plant exceeds the calculations by approximately 10 %; the energy demand for the provision of space heating and domestic hot water is almost 30 % lower than expected (in total 58 kWh/m²a rather than the previously estimated 84 kWh/m²a). The heat gain generated by the solar thermal collectors in summer noticeably exceeds the requirements of the family of four. The power consumption of the technical facilities, however, is higher than what was estimated on paper. All in all, there was a discrepancy of about 55 %, or in figures approximately 2500 kWh, which meant that the target of achieving a net zero energy demand was missed by about 2300 kWh in the first year of operation. Among other things, this is due to the oversized solar thermal collector plant, which necessitated the use of the heat pump to dissipate excess heat to the outside air. In order to make better use of these summer heat gains, the building services were augmented by adding a geothermal plant, which functions as a seasonal thermal storage system, for the second year of the test phase. The heat that is fed into the ground in summer is now used in winter to heat the home. According to standards of thermal comfort [10], the quality of the room air and the conditions of thermal comfort monitored in both the old and new parts of the residential building are excellent throughout the year. Overheating was an issue only on very few days [11]. The annual distribution of temperature (fig. 6.30, p. 114) at different measuring points in the building shows that the rooms on the ground floor of the old building, in particular, heated up and cooled down less than the other rooms due to the availability of storage mass. The solid brickwork and the ventilation of the stairwell help to achieve the desired stack effect. The performance of the light timber-framed extension is similar to that of the rooms on the first floor of the old building where the (light) roof structure forms the largest part of the building envelope. Despite the use of sun shading devices, the residents felt that the rooms in the extension were too hot in summer. Uncomfortable draughts were an issue on cold winter days. The automatic sensor-controlled opening and closing of windows is noisy and was criticised as a disturbance, especially in the bedrooms of the older building. This was also a reason for switching off the automatic control systems at night [12].

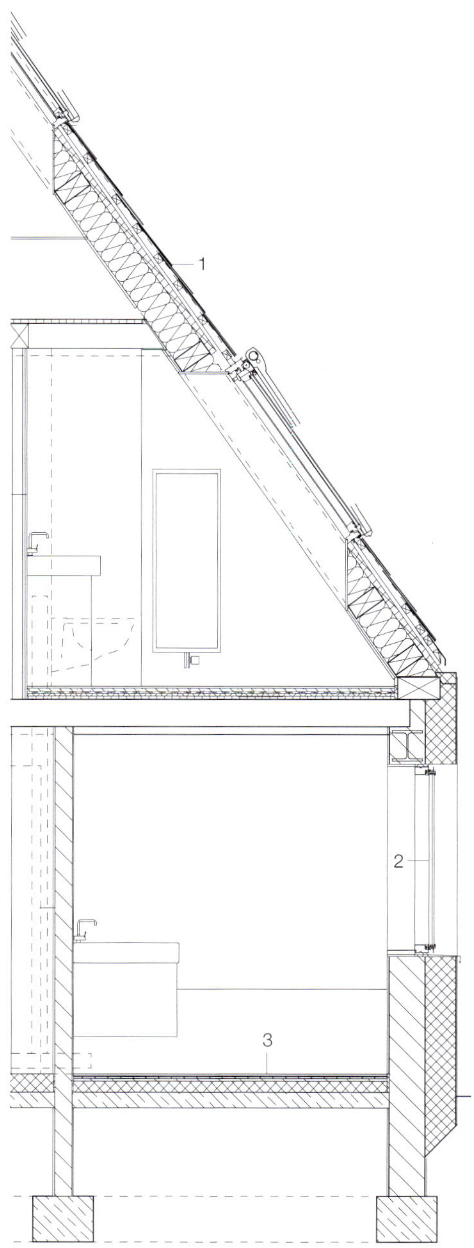

6.29

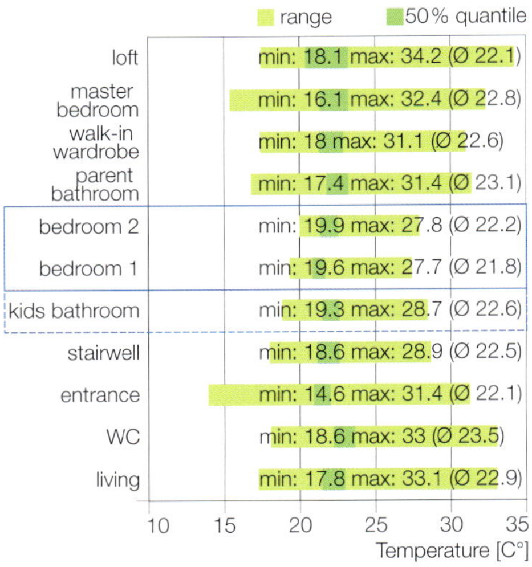

6.30

6.31

Indoor air hygiene

Alongside temperature and air humidity, sensors in the building also measure the concentrations of VOCs and CO_2. The windows open automatically as soon as one of the threshold values is exceeded. Whereas the CO_2 concentration in the room air is attributable to the residents, the level of VOCs is dependent mainly on the choice of materials. The well-considered choice of low-emission products in the LichtAktiv Haus is most visible in the choice of floor coverings: there are no carpets, laminates or vinyls, which contribute to higher emissions and form dangerous gases in the case of fire. The old building features parquet flooring. Because the anhydrite screed in the new build is coated with oil, it was not necessary to use epoxy resin. The gypsum plasterboard walls in the interior are finished with casein paint – a milk-product based paint. Despite all of these environmentally friendly measures, detailed advice on building materials was never received. The measurements taken in the first year indicate that the VOC concentration in the room air was on average below the normal level and even the maximum value was below the benchmark set by the Association of Ecological Research Institutes (Arbeitsgemeinschaft ökologischer Forschungsinstitute e. V. – AGÖF) [13]. The indoor air quality is thus regarded as ecologically sound (see Objectives, criteria and assessment methods, pp. 16ff.). One-off overruns of the target values are usually due to resident behaviour, such as cooking. The family members describe the air quality as having improved their standard of living significantly [14].

Life cycle assessment

In order to assess the energy efficiency and environmental impact on a material level, the construction process – a late stage that only offers a limited opportunity to control the choice of materials – was accompanied by a life cycle assessment [15]. The assessment took into account all new components and layers introduced into the building throughout their entire life cycle, including production, use, maintenance, removal and disposal. The original, retained parts of the residential building were not part of the analysis. The primary construction of the existing building, which did not have to be built this time round, was regarded as an available resource. The removal of parts no longer required in the new build, including the demolition waste, was also not taken into consideration. The life cycle assessment is based on the DGNB guidelines and designed to illustrate an operation period of 50 years (fig. 6.31, 6.33, 6.37, p. 116). The analysis differentiates between old (refurbished building) and new parts (extension). The results are differentiated according to their environmental impact and expressed per m² of surface area or as absolute values. In order to assess the impact the results have on the project, the indicators are summed up according to their factors of significance in the appropriate DGNB profile [16]. The results show that the mass-intensive components of the building envelope have the largest environmental impact of the LichtAktiv Haus. Even though the floor area of both building parts is almost identical (NFA_{new}: 116.8 m²/NFA_{old}: 112.4 m²), the difference in environmental impact is significant in all categories (fig. 6.31). All in all, the old part of the dwelling is responsible for only approximately a third. The ground slab of the new build with around 22 % represents the component with the largest single impact (fig. 6.36, p. 116). Due to

6.32

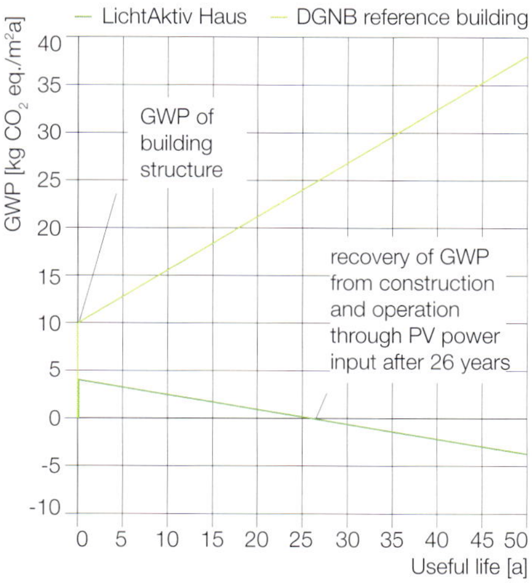

6.33

6.30 Annual distribution of room temperatures (January to December 2011) based on mean hourly measurements
6.31 Comparison of environmental impact (operating energy excluded) of new and old build over a course of 50 years
6.32 View from north-east (garden)
6.33 Global warming potential of the LichtAktiv Haus in comparison to DGNB reference building
6.34 Section through extension, scale 1:50
1 Roof connecting corridor (entrance area): bituminous waterproofing membrane, two layers
45 mm laminated veneer lumber
60 mm wood fibre insulation
roof beams with 190–240 mm mineral wool infill insulation, sloped
15 mm OSB panel; vapour barrier
12.5 mm gypsum board
2 Roof of extension:
18 mm photovoltaic module glass/glass
approx. 55 mm substructure
60 mm wood fibre insulation
EPDM roofing membrane, two layers
80/240 mm roof beam, laminated timber with mineral wool infill insulation (WLG 035)
vapour barrier (s_d = approx. 420 m)
15 mm OSB panel
12.5 mm gypsum board
3 Exterior wall:
single-pane safety glass in wood/aluminium frame
24/60 mm batten substructure, set into
80 mm wood fibre insulation
roofing membrane (s_d = approx. 0.02 m)
80/200 mm laminated timber post with mineral wool infill insulation (WLG 035)
15 mm OSB panel as vapour barrier (airtight-sealed joints)
30/50 mm battens with mineral wool infill insulation (installation zone)
2x 12.5 mm gypsum board
4 Floor:
75 mm screed (cement) with underfloor heating system, polished
PE separating layer
125 mm EPS insulation (WLG 035)
bituminous waterproofing membrane
250 mm reinforced concrete ground slab
PE separating layer
180 mm foamed glass insulation
6.35 Dining and living area in extension

the high groundwater level on the Elbe peninsula and the difficulties involved in constructing strip or deep foundations, the slab had to be executed as a raft foundation. For technical reasons, the concrete was poured to form a single solid slab underneath the living area, the carport, terrace and the connecting element between the new and the old part of the single-family dwelling. The amount of cement and steel are mainly responsible for the, in comparison, very high environmental impact of the ground slab. In the cement manufacturing process, for example, CO_2 is emitted not only for the transformation of the raw materials lime stone, clay, sand and iron ore, but also for the primary energy input for firing the kilns. The world-wide production of cement, including both of these aspects, is responsible for approximately 5–7 % of the total annual CO_2 emissions [17]. So, in terms of life cycle assessment, the old building benefits from retaining the primary construction. The existing ground slab was merely supplemented by a new screed, which reduces the amount of newly added mass and the resulting environmental impact.
With regard to the exterior wall constructions, both parts of the building are, in terms of absolute values, very similar. Even though the load-bearing structure of sand lime brick was retained, the added thermal insulation composite system has a comparatively short life cycle. Within the 50-year assessment period, the insulation has to be fully exchanged once, i.e. it has to be removed, disposed of and replaced.
A light timber-framed construction is used for the opaque wall elements of the new build. The ends are clad with fibre cement panels and therefore account for

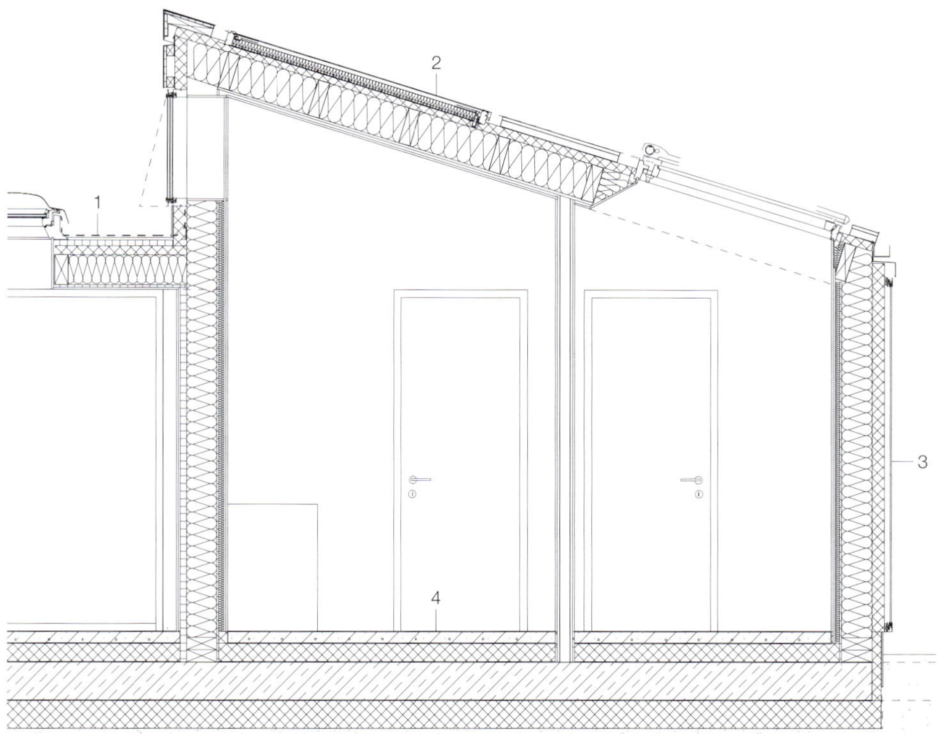

6.34

6.35

only approximately 1.4 % of the total environmental impact. The longer sides, on the other hand, are built using aluminium frames with tempered safety glass. In the manufacturing process of TG, the glass is tempered twice; in the second process, it is heated above the transition point (800 °C) and then cooled very quickly. The tension created in this process gives the material its greater strength and resistance. The use of tempered safety glass is valid in the case of this project; however, due to its complicated manufacturing process, a large proportion of the emissions induced by this building component are generated by the TG (9.7 % of the new build's total environmental impact).
The building component with the lowest CO_2 emissions is the ceiling above the first floor in the old part of the house. Within the total life cycle assessment, it even reduces the environmental impact of the building by 0.05 %. The original timber beams were retained and covered with a new layer of wooden floorboards. Untreated floorboards were used here, which can be thermally recycled (incinerated) at the end of their service life. The energy generated through incineration compensates for the energy used in the production of the floorboards, which means that this component is almost carbon neutral.
A life cycle assessment can be improved, in particular, by light, durable, reversible and recyclable constructions, as well as the use of renewable resources. So the use of a timber-framed construction in the new build is beneficial for the overall result. A further key factor is the reuse of the existing building stock. This is made especially clear by comparing the environmental impact of the LichtAktiv Haus with that of the DGNB reference building (fig. 6.37). The reduced amount of newly introduced high-mass and solid components leads to a much lower environmental impact of the LichtAktiv Haus than is the case for the reference building. The load-bearing structure, which usually makes up approximately 50 % of a building's environmental impact during its service life, was, for example, revitalised in the old building. The primary energy input is the only criterion where the LichtAktiv Haus exceeds the reference value. This can, however, be attributed to the comparably low compactness of the building.

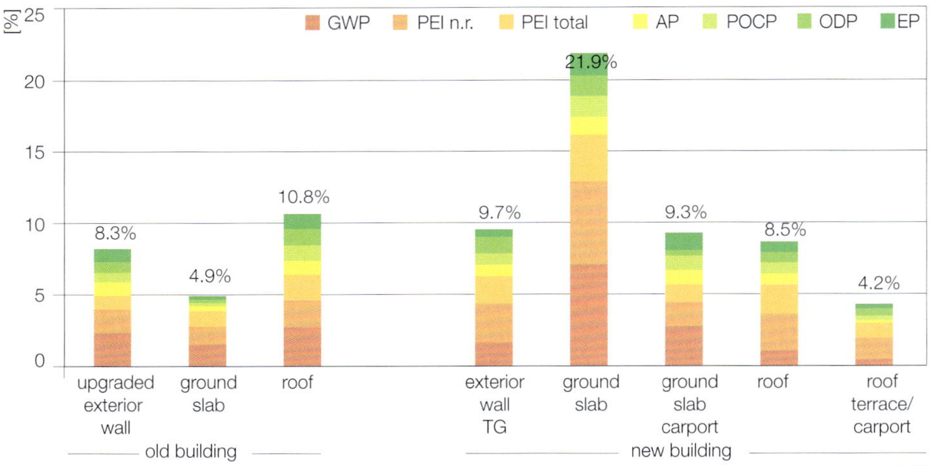

6.36

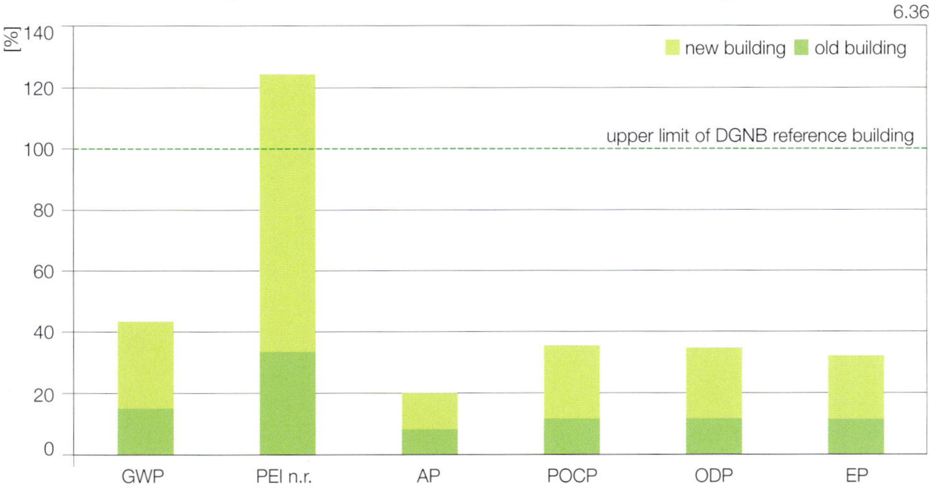

6.37

Because the building generates more energy than it consumes in its operation, the emissions accumulated through the construction, maintenance and disposal can be compensated during the use phase. Based on these calculations, the residential home is carbon neutral after an operation period of approximately 26 years (fig. 6.33, p. 114).

Conclusion

The significance of the load-bearing structure for the life cycle assessment of smaller buildings is perfectly illustrated by the LichtAktiv Haus. The floor slab, in particular, accounts for a large proportion of the environmental impact. A long-term and ecological solution for the thermal insulation composite system used to upgrade the existing walls would also have been beneficial for the life cycle assessment. However, the assessment also shows that the reuse of existing structures, even if a building is totally stripped, has significant potential.
The analysis goes beyond the environmental impact and highlights that the old and new parts of the building have a symbiotic relationship. Their different availability of storage mass allows for an energy-based zoning of the layout and, for example in terms of insolation, an optimised arrangement of functions during the day. The old part is sluggish and enables intense natural ventilation due to its height. The new build, in contrast, immediately transfers the outside climate to the interior space and thus provides, in terms of inside climate, a smooth transition to the garden. As a consequence, the private bedrooms are located in the older part; the communal areas, on the other hand, in the new build.
The original building stock reduces the environmental impact of the scheme by retaining its primary construction; the new build improves the life cycle assessment by generating energy with the building envelope. Together, both parts account for a much improved spatial, thermal and functional diversity. As a pilot project, they illustrate in a perfect way the opportunities inherent in the efficient use of existing building stock.

6.36 Cumulative environmental impact of the individual components (percentage comparison). The dominant role of the reinforced concrete ground slab in the extension (incl. carport) clearly stands out with a percentage of over 30 %.
6.37 Percentage comparison of the environmental impact of the LichtAktiv Haus and the DGNB reference building

Mixed residential and commercial building in Zurich

In the field of ecological and resource-efficient building, timber has the aura of being the all-around solution for every situation. It is a natural building material, resource efficient, pollution-free and 100% recyclable. What is more, the minimalist timber buildings completed throughout Europe in the last 20 years have no longer got anything to do with the eco houses characteristic of the environmental movement in the 1980s. The technical performance of these timber buildings is on a par with the high quality of their design. It is for this reason that timber is usually applied as a visible and characteristic feature: timber cladding in the facades, timber walls, ceilings, floor coverings and structures, which clearly have an impact on the atmosphere and style of the building, dominate today's image of modern timber structures. This is one of the reasons why, alongside the omnipresent issue of fire protection, timber constructions are usually an exception in town centres where the cityscape tends to be characterised by mineral or metal-based building materials.

Inner values

The mixed residential and commercial building, a housing cooperative building, on Badener Straße in Zurich is a novelty in this respect. In contrast to many timber-clad hybrid or solid brick buildings, this multi-storey building is made entirely of wood. Even though wood was primarily used for ecological reasons, the choice of the construction material, as would have been the case for buildings made of concrete or brick, focussed mainly on its technical and functional properties. The building does not reveal itself at all as a timber construction - neither inside or outside. The design of the facades and floor plans is a reaction to the very demanding urban situation with the heavily trafficked Badener Straße in the south and the new town park in the north; apart from the oak parquet flooring, the style and finishes of the apartments give no indication of a timber construction.

Project description

The Housing Cooperative Zurlinden is a private, non-profit corporation, which has decided to develop all new builds according to the framework of the 2000-Watt Society (see Optimisation of the building life cycle, pp. 57ff.). The design competition, initiated in 2006, for the development of inexpensive inner-city apartments on Badener Straße in Zurich was the first pilot project implementing this strategy. An architects' practice,

Project participants
Client: Baugenossenschaft Zurlinden (BGZ), Zurich
Architecture: pool Architekten, Zurich
Site management: Caretta Weidmann Baumanagement, Zurich
Sustainability consultant: Architekturbüro H. R. Preisig, Zurich
Timber engineer: SJB Kempter Fitze AG, Frauenfeld
Structural engineer: Henauer Gugler AG, Zurich
Building physics: Wichser Akustik + Bauphysik AG, Zurich
Building services: Amstein + Walthert AG, Zurich

Building parameters
Location: Zurich, Switzerland
Design period: 2006–2008 (20 months including competition)
Construction period: 2008–2010 (18 months)
Use: 54 apartments (2.5 and 3.5-room units), supermarket
Plot: 2700 m^2
Built surface area: 2700 m^2
Gross floor area (GFA): 13876 m^2
Living area (usable floor area): 7050 m^2
Treated floor area: 9150 m^2
Construction costs (German DIN cost groups 300/400): Total construction costs CHF 34 mil; CHF/m^2 living area: CHF 3900

Objective
2000-Watt compatibility (according to SIA Energy Efficiency Path)

Energy parameters (SIA 380/1)
Space heat demand, all zones: 17.5 $kWh/m^2_{TFA}a$
Space heat demand, only living: 14.7 $kWh/m^2_{TFA}a$
Heat demand DHW: 19.4 $kWh/m^2_{TFA}a$
(proportion covered by waste heat from supermarket: 15.8 kWh/m^2a)
Power output photovoltaics: 10000 kWh/a
Energy coefficient: 62 kWh/m^2a
Embodied energy (SIA 2032 fact sheet): 24.1 kWh/m^2a

6.38 Mixed residential and commercial building in Zurich (CH), pool Architekten 2010; view from the south

6.38

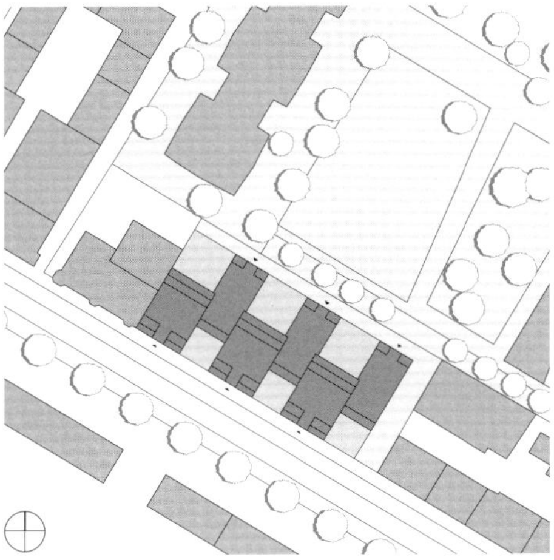
6.39

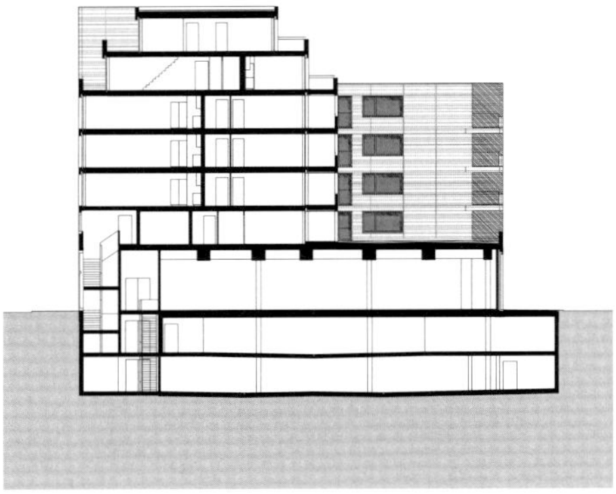
6.40

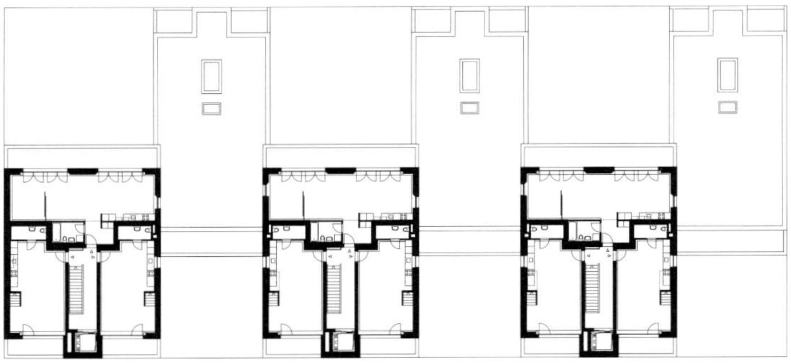
6.41

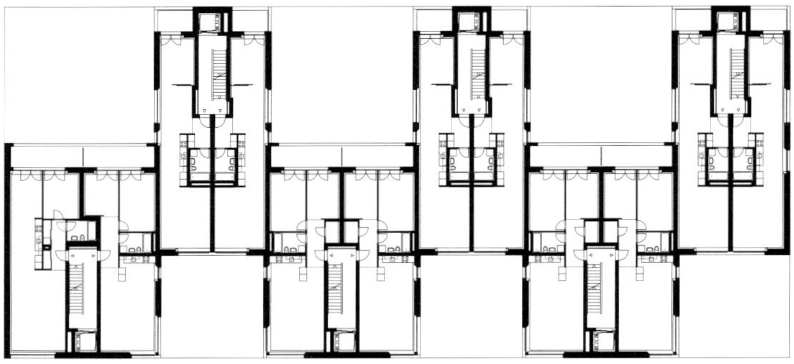
6.42

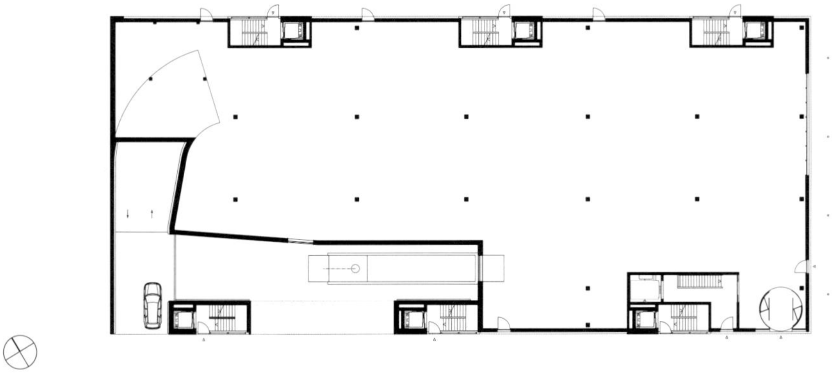
6.43

specifically chosen to support the model character of the scheme, already accompanied the development and implementation of sustainability strategies during the competition preparation phase. Alongside the development of approximately 50 apartments, the specifications included the creation of a large clear-span area on the ground floor for a new supermarket including all necessary facilities, such as a goods delivery zone. The above-ground car parking originally located on the site was to be replaced by an underground carpark.

The building, which is up to seven storeys high, covers the whole of the 2700 m² site formerly owned by the retail chain Migros on Badener Straße (fig. 6.39). Alongside the retail store, the ground floor also provides space for the goods delivery zone, the entrance and exit ramps to the underground carpark, as well as the entrances to the apartments. The six upper storeys accommodate a total of 54 dwelling units with 2.5 to 3.5 rooms each. The building, which, due to a number of setbacks, becomes narrower towards the top, features two equally important facades. Its comb-like structure allows each unit to be opened up to both sides, which in spatial terms are very different: the quiet north side with a view to the newly planned park and the busy road to the south (fig. 6.40–6.42). The various cutouts in the structure produce courtyards and help to reduce noise in the rooms positioned further back. The result is that all living rooms facing the street can also be ventilated naturally. Owing to the open-plan layouts – one room can be separated off with a sliding door if the need arises – views are provided from one side to the other side of the building.

The two basement levels, the ground floor and the two stairwells are solid constructions made of reinforced concrete. The ceiling above the ground floor is designed as a load-bearing plane to support the six residential storeys above consisting of load-bearing solid timber walls and hollow-core timber floor elements. The exterior cavity walls are clad with glass fibre concrete panels, which are fixed to an aluminium substructure (fig. 6.47, p. 120 and 6.55, p. 124). The energy for the generation of heat is mainly extracted from the waste heat of the supermarket's refrigeration units. The remaining heat demand is supplied by a groundwater heat pump, the electricity for which, by way of calculation, is covered by the 82 m² PV system on the roof of the building. Underfloor heating systems are used to distribute the heat in the rooms. Decentralised mechanical ventilation units, conceived as floor-to-ceiling elements, are incorporated in the facade next to each window to provide a controlled supply and extraction of air (fig. 6.51, p. 122). Due to the nature of the floors, it was not possible to incorporate any services, such as air ducts, into the structural elements; suspended ceilings were not an option owing to the low ceiling height. Each mechanical ventilation unit has an extractor fan and a heat recovery system with an efficiency coefficient of 80 %. The extracted heat is used to preheat the fresh air, which means that each room is totally independent. The stale air extracted from the bathrooms is guided up through the roof without any form of heat recovery.

Construction and material specifications

The use and construction of the lower levels is fundamentally different to the upper floors. The basement levels, the ground floor and the stairwells are made of concrete (fig. 6.44). Whereas it was possible to use recycled concrete in the stairwells, new concrete was, for technical and structural reasons, used for all components in contact with the ground as well as the ground floor. A load-bearing solid timber construction method, which was developed by the timber engineer Herman Blumer, was used for the first time in the residential storeys of this building. The walls are made of regional spruce using storey-high solid timber studs measuring 100/195 mm. The studs, each with a central drilled hole at the top and bottom, are connected to timber plates by means of dowels (fig. 6.48, p. 121). A ribbon plate, which is designed to tie-in the prefabricated hollow-core floor elements, completes the walls.
The ceiling elements are interlinked using steel shear connectors, thus forming a horizontal plane, which is anchored into the stairwell walls to provide earthquake resistance. Due to the optically very heterogeneous surface structure of the timber walls and the danger of fire and noise transmission, the 100-mm-thick interior walls are sheathed with gypsum fibreboard on both sides. The party walls are constructed as double walls with a mineral wool-filled cavity (40 mm) and gypsum fibreboard sheathing.
In the case of the exterior walls, the load-bearing timber structure is insulated on both sides. Work on site included adding 80-mm-thick mineral wool board

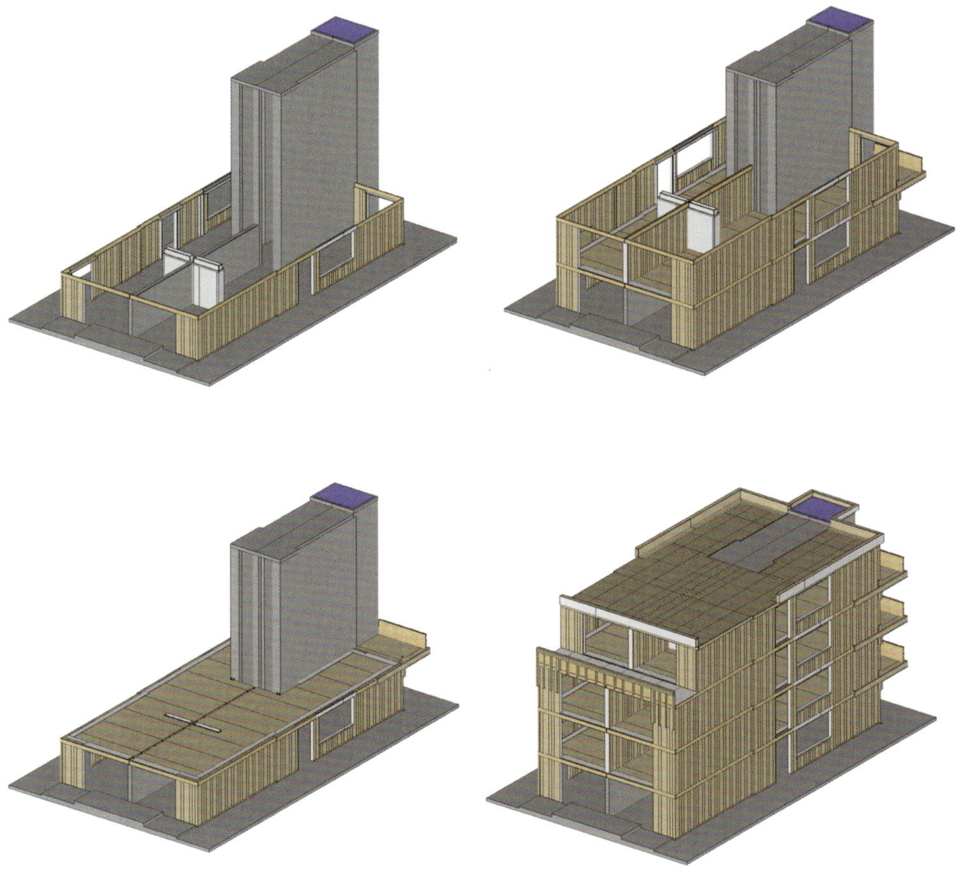

6.44

6.39 Site plan, scale 1:2500
6.40 Section, scale 1:750
6.41 5th floor plan, scale 1:750
6.42 3rd floor plan, scale 1:750
6.43 Ground floor plan, scale 1:750
6.44 Assembly sequence of the timber structure above the ground floor (supermarket) ceiling. This mixed residential and commercial building was the first building ever to use the newly developed solid timber construction method with storey-high spruce studs.

6.45 South-west facade with an "art in architecture" project completed by Superflex. According to the contract displayed here, the residents are obliged to limit their energy consumption to a maximum of 2000 Watt, including all personal areas of everyday life (home, consumer goods and transportation).
6.46 Apartment with kitchen block and floor duct (alongside left wall)

6.45

6.46

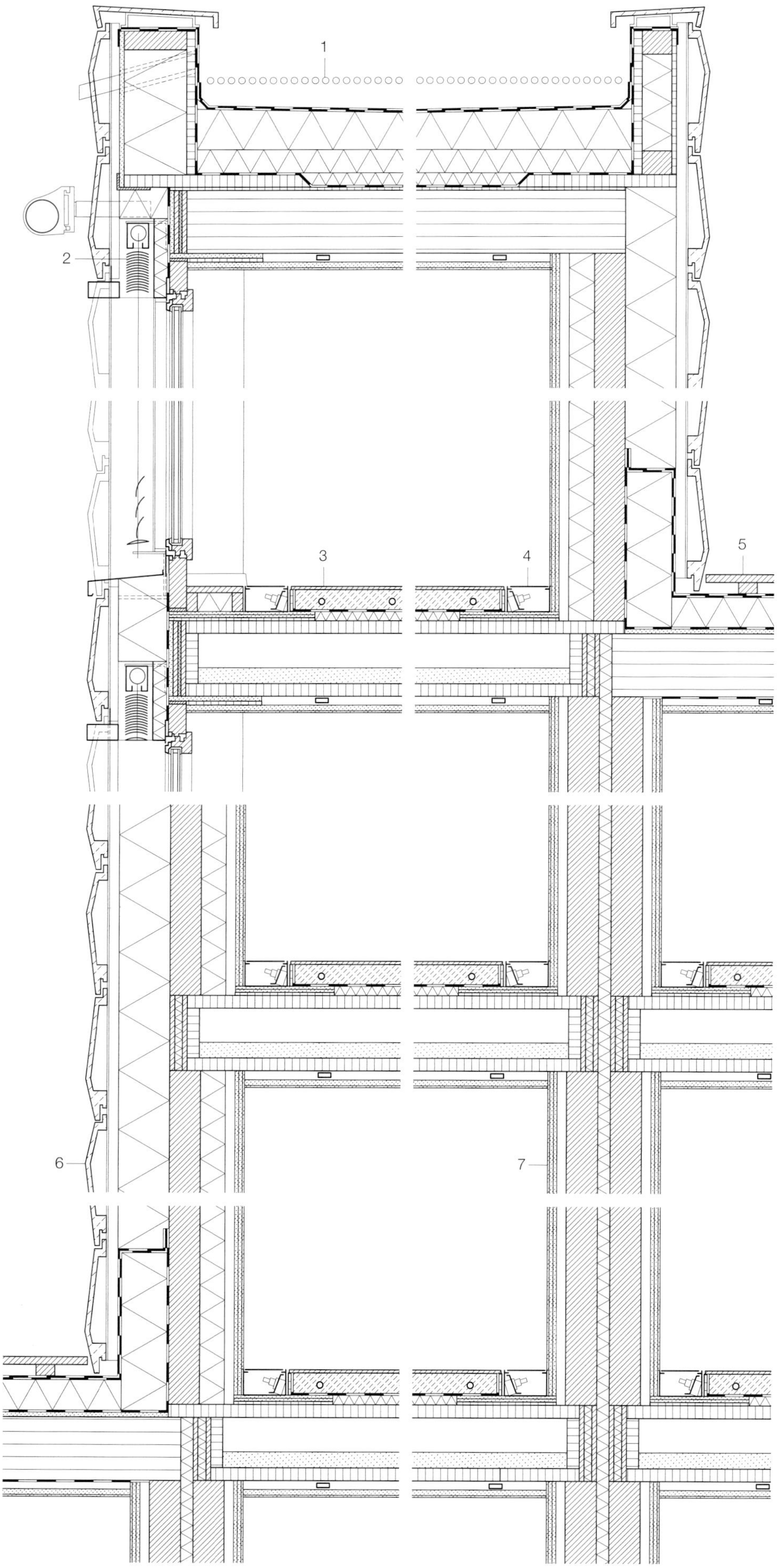

6.47

6.47 Vertical section through facade/roof, scale 1:20

1 Roof:
80 mm pebbles
10 mm protective layer
bituminous waterproofing membrane, two layers (top layer root resistant)
150–250 mm mineral wool insulation, sloped (along edges next to parapet: 130 mm PUR insulation, aluminium coated, pressure resistant)
3.5 mm EVA waterproofing membrane
3.5 mm OSB panel
200 mm roof slab, cross laminated timber
airtightness membrane
27 mm substructure with spring hangers
18 mm gypsum board (fire protection)
5 mm thin coat plaster

2 Aluminium venetian blind, with 50 mm mineral wool insulation behind
aluminium cover, gold anodized

3 Floor structure:
10 mm parquet flooring
70 mm cement screed with underfloor heating
PE separating layer
30 mm thermal and impact sound insulation, mineral wool
hollow core element (total height 240 mm) comprising:
40 mm laminated veneer lumber
160 mm joists
with infill of chippings, approx. 50 mm
40 mm laminated veneer lumber
27 mm substructure with spring hangers
18 mm gypsum board (fire protection)
5 mm thin coat plaster

4 Floor duct with steel cover plate, 80 × 150 mm screwed into gypsum board

5 Roof terrace:
timber deck, solid larch, varnished
35 mm battens
8 mm separating layer/roofing membrane
bituminous waterproofing membrane, two layers
60–100 mm PUR insulation, sloped, aluminium coated, pressure resistant
vapour barrier
15 mm gypsum fibre board
200 mm Brettstapel panel
airtightness membrane
27 mm substructure with spring hangers
18 mm gypsum board (fire protection)
5 mm thin coat plaster

6 Exterior wall:
70 mm glass fibre concrete facade cladding
30 mm substructure/cavity ventilation
160 mm mineral wool insulation
windtight membrane
100 mm timber stud wall
80 mm mineral wool insulation
30 mm substructure
felt membrane
25 mm gypsum board, two layers
5 mm thin coat plaster
glass fibre fleece

7 Apartment partition wall:
glass fibre fleece
5 mm thin coat plaster
25 mm gypsum board, two layers
felt membrane
30 mm substructure
100 mm timber stud wall
40 mm mineral wool insulation
100 mm timber stud wall
30 mm substructure
felt membrane
25 mm gypsum board, two layers
5 mm thin coat plaster
glass fibre fleece

6.48 Assembly sequence of timber construction system (exterior wall and floor)

6.49 View from north-east

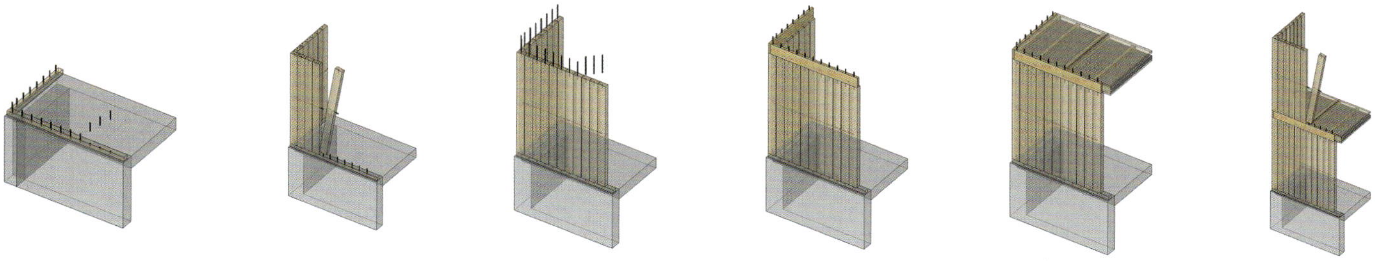

6.48

and a double layer of gypsum fibreboard to the inside. The wall configuration is completed by adding a wind-tight membrane, insulation consisting of 160-mm-thick mineral wool board and rear-ventilated cladding using grooved glass fibre concrete panels fixed to an aluminium substructure on the outside (fig. 6.47). Noise abatement and summer heat protection are improved by incorporating a 50-mm-layer of chippings into the cavities of the 240-mm-thick hollow core floor elements. This measure adds a mass of 60 kg/m² to the ceilings. For noise abatement and fire protection purposes, the lower side is finished with 18-mm-thick decoupled plasterboard; the top side includes a 70-mm-thick layer of floating screed, incorporating an underfloor heating system, and 10-mm-thick solid parquet flooring. The full height of the floor structure is 400 mm, which means it is at the top end of floor thicknesses commonly used in solid structures (approximately 330–420 mm).

For issues concerning building physics, the flat roof is made of 200-mm-thick Brettstapel panels instead of the hollow-core floor elements (to prevent the formation of condensation in the cavity). The upper side has been finished by adding sloped insulation using 150–200-mm-thick mineral wool board. In terrace areas, the good insulation properties of the Brettstapel panels mean that the height of the construction is only approximately 150 mm, thus providing almost level access to the outside living areas. The height of the construction inside did not have to be raised nor was it necessary to install vacuum insulation panels outside. The height of the terrace structure would have even been slightly less if cement tiles had been chosen for the surface finish instead of wood decking.

The vertical service lines are accommodated in continuous shafts equipped with reversible fire protection panels next to the stairwells, which eases the burden of retrofitting measures considerably. A cavity wall system was used for the installation of plumbing and sanitary equipment. The horizontal wiring in the apartments is contained in visible floor ducts with the result that there are no unsightly cables on the ceilings and walls (fig. 6.46).This solution is comparatively expensive, however, it not only makes planning the cable layout and a possible change of use at a later date easier but also provides more flexibility for the residents who have access to power and communications throughout the apartment without any visible cable clutter.

Swiss fire regulations permit a maximum of six storeys for timber structures, and they may not exceed an eaves height of 25 m. The construction chosen for this scheme, with the ground floor made of concrete, meant that the actual timber structure could be limited to six storeys and planning permission was granted. All load-bearing components meet the requirements of EI60 specified by the

6.49

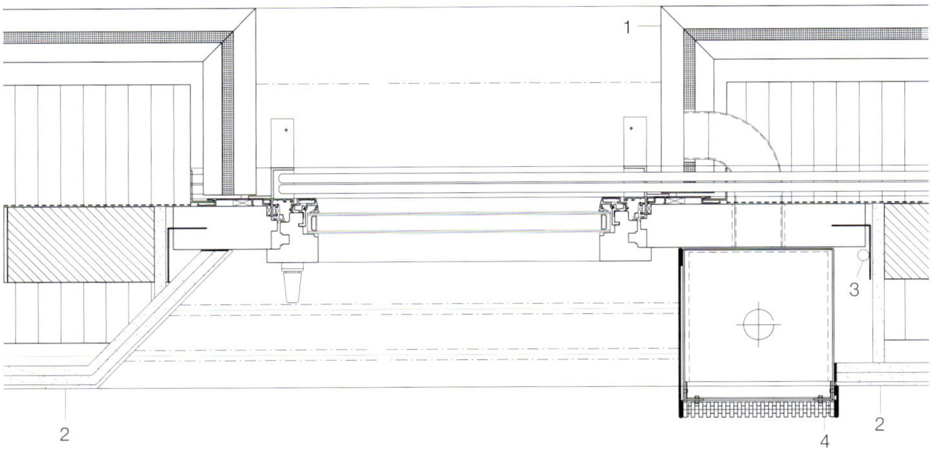

6.50

Association of Swiss Canton Fire Insurances (VKF); the ground floor and the stairwells have been executed according to EI60 nbb.
The clients did not specify any additional requirements concerning noise abatement. The facades, floor and wall structures were tested by the Swiss Federal Laboratories for Materials Science and Technology (EMPA) during the planning phase and produced very good results (facade: R_w 67 dB, max. deviation 11 dB at 125 Hz). No acoustic measurements were taken after completion of the building even though this would have been interesting for the companies in charge of the very sophisticated detailing and the use of floor ducts. Nevertheless, the residents have confirmed that the insulation is very good in terms of airborne sound, whereas impact and low-frequency noise from the neighbours is audible (e.g. washing machines, lifts).

Design and construction process
The development of the, in some respects, highly unusual concepts and strategies was partly determined by following the principles of SIA 2040 (SIA Energy Efficiency Path), which specifies clear benchmarks in the categories embodied energy, operation and mobility. The specifications are derived from the overall objectives of the 2000-Watt Society in the field of residential building and provide the framework for a detailed account of the energy consumption and the greenhouse gas emissions. The president of the building society had been involved in the development of the SIA Energy Efficiency Path and was therefore interested in demonstrating the possibilities and advantages of this approach in comparison to using established labels.
By commissioning a specialist for sustainability, the client was able to clarify important issues concerning quality assurance at a very early stage and take into consideration the various aspects in the design. All competition designs were checked during the preliminary evaluation stages according to their input of embodied and operating energy. While the award-winning design was not the most compact entry, it provided the best solution for the many requirements inherent in a situation which from an urban design point of view was very difficult for the development of a residential building. Many decisions made during later design phases were based on the preliminary studies and analyses of alternative solutions.
At the competition entry stage, the housing scheme was not planned as a timber structure but as a conventional solid construction. However, first assessments showed that the design, which from an energy efficiency viewpoint was not perfectly compact, would not be able to meet the target values of the SIA Energy Efficiency Path if built in a conventional way. It was for this reason that the client and architect searched for solutions to improve the load-bearing structure, which they eventually found in the new timber construction method. It was originally planned to combine the solid timber walls with conventional concrete floor slabs. However, the further development of the system finally led to a combination with timber floors.
As a consequence of these fundamental decisions, new solutions had to be found for other details, such as the decentralised ventilation units or the accessibility of the floor ducts. The technical elements were not concealed, but considered as a design feature and thus arranged carefully in the planning process (fig. 6.51). The client was often willing to accept more expensive solutions if they promised to provide added value for the users of the building or reduce the carbon footprint.

6.51

6.52

6.50 Horizontal section through window, scale 1:10
1 corner element, glass fibre concrete
2 2× 12 mm gypsum board sheathing, smooth finish
3 cable for aluminium venetian blind
4 ventilation unit
6.51 Decentralised ventilation unit with heat recovery system in one of the apartments
6.52 View from the balcony at the rear of the building looking out north towards the high-rise housing blocks
6.53 Comparison of the SIA Energy Efficiency Path benchmarks with the values achieved by the mixed residential and commercial building in Zurich
6.54 Comparison of different facade cladding systems
a in terms of quantity
b in terms of quantity and quality

This interaction between the project participants is expressed most clearly in the cladding of the facade: for reasons of durability, the clients had originally requested a rear-ventilated facade. The architects, however, wanted the building to blend into the urban neighbourhood with its mainly stone buildings (fig. 6.52). Consequently they favoured a facade with a compact and solid appearance. When comparing the environmental impacts of different sheathing materials, the only 13-mm-thick and comparatively light glass fibre concrete panels, which are extruded and then air-dried in the manufacturing process, performed well. Moreover, the manufacturer's production site was only approximately 50 km away from the building site. The folds in the elements give the facade greater plasticity and ensure that the horizontal joints are less prominent. This measure also increases the stability of the facade panels, allowing the distance between the aluminium elements of the substructure, which is mainly responsible for the environmental impact and costs of the facade, to be increased by 40 cm, from 80 cm to 120 cm (fig. 6.55, p. 124).
It was difficult to determine the embodied energy and the global warming potential according to the SIA Energy Efficiency Path, because there are no benchmarks for retail stores. Moreover, the city of Zurich stipulated that an underground garage be built to accommodate the car parking which was originally available on the site; however, this was not to be used by the residents of the building. It is for this reason that the first basement level and the ground floor including the ceiling above were not taken into consideration in the calculations. Nevertheless, the planners also made some suggestions for the improvement of the ceiling above the ground floor. Instead of opting for the originally planned flat plate, the height of the construction was reduced by adding downstand beams to the concrete floor slab.

Environmental impact

The use of load-bearing solid timber elements combines some of the advantages of solid construction with those of timber construction. In comparison to clay or sand lime brick, timber has a much better relation between U-value and specific heat storage capacity. The result is that, in contrast to a timber framework construction, the storage mass in the building rises considerably without increasing the

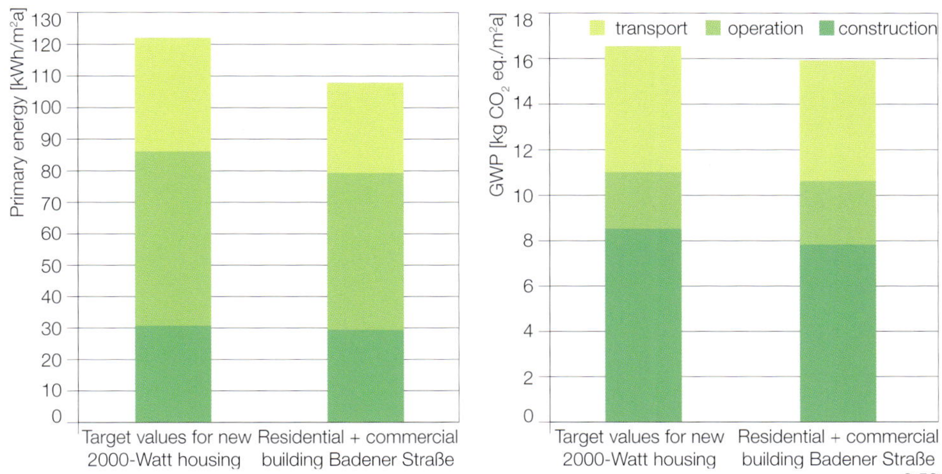

6.53

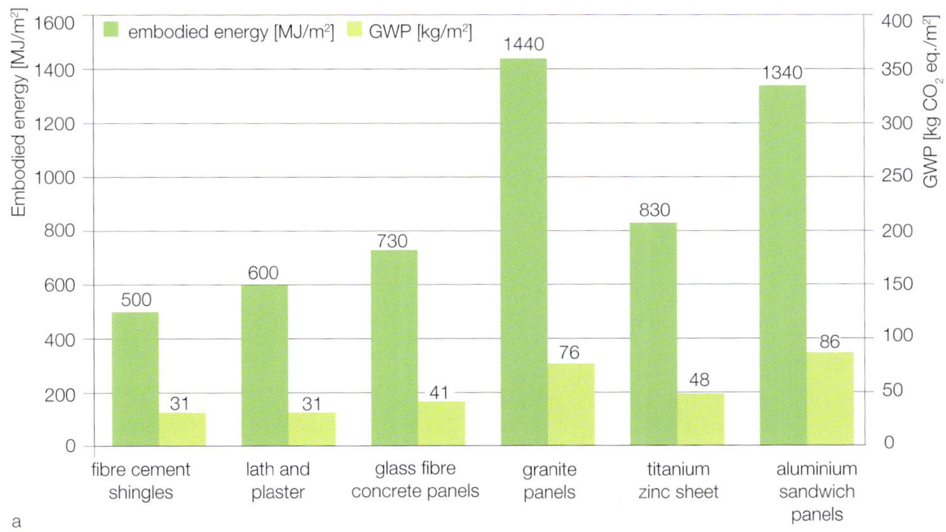

a

Material	Fibre cement shingles	Lath and plaster	Glass fibre concrete panels	Granite panels	Titanium zinc sheet	Aluminium sandwich panels
Description	small-size fibre cement panels	lath made of recycled glass granulate and epoxy resin as binding agent, organic render	16 mm glass fibre concrete panel	natural stone panel from Northern Italy, heavy panel with complicated fixing system	premium titanium zinc sheet, folded, 5 kg/m²	sandwich made of power-coated aluminium panels with foamed plastic core, special light metal substructure
Attachment/ structure	bracket/ wall tie, fibre cement shingles 6 mm	bracket/ wall tie, lath, 12 mm render	bracket/ wall tie, 16 mm glass fibre concrete, extruded	special substructure, 30 mm granite panels	bracket/ wall tie, 7 mm sheet metal, folded, on timber sheathing	special substructure, 4 mm sandwich panel
Embodied energy [1] [MJ/m²]	500	600	730	1440	830	1340
GWP [kg CO_2-eq./m²]	31	31	41	76	48	86
Material ecology	safe	hazardous disposal, reactor disposal site/ special waste	safe	large amount of transport energy, environmental impact, safe	high removal through washout, enters food chain via water	resource inefficient, high greenhouse gas emissions for production

[1] The outermost layer including the substructure (fixing devices) is responsible for approximately 50 % of the exterior walls' total embodied energy. This corresponds to approximately 15 % of the building's total embodied energy. This means that the differences between the variants listed above have an impact of approximately ± 5 % on the energy input into the construction of the building.

b

6.54

6.55

6.56

thickness of the exterior walls. Furthermore, the system used here is comparable with a brick wall due to the linear load transfer and the assembly of squared timber on site. The homogenous structure of layers with a small degree of prefabrication results in a simple sequence of trades on site and theoretically enables the development of buildings with more than ten storeys. Due to the quick assembly of walls and the simple installation of prefabricated floor elements, the construction time is reduced noticeably. The construction time of the new build on Badener Straße was approximately three months shorter than would have been the case for a comparable solid concrete or masonry construction. In contrast to a timber-frame building, a solid timber construction requires greater wall thicknesses to achieve the same U-values, and the embodied energy is higher. However, in order to reach a level of summer heat protection comparable to that of a solid timber construction, it would be necessary to compensate for the lack of storage mass in the exterior walls of the timber-frame building by using, for example, concrete floor slabs or timber-concrete composite floors. In comparison to timber floors, this, in turn, would lead to an increased environmental impact.
The completed facade structure reveals a further conflict of objectives arising from highly insulated, rear-ventilated solid timber exterior walls: if the thickness of exterior insulation exceeds 20 cm, the number and size of brackets to fix the cladding, and thus also the impact on the environment, rises disproportionately. If the load-bearing component is insulated on both sides, as is the case here, the inner layer of insulation prevents the activation of the timber's storage mass. The exterior walls can then no longer be considered as making a positive contribution to the improvement of summer heat protection.
The use of hollow-core timber floor slabs leads to a significant reduction of embodied energy since the floor slabs usually make up the largest surface area in a building. The degree of reduction, however, is very much dependent on the requirements concerning fire and noise protection. Large-scale gypsum plasterboard or gypsum fibreboard finishes increase the embodied energy to such a degree that the savings are often lost (fig. 4.4, p. 70).
Thanks to the floor elements, which span the full width of an apartment without intermediate supports, it is easy to change the use of the building within the units. Due to the selected construction system, it is not possible to create larger units by connecting two or more apartments; however, the need to do this is considered highly unlikely based on the urban situation and the shape and size of the building.
The system building method chosen allows for an orderly deconstruction and removal of all parts. It is possible to meet new insulation standards by adding a thicker layer of insulation or changing the facade cladding. Outside the heating period, these measures can be performed while the apartments are in use. The strict separation of all building services installations provides for easy retrofitting of cables, pipes and ducts as well as any adjustments necessary to meet future requirements and to use better technologies without having to interfere with the primary structure (fig. 6.56).
The use of decentralised ventilation units is a more complicated matter. Decentralised solutions may still be available in future, but it is difficult to foresee whether these will fit into the existing facade. The sound of the fan can be heard in the bedrooms, especially at night. The further development of the system, however, will hopefully reduce noise emissions to an acceptable level.
Due to the good access to public transport and the consistent reduction of environmental loads in the development and operation, the project Badener Straße 380 undercuts the target values of the Efficiency Path in all three categories. Thus, it is the first 2000-Watt-compatible building ever to have been completed in Switzerland (fig. 6.54, p. 123).

Conclusion

Several factors were critical for meeting the high demands of the project: on the one hand, the client's own interest to systematically implement the objectives of the SIA Energy Efficiency Path and the early involvement of a sustainability specialist to oversee the design and perform quality assurance measures. This was complemented by the willingness and capability of the architects and planners to incorporate the specifications concerning energy efficiency and sustainability, as well as the results of comparisons between different variations and components in the design and planning processes. The aim here was to generate synergy and thus increase the overall quality of the project. Alongside the commitment to finding creative solutions, one of the planning team's main achievements was the positive and open-minded approach to wood.
The advantage of the SIA Energy Efficiency Path is the comprehensive and target-oriented assessment of material and energy flows, as well as the great openness in terms of requirements. The involvement of a sustainability specialist to provide advice and quality assurance is of great importance in this case, since it is not yet common practice to have an external assessment of the design conducted.

6.55 Mixed residential and commercial building in Zurich: facade during the construction phase (corner detail)
6.56 Cavity wall before sheathing
6.57 Office building in Krems: view from Ringstraße in the south

Office building in Krems

The slogan "Let's hope it's concrete!", invented for an image campaign in 1991, aimed at counteracting the commonplace prejudice that this material is cold and hostile. The sentence could, however, also be interpreted as a manifestation of a universal phenomenon among architects, who – in stark contrast to public opinion – had already selected concrete as their favourite material a very long time ago.

Let's hope it's concrete!

The reasons for this wish are, among other things, based on the fact that no other material is so closely linked to contemporary architecture. The range of surface structures and atmospheres reach from the archaic roughness of "béton brut", a name that Le Corbusier coined in the 1920s, to the perfectly smooth visual concrete facades of Kunsthaus Bregenz designed by Peter Zumthor.
The innate malleability, the monolithic appearance and the homogeneous surface structure of exposed concrete can turn buildings into almost perfect sculptures. The worldwide availability, the low production costs and the simple implementation on site are further technical advantages. The benefits in terms of building physics, such as the thermal storage capacity, noise reduction and the excellent fire protection properties, also express that concrete is a universal construction material suitable for a large range of different applications.
However, the production of cement is an extremely energy-intensive process and large amounts of CO_2 are released during manufacture, making the use of concrete controversial from an environmental viewpoint. It is for this reason that ways and means are being investigated to reduce the environmental impact of concrete constructions.
The desire for resource efficiency also determined the design of the Niederösterreichhaus in Krems. The administrative offices of the Lower Austrian State Government completed in 2011 were not only supposed to reach Passive House standard but also to reduce the energy embodied in the executed constructions to an absolute minimum.
In addition to the strategies and systems to optimise concrete constructions mentioned in the chapter "Strategies for material use in the construction process" (p. 46), such as reduction of the slab's span and thickness, use of precast concrete hollow core slabs, minimisation of load-bearing concrete walls and the use of recycled concrete as aggregate, the production processes and the configura-

Project participants
Client: LIG NÖ – Landesimmobiliengesellschaft mbH, St. Pölten
Project design: ARGE NÖHK – AllesWirdGut, Vienna/feld72, Vienna/Fritsch, Chiari & Partner, Vienna
Building services: ZFG Projekt GmbH, Baden near Vienna
Building physics: DI Walter Prause, Vienna
Electrical design: Kubik Project GmbH, Gießhübl
Fire protection planning: Ingenieurbüro H. Redl, Getzersdorf
Preliminary study on energy and ecology: Stockinger & Partner, Limbach
Ecology consultant: bauXund Forschung und Beratung GmbH, Vienna

Building parameters
Location: Krems, Austria
Design period: 2005–2011
Construction period: 2009–2011
Use: office and administration
Plot: 4781 m²
Built surface area:
2179 m² building + 1288 m² car park
Gross floor area (GFA):
12556 m² building + 5697 m² car park
Usable floor area (UFA): 9915 m²
Treated floor area (according to PHPP): 8756 m²
Volume: 36805 m³
Total construction costs: €25 mil

Objective
Passive House standard

Energy parameters according to OIB energy certificate (in reference to site climate)
Space heat demand (SHD): 7.79kWh/m²a
Primary energy demand, non-renewable (according to PHPP; for heating, DHW, cooling, auxiliary power for ventilation, lighting and office equipment): 115.5 kWh/m^2a_{TFA}
Power output photovoltaics: 9.45 kW_{peak}
DHW demand: 4.71 kWh/m²a
Energy demand for space heating: 18.87 kWh/m²a
Energy demand for cooling: 29.44 kWh/m²a
Energy demand for lighting: 18.4 kWh/m²a
OI3 $index_{GFA}$: 109

6.57

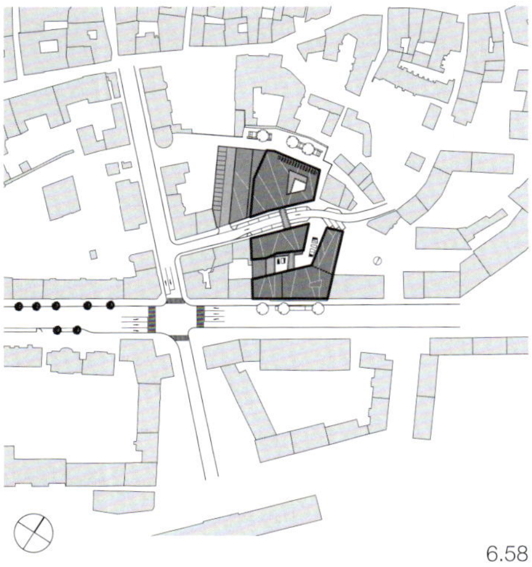

6.58

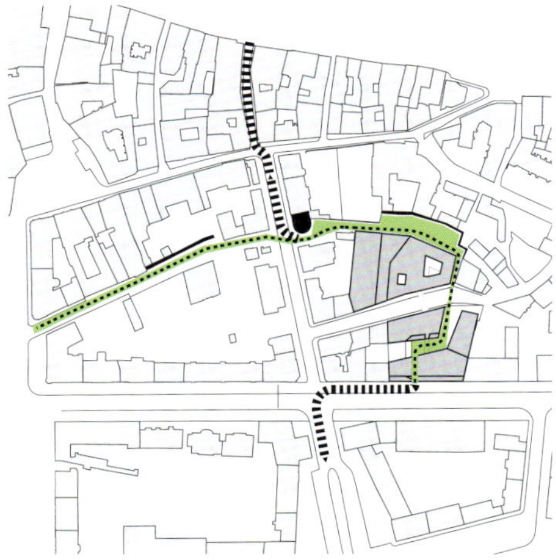

6.59

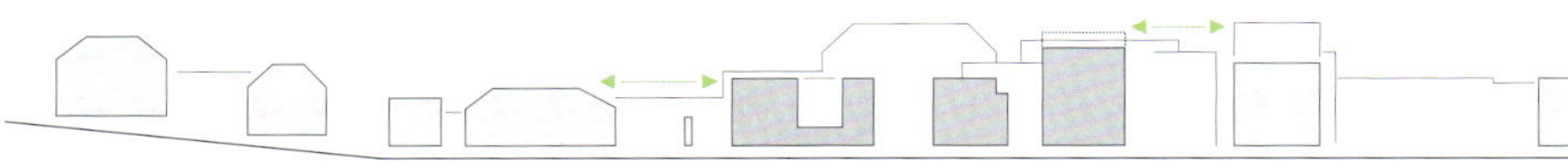

Scale

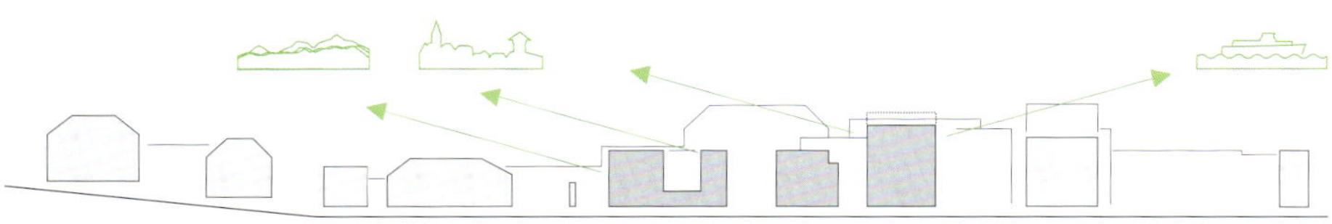

Views

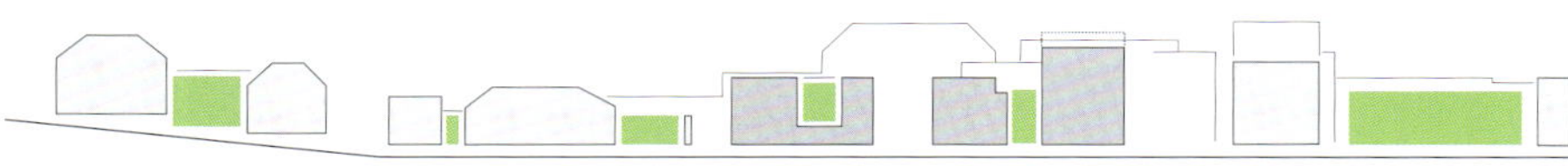

Courtyards

6.60

6.61

tion of the cement mixture also offer sizable potential for decreasing the impact on the environment. Alongside the most frequently used cement mixtures (CEM I B and CEM II B) featuring large proportions of Portland cement, recent years have seen the introduction of cements with greater amounts of blast furnace slag sand (CEM III B with 70 % blast furnace slag sand and sulphate blast furnace slag cement with 90 % blast furnace slag sand; see Substitution processes, p. 46). Blast furnace slag sand is a waste product (slag) left over from steel production. On account of its excellent watertightness, it has been used in road construction and underground engineering for a long time. The CO_2 savings potential is between 47 % (CEM III B) and 65 % (sulphate blast furnace slag cement) in comparison to cement mixtures usually used in Central Europe.
The Niederösterreichhaus is one of the first buildings in Europe to make extensive use of CEM III B to reduce the primary energy input. It can therefore be regarded as a role model project when investigating improvement potentials in the construction industry.

Project description

The two-stage competition for the Niederösterreichhaus initiated in 2005 called for the design of an office building to house the administration of the district capital Krems, various regional authorities and the district's Chamber of Commerce in a part of the old town, which at that time was still fairly rundown. The plot, in the immediate vicinity of the main station, had lain idle and had predominately been used as a car park for many years. To the south it is bordered by the ring road; to the north it backs onto the medieval town wall. The proposal submitted by the team of architects AllesWirdGut and feld72, and the structural engineers Fritsch, Chiari & Partner was the most convincing competition entry, in particular due to the way in which the new build blends into the existing building stock. In response to the small-scale structures in the immediate neighbourhood, the architects subdivided the approximately 60 000-m³-large volume into three blocks, which are all interconnected by bridges on the upper storeys (fig. 6.67, p. 129). This arrangement and the different heights of the blocks help to embed the complex in the ensemble of historic buildings and continue the existing structure of alleyways, squares and public thoroughfares (fig. 6.59–6.61).

All three blocks are connected by a central north-south axis incorporating not only the two bridges but also the four entrances on ground floor level. These connecting ties ensure that the three components form a functional unit. Only the Chamber of Commerce located on the ground floor of the most northern block is treated as a separate element with its own entrance. Alongside the approximately 200 work spaces, the office complex includes a number rooms for special purposes, ranging from an X-ray room for the Public Health Officer to a civilian safe room for the District Commission. Local residents were strongly opposed to the erection of a multi-storey public car park with 159 spaces on the west side of the northern block. However, due to the vicinity of the Danube and the inherent high groundwater levels, it was not possible to locate all car parking spaces below ground at reasonable cost. The compromise was to reduce the number of parking spaces and make them accessible to the public.
An extraordinarily high density is achieved through the good utilisation of the site with a floor space index of almost 4.0 and the structure of offices with single and double offices only, which was specifically requested by the client. A full-height atrium and a courtyard open up the blocks and allow daylight to penetrate into the access and recreation zones at the centre of the buildings (fig. 6.62–6.64 and 6.68, p. 129).
The light beige punctuated facade with a window-to-wall ratio of only 25% is the characteristic design feature unifying all three blocks and the multi-storey car-park. The limit to the amount of window surface area was added as a contract specification after the Federal State of Lower Austria decided in 2007 to complete all public new builds according to Passive House standard. To avoid the building looking too closed, the architects increased the overall size of the openings by adding opaque ventilation sashes at the sides of the fixed-glass aluminium frame windows. Exterior-mounted aluminium blinds, of which the top third can be operated separately to control the entry of daylight, provide shade from the sun. Furthermore, all offices are equipped with plain full-height and full-depth curtains to provide privacy from the outside world. In the case of the framed glazing at ground floor level, the blinds have been fitted into the space between the panes to prevent damage through vandalism.

6.62

6.63

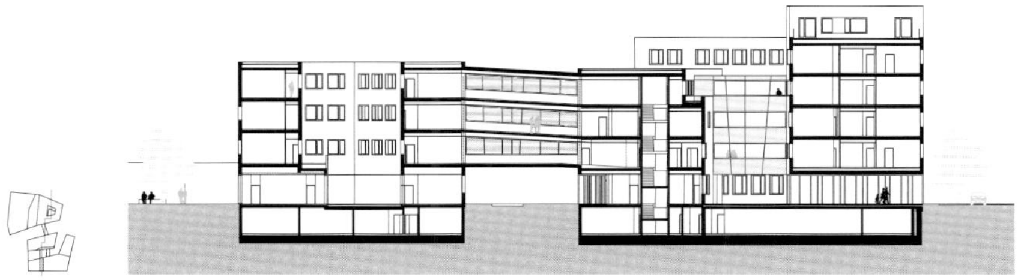

6.64

6.58 Site plan, scale 1:5000
6.59 Schematic diagram of new paths created in the neighbourhood
6.60 Integration of new build in the urban surroundings
6.61 Aerial view from the north
6.62 First floor plan, scale 1:1000
6.63 Ground floor plan, scale 1:1000
6.64 Section, scale 1:1000

1 car park
2 courtyard
3 offices
4 canteen
5 atrium
6 meeting rooms
7 reception area of the Chamber of Commerce
8 Citizen Office

6.65 View from south-west
6.66 Vertical section through south-facing facade scale 1:20
1 Flat roof, extensive planting:
70 mm growing medium
5 mm filter fabric
25 mm drainage panel
160 mm XPS insulation
waterproofing membrane, three layers (top two layers root resistant)
120–280 mm (on average 200 mm) EPS insulation, sloped
bituminous coating
250 mm reinforced concrete roof slab
silicate paint finish
2 Fixed glazing (flush with interior surface):
triple glazing in aluminium frame,
U_w = 0.90 W/m²K;
g-value = 50 %; light transmission = 70 %
3 Opaque sash (flush with exterior surface):
aluminium sandwich panel with PIR core insulation, tilt and turn mechanism,
U = 0.91 W/m²K
4 Exterior wall, upper storeys:
silicate scraped render with Lotus effect paint finish
200 mm EPS insulation
200 mm reinforced concrete wall
flat coat
silicate paint finish
5 Floor slab:
10 mm linoleum floor covering
60 mm cement screed
PE separating layer
30 mm EPS impact sound insulation
vapour barrier
50 mm layer of chippings
250 mm reinforced concrete floor slab
silicate paint finish
6 Exterior wall, ground floor:
framed glazing system, triple glazing in aluminium frame (U_g = 0.5 W/m²K)
sun protection blinds incorporated in window cavities, silk screen printing on exterior surface
6.67 View into corridor connecting block B and C
6.68 Atrium in block A

6.65

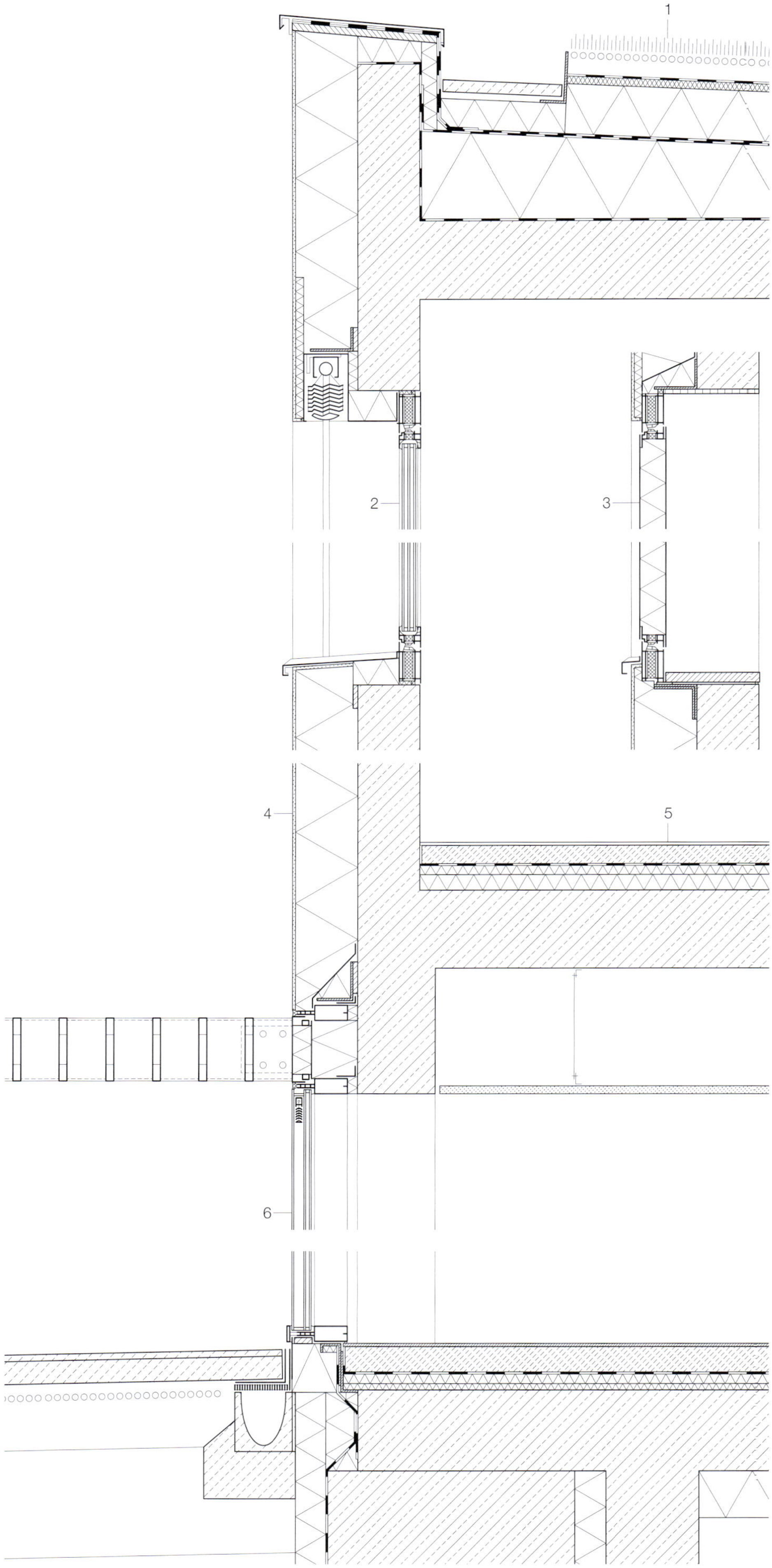

6.66

The building's energy concept combines passive structural measures with, from a technical viewpoint, simple building services systems. The local district heating grid supplies the building with heat. For cost reasons and due to the high forward flow temperatures available, all offices are equipped with conventional radiators. The only rooms actively cooled are the server rooms (decentralised split air conditioning units) and the Chamber of Commerce (compression cooling machine and cooling ceiling). In the remaining rooms, overheating in summer is prevented not only by the limited heat input through the small amount of window surface area and the use of sun shading devices but also by taking advantage of the concrete's thermal mass. Thus, there are no suspended ceilings in the offices. The concrete slabs are simply painted white and ceiling panels are added for acoustic purposes only. The outside air is preconditioned by drawing it in through a 2000-metre-long ground collector (fig. 6.69, p. 130). The exhaust air is cooled adiabatically by a cold water spray in summer, reducing the temperature by four to five degrees before entering the heat exchanger. This method enables more efficient cooling of the outside air in the air conditioning unit. The building can also be cooled at night by making use of the air handling unit, which is only equipped with a duct system for the supply of air. The fresh air reaches the offices through ducts that are fitted above the suspended ceilings of the corridors; the waste air, on the other hand, flows into the corridors via vents in the door frames, and from there into the stairwells, from where it is finally extracted.
The demand for drinking water is covered by the municipal utilities, whereas groundwater from a purpose-built extraction well is used for flushing toilets and adiabatic cooling. Unfortunately, it was not possible to make further use of the groundwater for heating and cooling purposes due to the limitations imposed on account of the fluctuating water levels. Due to the low demand for domestic hot water and the danger of Legionella, decentralised instantaneous water heaters are used for the production of hot water.
The daylight conditions in the offices are regulated by the centrally controlled sun shading systems; however, the blinds can be operated manually, too. Standing lamps cover the demand for artificial light in the offices. A PV plant with a capacity 9.45 kW_p installed on the roof supplies the building with electricity.

Construction and material specifications

The building was built as a solid construction using in situ concrete. The load-bearing exterior concrete walls are insulated with a 20-cm-thick composite thermal insulation system using grey EPS. The insulation has been continued in front of the blind boxes, which means that the thermal envelope is not one hundred per cent homogeneous in these areas. However, in the overall assessment, this slight flaw is compensated by the excellent surface area-to-volume ratio and an average insulation thickness of 36 cm on the roof.
The exterior walls have been completed with a mineral scraped render and a Lotus effect paint finish.
Alongside meeting Passive House standard, the "Specifications for energy efficiency in public buildings" issued in 2007 include a variety of additional ecological provisions. The energy and environment concept for the project is based on the following five pillars:

- Reduction of embodied energy, in particular by using low-CO_2 concrete: by using CEM III B with a 70 % content of blast furnace slag sand for a large part of the in situ concrete, the primary energy input and the greenhouse gas emissions are lowered significantly.
- Implementation of a building logistics concept in order to lower the emissions of building operations that are most important in terms of quantity (earth and construction works). The emission class Euro 4 was specified as the minimum standard for all trucks used during the earth and construction works.
- Chemical and product management policies to minimise products and chemicals hazardous to health and the environment: in contrast to a conventional development, the measures implemented in the design, tendering and construction phases resulted in reducing the amount of VOCs introduced into the building through construction materials by approximately 2700 kg. This also significantly lowered the VOC emissions in the room air (fig. 6.73–6.75, p. 132). Floor coverings, pipes and electric cables with PVC and halogens were avoided, lead-

6.67

6.68

ing to a reduction of about 8000 kg in the total amount of plasticizers while also reducing the danger of corrosive fumes in the case of fire. These measures increased the costs of the electrical installations by only approximately 0.4 % of the total building costs (extra of €95 000).
- Promote the use of renewable resources, in particular in the interior by fitting 5200 m² of linoleum and using local timbers.
- Completion of low-emission interiors: an indoor air measurement was taken one month after commissioning the building to evaluate the air quality. The results showed good to very good levels for VOC and formaldehyde.

Design and construction process

The ecological conditions of the project changed fundamentally in 2007 when Passive House standard was introduced for all public buildings. The competition specifications issued in 2005 had not included any enhanced energy efficiency or ecological requirements. The budget was thus increased by 10 % to cover the alterations needed to meet Passive House standard and fulfil the criteria of the additional specifications listed in the "Pflichtenheft Energieeffizienz". The maximum permitted window-to-wall ratio of 25 % had a significant impact on the building's appearance.
Due to the intended role model effect of the Niederösterreichhaus and the desire to complete a building with a commendable overall result, the client commissioned several studies designed to accompany the design process. An energy and building ecology specialist already completed a study during the planning phase of the preliminary scheme that highlighted means to reduce the environmental impact caused by the construction and operation phases, as well as indicating the effects these have on the design. Based on the preliminary design, the study determined that the floor and roof slabs of the building accounted for approximately 70 % of the GWP emissions in the construction, and thus presented the largest potential for savings. By reducing the architectural volume and using sulphate blast furnace slag cement, the OI3 index (see TQB, p. 39) was decreased from 58 to 48 and the GWP by approximately 40 % on paper.
According to the preliminary studies, the specialists also recommended the use of clay boards and tiles, or porcelain stoneware flooring, in the interior, planting green roofs and replacing the asphalt surfaces outside with water-absorbing materials.
A further specialist for sustainability issues was commissioned to oversee the execution phases in terms of advisory and quality assurance matters. He accompanied the team of general contractors as an independent consultant during the entire development stage and evaluated the efficiency of individual measures upon their completion.
The sometimes slightly controversial requirements of the client, the user and the specifications became apparent during the design process. And several questionable decisions were made concerning the very demanding objectives and innovative concepts involving construction materials and building services. It is not only the number of parking spaces requested by the user for a city centre building less than 250 m from the main station that is extremely debatable, but also the schedule of rooms with one and two-person offices throughout almost the entire building. In the meantime, experience has revealed that the general and uniform limitation on the maximum window surface area is fraught with problems. Due to the minimum window surface area imposed by the Workplace Ordinance, it was not possible to differentiate the size of openings according to their level in the building or the direction they face. The result is that rooms on the lower floors need more artificial light and some south-west facing offices on the top floors are subject to overheating in summer.
Concrete with a 70 % content of blast furnace slag sand (CEM III B) was used wherever possible in place of regular concrete (CEM I B or CEM II B) in the Niederösterreichhaus. In detail this means that out of all of the in-situ concrete poured (a total of 12 304 m³) 9627 m³ was CEM III B (78 %) and 2677 m³ was regular concrete. The use of sulphate blast furnace slag cement with a 90 % content of blast furnace slag sand was avoided since this demand would have limited the number of possible suppliers at the time of tendering and the client was concerned about restricting competition. At temperatures above 10 °C (24-hour average), CEM III B is similar in its workability and setting time to regular concrete. At temperatures below 5 °C, the setting time increases significantly; at temperatures below 0 °C, the setting time can be three to four times as long as that of regular concrete. It

6.69

6.70

would have been necessary to take these potentially longer periods into account in the construction schedule from the very beginning and they would have resulted in higher costs. The time pressure might possibly have also led to damage at the edges and corners of the softer concrete, which in turn would have meant more work and expense involved in remedying the defects. It is for these reasons that CEM III B was not used at temperatures below 5 °C.

Even though in-situ concrete was poured throughout winter, it was possible to use blast furnace slag concrete for 78 % of the total volume of concrete. The original worries of the project participants concerning the limited temperature range for the setting of blast furnace slag cement proved unfounded.

Due to a mistake made in the ordering process, the waterproof concrete in the Niederösterreichhaus was not executed using CEM III B although it would have been particularly suitable in terms of its technical properties. The extra costs for using CEM III B accounted for a rise of approximately 2 to 3 % (€2.25/m^3 of concrete).

From an economic viewpoint, it generally does not make sense to use CEM III B in winter at temperatures below 10 °C (24-hour average). At temperatures above the critical zone, CEM III B is identical to regular concrete in terms of workability and load-bearing capacity. The curing period of sulphate blast furnace slag cement is between that of CEM III B and CEM I B and is therefore ideal for the in-between seasons. Extensions of time should be incorporated into the construction schedule in spring and autumn; alternatively, the bill of quantities could include alternative items for the use of regular concrete. Ideally, the construction schedule should be drawn up in such a way that it allows for long periods of suitable temperatures for the placing of concrete.

Environmental impact

Calculations performed by the Austrian Institute for Healthy and Ecological Building (IBO) revealed that, by changing the binding agent from Portland cement to CEM III B, the CO_2 emissions for producing the concrete structure were reduced by around 50 % (fig. 6.76, p. 132).

The use of sulphate blast furnace slag cement would have produced an even larger reduction of over 75 %. The total savings achieved in the Niederösterreichhaus amount to 1092 t of CO_2 in comparison to a building using conventional construction methods. This amount almost matches the difference that is achieved by reducing the heat demand in the first 19 years after commissioning the building through changing from meeting statutory requirements only to Passive house standard. In comparison to other structural solutions, the floor slabs achieve considerable PEI and CO_2 savings. A comparable structure using a composite wood concrete construction method with regular concrete, similar fire protection standards and ceiling cladding would have meant a deterioration of 65 %. Due to the savings that can be achieved by using CEM III B and sulphate blast furnace slag cement, the completed floor slabs are, from an environmental impact point of view, equivalent to timber floors. In regard of the OI3 index, the improved concrete slabs actually perform better since the acidification potential of timber is greater than that of concrete (fig. 5.7, 5.8, p. 91). The fact that in-situ concrete floor slabs span in two directions is a further advantage. Hence, they are more suitable for framed structures than timber structures, which usually span only one way and provide greater flexibility when it comes to conversions. In terms of their environmental impact, concrete floor slabs with sulphate blast furnace slag cement are one of the best options at this point in time. In terms of recyclability, on the other hand, concrete is less environmentally friendly than wood, since concrete can only be downcycled. The assessment is less positive concerning the use of CEM III B in facade constructions. In comparison to other load-bearing constructions, the concrete facade is still acceptable, however, there are a number of alternative solutions which not only achieve better results with regard to GWP and embodied energy but also offer advantages in terms of deconstruction and recyclability. To achieve comparable U-values, timber constructions are also less thick (fig. 5.11. 5.12, p. 93). However, as regards the OI3 index, the benefits of CEM III B are once again more convincing.

The savings potential is also considerable in comparison to facade constructions made of regular concrete. In contrast to regular concrete, the environmental impact is less than that of a comparable load-bearing facade made of clay or sand lime brick. However, a reliable comparison of load-bearing and non-load-bearing facades can only be made by taking all load-bearing and space-enclosing components into consideration, simply because the interdependencies of the elements are so complex. Moreover, the choice of the right construction system is very much dependent on what the building is used for and the desired result. Owing to the almost white hue, CEM III B

6.71

6.72

6.69 Installation of ground collector below base slab
6.70 Concrete structure
6.71 Bridge connecting block B and C
6.72 Courtyard between block A and B

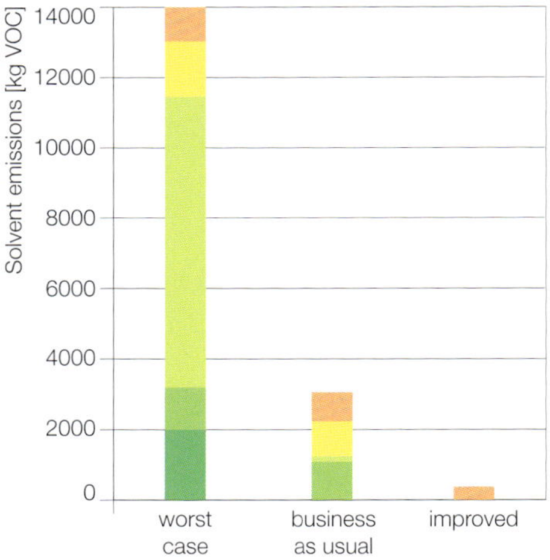

6.73

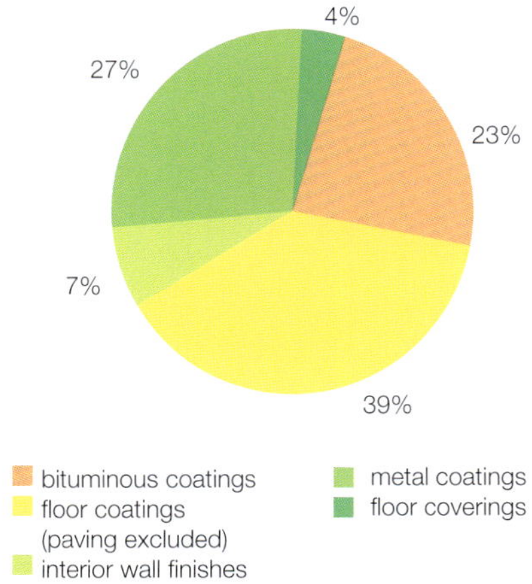

6.74

VOC emissions compared [kg]

Product group	worst case	business as usual	improved
bituminous coatings	906	755	125.8
floor coatings (paving excluded)	1565	1113	0
interior wall finishes	8038	246	49.5
metal coatings (fire protection included)	1137	758	1.6
floor coverings	2035	102	2.8
Total	**13680**	**2974**	**179.6**

6.75

CO_2 emissions through concrete production

Binding agent	GWP/m² [kg CO_2 eq./m³]	total GWP [t CO_2 eq.]	comparison [%]
average Austrian cement	254	3125	100 %
CEM I (Portland cement)	310	3814	122 %
CEM IIIB (blast furnace cement)	120	1476	47 %
sulphate blast furnace slag cement (EN 15743)	55	677	22 %
concrete mix for Niederösterreichhaus in Krems	165	2033	65 %

6.76

and sulphate blast furnace slag concrete are highly suitable for use as exposed concrete.
Alongside the savings achieved through improving the structure, building site logistics and ecological requirements with regard to construction site operations helped to reduce emissions. All vehicles involved in the earthworks and construction operations had to meet at least emission class Euro 4 or 5. Thus, it was possible to reduce the emissions caused by construction site vehicles (carbon monoxide [CO], hydrocarbons [HC], nitrous gases [NO_x]) by 30 % and the particulate matter pollution by as much as 80 % in comparison to Euro 3 vehicles.
There were no specifications at the design stage concerning maximum distances. A study made following completion of the development identified the savings potential associated with this category: approximately 3410 trips were necessary to take the loose excavated soil (34 100 m³) to a disposal site 14 km away. So the total distance covered amounted to 88 680 km. The approximately 13 000 m³ of in-situ concrete required around 2200 trips to the concrete mixing plant only 5 km away, which adds up to a total distance of 22 000 km. This figure could easily increase to over 150 000 km if the trip to the concrete mixing plant had been 35 km (maximum permitted distance according to Minergie-ECO). By limiting the distance to the disposal site and concrete mixing plant, a comparable building would be able to prevent the emissions accumulated over a distance of 100 000 km (fig. 4.25, p. 88).
All in all, the measures introduced in the Niederösterreichhaus concerning improved use of material and construction processes have significantly reduced the environmental impact. The findings could benefit many other projects. Nevertheless, the interplay of materials, functions and technologies is debatable. Due to the fact that the mechanical ventilation system is designed to cater for larger capacities but the layout is based largely on small-scale units, the amount of concrete incorporated in the building cannot adequately fulfil its purpose as storage mass. Open-plan layouts and the ability to control the ventilation system in smaller units would have been better suited to the material properties of concrete.

Conclusion

The Niederösterreichhaus illustrates the great potential of low-CO_2 concrete for reducing the environmental impact of buildings. The 850 000 t of slag accumulated annually in Austria's steel production could be used to create approximately 1 million tonnes of sulphate blast furnace slag cement. At an average annual production of 5 million tonnes of cement, this represents approximately 20 % of the total demand [18]. It makes no sense to import slag sand from abroad due to the transport distance. One way to cover the demand, would be to process the slag deposits from former steel production processes. It definitely makes sense to use existing deposits efficiently and continue the search for alternative methods to help improve the environmental impact of the building industry.
The missed opportunity to reduce emissions by improving the user requirements is considered a flaw in this project. A mobility concept in combination with a 50 % reduction of the car park size, for example, would have saved approximately 435 t of CO_2. A more contemporary organisation of at least some of the work spaces in group offices (50 % in four or six-person offices) would have allowed for a further reduction of 125 t of CO_2. These two measures would not only have saved an extra 560 t of CO_2 on top of the 1092 t of CO_2 already saved, they would have also cut costs by around €2.5 million, which represents approximately 7 % of the total building costs.

6.73 Solvent reduction through chemicals management plan: comparison of Niederösterreichhaus (right bar) with a "business as usual" and a "worst case" scenario
6.74 Solvent reduction according to trade
6.75 VOC reduction through chemicals management plan
6.76 Analysis comparing the use of different cements in the load-bearing structure. 78 % of the concrete used In the Niederösterreichhaus had a blast furnace sand content of 70 %.

Lower secondary school in Langenzersdorf

When upgrading existing buildings using resource-efficient methods, the intricate nature of the requirements and measures is far greater than when dealing with new builds. The question concerning the scope of the necessary actions – replacement, extension, conversion or refurbishment – tends to be so complex that it is almost impossible to make a general statement on how to deal with existing building stock. In order to identify the right depth of measures, a balance has to be found between the necessary energy-related and economic investments and their impact throughout the design life of the building (fig. 4.5, p. 70).
In the case of most published refurbishment projects, the approach taken is usually that of extensive and fundamental change – both in terms of technical and structural features and appearance. One reason for choosing this strategy is the project participants' desire to make the upgrade visible instead of limiting the alterations to technical and structural measures only. The impression arises that comprehensive studies of requirements and consequences were performed to explain the greater amount of work executed. However, especially in terms of minimising the use of resources, this approach is highly controversial.
The principle applied in the case of the school refurbishment in Langenzersdorf was that the measure requiring the least resources is the one that can be avoided. In detail this means that only those components and layers which desperately needed exchanging were actually replaced and renewed. The measures implemented were generally those with little impact. A large proportion of the components with a high primary energy input, such as the load-bearing structure or the floor constructions, were retained. An excellent result was achieved with little expense and effort by restructuring the inner functions, adding a bespoke extension to the existing building and upgrading the building services and the building envelope using energy-saving methods. Moreover, a proportion of the investment was put into improving the educational infrastructure.

Project description

The lower secondary school in Langenzersdorf in the immediate vicinity of the train station has undergone a total of five conversions and extensions since the erection of the original school building in 1876. Past extensions include the small gymnasium added in 1952 and a larger one in 1985, which are both also used regularly by local sports clubs (fig. 6.83, p. 135). The negotiated procedure for the school refurbishment in the market town of Langenzersdorf initiated in 2008 sought proposals for a variety of individual measures: upgrade of the building envelope, addition of a lift, provision of rooms for after school care, as well as a central cloakroom and recess hall. Because all the work was to be performed outside school opening hours,

Project participants
Client: Marktgemeinde Langenzersdorf, Lower Austria
Project design: ah3 Architekten ZT GmbH, Horn
Structure: Schindler & Partner ZT GmbH
Building physics: IBO – Austrian Institute for Healthy and Ecological Building, Vienna
Building Services: New Energy Consulting, Kirchschlag near Linz
Site management: ah3 Architekten ZT GmbH, Horn

Building parameters
Location: Langenzersdorf, Lower Austria
Design period: 2008–2010
Construction period: 2009/10 (16 months)
Use: Lower secondary school with small and large gymnasium, youth centre
Plot: 5157 m^2
Built surface area: 2130 m^2
Gross floor area (GFA): 5581 m^2
Usable floor area (UFA): 3601 m^2
Treated floor area (TFA): 3101 m^2
Volume: 17 441 m^3
Construction costs: €1100/m^2_{GFA} (new build and refurbishment)
Total construction costs: approx. €4 mil

Objective
Refurbishment according to Passive House standard

Energy parameters (OIB energy certificate)
Space heat demand Q_h (all zones): 13.5 kWh/(m^2_{TFA} · a)
Primary energy demand Q_p (DHW, heating and auxiliary power): 21 kWh/(m^2_{TFA} · a)
Primary energy demand Q_p (DHW, heating, cooling, auxiliary and domestic power): 49 kWh/(m^2_{TFA} · a)
Power output photovoltaics: 5 kW_{peak}
OI3 index: 50

6.77 View from the terrace of the after school care centre into the recess hall and new gymnasium

6.77

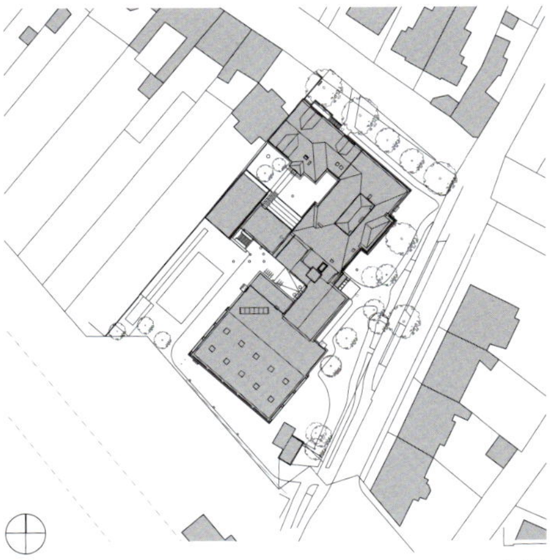

6.78

6.79

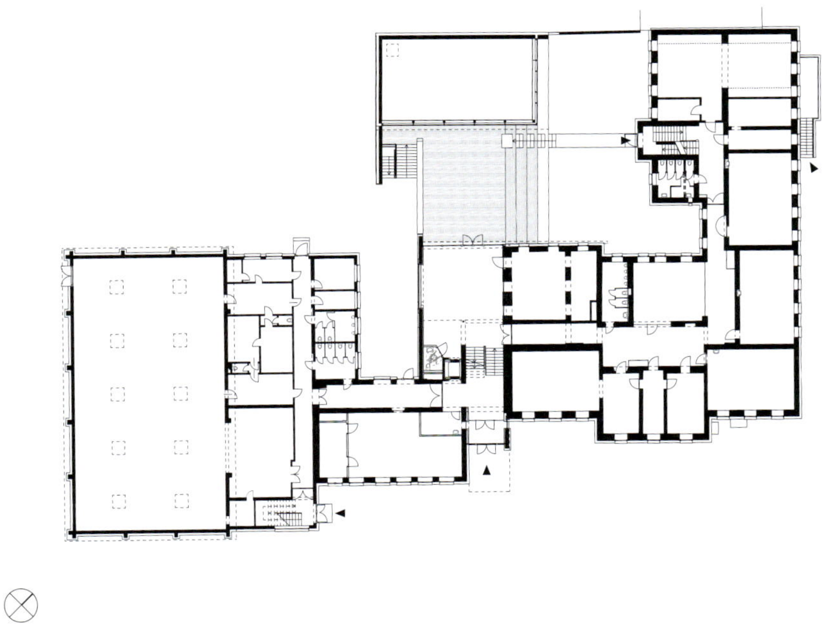

6.80

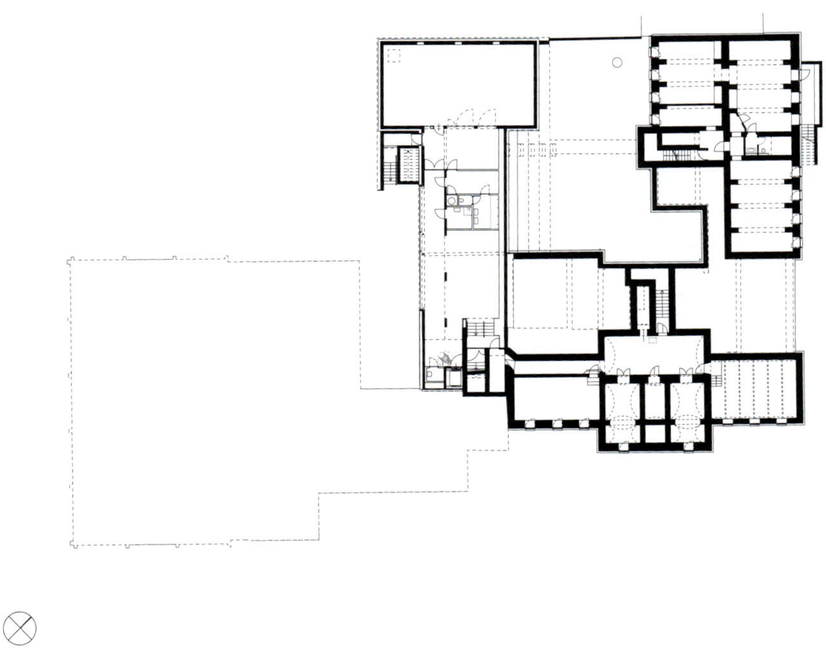

6.81

principally during the summer holidays, a decision was made to carry out the refurbishment over a period of three school years.

The proposal submitted by ah3 Architekten involved the addition of a new building accommodating the central cloakroom and the multifunctional recess hall. The three current entrances were combined to form a single one in this added space (fig. 6.79). The new build is also where the architects have accommodated the lift and disabled toilet facilities to meet the requirements of barrier-free access. The bracket formed by the new gymnasium and the entrance area reorganises the existing structures while at the same time accommodating a multitude of additional features and functions (fig. 6.83 and 6.84). One objective of the restructuring measures was to increase the quality and usefulness of the space by making existing areas more efficient and functional. So the school caretaker's apartment was replaced by a library and the caretaker's workshop by a changing room with shower facilities for the new 120 m^2 gymnasium, which was erected in the lowered courtyard. The restructuring measures also provided the opportunity to create an after school care centre with an outside deck, new science rooms as well as a youth centre. Approximately 350 m^2 of new space has been provided of which 70 m^2 are taken up by the new multipurpose hall, which doubles as a recess hall and auditorium and opens to the outdoors via a terrace (fig. 6.89, p. 138).

The building envelope underwent a thorough energy efficiency refurbishment. All facades and roofs were insulated according to Passive House standard, the windows were replaced and, where necessary, supplemented by exterior sun shading devices. The gymnasium built back in 1952 was replaced by a new timber-frame structure accommodating a new sports hall and the indoor recess area. What was once the school caretaker's private garden is now used as a terrace, and seating steps lead down to the remodelled school yard. A new long-jump pit and volleyball field complement the exteriors.

The roofs of the gymnasium and the extension completed in 1964 are used to accommodate a solar collector plant for the provision of hot water and a photovoltaic array with a capacity of 5 kW_{peak} for the generation of electricity. A mechanical ventilation system with a heat recovery unit ensures that the classrooms are sup-

plied with fresh air. All existing radiators in the classrooms were replaced by new ones. A long-term contract with a gas supplier means that the heating system cannot switch to wood chip until 2015. Before the refurbishment, the heating energy consumption of the existing building accounted for 220 kWh/m²a.
As a result of using the Passive House Planning Package (PHPP), the space heat demand has been reduced to 13.5 kWh/m^2a_{TFA}. The primary energy demand (DHW, heating, cooling, auxiliary and domestic power) at 49 kWh/m^2a_{TFA} is well below the permitted Passive House value of 120 kWh/m^2a_{TFA}.

Construction and material specifications

Except for the walls of the gymnasium built in 1984, which are made of hollow blocks with a 70-mm-thick layer of insulation, all buildings were executed using solid, load-bearing masonry. Before the refurbishment, the facade materials included a colourful mix of rear-ventilated fibre cement panels, different render finishes and exposed aggregate concrete cladding. The street facade of the main building completed in 1876 is structured with pilasters, string courses and window surrounds. There is a similar variety of roof finishes including gravel-covered flat roofs, corrugated cement roofing panels and fibre cement shingles on the pitched surfaces.
The facade upgrade involved removing all the render and insulation from the existing facades. The walls were then upgraded using a 260-mm-thick composite thermal insulation system with expanded polystyrene (grey EPS with graphite particles to reflect infrared radiation) and a rough mineral render. The flat roofs were insulated using 400-mm-thick EPS panels, resealed and covered with gravel. In the case of the two oldest buildings with pitched roofs, the historical solid timber floor structure beneath the attic was insulated using a 400-mm-thick layer of mineral wool in order to conserve the existing roof structure. This solution also made it possible to use a thinner layer of insulation on the outside of the low jamb walls and thus retain the profiled structure of the cornice. The junction between the two different insulation thicknesses was finished using a strip of metal flashing to prevent water from collecting on top of the composite thermal insulation system (fig. 6.88, p. 137). The plinth, which used to project slightly, was made flush with the main facade by adjusting the thickness of insulation. The original jut in the

6.82

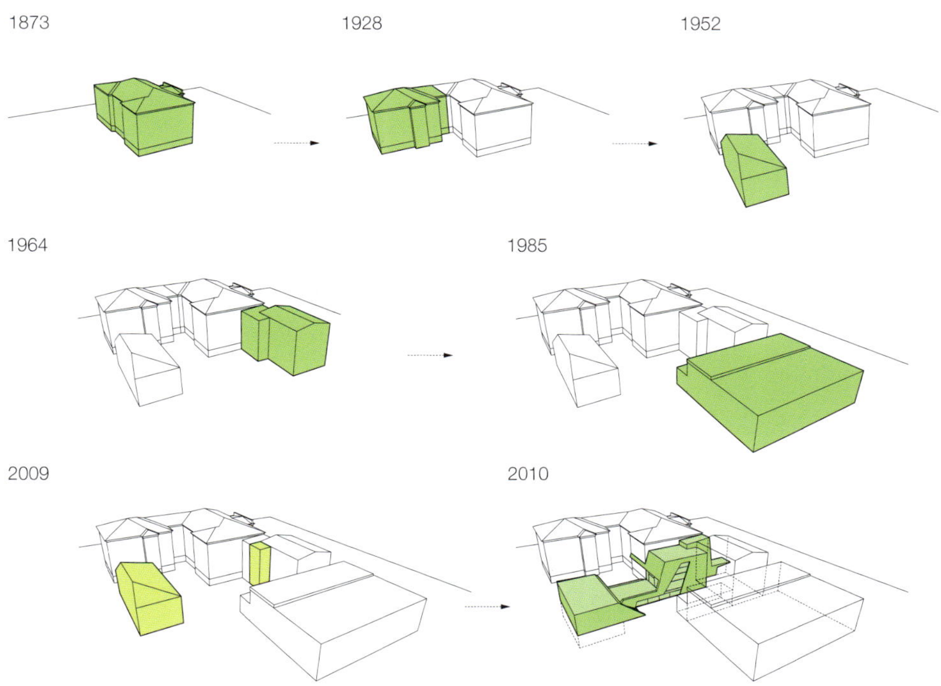

6.83

6.78 Site plan, scale 1:2500
6.79 Street view of the refurbished school building
6.80 Ground floor plan, scale 1:1000
6.81 Basement floor plan, scale 1:1000

6.82 Section, scale 1:500
6.83 Development of the school since its foundation; the elements changed are highlighted in green
6.84 Multifunctional recess hall with terrace

6.84

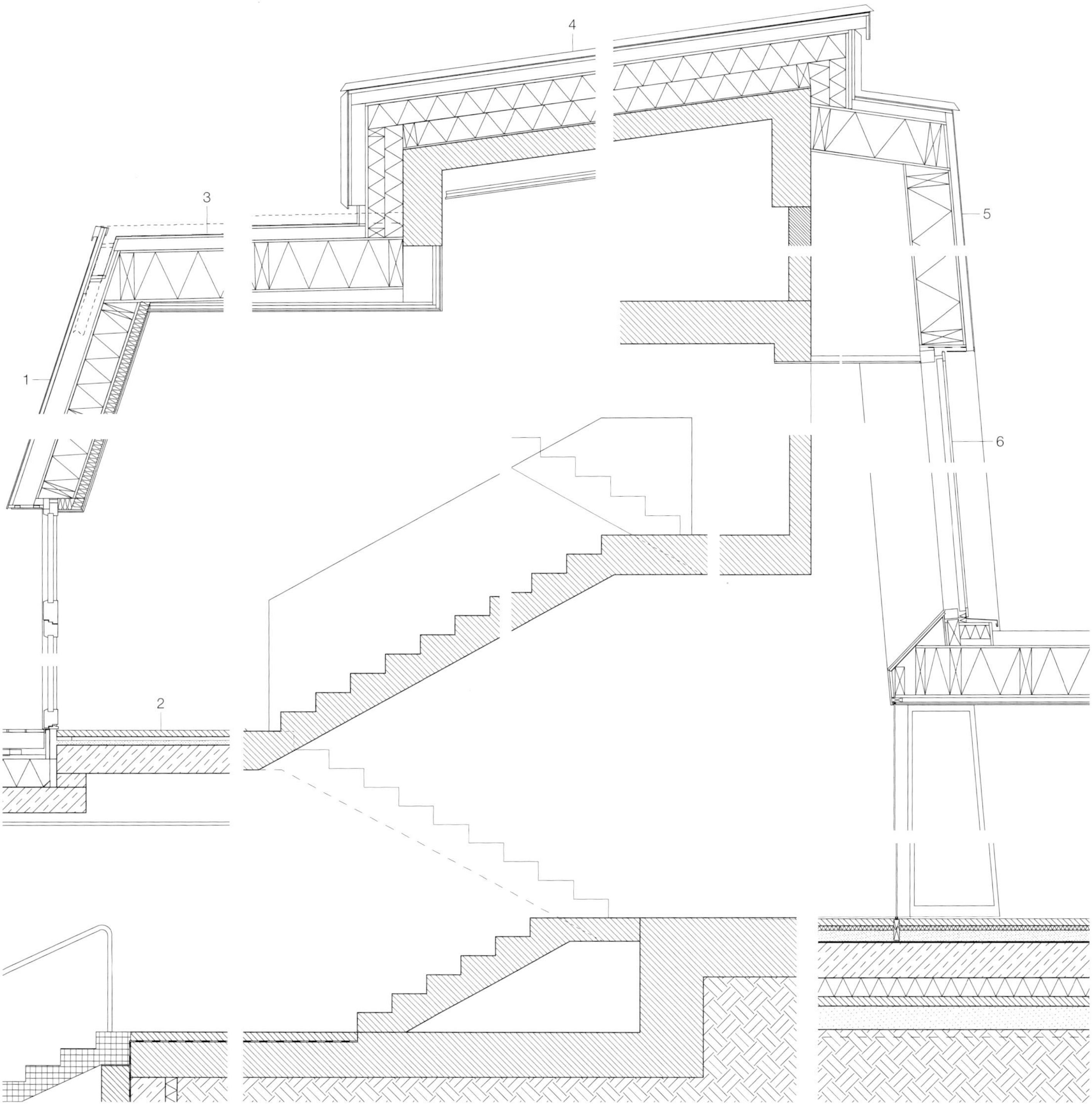

6.85 Vertical section through entrance building/auditorium, scale 1:50
1 Exterior wall auditorium (U = 0.126 W/m²K):
8 mm fibre cement facade panels
200 mm substructure/ventilation cavity
EPDM waterproofing membrane
22 mm OSB panel
280 mm timber post, mineral wool insulation-filled cavities
vapour barrier, PE sheet (s_d = 180 m)
18 mm OSB panel
80 mm battens, insulation-filled cavities
2 × 12.5 mm gypsum board sheathing
2 Floor structure, ground floor:
20 mm terrazzo tile floor covering
60 mm screed, PE separating layer
30 mm impact sound insulation
40 mm filler course, sand
240 mm reinforced concrete floor slab
15 mm suspended ceiling, gypsum board
3 Roof (new) (U-value: 0.125 W/m²K):
1.3 mm EPDM waterproofing membrane
20 mm OSB panel
100 mm battens, insulation-filled cavities
permeable roofing membrane (s_d = 0.05 m)
22 mm OSB panel
400 mm timber beam, insulation-filled cavities
vapour barrier, PE sheet (s_d = 180 m)
18 mm OSB panel
12.5 mm suspended ceiling, gypsum board
4 Roof (upgraded original) (U = 0.097 W/m²K):
1 mm zinc sheet roof covering (standing seam)
0.8 mm permeable roofing membrane
24 mm sheathing
100 mm battens, insulation-filled cavities
0.8 mm permeable roofing membrane
24 mm sheathing
400 mm mineral wool insulation
5 mm vapour barrier
approx. 200 mm reinforced concrete roof slab (original)
5 Exterior wall, lobby (U = 0.131 W/m²K):
8 mm fibre cement facade panels
120 mm aluminium substructure
1 mm EPDM waterproofing membrane
22 mm OSB panel
360 mm timber post, insulation-filled cavities
vapour barrier, PE sheet (s_d = 180 m)
18 mm OSB panel
12.5 mm gypsum board sheathing
6 Lobby window: wood/aluminium framed glazing system with triple glazing

6.86 View of recess hall from outside
6.87 View of refurbished existing building
6.88 Vertical section through existing building facade, scale 1:50
7 Exterior wall (U = 0.109 W/m²K):
5 mm thin-layer render
260 mm EPS insulation (180 mm below cornice)
approx. 600 mm masonry wall (original)
8 Window: triple glazing in wood/aluminium frame (former position of the window is marked in green)

facade is now only highlighted by a recessed horizontal joint in the render (fig. 6.87). The ventilated roof structure of the 1962 extension was also retained by insulating the attic floor with a 400-mm-thick layer of mineral wool (fig. 6.88). The small gymnasium, in urgent need of renovation, was demolished and replaced by a new construction. Alongside a new small gymnasium, the new build accommodates the main entrance to the school, a cloakroom and a new auditorium. The roof of the single-storey element functions as a terrace and extension of the indoor recess area-come-multipurpose hall. All newly constructed components in contact with the ground and accessible roof decks are made of reinforced concrete and insulated on the outside with a 240-mm-thick layer of extruded polystyrene insulation (XPS). The exterior walls and the roof, on the other hand, were planned as a timber frame construction with an insulation thickness of 400 mm. The roof and the facades of the existing stairwell were insulated on the outside and clad with a timber frame curtain wall (fig. 6.85). The entire new build has been finished with rear-ventilated cladding made of large-size fibre cement panels visibly fixed to an aluminium substructure. For reasons of building physics and in order to maintain the depth of the window reveals, and thus not change the appearance of the building too severely, the facade refurbishment was used to move the windows further out into the insulation layer. The classroom windows and those of the teachers' room have been equipped with exterior aluminium blinds featuring a daylight control system. Alongside creating new classrooms and ancillary rooms, the conversion of the interior involved integrating a mechanical ventilation system and a lift into the existing structures, as well as performing all the associated restructuring work. In order to minimise the amount of ductwork, the central ventilation station has been accommodated in the attic of the old school house, with the effect that the supply and exhaust air ducts penetrate the roof. Suspended ceilings have not been installed in the access and recess zones to reduce resource consumption and costs. The ducts have also not been clad or coated with fire-resistant materials. Instead, fireproof dampers have been installed at the transition points between the fire compartments. Most of the floor and wall finishes in the staircases and corridors have been retained.
The floor and wall finishes in the classrooms, on the other hand, have been renewed and suspended gypsum board ceilings have been fitted to accommodate all technical installations (lighting, ventilation, acoustics). There is a one metre gap between the suspended ceiling (void depth: 70 cm) and the facade, which allowed the full height of the window openings to be retained. Great attention was paid to the ecological qualities of materials. In the case of the floor coverings, only local wood and linoleum was used. Thanks to the use of low-emission paint and floor coverings, it was possible to reduce the VOC and formaldehyde emissions considerably.

Design and construction process

The initial situation of this design and construction project was unusual. In contrast to many other school refurbishments, there was no demand for extra space due to a decline in the number of pupils. However, the available space was badly structured in terms of layout and function, and urgently required reorganisation. And what the school really needed was an outdoor play area for pupils. The other aspects of the negotiated procedure were very precise. They did not specify a comprehensive refurbishment concept, but

6.86

6.87

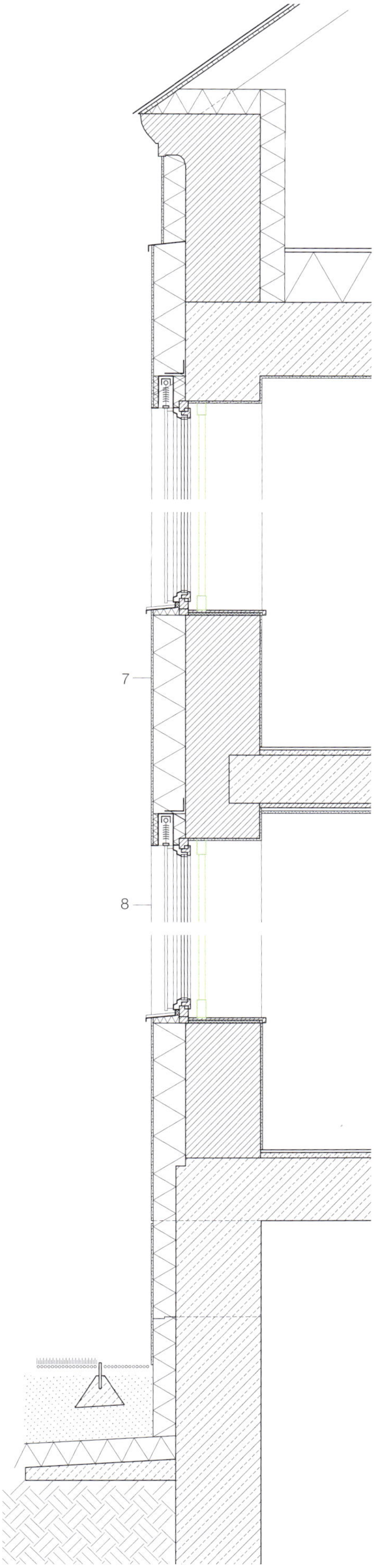

6.88

6.89

6.90

alongside the upgrade of the building envelope, defined a range of clearly described individual measures. Initially, planners were only sought for the construction design.
The architects' proposal included not only a new extension to the existing structure to reorganise and restructure the total complex but also a comprehensive energy efficiency refurbishment according to Passive House standard. The extended design contract meant a duplication of the originally calculated construction costs of which a large proportion was covered by a subsidy scheme initiated by the Federal State of Lower Austria for energy efficiency refurbishments meeting Passive House standard. However, to obtain these subsidies, the refurbishment costs were not allowed to exceed 60 % of the construction costs for a replacement new build.
From the very beginning, the teachers were involved in the many studies accompanying the design process. Thanks to a life cycle cost analysis, it was possible to prove that a timber structure would, in the long-term, be the best solution for the reconstruction of the hall in terms of both costs and environmental impact. The calculations of the energy and CO_2 savings potential of various scenarios illustrated that the variant including a refurbishment according to Passive House standard in combination with a wood chip heating system was not only the solution with the lowest CO_2 emissions but also the one with the lowest operating costs (fig. 6.91, 6.93).
A committee of teachers helped to assess and channel the user requirements.
Close collaboration with the teachers and parents during the construction phase made it possible to shorten the originally planned construction period from 26 to 16 months by allowing work to continue during term time and not restricting it to the school holidays.
The certification systems ÖGNI and ÖGNB were compared for their suitability for the scheme in a master's thesis that was supervised and completed during the project development. The ÖGNB system was eventually chosen due to the lower costs and shorter amount of time needed for the certification procedure. Moreover, ÖGNB offered to support the certification process in order to then use the results for the compilation of new assessment criteria for school buildings.
IBO, the Austrian Institute for Healthy and Ecological Building, completed a life cycle assessment during the design phase of the project. This enabled the biological requirements concerning construction materials to be incorporated in the tender specifications. Among other things, these included no use of PVC in the installations and observing the limits of VOC and formaldehyde in the floor coverings and paintwork. Simulations were performed to check that the existing window openings would be able to provide good daylight conditions. The results showed that suitable daylight levels would be met by increasing the reflective qualities of the floor and wall surfaces.

Environmental impact

In contrast to new builds, there tends to be a lack of suitable benchmarks and reference values for the assessment of a refurbishment's environmental impacts. Should the assessment take into consideration only the completed measures and the installed building materials, or should it also examine the building as a whole functional unit? How should the reuse of structural components, building materials and layers be evaluated? What is the relation between the reduced use of material achieved by retaining existing structures and the usually slightly higher energy demand for the operation of the building? One possible approach is to determine and then compare the environmental impacts of different measures throughout their total life cycle (see Refurbishment and conversion of single-family home in Hamburg, pp. 109ff.). Applied to the school in Langenzersdorf, this method shows that a refurbishment fares better than a comparable new build. By retaining almost the entire existing structure, the embodied energy and the CO_2 emissions for the construction could be lowered by approximately 40 to 45 % in comparison to building from scratch [19].
Moreover, the refurbished school building meets Passive House standard, and a further reduction of the space heat demand is something that, even in the case of new builds, is rarely thought to be worthwhile from a present-day perspective. So, it can be assumed that the results of the refurbished building are also better than those of a comparable new build when considering the total life cycle in terms of resource consumption and environmental impact. A very detailed analysis would have to be performed to see whether a new build would be able to make do with less area and volume, as well as providing better daylight conditions, and thus lead to a considerable reduction of the total energy demand.
An assessment which is limited to the evaluation of environmental impacts takes absolutely no account of the building's overall purpose, in this case the communication of knowledge to children and teenagers. Analyses assessing the future benefits and use of an existing building must establish at a preliminary design stage whether the available floor plans and functional layouts are able to fulfil their purpose in the long term.
The additions and changes made in the project are exemplary in terms of both ecological and biological aspects, and most of the building materials can be classified as safe. The new build is designed using a timber frame construction with mineral wool insulation, which has a very low environmental impact (fig. 5.11 and 5.12, p. 93). The rear-ventilated facade cladding with visibly fixed fibre cement panels is excellent in terms of building physics, durability and maintenance.
A marginal improvement could have been achieved by using a timber substructure

rather than an aluminium one; however, this change would have been made at the expense of durability. The conditions of the facade surrounding the courtyard show that the cladding does not perfectly meet the mechanical requirements of a school. Some of the components, such as the seating steps and parts of the facade to the gymnasium, have been clad in timber and are thus not protected from the weather. The shorter replacement cycle of the timber cladding is insignificant in terms of ecological aspects due to the fact that the wood is neither treated nor difficult to reach and replace.
The insulation of the existing facades with grey EPS panels is a good solution in terms of energy demand and CO_2 emissions; with regard to recyclability, however, the panels are fraught with problems. Nevertheless, there is a lack of good alternatives for the energy efficiency upgrade of rendered facades, particularly where the appearance of the building is to be maintained.
Concerning the interior fit-out, close attention was paid to the separation of layers and ensuring the accessibility of building materials and installations. Low-emission products were used for all floor, wall and ceiling surface finishes in order to ensure good air quality in the classrooms. The measurements taken one year after commissioning the building show that the emissions remained well below the targeted maximum acceptable levels (total VOC: 200 µg/m³ [20], formaldehyde: 0.032 ppm [21]).
The school was certified by ÖGNB and achieved 929 of 1000 possible points. Alongside the category "Thermal comfort and fit-out", the project did especially well in the areas "Health and thermal comfort" as well as "Building materials and construction" (fig. 6.92).

Conclusion

The resource "existing building stock" has priority over all other aspects of sustainability in this project. The assessment of the selected upgrade strategy only does justice to the project if the measures which were not performed are also taken into account. At the school in Langenzersdorf, the sufficiency strategy was applied consistently to the energy efficiency upgrade and conversion of the building. Whereas in most refurbishment projects building components and layers are removed and replaced on a large scale before the end of their service life for aesthetic reasons only, the constructional measures performed in this project were chosen and carried out with great care. For a successful outcome, it was therefore necessary to question standard design and construction procedures, and use new sustainability-related parameters as a basis for the design process. The measures affecting the appearance and the layout of space are the result of a thorough analysis of the technical, economic, ecological and functional requirements. The way in which the measures were implemented is also based on the courage to break with conventional approaches and explore new ways and methods. The decision to use exposed air ducts, for example, was made not only to reduce costs and embodied energy, but as a creative statement with reference to the objectives and principles of high-tech architecture as practised in the 1980s and 1990s. Instead of concealing technology behind false walls and suspended ceilings, the "serving" components and technical installations are used as an architectural feature. This didactic approach seems predestined for educational institutions in particular as a way of visually expressing the requirements which have to be met by buildings today and their possible solutions.

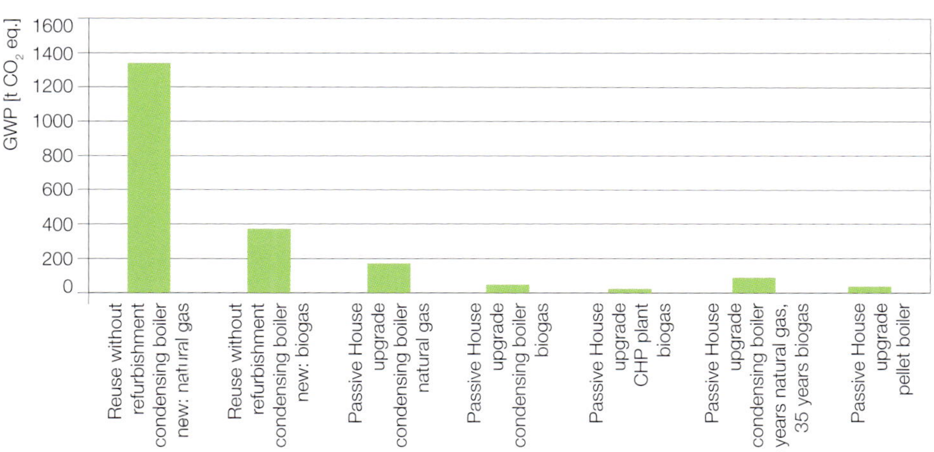

6.91

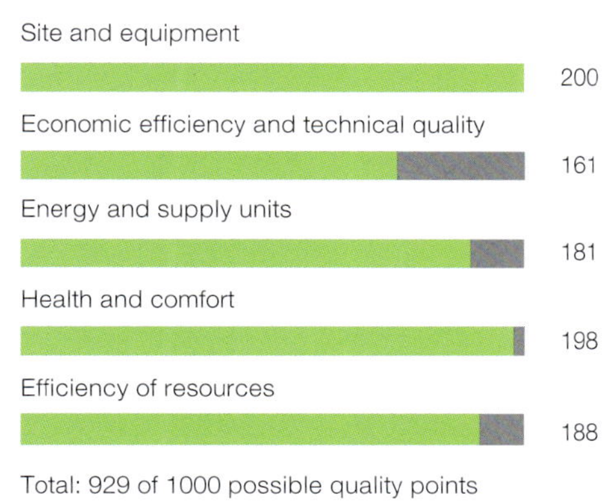

6.92

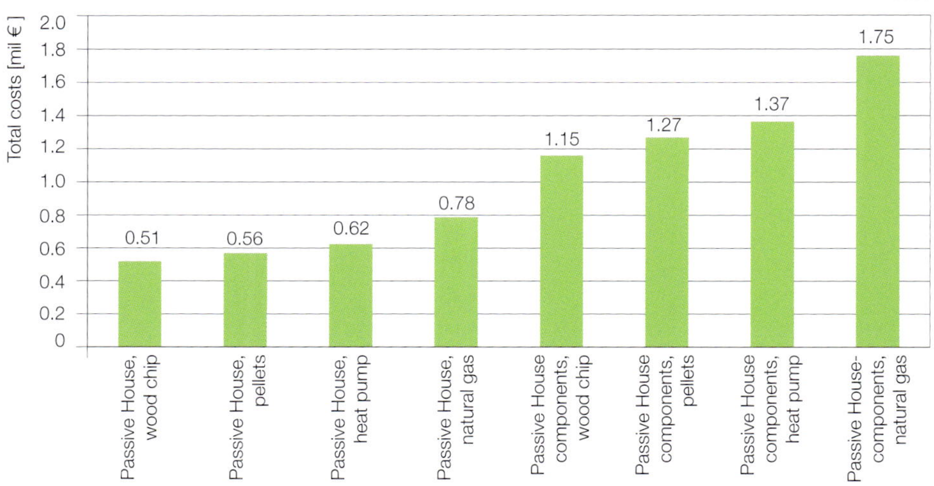

6.93

6.89 Multifunctional recess hall with terrace
6.90 Access zone in the old building with group work areas
6.91 Cumulative global warming potential from space heating (operation period of 50 years) for a variety of refurbishment strategies, including the further use of the unrefurbished building
6.92 Assessment of the refurbished school building according to the certification system, Total Quality Building (TQB) managed by the Austrian Sustainable Building Council (ÖGNB)
6.93 Feasibility assessment of the heating system's operation and maintenance according to different refurbishment strategies (cash value over 50 years; assumptions: discount interest rate 5%; energy price increase 10%/a)

Acknowledgements

The authors would like to thank all those who contributed towards the production of this book whether through discussion, written content, sponsorships or simply by offering moral support during the development stages.
Our special thanks go to Thomas Belazzi, Hans Drexler, Lone Feifer, Maria Fellner, Matthias Fuchs, Roman Güntensperger, Guillaume Habert, Franziska Hartmann, Joost Hartwig, Mathias Heinz, Angela John, Johannes Kislinger, Alexander Mössinger, Christoph Österreicher, EunJu Oh, Alexander Passer, Katrin Pfäffli, Astrid Unger, Christian Waldner, Carin Whitney, Thomas Wilken, Karin Zeder, Patrick Zimmermann and, in particular, Jakob Schoof.
We would also like to thank all other persons not mentioned above for participating in and supporting the making of this book.

Authors

Sebastian El khouli
1972 born in Hamburg
1993–2000 studied architecture at TU Braunschweig
1999 studied architecture at Universidad Politecnica de Valencia
1998–2000 employed at Architekturbüro Möhlmann & Urbisch, Braunschweig
2001–2006 member of staff at Atelier 5, Bern
2006 Certificate of Advanced Studies (CAS) in the field Systematic Project Management, Managementzentrum HTI Bern
2006–2009 research assistant at TU Darmstadt in the department design and energy efficient building (Prof. Hegger)
2008 further training as energy consultant at TU Darmstadt
2009 lecturer at TU Darmstadt in the department design and energy efficient building
since 2009 project manager at Bob Gysin + Partner BGP Architekten ETH SIA BSA, Zurich
2008–2011 director of the UIA Work Programme "Architecture for a sustainable future", Region I
2010 visiting critic at MSA Münster, Sustainable Building Design Studio
since 2010 consultant of the architects' council Kulturkreis der deutschen Wirtschaft
since 2010 lecturer at various architects' chambers (i.a. Berlin, Lower Saxony)
2013 visiting critic at the Summer School "Energy and the City", ETH Zurich

Viola John
1977 born in Wiesbaden
1997–2005 studied architecture at TU Darmstadt
2003/04 Postgraduate Diploma in "Energy Efficient Building" at Oxford Brookes University in Oxford, UK (ERASMUS scholarship)
2006/07 free-lance work at TU Darmstadt in the department design and energy efficient building (Prof. Hegger) and free-lance work as energy and sustainability consultant
2007–2012 teaching and research assistant at ETH Zurich, Chair of Sustainable Building (Prof. Wallbaum)
2008–2012 completion of doctoral programme with title "Doctor of Sciences" at ETH Zurich, Chair of Sustainable Building (Prof. Wallbaum), dissertation title: Derivation of reliable simplification strategies for the comparative LCA of individual and "typical" newly built Swiss apartment buildings
2012–2014 post doctorand at ETH Zurich, Chair of Sustainable Building (Prof. Habert)
since 2014 chief assistant at ETH Zurich, Chair of Sustainable Building (Prof. Habert)

Martin Zeumer
1977 born in Siegen
1997–2005 studied architecture at TU Darmstadt
since 2003 free-lance work as energy and sustainability consultant, speaker and author on the topics energy efficiency, sustainability, life cycle assessment and building materials
2005 member of staff at Eurolabors, Kassel
2005/06 lecturer and free-lance work at TU Darmstadt in the department design and energy efficient building (Prof. Hegger)
2007–2010 lecturer and research assistant at TU Darmstadt, in the department design and energy efficient building (Prof. Hegger)
since 2007 doctoral programme at TU Darmstadt, architecture department (Prof. Hegger), dissertation title: Facade systems for refurbishments – construction and energy efficiency improvement of plastic refurbishment systems for residential buildings
2010 lecturer at Hochschule Bochum for the fields building construction / sustainable building / upgrades of existing buildings
2010/11 lecturer and research assistant at TU Darmstadt in the department design and energy efficient building (Prof. Hegger) as well as design and building composition (Prof. Eisele)
2012 lecturer at TU Darmstadt in the department design and building composition (Prof. Eisele)
2012 further training as certified building biologist and energy consultant
since 2012 cooperation with ee concept GmbH Darmstadt, manager of the department "building material consultants", since 2013 authorised signatory of ee concept GmbH
since 2012 lecturer at various architects' chambers (i.a. Saxony, Baden-Wuerttemberg) as well as DGNB

Supplementary notes

Sustainable construction techniques – current situation

[1] Federal Environmental Agency Berlin, 2005
[2] Zeumer, Martin: Baubiologie und Bauökologie (IFBau seminar). Stuttgart 2013
[3] Hegger, Manfred et al.: Baustoff Atlas. Munich 2005
[4] Articles of Deutscher Werkbund, preamble, Berlin 1907
[5] Boyd Whyte, Iain; Schneider, Romana (pub.): Die gläserne Kette. Berlin 1986
[6] Ruskin, John; Kemp, Wolfgang (pub.): Die sieben Leuchter der Architektur, chapter V-1. Dortmund 1994
[7] Lorenz, Peter: Das Neue Bauen im Wohnungs- und Siedlungsbau, dargestellt am Beispiel des Neuen Frankfurt. Stuttgart 1986
[8] Goodwin, Philipp L.: Preface; in Mock, Elisabeth: catalogue for travelling exhibition "In USA erbaut 1933–1944". Wiesbaden 1948
[9] Buckminster Fuller, Richard: Operating Manual for Spaceship Earth. Carbondale/Edwardsville 1969
[10] Exhibition: Architecting the Future: Buckminster Fuller & Lord Norman Foster. Miami 2011
[11] Palm, Hubert: Das gesunde Haus. Das kranke Haus und seine Heilung. Die Zivilisationskrankheiten der Architektur. Zur architectura perennis. Constance 1979
[12] Minke, Gernot: Alternatives Bauen. Kassel 1980
[13] Aicher, Otl: Die Welt als Entwurf. Berlin 1991
[14] Stryi-Hipp, Gerhard; Rockendorf, Gunter; Reuß, Manfred: Das Technologienentwicklungspotenzial für die Nutzung der Solarwärme. In: FVEE-Tagungsband 2010: Forschung für das Zeitalter der erneuerbaren Energien. Berlin 2010
[15] Interview with Kieran Timberlake. In: Detail Green 1/2009. Munich 2009
[16] World Commission on Environment and Development – WCED (pub.): Our Common Future. Oxford 1987
[17] International Council for Research and Innovation in Building and Construction – CIB (pub.): Agenda 21 on sustainable construction. Rotterdam 1999
[18] United Nations Human Settlements Programme: Istanbul Declaration on Human Settlements, 1996
[19] Hoinka, Thomas: Transparenz für Bauprodukte im LEED und DGNB-System. In: greenbuilding 1–2/2011. Berlin 2011
[20] AGÖF (pub.): AGÖF-Orientierungswerte für flüchtige organische Verbindungen in der Raumluft. Springe-Eldagsen 2013
[21] Building product guideline 89/106 (EWG)
[22] AgBB (pub.): Vorgehensweise bei der gesundheitlichen Bewertung der Emissionen von flüchtigen organischen Verbindungen (VOC) aus Bauprodukten. In: DIBt-Mitteilungen 1/2001, pp. 3–12
[23] Building product directive 305/2011 (EU)
[24] Schmidt-Bleek, Friedrich; Bierter, Willy: Das MIPS Konzept. Weniger Naturverbrauch, mehr Lebensqualität durch Faktor 10. Munich 2000
[25] Mettke, Angelika et al.: Wiederverwendung von Plattenbauteilen in Osteuropa. Endbericht – Bearbeitungsphase I. Cottbus 2008
[26] Waltjen, Tobias; Mötzl, Hildegund: Ökologischer Bauteilkatalog. Berlin 1999
[27] ee concept GmbH (pub.): Entwicklung und Erprobung eines Bewertungssystems "BNB für Forschungs- und Laborgebäude (Neubau)". Darmstadt 2014
[28] Hegger, Manfred et al.: Energie Atlas. Munich 2007
[29] Sloterdijk, Peter: Gebäude sind Partner ihrer Bewohner. In: Goehler, Adrienne: zur nachahmung empfohlen! expeditionen in ästhetik und nachhaltigkeit. Ostfildern 2010

Environmental objectives, criteria and assessment methods

[1] German Federal Ministry of Traffic, Building and Housing (pub.): Leitfaden Nachhaltiges Bauen. Berlin 2001, p. 11
[2] Federal Ministry of Health (BMG) (pub.): Formaldehyd in der Innenraumluft. Informationen und Tipps für Verbraucher. Bern 2010
[3] Kohler, Niklaus; Hassler, Uta; Paschen, Herbert (pub.): Stoffströme und Kosten in den Bereichen Bauen und Wohnen. Berlin/Heidelberg 1999, p. 18
[4] all AGÖF values according to: AGÖF Association of Ecological Research Institutes e.V. (pub.): AGÖF-Orientierungswerte für flüchtige organische Verbindungen in der Raumluft. Springe-Eldagsen 2013
[5] German Federal Ministry of Environment, Nature Conservation, Building and Nuclear Safety (BMUB): WECOBIS – Ecological Building Material Information System. www.wecobis.de
[6] ECHA European Chemicals Agency: ECHA. echa.europa.eu/de/
[7] BG BAU – GISBAU Berufsgenossenschaft der Bauwirtschaft: GISCODE Produktgruppen. www.bgbau.de/gisbau/giscodes
[8] DIN German Institute for Standardization (pub.): Environmental management – life cycle assessment – principles and framework. DIN EN ISO 14040. Berlin 2006
[9] DIN German Institute for Standardization (pub.): Environmental management – life cycle assessment – requirements and guidelines. DIN EN ISO 14044. Berlin 2006
[10] DIN German Institute for Standardization (pub.): Sustainability of construction works – assessment of environmental performance of buildings – calculation method. DIN EN 15978. Berlin 2012
[11] John, Viola: Derivation of reliable simplification strategies for the comparative LCA of individual and "typical" newly built Swiss apartment buildings. Dissertation, Zurich 2012 dx.doi.org/10.3929/ethz-a-007607252, p. 8
[12] see note at 11
[13] Holliger Consult: Elektronischer Bauteilkatalog. www.bauteilkatalog.ch
[14] Swiss Society of Engineers and Architects (SIA) (pub.): Graue Energie von Gebäuden. SIA 2032. Zurich 2010
[15] Frischknecht, Rolf; Jungbluth, Niels; Althaus, Hans-Jörg; Bauer, Christian; Doka, Gabor; Dones, Roberto; Hischier, Roland; Hellweg, Stefanie; Humbert, Sébastien; Köllner, Thomas; Loerincik, Yves; Margni, Manuele; Nemecek, Thomas (pub.): Implementation of Life Cycle Impact Assessment Methods. Ecoinvent report No. 3. Dübendorf 2007
[16] Association of German Engineers (VDI) (pub.): Kumulierter Energieaufwand (KEA) Begriffe, Berechnungsmethoden. VDI 4600. Berlin 2013
[17] Federal Environmental Agency (pub.): Daten zur Umwelt Ausgabe 2009. Dessau-Roßlau 2009, p. 9
[18] Guinée, Jeroen B.; Gorrée, Marieke; Heijungs, Reinout; Huppes, Gjalt; Kleijn, René; Koning, Arjan de; Oers, Lauran van; Sleeswijk, Anneke Wegener; Suh, Sangwon; Haes, Helias A. Udo de; Bruijn, Hans de; Duin, Robbert van; Huijbregts, Mark A. J. (pub.): Handbook on life cycle assessment. Operational guide to the ISO standards. Dordrecht 2002
[19] see note at 18
[20] see note at 18
[21] see note at 18
[22] see note at 18
[23] Frischknecht, Rolf; Steiner, Roland; Jungbluth, Niels (pub.): Ökobilanzen: Methode der ökologischen Knappheit – Ökofaktoren 2006. Methode für die Wirkungsabschätzung in Ökobilanzen. Öbu SR 28/2008. Zurich 2008
[24] Goedkoop, Mark; Heijungs, Reinout; Huijbregts, Mark; De Schryver, An; Struijs, Jaap; van Zelm, Rosalie (pub.): ReCiPe 2008 A life cycle impact assessment method which comprises harmonised category indicators at the midpoint and the endpoint level; Report I: Classification. Den Haag 2008
[25] Ecoinvent Centre: Database ecoinvent data. www.ecoinvent.org
[26] IPCC (pub.): Climate Change 2007 Working Group I. The Physical Science Basis. Cambridge 2007
[27] European Commission Joint Research Centre JRC: European Platform on LCA – LCA Resources Directory – Services & Tools. eplca.jrc.ec.europa.eu/ResourceDirectory/providerList.vm
[28] German Institute for Standardization (pub.): Sustainability of construction works - environmental product declarations - core rules for the product category of construction products. DIN EN 15804. Berlin 2012
[29] Federal Ministry of Transport, Building and Urban Development (BMVBS) (pub.): Leitfaden Nachhaltiges Bauen. Berlin 2013
[30] German Federal Ministry of Environment, Nature Conservation, Building and Nuclear Safety (BMUB): Informationsportal Nachhaltiges Bauen, www.nachhaltigesbauen.de
[31] see note at 5
[32] BG BAU – GISBAU Berufsgenossenschaft der Bauwirtschaft: WINGIS Online Gefahrstoff-Informationssystem, www.wingis-online.de
[33] Landesverband Steiermark und Kärnten (pub.): Nutzungsdauerkatalog baulicher Anlagen und Anlagenteile. Graz 2006
[34] Austrian Institute for Building Biology and Ecology (IBO): OI3-INDIKATOR Leitfaden zur Berechnung von Ökokennzahlen für Gebäude. Vienna 2011
[35] Austrian Institute for Building Biology and Ecology (IBO): ECOSOFT / Eco2Soft. www.baubook.at/eco2soft/
[36] Swiss Society of Engineers and Architects (SIA) (pub.): Empfehlung SIA 112/1 – Nachhaltiges Bauen (Hochbau). Zurich 2004
[37] see note at 14
[38] Swiss Society of Engineers and Architects (SIA) (pub.): Mobilität – Energiebedarf in Abhängigkeit vom Gebäudestandort SIA 2039. Zurich 2011
[39] Swiss Society of Engineers and Architects (SIA) (pub.): SIA D 0200 SNARC Systematik zur Beurteilung der Nachhaltigkeit von Architekturprojekten für den Bereich Umwelt. Zurich 2004
[40] see note at 13
[41] E4tech: Lesosai, www.lesosai.com/de
[42] Geschäftsstelle eco-bau (pub.): Eco-BKP 2013 Merkblätter ökologisches Bauen nach Baukostenplan BKP. Zurich 2013
[43] www.bre.co.uk/greenguide/page.jsp?id=2069
[44] www.rics.org/Documents/Methodology_embodied_carbon_final.pdf
[45] Passer, Alexander; Mach, Thomas; Kreiner, Helmuth; Maydl, Peter: Predictable Sustainability? The role of building certification in the design of innovative facades. Graz 2012
Ebert, Thilo; Essig, Natalie; Hauser, Gerd: Zertifizierungssysteme für Gebäude. Munich 2010
Wallbaum, Holger; Hardziewski, Regina: Minergie und die anderen – Vergleich von vier Labels. In: TEC 21, 47/2011
[46] BRE Building Research Establishment: BREEAM, www.breeam.org
[47] U.S. Green Building Council: LEED, www.usgbc.org/leed
[48] Department for Communities and Local Government (pub.): Code for Sustainable Homes. A step-change in sustainable home building practice. London 2006.

[49] Department for Communities and Local Government (pub.): Code for Sustainable Homes Technical Guide. London 2010
[50] www.minergie.ch
[51] Sustainable Construction Network Switzerland (NNBS): SNBS Standard für Nachaltiges Bauen der Schweiz, www.nnbs.ch/standard-snbs
[52] German Sustainable Building Council (DGNB): DGNB, www.dgnb.de
[53] Austrian Sustainable Building Council (ÖGNB): TQB, www.oegnb.net/tqb.htm
[54] www.oegnb.net
[55] IBO: Ökokennzahlen, www.ibo.at/de/oekokennzahlen.htm
[56] see note at 34
[57] www.behqe.com
[58] SCERT Schweizer Zertifizierungsstelle für Produkte und Personen im Bauwesen: GI Gutes Innenraumklima, www.s-cert.ch/index.php/gutes-innenraumklima.html
[59] Sentinel House Institute: Der SHI-Gesundheitspass, www.sentinel-haus.eu/leistungen/zertifizierung/gesundheitspass/
[60] Weidema, Bo Pedersen; Wesnæs, Marianne Suhr: Data quality management for life cycle inventories – an example of using data quality indicators. Journal of Cleaner Production 1996
[61] European Commission Joint Research Centre JRC: European Reference Life Cycle Database. eplca.jrc.ec.europa.eu/ELCD3/
[62] Federal Ministry of Transport, Building and Urban Development (BMVBS): Ökobau.dat 2013, www.nachhaltigesbauen.de/baustoff-und-gebaeudedaten/oekobaudat.html
[63] see note at 55
[64] KBOB: Ökobilanzen im Baubereich (2009/1), www.eco-bau.ch/index.cfm?Nav=15&ID=18&js=1#CustomDetails59
[65] www.lcacommons.gov/nrel/search
[66] see note at 25
[67] PE International: GaBi Software und Datenbank, www.gabi-software.com
[68] Product Ecology Consultants: SimaPro LCA Software, www.pre.nl/simapro/
[69] Ifu Hamburg GmbH: Umberto, www.umberto.de
[70] GreenDelta: OpenLCA, www.openlca.org
[71] König, Holger: LEGEP Software, www.legep.de
[72] www.sbs-onlinetool.com
[73] www.lesosai.com/en/
[74] www.ecat-buildings.com
[75] www.athenasmi.org/
[76] www.izuba.fr
[77] www.elodie-cstb.fr/Presentation-EN.aspx

Strategies for material use in the construction process

[1] German Federal Ministry of Environment, Nature Conservation, Building and Nuclear Safety (BMUB) (pub.): Strategie Ressourceneffizienz – Impulse für den ökologischen und ökonomischen Umbau der Industriegesellschaft. Berlin 2008
[2] Davis Langdon Managment Consulting (pub.): World Construction Review – Outlook 2004/05. London 2004
[3] International Labour Organization (pub.): The construction industry in the twenty-first century: its image, employment prospects and skill requirements. Geneva 2001
[4] Knappe, Florian: Recyclingbaustoffe in Hoch- und Tiefbau. Presentation at RECYCLING-TECHNIK 2012. Dortmund
[5] Bleck, Wolfgang: Ressourcenschonung mit neuen Stählen/Technologien/Methoden; Lecture within the project "Verbesserung von Rohstoffproduktivität und Ressourcenschonung". Düsseldorf 18 April 2007
[6] Lemken, Thomas et al.; Wuppertal Institut für Klima, Umwelt, Energie GmbH (pub.): Stahl – ein Werkstoff mit Innovationspotenzial. Wuppertal 2008
[7] Glücklich, Detlef (pub.): Ökologisches Bauen. Munich 2005
[8] Siebers, Raban; Hauke, Bernhard: Ökobilanzieller Vergleich von Hallen unterschiedlicher Bauweisen. Düsseldorf 2012
[9] Kaufmann, Hermann et al.: Holzbau der Zukunft in der High-Tech-Offensive Zukunft Bayern. Ganzheitliche Planungsstrategien: Konzeption und Umsetzung. Munich 2008
[10] König, Holger: Bauen für die Zukunft – Bauen mit Holz. Nachwachsende Rohstoffe und ihre Rolle in der Zertifizierung. Presentation. Munich 2012
[11] Gärtner, Sven; Holzkaskadennutzung vs. Holzenergie: Was nützt der Umwelt mehr? Augsburg 2012
[12] Plugge, Daniel: Holzwerkstoff – Spanplattenherstellung. Hamburg 2006
[13] Rudolphi, Alexander: Lecture at the symposium "Beyond Green!" Stuttgart, 11 October 2012
[14] John, Viola: Derivation of reliable simplification strategies for the comparative LCA of individual and "typical" newly built Swiss apartment buildings. Zurich 2012
[15] according to Frischknecht, Rolf et al.: The ecoinvent Database: Overview and Methodological Framework. In: International Journal Of Life Cycle Assessmant 2005/10, pp. 3–9
[16] Knippers, Jan et al.: Atlas Kunststoffe und Membrane. Munich 2010
[17] see note at 14
[18] Preisig, Hansruedi: Massiv- oder Leichtbauweise? Zurich 2002
[19] Zeumer, Martin; Hartwig, Joost: Umweltwirkungen von Kunststoffen. In: Knippers, Jan et al.: Atlas Kunststoffe und Membrane. Munich 2010
[20] Widman, Joakim; Swedish Institute of Steel Construction (pub.): Sustainability of Modular Construction. SBI Report 229-2. Stockholm 2004
[21] König, Holger: Umweltorientierte Datenerfassung für Beschaffer. Nachwachsende Rohstoffe und ihre Rolle in der Zertifizierung. Presentation. Munich 2011
[22] Badr, Amani; Fuchs, Matthias; Zeumer, Martin: 6th Interim report on the project "Ganzheitliche Optimierung und Umsetzung des Neubaus der Propsteipfarrei St. Trinitatis in Leipzig als ökologisches Modellvorhaben". Darmstadt 2013
[23] see note at 22
[24] Brenner, Valentin: Recyclinggerechtes Konstruieren: Konzepte für eine abfallfreie Konstruktionsweise im Bauwesen. Stuttgart 2010
[25] Mettke, Angelika et al.: Interim report on the research project "Ökonomische und ökologische Bilanzierung des Transportes von Betonplattenbauteilen aus dem Rückbau von Wohnbauten in Deutschland in Länder Osteuropas und dortige Wiederverwendung beim Neubau von Wohngebäuden". Cottbus 2011
[26] Hellerich, Walter; Harsch, Günther; Haenke, Siegfried: Werkstoffführer Kunststoffe. Munich 2004
[27] Plugge, Daniel: Holzwerkstoff – Spanplattenherstellung. Hamburg 2006
[28] Mötzl, Hildegund: Entsorgungseigenschaften von Gebäuden. Vienna 2009
von Gleich, Arnim et al.: Effizienzgewinne durch Kooperation bei der Optimierung von Stoffströmen in der Region Hamburg. Hamburg 2004
Brenner, Valentin: Recyclinggerechtes Konstruieren: Konzepte für eine abfallfreie Konstruktionsweise im Bauwesen. Stuttgart 2010
Thormark, Catarina: Recycling Potential and Design for Disassembly in Buildings. Lund 2001
[29] William McDonough, Michael Braungart: Cradle to Cradle: Remaking the Way We Make Things. New York 2003
[30] Schmidt-Bleek, Friedrich: Wieviel Umwelt braucht der Mensch? Faktor 10 – Das Maß für ökologisches Wirtschaften. Basel 1993
[31] Sobek, Werner: Bauen im 21. Jahrhundert: High-Tech und Ökologie. Berlin 2007; also available at: http://www.bvbaustoffe.de/root/img/pool/downloads/praesentationen/071211_sobek_geschuetzt.pdf
[32] DGNB: www.dgnb.de
[33] see note at 22
[34] Hegger, Manfred; Fuchs, Matthias; Zeumer, Martin: Nachhaltigkeitskennwerte von Baumaterialien nach Bauteilschichten. Darmstadt 2005
[35] Sigg, René; Kälin, Werner; Plattner, Hugo: LUKRETIA – Lebenszyklus – Ressourcen – Technisierung. Zurich 2006
[36] Zeumer, Martin: Vortrag Linoleum – ein nachhaltiges Produkt. Bremen 2006; with excerpts from Hegger, Manfred et al.: Linoleum – ein nachhaltiges Produkt. Darmstadt 2006
[37] DGNB (pub.): Steckbrief Risiken für die lokale Umwelt. Stuttgart 2008
[38] Gesellschaft für ökologische Bautechnik Berlin (pub.): Instrumente zur qualitätsabhängigen Abschätzung der Dauerhaftigkeit von Materialien und Konstruktionen. Berlin 2006
[39] König, Holger et al.: Lebenszyklusanalyse in der Gebäudeplanung. Munich 2009
[40] Bundesamt für Konjunkturfragen, Impulsprogramm IP Bau (pub.): Alterungsverhalten von Bauteilen und Unterhaltskosten: Grundlagendaten für den Unterhalt und die Erneuerung von Wohnbauten. Bern 1994
[41] Bahr, Carolin; Lennerts, Kunibert: Lebens- und Nutzungsdauer von Bauteilen. Karlsruhe 2010
[42] Gesellschaft für ökologische Bautechnik Berlin mbH (Hrsg): Instrumente für die qualitätsabhängige Abschätzung von Dauerhaftigkeiten von Materialien und Bauteilen. Berlin 2005
[43] Hegger, Manfred et al.: e-life – Lebenszyklusbetrachtung und Optimierung von Instandsetzungsprozessen im Wohnungsbau. Stuttgart 2008
[44] Kortmann, Konstantin; Hegger, Manfred: Planung im Lebenszyklus – Aufgaben des Architekten. In: Bundesingenieurkammer (pub.): Der Lebenszyklus von Wohngebäuden. Berlin 2006
[45] DGNB (pub.): Steckbrief Rückbau und Demontagefreundlichkeit. Stuttgart 2012
[46] Brenner, Valentin: Recyclinggerechtes Konstruieren: Konzepte für eine abfallfreie Konstruktionsweise im Bauwesen. Stuttgart 2010
[47] see note at 40
Hegger, Manfred et al.: Energie Atlas. Munich 2007
[48] see note at 24

Design phases and processes

[1] Royal Institute of British Architects: Green Overlay to the RIBA Outline Plan of Work. London 2011
[2] BNB-Steckbrief 1.1.6.: Risiken für die lokale Umwelt, 2011 edition

Environmental impacts of building components

[1] Kaufmann, Hermann et al.: Holzbau der Zukunft in der High-Tech-Offensive Zukunft Bayern: Ganzheitliche Planungsstrategien: Konzeption und Umsetzung. Munich 2008
[2] Mergl, Oliver: Flexibilisierung von Baustrukturen durch Modularisierung zur Verbesserung des Nutzungspotenzials am Beispiel industrieller Produktionsstätten des Automobilbaus. Kassel 2007
[3] Waltjen, Mück, Thorghele, Zelger; Ökologischer Bauteilkatalog; Österreichisches Institut für Baubiologie- und -ökologie (IBO). Vienna 1998
[4] Rudolphi, Alexander: Vortrag im Rahmen der Consense. Stuttgart 2011
[5] see note at 2

[6] CSD-Ingenieure; Ökologische Lebenszyklusanalyse. Stahlbetondeckensystem Cobiax. Berlin 2012, Appendix A, p. 1
[7] Quack, Dietlinde; Liu, Ran: Ökobilanz Betondecken. Freiburg 2010, p. 75
[8] see note at 7, p. 63
[9] Mück, Wolfgang: baubiologie24, Modul 3 – Konstruktion und Innenausbau. Hamm 2011, p. 12
[10] eco-bau (pub.): Normpositionenkatalog (NPK) 651–653 Deckenbekleidungen. Bern 2007
[11] see note at 10
[12] Gesellschaft für ökologische Bautechnik Berlin mbH (pub.): Instrumente für die qualitätsabhängige Abschätzung von Dauerhaftigkeiten von Materialien und Bauteilen. Berlin 2005
[13] Sprengard, Christoph; Treml, Sebastian; Holm, Andreas: Technologien und Techniken zur Verbesserung der Energieeffizienz von Gebäuden durch Wärmedämmstoffe. Metastudie Wärmedämmstoffe – Produkte – Anwendungen – Innovationen. Gräfelfing 2013, p. 119
[14] Austrian Institute for Building Biology and Ecology (IBO); Mötzl, Hildegund; Bauer, Barbara; Lerchbaumer, Siegfried; Torghele, Karl: Planungsleitfaden: Ökologische Baustoffwahl. Vienna 2007
[15] Hegger, Manfred et al.: Energie Atlas. Munich 2007, p. 264
[16] compare data sets ökobau.dat 2012
[17] see note at 14
[18] Hegger, Manfred et al.: Energie Atlas. Munich 2007, p. 262
[19] see note at 16
[20] Hegger, Manfred; Fuchs, Matthias; Zeumer, Martin: Integration vergleichender Nachhaltigkeitskennwerte von Baumaterialien nach Bauteilschichten. Darmstadt 2005 and see note at 15
[21] Richter, Klaus; Künniger, Tina; Brunner, Kaspar: Ökologische Bewertung von Fensterkonstruktionen verschiedener Rahmenmaterialien (ohne Verglasung). Study performed on behalf of the Swiss Centre for Windows and Facades (SZFF) in cooperation with the German Window and Facade Association (VFF). Frankfurt/Main 1996
[22] see note at 12
[23] German Sustainable Building Council (DGNB): DGNB System, Steckbrief Env. 1.1.6.
[24] see note at 3
[25] see note at 12
[26] see note at 15
[27] see note at 23
[28] see note at 3
[29] see note at 14
[30] see note at 16
[31] from Arx, Urs: Bauprodukte und -zusatzstoffe in der Schweiz, Bundesamt für Umwelt, Wald und Landschaft (BUWAL), 1995
[32] see note at 16
[33] see note at 23
[34] see note at 12
[35] Tichelmann, Heller: Vergleichende Ökobilanzbetrachtung und Lebenszyklusanalyse mit erweiterten Betrachtungen. Darmstadt 2011
[36] see note at 15
[37] eco-bau (pub.): eco-devis 671: Gipserarbeiten – Innenputze und Stuckaturen. Bern 2001
[38] see note at 14
[39] see note at 16
[40] eco-bau (pub.): eco-devis 661: Unterlagsböden und Zementüberzüge. Bern 2001
[41] see note at 12
[42] see note at 40, 14 and 23
[43] see note at 16
[44] see note at 16
[45] eco-bau (pub.): eco-devis 662: Bodenbeläge für leichte bis schwere Beanspruchung. Bern 2001
[46] see note at 45
[47] see note at 23
[48] see note at 23

Case studies

[1] Umweltbundesamt Dessau: Daten zur Umwelt – Umweltzustand in Deutschland, Abfall- und Kreislaufwirtschaft, Abfallaufkommen, www.umweltbundesamt.de/daten/umweltdaten/public/theme.do?nodeIdent=2320
[2] Velux Deutschland GmbH (pub.): LichtAktiv Haus – Velux Modell Home 2020. Hamburg 2012
[3] Hegger, Manfred et al.: Abschlussbericht Ökobilanzierung Velux Model Home 2020 "LichtAktiv Haus" Hamburg. Darmstadt 2011
[4] Diefenbach, Nikolaus et al.: Datenbasis Gebäudebestand – Datenerhebung zur energetischen Qualität und zu den Modernisierungstrends im deutschen Wohngebäudebestand. Darmstadt 2010
[5] www.velux.de/privatkunden/wohnqualitaet_energieeffizienz_nachhaltigkeit/model-home2020/lichtaktivhaus/architekturkonzept/herausforderungen
[6] see note at 2
[7] Hegger, Manfred et al.: Aktivhaus – Das Grundlagenwerk. Munich 2013
[8] Deutsche Gesellschaft für nachhaltiges Bauen: Neubau kleine Wohngebäude – 2013 edition, Steckbrief SOC 1.4: Visueller Komfort
[9] see note at 7
[10] DIN EN 13779:2007-09: Ventilation for non-residential buildings - Performance requirements for ventilation and room-conditioning systems; DIN EN ISO 7730:2006-05: Ergonomics of the thermal environment - Analytical determination and interpretation of thermal comfort; DIN EN 15251:2012-12: Indoor environmental input parameters for design and assessment of energy performance of buildings addressing indoor air quality, thermal environment, lighting and acoustics
[11] Wilken, Thomas; Rosebrock, Oliver: Monitoring LichtAktiv Haus Hamburg. Braunschweig 2013
[12] Rohde, Sven: Hilfe, unser Haus lebt! In: stern extra Energie, 2013
[13] Association of Ecological Research Institutes e.V. (AGÖF): Orientierungswerte für flüchtige organische Verbindungen in der Raumluft. Springe-Eldagsen 2013
[14] Federal Ministry of Education and Research: Pressemitteilung – Öko-Zement reduziert CO_2-Emissionen. Berlin 2010
[15] see note at 3
[16] see note at 8
[17] see note at 14
[18] Zement- und Betonhersteller Wopfinger Baustoffindustrie GmbH
[19] The target values of the SIA Energy Efficiency Path for embodied energy and CO_2 emissions in schools are 45% (embodied energy) and 40% (CO_2) lower in the case of refurbishments in comparison to new builds. The results from case studies performed by ZHAW Zurich are used as a basis for the assumptions.
[20] Target value according to the Austrian scheme for the assessment of VOC concentrations: 300 $\mu g/m^3$
[21] Reference value used by the Swiss Federal Institute for Health (BAG): 0.1 ppm

Picture credits

The authors and editors wish to extend their sincere thanks to all those who helped realise this book by making illustrations available, granting permission to reproduce them and supplying information. Photos without credits are from the architects' own archives or the archives of DETAIL. Despite intensive efforts, it was not possible to identify the copyright owners of all photos and illustrations. However, their rights remain unaffected, and we request them to contact us. The numbers refer to the figures in the text.

Title Temporary residential units in Iwaki (JP), Kunihiro Ando + Satoyama Architecture 2011. Photo: Sadamu Saito, J-Tsukuba

Introduction
0.1 Jesper Ray, DK-Birkerød

Sustainable construction techniques – current situation
1.1 karnizz/Fotolia.com
1.2 according to Fuchs, Matthias; Hartmann, Franziska; Henrich, Johanna; Zeumer, Martin: SNAP Systematik für Nachhaltigkeitsanforderungen in Planungswettbewerben – Endbericht. Berlin 2013, p. 99, und Hartwig, Joost / ina Planungsgesellschaft mbH, Darmstadt
1.3 Martin Zeumer, Darmstadt
1.4 Jakob Schoof, Munich
1.5 Jakob Schoof, Munich
1.6 Kim Zwarts, NL–Maastricht
1.7 Kandschwar/ Wikipedia
1.8 Matthias Planitzer, Berlin
1.9 Hansruedi Riesen, CH–Zuchwil
1.11 Martin Zeumer, Darmstadt
1.12 Jakob Schoof, Munich
1.13 Jakob Schoof, Munich
1.14 Martin Zeumer, Darmstadt
1.15 Jakob Schoof, Munich
1.16 Mathias Koslik, Berlin

Environmental objectives, criteria and assessment methods
2.1 own illustration
2.2 Viola John, CH–Zurich
2.3 Åke E:son Lindman, S–Stockholm
2.4 own illustration
2.5 Hisao Suzuki, E–Barcelona
2.6 Bünger, Sven: Schadstoffe in Gebäuden – Überblick über die wichtigsten Problemfelder. 31. Jahresfachtagung der VDSI-Fachgruppe Hochschulen und wissenschaftliche Institutionen. TU Hamburg, 2006, p. 78
2.7 Wikipedia: VOC-Anteile Deutschland 1990 und 2003. commons.wikimedia.org/wiki/File:VOC-Anteile_Deutschland_1990_2003.svg
2.8 Lukas Jungmann / www.urlaubsarchitektur.de
2.9 own illustration
2.10 New build orientation values according to: Association of Ecological Research Institutes e.V. (AGÖF) (pub.): AGÖF-Orientierungswerte für flüchtige organische Verbindungen in der Raumluft. Springe-Eldagsen 2013; Reference values I and II according to indoor air values established by the ad-hoc working group of the Federal Environment Agency and Sagunski, Helmut: Formaldehyd, eine Innenraum-Geschichte. In: Bayerisches Landesamt für Gesundheit und Lebensmittelsicherheit (pub.): Materialien zur Umweltmedizin, Volume 13 Munich 2006, pp. 60–70
2.11 BG BAU – GISBAU Berufsgenossenschaft der Bauwirtschaft (pub.): Einstufung nach dem GISCODE für Epoxidharze. Frankfurt/ Main 2006
2.12 Wissenwiki: Bauproblem TVOC. www.wissenwiki.de/images/6/66/Wohngesundheit_UBA_TVOC.jpg
2.13 The Bunkie Co., CDN–Meaford
2.14 Ralph Feiner, CH–Malans
2.15 own illustration; recommendations according to: Die Verbraucher Initiative e. V.: Label Online, www.label-online.de
APUG Aktionsprogramm Umwelt und Gesundheit Nordrhein-Westfalen (pub.): Umweltzeichen für Bauprodukte. Bauprodukte gezielt auswählen – eine Entscheidungshilfe. Düsseldorf 2004
2.16 John, Viola: Derivation of reliable simplification strategies for the comparative LCA of individual and "typical" newly built Swiss apartment buildings. Dissertation, Zurich 2012 dx.doi.org/10.3929/ethz-a-007607252; S. 8
2.17 see 2.16
2.18 see 2.16, p. 10
2.19 see 2.16, p. 76
2.20 own illustration nach Eyerer, Peter; Reinhardt, Hans-Wolf; Kreissig, Johannes: Ökologische Bilanzierung von Baustoffen und Gebäuden. Wege zu einer ganzheitlichen Bilanzierung. Basel 2000, p. 11
2.21 Roland Tännler, CH–Zurich
2.22 Dratz & Dratz Architekten, Oberhausen
2.23 Zeumer, Martin; John, Viola; Hartwig, Joost: Nachhaltiger Materialeinsatz – Graue Energie im Lebenszyklus. In: Detail Green 1/2009
2.24 see 2.16, p. 17
2.25 Viola John, CH-Zurich
2.26 see 2.16, p. 84; mfd02
2.27 see 2.16, p. 91; mfd02
2.28 see 2.16, p. 89
2.29 see 2.16, p. 96
2.30 Möltner, Clemens: Life Cycle Assessment als Werkzeug zur Entwicklung umweltgerechter Produkte: Strategien zur Implementierung von Ecodesign. Hamburg 2009, p. 58
2.31 Econcept: Instrumente für ökologisches Bauen im Vergleich ein Leitfaden für das Planungsteam. SIA D 0152. Zurich 1998, p. 10
2.32 see 2.16, pp. 144f.
2.33 Hafner, Annette; Ott, Stephan; Winter, Stefan: Holzbauten Nutzung und Lebenszyklus – Ökobilanzen für Bauwerke: Standards und praktische Anwendung. Holzbau – die neue Quadriga 3/2012, p. 39
2.34 Hedrich Blessing Photography, USA–Chicago
2.35 own illustration
2.36 own illustration according to Passer, Alexander; Mach, Thomas; Kreiner, Helmuth; Maydl, Peter: Predictable Sustainability? The role of building certification in the design of innovative façades. Graz 2012
Ebert, Thilo; Essig, Natalie; Hauser, Gerd: Zertifizierungssysteme für Gebäude. Munich 2010, p. 97
Wallbaum, Holger; Hardziewski, Regina: Minergie und die anderen – Vergleich von vier Labels. TEC 21, 47/2011, p. 38
2.37 Eberhard Franke, Neufahrn/Egling
2.38 Austrian Institute for Building Biology and Ecology (IBO) (pub.): OI3-INDIKATOR Leitfaden zur Berechnung von Ökokennzahlen für Gebäude. Vienna 2011
2.39 MINERGIE: www.minergie.ch; und eco-bau
2.40 Weidema, Bo Pedersen; Wesnæs, Marianne Suhr: Data quality management for life cycle inventories – an example of using data quality indicators. In: Journal of Cleaner Production 1996
2.41 Viola John, CH–Zurich

Strategies for material use in the construction process
3.1 own illustration
3.2 Preisig, Hansruedi: Massiv- oder Leichtbauweise? Zurich 2002
3.3 own illustration according to Wirth, Stefan; Hildebrand, Torsten: Die Fabrik der Zukunft. In: IndustrieBau 4/2001, p. 56
3.4 Rechberger, Helmut: Recyclinggerechtes Bauen. Vienna 2012, p.7
3.5 according to Sustainum – Institut für zukunftsfähiges Wirtschaften. Berlin 2013
3.6 according to data from: Blum, Marc; Satzger, Falk; Arcelor Mittal (pub.): Nachhaltiges Bauen dank hochfester Stähle. Esch-sur-Alzette 2009
3.7 according to data from: Beton (pub.): Zemente und ihre Herstellung, Zement-Merkblatt Betontechnik 4/2014 und Proske, Tilo; Graubner, Carl-Alexander; Hainer, Stefan: Ökobetone zur Herstellung von Betonfertigteilen. Darmstadt 2012
3.8 Rechberger, Helmut: Recyclinggerechtes Bauen. Vienna 2012, p. 16, according to: Energie und Rohstoffe 2009. Tagungsband. Goslar 2009
3.9 according to data from: Mettke, Angelika; Heyn, Sören: Ökologische Prozessbetrachtungen – RC-Beton (Stofffluss, Energieaufwand, Emissionen). Cottbus 2010
3.10 according to data from: Mensinger, Martin et al.: Nachhaltiges Bauen mit Stahl: Ökologie. Munich 2009
3.11 Brenner, Valentin: Recyclinggerechtes Konstruieren: Konzepte für eine abfallfreie Konstruktionsweise im Bauwesen. Stuttgart 2010
3.12, 3.13 see 2.6, p. 89
3.14 in reference to EAWAG: Forum Chriesbach – Ein Neubau für die Wasserforschung. Dübendorf 2006
3.15 König, Holger: Bauen mit Holz als aktiver Klimaschutz. In: Kaufmann, Hermann; Nerdinger, Winfried: Bauen mit Holz. Wege in die Zukunft. Munich 2011, pp. 18ff.
3.16 König, Holger: Umweltorientierte Datenerfassung für Beschaffer. Nachwachsende Rohstoffe und ihre Rolle in der Zertifizierung, presentation. Munich 2011
3.17 Knippers, Jan et al.: Atlas Kunststoffe + Membranen. Munich 2010, p. 135
3.18 Renaud Araud, F–Couzon au Mont d'Or
3.19 Dominique Uldry, CH–Bern
3.20 Jasmin Schuller, A–Graz
3.21 according to data from: Hegger, Manfred; Fuchs, Matthias; Zeumer, Martin: Forschungsbericht Vergleichende Nachhaltigkeitskennwerte von Baustoffen und Bauteilschichten. Darmstadt 2005
3.22 Lignatec (pub.); Pfäffli, Katrin; Preisig, Hansruedi: Klimaschonend und energieeffizient bauen mit Holz – Umsetzung, p. 18, http://issuu.com/lignum/docs/lit26_d/18
3.23 according to data from: Hegger, Manfred; Fuchs, Matthias; Zeumer, Martin: Forschungsbericht Vergleichende Nachhaltigkeitskennwerte von Baustoffen und Bauteilschichten. Darmstadt 2005
3.24 Tichelmann, Karsten: Vergleichende Ökobilanzbetrachtung und Lebenszyklusanalyse für Konstruktionen nichttragender Innenwände und tragender Außenwände. Darmstadt 2010
3.25 see 3.24
3.26 Hartwig, Joost; Zeumer, Martin: Umweltwirkungen von Kunststoffen. In: Atlas Kunststoffe und Membrane. Munich 2010, p. 126
3.27 a Müller, Michael et al.: Ökologische/Ökonomische Bewertung zweier Fassadenkonzepte – Glasfassade vs. Kunststofffassade. Remscheid 2007, p. 84
b Tomas Riehle, Cologne
3.28 Hartwig, Joost; Zeumer, Martin: Umweltwirkungen von Kunststoffen, In: Knippers, Jan et al.: Atlas Kunststoffe und Membrane. Munich 2010
3.29 csd Ingenieure: Ökologische Lebenszyklusanalyse zum Stahlbetondeckensystem Cobiax. Berlin 2012
3.30 Martin Zeumer, Darmstadt according to data from ökobau.dat
3.31 Zeumer, Martin; John, Viola; Hartwig, Joost: Nachhaltiger Materialeinsatz: Holz und Holzwerkstoffe. In: Detail Green 2/2009, pp. 56f.

3.32 a Hermann Kaufmann ZT GmbH, A-Schwarzach
b Norman A. Müller, Ingolstadt
3.33 Goran Potkonjak, CH-Uster
3.34 Martin Zeumer; Darmstadt
3.35 according to AgBB – Bewertungsschema für VOC aus Bauprodukten, 2012 edition
3.36 ee concept GmbH, Darmstadt
3.37 Brenner, Valentin: Recyclinggerechtes Konstruieren: Konzepte für eine abfallfreie Konstruktionsweise im Bauwesen. Stuttgart 2010, p. 15
3.38 updated and extended according to: Hildegund Mötzl: Entsorgungseigenschaften von Gebäuden, IBO, 2007
3.39 Brenner, Valentin: Recyclinggerechtes Konstruieren: Konzepte für eine abfallfreie Konstruktionsweise im Bauwesen. Stuttgart 2010, p. 63
3.40 Rechberger, Helmut: Recyclinggerechtes Bauen. Vienna 2012, p. 38
3.41 in reference to the Association of Swiss Architects and Engineers (SIA) (pub.): SIA D 0216. SIA Effizienzpfad Energie. Zurich 2006
3.42 Eckhart Matthäus, Augsburg
3.43 Zooey Braun, Stuttgart
3.45 Martin Zeumer, Darmstadt
3.46 Martin Zeumer, Darmstadt
3.47 a http://www.zelenarchitektura.sk/wp-content/uploads/2010/12/073.pdf
b Allard van der Hoek, NL-Amsterdam
3.48 Glücklich, Detlef (pub.): Ökologisches Bauen. Von Grundlagen zu Gesamtkonzepten. Munich 2005, p. 56
3.49 Cree GmbH, A-Bregenz
3.50 a, b Hegger, Manfred; Fisch, Norbert et al.: Aktiv-Stadthaus. Entwicklungsgrundlage für städtische Mehrfamilienhäuser in Plus-Energie-Bauweise nach EU 2020 und zur Vorbereitung eines Demonstrativ-Bauvorhabens in Frankfurt am Main. Final report. Stuttgart 2014
c HHS Architekten und Stadtplaner, D-Kassel
3.51 Martin Zeumer, Darmstadt
3.52 Hegger, Manfred et al.: Energie Atlas. Munich 2007, p. 33, fig. A 6.2
3.53 Federal Ministry of Transport, Building and Urban Development (BMVBS) (pub.): Leitfaden Nachhaltiges Bauen. Berlin 2013
3.54 Federal Ministry of Transport, Building and Urban Development (BMVBS) (pub.): Leitfaden Nachhaltiges Bauen. Berlin 2001
3.55 see 3.54
3.56 Jakob Schoof, Munich
3.57 Klaus Mellenthin für Blocher Blocher View, Stuttgart
3.58 Jan Bitter, Berlin
3.59 according to German Federal Ministry of Traffic, Building and Housing: Leitfaden nachhaltiges Bauen. Berlin 2001, Appendix 6
3.60 ee concept GmbH, Darmstadt in reference to: Buergel-Goodwin, Ebba: Vergleichende Studie zu Erneuerung, Unterhalt und Betrieb von Bestandsgebäuden auf Bauteilebene. Karlsruhe 2004, p. 13
3.61 ee concept GmbH, Darmstadt
3.62 Bahr, Carolin; Lennerts, Kunibert: Lebens- und Nutzungsdauer von Bauteilen. Karlsruhe 2010, p. 20
3.63 Gesellschaft für ökologische Bautechnik Berlin mbH (pub.): Instrumente für die qualitätsabhängige Abschätzung von Dauerhaftigkeiten von Materialien und Bauteilen. Berlin 2005
3.64 ee concept GmbH, Darmstadt
3.65 Hegger, Manfred et al.: Energie Atlas. Munich 2007, p. 164, fig. B 5.62
3.66 Christen, Kurt; Meyer-Meierling, Paul: Optimierung von Instandsetzungszyklen und deren Finanzierung bei Wohnbauten: Forschungsbericht. Zurich 1999
3.67 see 3.66
3.68 Brenner, Valentin: Recyclinggerechtes Konstruieren: Konzepte für eine abfallfreie Konstruktionsweise im Bauwesen. Stuttgart 2010, p. 58
3.69 see 3.68, p. 57
3.70 see 3.68, p. 54

Design phases and processes
4.1, 4.2 own illustration
4.3 own illustration according to: Gesis: SIMon – Social Indicators Monitor;
Bundesamt für Statistik Schweiz (BFS);
Gesis: SIMon/Statistik Austria
4.4 own illustration
4.5 SIA Effizienzpfad Energie. Statusbericht Graue Energie, Grundlagen zur Dokumentation SIA D 0216, Bearbeitung: büro für umweltchemie, Ueli Kasser; 22 February 2004
4.6 Fischer, Roland; Schwehr, Peter: Module für das Haus der Zukunft. Luzern 2009, p. 21
4.7 see 4.6, p. 22
4.9 Hermann Kaufmann ZT GmbH, A-Schwarzach
4.10 Matthias Hampe, TU Darmstadt
4.11 Ökobilanzierung von Siedlungen unter Berücksichtigung von Lebensstilaspekten am Beispiel einer Gartenstadt- und Wohnhöfesiedlung in Karlsruhe; Thesis written by Holger Wolpensinger; revised edition from 20 December 2002
4.12 see 4.5
4.13 Roger Frei, CH-Zurich
4.14 Machbarkeitsuntersuchung IBA Hamburg (D), HHS Architekten und Stadtplaner (2008), competition drawings
4.15 Bob Gysin & Partner BGP Architekten, CH-Zurich
4.16 Austrian Institute for Building Biology and Ecology (IBO) (pub.): Passivhaus-Bauteilkatalog. Vienna 2009, p. 151
4.17, 4.18 Bob Gysin + Partner BGP Architekten, CH-Zurich
4.19 TimbaTec, CH-Zurich
4.20 eco-bau (pub.): Eco-Devis NPK 645 Plattenbeläge. Bern 2005
4.21 Jakob Schoof, Munich
4.22 www.hsmservices.caimagesenergy_efficiency_blower_door_test_5_large.jpg
4.23 ee concept GmbH, Darmstadt
4.24 Amt für Hochbauten der Stadt Zürich (pub.): LUKRETIA (Lebenszykluskosten – Ressourcen – Energie – Technisierung – Gebäudeautomation), final report. Zurich 2006, p. 9
4.25 own illustration according to BauXund Forschung und Beratung GmbH, A-Vienna
4.26 Richtlinie über bauliche und betriebliche Massnahmen zur Begrenzung des Baulärms gemäß Artikel 6 der Lärmschutz-Verordnung (Swiss guideline for the prevention of noise), 2011
4.27 Sebastian El khouli, CH-Zurich

Environmental impacts of building components
5.1 North Rhine Westphalia Ministry of Economic Affairs, Energy, Building and Transport (MWEBWV) (pub.): Wohnen ohne Barrieren – Komfort für alle. Beispielhafte Lösungen für Neubau und Bestand. Düsseldorf 2010
5.2 Zeumer, Martin; Baumgärtner, Steffen: Architektonische Vergleichbarkeit von Tragkonstruktionen – Ermittlung einer funktionellen Einheit, Darmstadt 2012
5.3 in reference to Austrian Institute for Building Biology and Ecology (IBO) (pub.): Mötzl, Hildegund; Bauer, Barbara; Lerchbaumer, Siegfried; Torghele, Karl: Planungsleitfaden: Ökologische Baustoffwahl. Vienna 2007
5.4–5.28 Martin Zeumer, Darmstadt

Case studies
6.2, 6.9, 6.13 Hans Drexler, Münster
6.3–6.8, 6.11, 6.14, 6.15, 6.16
Kieran Timberlake Architects, US-Philadelphia
6.10 Peter Aaron/Esto
6.12 Teicholz, Paul: Labor Productivity Declines in the Construction Industry: Causes and Remedies, aecbytes, Viewpoint 4, 14, April 2004, http://www.aecbytes.com/viewpoint/2004/issue_4.html (access: 21 May 2014).
6.14 Bosch Rexroth Corporation, US-Charlotte
6.17, 6.25, 6.28, 6.32, 6.35 Adam Mørk, DK-Kopenhagen
6.18–6.24, 6.26, 6.30, 6.31, 6.33, 6.36, 6.37 Fachgebiet Entwerfen und Energieeffizientes Bauen, TU Darmstadt
6.29, 6.34 Ostermann Architekten, D-Hamburg
6.38 Michael Meuter, CH-Zurich
6.39–6.44, 6.47–6.48, 6.50, 6.55 pool Architekten, CH-Zurich
6.45, 6.46, 6.51, 6.52, 6.56 Giuseppe Micchiché, CH-Zurich
6.49 Jakob Schoof, Munich
6.53, 6.54 Architekturbüro H. R. Preisig, CH-Zurich
6.57, 6.65, 6.67, 6.68, 6.71, 6.72 Rupert Steiner, A-Vienna
6.58–6.60, 6.62–6.64, 6.69, 6.70 AllesWirdGut Architekten, A-Vienna
6.61 Walter Scheibenpflug, A-Bischofshofen
6.73–6.76 bauXund Forschung und Beratung GmbH, A-Vienna
6.77, 6.84 Dieter Schewig, A-Horn
6.78, 6.80–6.83, 6.85, 6.88 ah3 Architekten ZT GmbH, A-Horn
6.79. 6.86, 6.87, 6.89, 6.90 Sebastian El khouli, CH-Zurich
6.91, 6.93 Austrian Institute for Building Biology and Ecology (IBO), A-Vienna
6.92 Österreichische Gesellschaft für Nachhaltiges Bauen (ÖGNB), A-Vienna

Literature

Standards and guidelines

(Federal Immission Control Act (BImSchG). 2002

CEN report CR 1752 Ventilation for Buildings: Design Criteria for the Indoor Environment. 1998

DIN EN ISO 14024 Environmental labels and declarations – Type I environmental labelling – Principles and procedures. 2001-02

DIN EN ISO 14021 Environmental labels and declarations – Self-declared environmental claims (Type II environmental labelling). 2001-12

DIN EN ISO 14025 Environmental labels and declarations – Type III environmental declarations – Principles and procedures. 2005-07

DIN EN ISO 14040 Environmental management – Life cycle assessment – Principles and framework. 2006

DIN EN ISO 14044 Environmental management – Life cycle assessment – Requirements and guidelines. 2006

DIN EN 15804 Sustainability of construction works – Environmental product declarations – Core rules for the product category of construction products. 2012

DIN EN 15978 Sustainability of construction works – Assessment of environmental performance of buildings – Calculation method. 2012

DIN 4108 Thermal insulation and energy economy in buildings. 2013

DIN 4109 Sound insulation in buildings; requirements and testing. 1989-11

Energy Performance of Buildings Directive (EPBD) – EU guideline "Energy Performance of buildings". 2002

Minergie-ECO catalogue and instructions on implementing criteria, 2014

Regulation regarding structural and operational measures preventing noise on building sites according to paragraph 6 of the Swiss Noise Abatement Ordinance 2011

SIA 112/1 Nachhaltiges Bauen – Hochbau. 2004

SIA D 0123 Hochbaukonstruktion nach ökologischen Gesichtspunkten. 1995

SIA D 0152 Instrumente für ökologisches Bauen im Vergleich – Ein Leitfaden für das Planungsteam. 1998

SIA D 0200/SNARC Systematik zur Beurteilung der Nachhaltigkeit von Architekturprojekten für den Bereich Umwelt. 2005

SIA D 0216 SIA Effizienzpfad Energie. 2006

SIA 2032 Graue Energie von Gebäuden. 2010

EU regulation No. 305/2011 laying down harmonised conditions for the marketing of construction products (EU-Bauproduktenverordnung – EU-BauPVO)

Ordinance on Hazardous Substances (GefStoffV)

Additional literature

Addis, Bill: Building with Reclaimed Components and Materials. A Design Handbook for Reuse and Recycling. London 2006

Arbeitsgemeinschaft Kreislaufwirtschaftsträger Bau (pub.): 4. Monitoring-Bericht Bauabfälle. Berlin 2005

Bahr, Carolin; Lennerts, Kunibert: Lebens- und Nutzungsdauer von Bauteilen. Karlsruhe 2010

Baumann, Henrikke; Tillman, Anne-Marie: The hitch hiker's guide to LCA an orientation in life cycle assessment methodology and application. Lund 2011

Baumann, Ruth et al.: Bewertung der Innenraumluft. Flüchtige organische Verbindungen – VOC. Allgemeiner Teil. Vienna 2003

Bauwelt 43/2001: Die neue Nutzung. Berlin 2001

Büro für Umweltchemie; Kasser, Ueli: SIA Effizienzpfad Energie, Statusbericht Graue Energie, Grundlagen zur Dokumentation SIA D 0216. Ein Projekt von Swiss Energycodes der KHE des SIA. 2004.

Bundesamt für Umwelt, Wald und Landschaft (BUWAL) (pub.): Bewertung in Ökobilanzen mit der Methode der ökologischen Knappheit. Schriftenreihe Umwelt Nr. 297. Bern 1998

Federal Ministry of Transport, Building and Urban Development (BMVBS) (pub.): Leitfaden nachhaltiges Bauen. Berlin 2013

Brenner, Valentin: Recyclinggerechtes Konstruieren: Konzepte für eine abfallfreie Konstruktionsweise im Bauwesen. Stuttgart 2010

Ebert, Thilo; Eßig, Natalie; Hauser, Gerd: Zertifizierungssysteme für Gebäude. Munich 2010

Eyerer, Peter; Reinhardt, Hans-Wolf; Kreissig, Johannes: Ökologische Bilanzierung von Baustoffen und Gebäuden Wege zu einer ganzheitlichen Bilanzierung. Basel 2000

Frischknecht, Rolf et al. (pub.): Implementation of Life Cycle Impact Assessment Methods. Ecoinvent report No. 3. Dübendorf 2007

Frischknecht, Rolf: LCI modelling approaches applied on recycling of materials in view of environmental sustainability, risk perception and eco-efficiency. International Journal of Life Cycle Assessment 2010

Gething, Bill (pub.): Green Overlay to the RIBA Outline Plan of Work 2011. London 2011

Gauzin-Müller, Dominique; Favet, Nicolas: Nachhaltigkeit in Architektur und Städtebau. Konzepte, Technologien, Beispiele. Basel/Berlin/Boston 2002

Gesellschaft für ökologische Bautechnik: Instrumente für eine qualitätsabhängige Abschätzung der Dauerhaftigkeit von Materialien und Konstruktionen. Berlin 2005

Glücklich, Detlef (pub.): Ökologisches Bauen. Von Grundlagen zu Gesamtkonzepten. Munich 2005

Goffin, Philippe et al.: Analyzing the potential of low energy building refurbishment by simulation. Sydney 2011

Graubner, Carl-Alexander; Hüske, Katja: Nachhaltigkeit im Bauwesen. Berlin 2003

Häfele, Gottfried (pub.); Oed, Wolfgang; Sambeth, Burkhard M.: Baustoffe und Ökologie. Bewertungskriterien für Architekten und Bauherren. Tübingen/Berlin 1996

Heeren, Niko et al.: A component based bottom-up building stock model for comprehensive environmental impact assessment and target control. Renewable & Sustainable Energy Reviews 2013

Hegger, Manfred; Auch-Schwelk, Volker; Fuchs, Matthias; Rosenkranz, Thorsten: Baustoff Atlas. Munich 2005

Hegger, Manfred; Fuchs, Matthias; Zeumer, Martin: Nachhaltigkeitskennwerte von Baumaterialien nach Bauteilschichten. Darmstadt 2005

Hegger, Manfred; Fuchs, Matthias; Stark, Thomas; Zeumer, Martin: Energie Atlas. Munich 2007

Hegger, Manfred; Drexler, Hans; Zeumer, Martin: Basics Materialität. Basel/Berlin/Boston 2007

Hegger, Manfred et al.: e-life – Lebenszyklusbetrachtung und Optimierung von Instandsetzungsprozessen im Wohnungsbau. Stuttgart 2008

John, Viola; Gut, Silvan; Wallbaum, Holger: Hoch oder quer? Ökologische Lebenszyklusanalyse eines Hochhauses im Vergleich zu einem Riegelbau. Bauingenieur, Volume 85, July/August 2010

John, Viola: Derivation of reliable simplification strategies for the comparative LCA of individual and "typical" newly built Swiss apartment buildings. Dissertation, Zurich 2012. dx.doi.org/10.3929/ethz-a-007607252

John, Viola; Habert, Guillaume: Graue CO_2-Emissionen im Gebäude – wo sind sie hauptsächlich verortet? Ökobilanzanalyse mittels zweier verschiedener virtueller Blickwinkel auf die Konstruktionsweisen und Bauteile von vier unterschiedlichen Mehrfamilienhäusern. In: Bauingenieur, Volume 88, July/August 2013

Kasser, Ueli; Pöll, Michael; Graffe, Kathrin: Deklaration ökologischer Merkmale von Bauprodukten nach SIA 493. Erläuterung und Interpretation. Zurich 1997

Kaufmann, Hermann et al.: Holzbau der Zukunft in der High-Tech-Offensive Zukunft Bayern. Ganzheitliche Planungsstrategien: Konzeption und Umsetzung. Munich 2008

Kellenberger, Daniel; Althaus, Hans-Jörg: Relevance of simplifications in LCA of building components. In: Building and Environment 1/2009

Klöpffer, Walter; Grahl, Birgit: Ökobilanz (LCA) – ein Leitfaden für Ausbildung und Beruf. Weinheim 2012

Knappe, Florian et al.: Einsatz von Recyclingmaterial aus mineralischen Baustoffen als Zuschlag in der Betonherstellung am Beispiel einer Wohnbebauung an der Rheinallee in Ludwigshafen. Heidelberg, Cottbus, Ludwigshafen 2011

Kohler, Niklaus: Grundlagen zur Bewertung kreislaufgerechter, nachhaltiger Baustoffe, Bauteile und Bauwerke. Karlsruhe 1998

König, Holger; Kohler, Niklaus; Kreißig, Johannes; Lützkendorf, Thomas: Lebenszyklusanalyse in der Gebäudeplanung. Munich 2009

Krusche, Per et al.: Ökologisches Bauen/Umweltbundesamt. Wiesbaden/Berlin 1982

Löfflad, Hans: Das global recyclingfähige Haus. Eindhoven 2002

Lieblang, Peter: Nachhaltiges Bauen mit Beton. In: Detail Green 1/2010

Meier, Thorsten: Solarenergie. Munich 2000

North Rhine Westphalia Ministry of Environment and Conservation, Agriculture and Consumer Protection: Aktionsprogramm Umwelt und Gesundheit Nordrhein-Westfalen. Umweltzeichen für Bauprodukte. Bauprodukte gezielt auswählen – eine Entscheidungshilfe. Düsseldorf 2004

Mittag, Martin: Baukonstruktionslehre. Ein Nachschlagewerk für den Bauschaffenden über Konstruktionssysteme, Bauteile und Bauarten. Braunschweig/Wiesbaden 2000

Möltner, Clemens: Life Cycle Assessment als Werkzeug zur Entwicklung umweltgerechter Produkte: Strategien zur Implementierung von Ecodesign. Hamburg 2009

Mötzl, Hildegund: Entsorgungseigenschaften von Gebäuden. Vienna 2009

Nemry, Francoise; Uihlein, Andreas (pub.): Environmental Improvement Potentials of Residential Buildings (IMPRO-Building). JRC Scientific and Technical Reports, Luxemburg 2008

Passer, Alexander: Zur Bewertung der umweltbezogenen Qualität von Gebäuden. Dissertation, Graz 2010

Passer, Alexander; Mach, Thomas; Kreiner, Helmuth; Maydl, Peter: Predictable Sustainability? The role of building certification in the design of innovative façades. Excerpt from the conference "Advanced Building Skins", Graz 2012

Preisig, Hansruedi: Massiv- oder Leichtbauweise? Zurich 2002

Rau, Johannes: Die große Ratlosigkeit. Was ist Baukultur? In: Baumeister 5/1998

Ritter, Volker: Optimizing the combination of active and passive building components in refurbishment projects to allow for net-zero emission architecture. Dissertation, Zurich 2012, dx.doi.org/10.3929/ethz-a-009937203

Schmidt-Bleek, Friedrich: Wieviel Umwelt braucht der Mensch? Faktor 10 – das Maß für ökologisches Wirtschaften. Munich 1997

Schmidt-Bleek, Friedrich; Käo, Tönis; Huncke, Wolfram (pub.): Das Wuppertal-Haus. Bauen nach dem Mips-Konzept. Basel/Berlin/Boston 1999

Schwarz, Jutta: Ökologie im Bau. Entscheidungshilfen zur Beurteilung und Auswahl von Baumaterialien. Bern/Stuttgart/Vienna 1998

Siebers, Raban; Hauke, Bernhard: Ökobilanzieller Vergleich von Hallen unterschiedlicher Bauweisen. Düsseldorf 2012

Sigg, René; Kälin, Werner; Plattner, Hugo: LUKRETIA – Lebenszyklus – Ressourcen – Technisierung. Zurich 2006

Steiger, Peter et al.: Hochbaukonstruktionen nach ökologischen Gesichtspunkten. SIA-Dokumentation D 0123. Zurich 1995

Thormark, Catarina: Recycling Potential and Design for Disassembly in Buildings. Lund 2001

Tichelmann, Karsten: Vergleichende Ökobilanzbetrachtung und Lebenszyklusanalyse für Konstruktionen nichttragender Innenwände und tragender Außenwände. Darmstadt 2010

von Gleich, Arnim et al.: Effizienzgewinne durch Kooperation bei der Optimierung von Stoffströmen in der Region Hamburg. Hamburg 2004
Voss, Karsten et al.: Ökologische/ökonomische Bewertung zweier Fassadenkonzepte – Glasfassade versus Kunststofffassade – zur Sanierung eines Verwaltungsgebäudes der 1960er-Jahre. Wuppertal 2007
Wallbaum, Holger; Hardziewski, Regina: Minergie und die anderen – Vergleich von vier Labels. TEC 21, 47/2011
Waltjen, Tobias (pub.); Mötzl, Hildegund: Ökologischer Bauteilkatalog. Bewertete gängige Konstruktionen. Vienna / New York 1999
Weidinger, Hans: Patina. Neue Ästhetik in der zeitgenössischen Architektur. Munich 2003
Weston, Richard: Material, Form und Architektur. Stuttgart 2003
Wittstock, Bastian; Albrecht, Stefan; Colodel, Cecilia Makishi; Lindner, Jan Paul: Gebäude aus Lebenszyklusperspektive – Ökobilanzen im Bauwesen. In: Bauphysik Volume 31, 2009, Jounal 1, pp. 9–17
Wolpensinger, Holger: Ökobilanzierung von Siedlungen unter Berücksichtigung von Lebensstilaspekten am Beispiel einer Gartenstadt- und Wohnhöfesiedlung in Karlsruhe. Diplomarbeit, überarbeitete Fassung 2002
Zapke, Wilfried: Der Primärenergiegehalt der Baukonstruktionen unter gleichzeitiger Berücksichtigung der wesentlichen Baustoffeigenschaften und der Herstellungskosten. Stuttgart 1998
Zea Escamilla, Edwin; Habert, Guillaume: Environmental impacts of bamboo-based construction materials representing global production diversity. In: Journal of Cleaner Production, Volume 69, 2014, pp. 117–127
Zeumer, Martin; Hartwig, Joost: Umweltwirkungen von Kunststoffen. In: Knippers, Jan et al.: Atlas Kunststoffe und Membrane. Munich 2010
Zeumer, Martin; John, Viola; Hartwig, Joost: Nachhaltiger Materialeinsatz – Graue Energie im Lebenszyklus. In: Detail Green 1/2009
Zeumer, Martin; John, Viola; Hartwig, Joost: Nachhaltiger Materialeinsatz: Holz und Holzwerkstoffe. In: Detail Green 2/2009
Zwiener, Gerd; Mötzl, Hildegund: Ökologisches Baustoff-Lexikon. Bauprodukte, Chemikalien, Schadstoffe, Ökologie, Innenraum. Heidelberg 2006

Links

www.2000watt.ch
Information for the planning of buildings and urban quarters according to the 2000-Watt Society guidelines for communities, companies and private clients; Excel calculation tool for 2000-Watt estates

www.agoef.de/agoef/oewerte/orientierungswerte.html
AGÖF orientation values for volatile organic compounds in indoor air

www.baubook.at
Online tool for the life cycle assessment of building components

www.baunetzwissen.de/index/Nachhaltig-Bauen_648364.html
General information on sustainable and energy-efficient building practices and products. Schedule of events and links to the most important sources

www.bauteilkatalog.ch
Component catalogue for the determination of U-values and environmental parameters

www.bbl.admin.ch/kbob/00493/00495/index.html
KBOB recommendations for sustainable building; life cycle assessment data for construction operations including information on the NNBS network and Standard Sustainable Building

www.bgbau.de/gisbau/giscodes
BG BAU – GISBAU Berufsgenossenschaft der Bauwirtschaft: information on GISCODE

www.bine.info/hauptnavigation/publikationen/projektinfos
Practical results in the field of energy research

www.bmwi.de/DE/Themen/energie.html
Information published by the Federal Ministry for Economic Affairs and Energy (BMWi) on energy-related issues

www.bnb-nachhaltigesbauen.de
Assessment System for Sustainable Building (BNB)

www.bre.co.uk
BRE Building Research Establishment; information on the building certification system BREEAM

www.bau-umwelt.de/hp6253/EPDs.htm
EPDs established by the Institute Construction and Environment (IBU)

www.dena.de
Website of the German Energy Agency (dena)

www.dgnb.de
DGNB; information on the German Sustainable Building Council

www.echa.europa.eu/de/
ECHA European Chemicals Agency; information on chemicals

www.eco-bau.ch
Recommendation SIA 112/1 “Sustainable building construction”; methodology for the consideration of criteria for a sustainable development in the strategic planning of public buildings (Albatros); system for the assessment of sustainability in projects at competition stage (Snarc); electronic building component catalogue; guidelines on ecological building according to construction cost plan (ECO-BKP); graphical illustration of ecologically interesting materials according to construction cost plan (eco-devis); design tool for a healthy indoor climate (GI); decision making tool for environmentally favourable building products (ECO products)

www.energieinstitut.at
Website of the Energy Institute Vorarlberg

www.energytools.ch
Excel calculation tool for 2000-Watt buildings

www.enob.info/de
Information on research projects for energy-improved buildings sponsored by the Federal Ministry for Finance and Technology

www.eplca.jrc.ec.europa.eu/ResourceDirectory/providerList.vm
European Commission Joint Research Centre JRC: European platform for the subjects life cycle assessments and life cycle assessment tools

www.gabi-software.com
Analysis software for the life cycle assessment of buildings and building components

www.grisli.net
Tool for the calculation of embodied energy and greenhouse gas emissions of buildings and building components

www.hausderzukunft.at
Case studies including various approaches concerning the use of ecological building materials and renewable resources in the construction industry

www.hslu.ch
Tool for recording and assessing requirements for sustainable building with the aim of meeting target agreements

www.ibo.at
Austrian Institute for Building Biology and Ecology (IBO); research projects; labels material ecology; consultants for projects that are innovative in terms of building ecology and building physics; publications and events

www.ibp.fraunhofer.de
Website of the Fraunhofer Institute for Building Physics

www.iwu.de
Website of the Institute Living and Environment with information on sustainable building

www.label-online.de
Information and recommendations on labels for building products

www.minergie.ch
All about the Minergie standard: events, publications, general information, links
Assessment system for the ecology and health standard of building projects

www.nachhaltigesbauen.de
Information platform for sustainable building generated by the German Federal Ministry of Environment, Nature Conservation, Building and Nuclear Safety (BMUB); guidelines for sustainable building; brochures and Excel tools for the integration of sustainability objectives in competitions, tools for the BNB assessment system; Ökobau.dat; Wecobis database; durability of building components

www.nnbs.ch
SNBS and NNBS; information on the network and the Swiss Standard Sustainable Building

www.novatlantis.ch
Information on the 2000-Watt Society of Novatlantis, a network of several Swiss universities and research institutes

www.ogni.at
Austrian Association for Sustainable Real Estate Industry (ÖGNI); DGNB certification systems (Ö) and blueCard

www.oegnb.net
Austrian Association for Sustainable Real Estate Industry (ÖGNI); online tool for the comprehensive assessment of buildings according to ÖGNB using the assessment system TQB (Total Quality Building)

www.oekobilanz-bau.de
Online tool for the life cycle assessment of buildings

www.s-cert.ch/index.php/gutes-innenraumklima.html
SCERT Swiss certification body for construction products; information on the certification system GI (Gutes Innenraumklima)

www.sbd2050.org
International online databank for sustainable architecture

www.sbs-onlinetool.com
Online tool for the life cycle assessment of buildings

www.sentinel-haus.eu/leistungen/zertifizierung/gesundheitspass
Information concerning the health certificate issued by the Sentinel House Institute

www.umweltbundesamt.de
Information published by the Federal Environmental Agency (UBA) with regard to environment-related subjects; ad-hoc working group for the provision of Federal guideline values for indoor air

www.umweltbundesamt.de/sites/default/files/medien/pdfs/agbb_bewertungsschema_2012.pdf
Procedures for the health-related assessment of emissions deriving from volatile organic compounds used in building products (AgBB assessment system of emissions)

www.usgbc.org/leed
U.S. Green Building Council; information on LEED certification system

www.wecobis.de
WECOBIS ecological building material information system

www.wingis-online.de
Information system on hazardous substances generated by the German Association of the Building and Construction Industry (BG Bau)

Index

With friendly support of

KEIMFARBEN GmbH
Keimstraße 16
D–86420 Diedorf
Tel.: +49 821 4802-0
Fax: +49 821 4802-210
www.keimfarben.de